Edward Behr was born in Paris and educated at the Lycée Janson de Sailly and St Paul's School, London. After service in the Indian Army (in South-East Asia and in Peshawar during Partition) he graduated from Cambridge and joined Reuter's. In 1957 he became a *Time–Life* correspondent, covering events in France, North Africa and the Middle East, then their Bureau Chief in Delhi. From 1963 to 1965 he was a roving correspondent for the *Saturday Evening Post*, also making TV documentaries, before joining *Newsweek* in 1965.

As South-East Asia Bureau Chief, he covered the Chinese cultural revolution and the Vietnam war, returning to Paris as Bureau Chief, then as European Editor of *Newsweek International* in 1973. In 1983 he became Cultural Editor. Since 1988 he has been a contributing editor of *Newsweek International* and has made several TV documentaries (for BBC 1), including *Hirohito – Behind the Myth* and, more recently, *Red Dynasty*. He is currently making a TV documentary for BBC 1 entitled *Ceausescu – Behind the Myth*.

His books include *The Algerian Problem* (1963), *The Thirty-Sixth Way* (1969), which is about the cultural revolution, *Anyone Here Been Raped and Speaks English?* (1978), *Getting Even* (1981), a novel, and *The Last Emperor* (1988), the tie-in book for Bertolucci's Oscar-winning film. It was research into the life of Pu Yi, the puppet emperor of Japanese-dominated Manchukuo, that led him to research the life of Emperor Hirohito. His latest book is *Les Misérables: History in the Making*, about the making of the internationally acclaimed musical, and he was involved as a consultant in the production of the new musical *Miss Saigon*.

HIROHITO:
Behind the Myth

Edward Behr

PENGUIN BOOKS

For P. B. and C. B.

PENGUIN BOOKS

Published by the Penguin Group
Penguin Books Ltd, 27 Wrights Lane, London w8 5tz, England
Viking Penguin, a division of Penguin Books USA Inc.,
375 Hudson Street, New York, New York 10014, USA
Penguin Books Australia Ltd, Ringwood, Victoria, Australia
Penguin Books Canada Ltd, 2801 John Street, Markham, Ontario, Canada l3r 1b4
Penguin Books (NZ) Ltd, 182–190 Wairau Road, Auckland 10, New Zealand

Penguin Books Ltd, Registered Offices: Harmondsworth, Middlesex, England

First published by Hamish Hamilton 1989
Published in Penguin Books 1990
1 3 5 7 9 10 8 6 4 2

Printed in England by Clays Ltd, St Ives plc

CONTENTS

LIST OF ILLUSTRATIONS

FOREWORD
AND ACKNOWLEDGEMENTS

It was while researching *The Last Emperor* that I determined that my next book had to be a biography of Emperor Hirohito.

Pu Yi, the puppet emperor of Manchukuo, and Emperor Hirohito had much in common: both were prisoners of an extremely rigid Court routine, both were treated, in their youth, like "living Gods", and both were singularly ill-equipped, physically, to assume the roles they were made to play. But, whereas Pu Yi's whole life was a tragi-comic failure, the saga of Hirohito is a barely credible one: one of the "three most hated men in the world" alongside Hitler and Mussolini, according to Allied wartime propaganda, he went on to become a universally respected constitutional monarch, his pre-war and wartime past forgotten – and certainly forgiven. Not only the sheer longevity of his reign, but the way he managed to extricate himself from responsibility for any of the pre-war and wartime decisions leading to millions of deaths, make him without doubt the ultimate survivor of all time.

Many of the events described in this book were initially only partially reported in the West: the irresistible rise of Japanese imperialism and militarism was overshadowed, in Western eyes, by the rise of fascism in Germany and Italy. Pearl Harbor came as a horrifying shock to most Americans even though the prospect of war between the United States and Japan had seemed inevitable to President Roosevelt and his advisers.

This book would not have been possible without the invaluable source material provided by two key books: the two-volume *Kido Diaries* and the two-volume *Sugiyama Memorandum*. From the moment he became confidential secretary to the Lord Privy Seal, a post he eventually assumed himself, Koichi Kido kept a detailed diary. After his arrest as a grade A war criminal suspect, he decided, on the advice of his son-in-law, to turn over this diary to the prosecution staff of the International Military Tribunal of the Far East, which eventually sentenced him to life imprisonment. It has since been published in Japanese, but never translated.

Many earlier books about Hirohito and the rise of the "Asian Co-prosperity Sphere" quote selected portions of Kido's diaries but, to my surprise, I discovered much in them that had never been utilized before; the *Sugiyama Memorandum*, another seminal work about the period, is a diary-like record of all meetings held during the time General Sugiyama was Army Chief of Staff; so detailed are the day-to-day entries that at times they read like tape recording transcripts.

For chapters 3 and 4, I have relied heavily on that monumental piece of research, the "civil Intelligence section's" *Brocade Banner* report; for chapter 5, I am indebted to Jerrold M. Packard's *Sons of Heaven* for the description of the wedding and coronation ceremonies; for chapters 8, 9, 10 and 11, to the *Honjo Diaries* and *Brocade Banner*. From chapter 12 onwards, I have drawn heavily on the *Kido Diaries* and *Sugiyama Memorandum*, State Department and OSS records, and the SCAP Archives at Suitland, Virginia.

My thanks, above all, to those who patiently translated thousands of pages of documents, diaries, books and newspaper articles for me: Fuyuko Nishisato, Motoko Suzuki, and Yukiko Shimahara, my interpreter; to the BBC's Janet Williams, in London and Tokyo; and to the numerous experts on the period and subject who were kind enough to submit themselves to lengthy interrogations: Faubion Bowers, General MacArthur's former aide; Robert Fearey, formerly with MacArthur's SCAP, Tokyo; Robert Donihi, former prosecution staff, IMTFE; Dr. Ikuhiko Hata, professor of history at Tokyo's Takushoku University, Tokyo, and author of *The Emperor's Five Decisions*; Professor Kyoshi Inouye, author of *The Emperor's Responsibilities*;

Dr. Roger Buckley, Associate Professor, International University of Japan, Tokyo; Dr. D. C. S. Sissons, Department of International Relations, Research School of Pacific Studies, Australian National University, Canberra, and H. I. H. Prince Takamado. John Taylor of the National Archives, Washington, DC, gave me invaluable guidance, and the staffs of both the National Archives and the Military Archives in Suitland were unfailingly helpful and patient, as were the staffs of the library of the School of Oriental and African Studies, at London University, the library staff of the Correspondents' Club and of the *Japan Times*, Tokyo.

Among veteran experts on Japan's pre-war and wartime period who talked to me I want particularly to thank Robert Guillain, Havas correspondent in Tokyo from 1938 to 1945 and *Le Monde* correspondent there from 1948 to 1971; Ambassador Jacques Bacyens; Ambassador Bernard Dorin; Sir John Pilcher; Rear-Admiral George C. Ross (retired); Colonel Eiku Arisue; Morio Tateno, ex-NHK; Torahiko Nagazumi, a "Peers' School" contemporary of Emperor Hirohito and later one of his Chamberlains; Peter McGill, Tokyo correspondent of the *Observer*; Masaki Shimosato of *Akahata*; Taro Kimura; Shizuto Haruna, ex-NHK; Toshiya Matsuzaki of Josei Jishin; Tetsuya Chikushi, Asahi Shimbun; Kyu Naruse, President of Hara Shobo; Mrs. Yoshiko Yashimoto, Ted Slate of *Newsweek*, Walter Harris, and many, many others. Thanks also to the Editor of the *Far Eastern Economic Review* for permission to publish the letter from Aristides George Lazarus that appears on pp. 421–2. Finally, I would like to thank Mrs. Penny Bergamini, for generously allowing me to use her late husband's archives and source materials, and Ed Victor, for his continued support and encouragement.

Edward Behr
London–Tokyo–Washington–New York and Ramatuelle,
1987–88

INTRODUCTION

On September 27, 1945, an extraordinary event took place, marking the end of an invincible era that had lasted in Japan for over 2,600 years. On that day, the oldest serviceable Imperial limousine (an ancient Mercedes) was coaxed into life in the Imperial Palace garage, and at 10 a.m. an unusual motorcade emerged through the palace gates, crossed the moat, and wended its way up the hill through flattened, charred, war-ravaged Tokyo. There were five cars in all (two of them filled with police and Palace bodyguards) and two motorcycle outriders, a modest enough attendance by Imperial standards.

Inside the Mercedes (which became known, later, to American forces, after its frequent appearances, as 'the cement mixer' – and has pride of place in West Germany's Mercedes museum) sat a small, dapper man with a neat moustache and a slightly receding chin, dressed in a black morning coat, striped trousers and top hat. The clothes, a witness noted, were almost as old as the Mercedes – and indeed, for the next three years, Emperor Hirohito would make it a practice to wear shabby, ill-fitting suits, to share, symbolically, the hardships and penury of his people. That September morning, Emperor Hirohito was on his way to meet General MacArthur, the Supreme Commander, Allied Powers (SCAP), the new American "shogun", in the main reception-room of the United States Embassy residence in Tokyo, a meeting that symbolized both Japan's defeat and the Emperor's own determination to render obeisance to the new master of Japan.

The encounter, immortalized in a faintly comic picture taken by a US Signals photographer sergeant, emphasized the difference between the two men. MacArthur, tieless, hands in pockets, in simple tan army shirt and trousers, stands next to the Emperor, who barely comes up to his shoulder. MacArthur is stern, unsmiling, his jaw set in something of a snarl. Emperor Hirohito's features are fixed in a somewhat nervous half-smile; he has a fatalistic but slightly apprehensive air, and looks incredibly young. The photographer, recalled ex-Major Faubion Bowers, MacArthur's personal aide, was only allowed a few seconds to operate. MacArthur wanted only one picture. As a good professional, the Sergeant begged for two, "in case the first doesn't come out", and MacArthur agreed, with a curt nod. (It was a wise decision: in the first picture, the Emperor's eyes are closed, and it would have been unusable.) With a snap of the fingers, the Sergeant was then dismissed.

Japanese editors were appalled by the contrast between the huge, towering MacArthur and their tiny Emperor, and were at first reluctant to publish it – but SCAP directives prevailed. Paradoxically, the photograph did more to endear the Emperor to the Japanese public than any of his later proclamations. He looked so vulnerable, and so clearly shared his people's predicament.

MacArthur's informal attire scandalized not only editors, but almost all Japanese readers as well. He should, they felt, at least have dressed up in his full general's uniform for the occasion. In MacArthur's eyes, there was nothing disrespectful about his appearance – his was, after all, the standard dress of all US personnel in US-occupied Japan. He was surprised later to learn of these Japanese reactions, for he had, he believed, done his utmost to protect the Emperor from prying eyes: there was no advance notice to the press of the visit, no mention of the appointment ever found its way into the MacArthur agenda, nor did the Honor Guard at the Embassy residence gates know whom to expect when the Mercedes, followed by two other cars, entered the small driveway. All they had been told was to "present arms" with exceptional "panache" to an expected VIP delegation. Even the US Army photographer who took the historic photograph had no inkling of the visitor's identity until he actually saw him. MacArthur did, however, deliberately stick his hands in his pockets, Bowers feels, "to show who was boss".

Emperor Hirohito must have found the whole morning's experience somewhat baffling. From the start there was a studied informality about it. An aide, General Bonner Fellers, greeted the Emperor with a hearty handshake. "Welcome, it's a pleasure to meet you, Sir," he said. The nine Palace aides who accompanied the Emperor caused MacArthur's staff something of a problem. "We expected him to come alone, or accompanied by only one equerry," Bowers remembered. Instead, the nine most senior officials of the Imperial Household Ministry, including Tsuneo Matsudaira, the Imperial Household Minister, and Marquis Koichi Kido, the Lord Privy Seal, and also the Emperor's closest adviser and lifelong friend (they had prepared together for the meeting the previous day for nearly three hours), remained downstairs in another, tiny adjoining sitting-room. Conversation was difficult. Bowers, MacArthur's personal interpreter as well as his military aide, did his best to amuse them with desultory small-talk. An expert on kabuki theatre, he tried to steer the conversation round to his pet subject. The Palace officials were polite but their minds were evidently elsewhere.

The Emperor's nervousness was apparent, and well-founded. He was – understandably – terrified. On the day of the signature of Japan's unconditional surrender aboard the *Missouri*, only some three weeks previously, the elderly Japanese Foreign Minister, Mamoru Shigemitsu, exhausted from his climb up the gangway of the battleship, an exceedingly painful ordeal for a seventy-year-old with only one leg (he had lost the other in a bomb outrage in Shanghai in the thirties), had asked for a glass of water – and Admiral Halsey had refused. Hirohito did not know what to expect. His request to see MacArthur had been curtly accepted ("about time, too," the "Supremo" had told his staff) and he did not know whether he would be humiliated, as his Foreign Minister had been aboard the *Missouri*, or perhaps even arrested on the spot.

For all these reasons, Bowers recalled, Hirohito "looked frightened to death. As I took his top hat I noticed his hands were trembling. On meeting MacArthur on the threshold of the drawing-room he bowed low, very low, a servant's bow." MacArthur shook hands with the Emperor, and said: "You are very, very welcome, Sir." He added that an American interpreter, Bowers, was standing by, but if he preferred the Emperor could use his own interpreter, and MacArthur would not insist on a second one being present. Hirohito immediately commanded his own interpreter, Katuzo Okamura, to remain by his side. On straight-backed, Louis XV-style chairs across a low table, decorated with valuable Japanese ceramics, the three of them talked in apparent secrecy. The Emperor's insistence on his own interpreter was understandable: what he had to say was so delicate, so difficult to express, that the idea of allowing a foreigner to translate would have been intolerable. How could he know that Jean MacArthur, the General's wife, was listening to every word behind a curtain?

Later, MacArthur was to tell his staff that the Emperor was both nervous and tense, but determined not to show it. "I tried to make it as easy for him as I could, but I knew how deep and dreadful must be his agony and humiliation," MacArthur said. "How painful it is to see someone raised so high brought so low." At one point he offered the Emperor a cigarette and Hirohito "was so nervous his hands shook". MacArthur lit it for him. The cigarettes had been an afterthought. "Does he smoke?" MacArthur asked Bowers minutes before the Emperor's arrival. MacArthur, of course, smoked only his corncob pipe. Bowers gave the General his own pack of Lucky Strikes.

If anyone on the American side could put the Emperor at ease, it was Douglas MacArthur, who, as ADC to his father General MacArthur, had accompanied him on a visit to Japan just after the 1905 Russo-Japanese war, during the reign of Emperor Meiji. MacArthur reminded the Emperor of this, and actually made him smile, thus breaking the ice. The new Supremo told Hirohito how preoccupied Emperor Meiji had been about a serious cholera epidemic which had broken out among the army units which had taken part in the campaign. The trouble was, the Emperor had told MacArthur's father, the soldiers simply refused to take their anti-cholera pills.

"My father," MacArthur told Hirohito, "had a piece of advice for your grandfather. He suggested that inside each box of pills there should be a notice: 'the Emperor requests that each soldier takes one capsule every four hours.' My father's advice was followed – and the cholera epidemic ceased."

From then on it was plain sailing, although there were a few awkward moments: Hirohito recognized the conduct and restraint of the US occupation troops; MacArthur congratulated Hirohito on the conduct of the Japanese people in this difficult time. The generalities then became a little less formal. After MacArthur had praised Hirohito for ending the war, the Emperor replied that others, too, deserved credit. "The peace party did not prevail," said Hirohito, "until the bombing of Hiroshima created a situation which could be dramatized."

MacArthur then asked a question many people have asked since. How was it that an emperor powerful enough to end the war had been unable to prevent it? "I felt my heart was breaking," said Hirohito, adding that the worst part of it was reflecting on the consequences of the war on the British Royal Family, "who had treated me with great kindness when I visited them as Crown Prince. But the idea of gainsaying my advisers in those days never even occurred to me. Besides, it would have done no good. I would have been put in an insane asylum or even assassinated."

"A monarch must be brave enough to run such risks," said MacArthur.

But Hirohito had another, unexpected rejoinder – and, considering the circumstances, it showed him to be both stubborn and a brilliant poker-player. "It was not clear to me that our course was unjustified," he said. "Even now I am not sure how historians will allocate the responsibility for the war." He then, in what must have been an excruciatingly difficult speech to make, told MacArthur that he came before him "to offer myself to the judgment of the powers you represent as the one to bear the sole responsibility for every political and military decision made and action taken by my people in the conduct of the war".

It was, of course, an empty gesture: the Emperor knew full well, by this time, nearly two months after Hiroshima, that MacArthur was on the whole against his indictment as a war criminal – and that his status as Emperor, though likely to change, would not be ended outright – he would almost certainly not be asked to abdicate. MacArthur knew that the Emperor knew that he knew this. But "bellytalk" is an essential part of formal Japanese social intercourse, and the Emperor, in offering himself up as a scapegoat, was in fact making the point that the new Occupation Authorities should not lean too hard on Japan, especially where "war criminals" were concerned. If they were determined to spare the Emperor, how could they possibly punish his loyal and devoted servants?

MacArthur, too, was at pains to tell the Emperor that America did not intend to behave as a colonizing power. In all, the meeting lasted thirty-five minutes. After it was over, according to Paul Manning, a veteran US correspondent who had covered the war in the Pacific, flown on bombing missions over Japan and witnessed the surrender aboard the *Missouri* and had privileged access to MacArthur's staff, "both knew they could work together to rehabilitate Japan and its people. Their respect was mutual, their courtesy and empathy marked ... They knew they were to be partners in the task of occupation that lay ahead." For Hirohito, the dreaded meeting had turned into a personal triumph. As he told Marquis Kido later, MacArthur had actually asked him for advice! As Kido recorded in his diaries, MacArthur had said "that the Emperor of Japan knows best about the important men in the Japanese political world. Therefore I want to get your advice from now on on various matters ..."

As he left, Emperor Hirohito was heard to ask Marquis Kido

for the name of the General who had ushered him into the Embassy, and later sent Bonner Fellers a photograph, signed in English. It was a surprising gesture, on the part of a still divine emperor, and proof that Hirohito, for all his palace seclusion, was fully aware of Western-style public relations techniques. More tokens of esteem followed: shortly after the meeting, Empress Nagako sent Jean MacArthur a huge basket of flowers, which she acknowledged in a thank-you letter addressed to "Your Majesty". And shortly after that came another gift, from the Emperor this time: a gold and lacquered writing box, for General and Mrs. MacArthur. Mrs. MacArthur promptly had it appraised and was slightly disappointed to learn that – though valuable – it was not all that old, probably dating back to the nineteenth-century Tokugawa era.

MacArthur was quick to acknowledge the Emperor's first post-war victory. He told his aides that Hirohito "was an emperor by inherent birth but at that instant I knew I faced the first gentleman of Japan in his own right". He said to a visitor that at first "I came here with the idea of using the Emperor more sternly. But it hasn't been necessary. He is a sincere man and a genuine liberal." At no time did MacArthur ever write for his titular chief, President Truman, an account of what had gone on in the Embassy residence between himself and Hirohito. This apparent dereliction of duty was deliberate: MacArthur, in this and all subsequent conversations with the Emperor (there were to be ten in all before the Occupation ended), respected Hirohito's wish that they be not only off-the-record but completely private, even though, after subsequent meetings, the Japanese Foreign Ministry immediately debriefed the Emperor's interpreter, with Hirohito's consent. Besides, as Faubion Bowers recalled, many years later, "anti-Japanese feeling ran so high in Washington at the time that had MacArthur reported back that the Emperor claimed full responsibility for the war, the pinkos in the State Department would have clamoured: fine, let's try him." (The substance of their subsequent talks has remained in a "top secret" file inside the Ministry, with the exception of one deliberate "leak", engineered by the Japanese Foreign Ministry, which led to the dismissal of one of Hirohito's interpreters, at MacArthur's request).

Three months later, in his New Year proclamation to the Japanese people, Hirohito formally renounced his "godliness" in a carefully prepared text he had mulled over for days. "The bondage between Us and you, the people," he said, "is constantly tied with mutual trust, love and respect. It is not brought about by mere mythology and legends. It is never founded on a chimerical conception which ascribes the Emperor as a living deity, and, moreover, [regards] the Japanese as superior to all other races of people, hence destined to rule the world."

The New Year proclamation also revealed the thrust of his preoccupations: "as a result of defeat in a war which lasted a long time, we think the people are apt to become fidgety and sink into an abyss of despondency. Certainly it is a cause of profound concern that there are signs of confusion of thought due to the marked decline of morality affected by the growing sophistries . . ." which some US correspondents interpreted, loosely but accurately, as meaning that "excessive radical tendencies are gradually spreading and the sense of morality tends to lose its hold on the people". By December 1945, the *Chicago Sun* reporter Mark Gayn noted, all pictures of Emperor Hirohito in Japanese schools showed him in civilian clothes, not in uniform. Already there was a new spirit afoot in SCAP. MacArthur's Deputy Chief of the Government Section, Colonel C. L. Kades, said MacArthur felt that "the Emperor had atoned for any past errors by his wholehearted support of the Occupation". General Courtney Whitney, MacArthur's Chief Aide, told reporters that "I would consider it a gross breach of faith if the Emperor were to be tried as a war criminal after all the services he has rendered to the allies".

The story of Hirohito is a complicated one to unravel, not least because, in the short space of time between the Emperor's decision to surrender and the arrival of the American occupying force, almost all Japanese confidential documents were destroyed. The Imperial Household Minister ordered the elimination of all "sensitive" Palace papers shortly before Japan's surrender, and the Foreign, Army and Navy Ministers, as well as the Army and Navy Chiefs of Staff, gave similar instructions, which were obeyed with rigorous thoroughness; so that when the time came for prosecutors of Japanese war criminal suspects to gather evidence they found almost no documents to work on, in marked contrast to the mass of papers left behind by the Nazi bureaucracy. It is, therefore, the image of a passive, blameless monarch that has, on the whole, prevailed.

At this remove in time, it is strange, however, to realize that back in August 1945 there was a very real possibility of Emperor Hirohito standing trial as a war criminal for his responsibility in the events leading up to Pearl Harbor. It was not just the Soviet Union (for reasons that had everything to do with furthering the cause of the Japanese Communist Party which had so long lain underground and nothing to do with justice *per se*) that sought his trial and the abolition of the Japanese monarchy. Australia wanted to identify Hirohito as the man who had condoned the summary execution of Australian prisoners-of-war and the systematic ill-treatment of tens of thousands of prisoners in defiance of all clauses of the Geneva Convention; New Zealand shared the Australian view; a strong current of opinion in the United States felt that Hirohito, who had failed to commute three of the death sentences passed on the first eight downed American aircrews captured on bombing raids over Japan, (five were executed as "war criminals"), deserved to suffer the same fate. In September 1945, a joint resolution in Congress declared that "it is the policy of the United States that Emperor Hirohito of Japan be tried as a war criminal". Many individual members of the US, British Commonwealth and Chinese prosecution teams preparing for the International Military Tribunal of the Far East (IMTFE, otherwise known as the "Tokyo trials") believed he deserved to be indicted. So of course did the surviving prisoners of war who emerged, in August 1945, their lives shattered by years of privation and sadistic treatment. Their indignation was nothing compared to that of the Chinese and *their* case against Hirohito for millions of Chinese deaths, starting with the "Mukden Incident" of September 1931 (which placed Manchuria under Japanese control in a carefully prepared "putsch" engineered by Japanese army officers) and encompassing the Shanghai "incident" of 1932, the later "China Incident" which led to the wholesale invasion of China in 1937, the infamous "rape of Nanking" and horrendous experiments on Chinese prisoners used as guinea-pigs in chemical and bacteriological warfare experiments in Japanese camps and laboratories in "Manchukuo" and on the Chinese mainland. Eisenhower even sent MacArthur a "Joint Chiefs of Staff Directive", drafted by the State/Navy/War Coordinating Committee (SNWCC) in Washington, reminding MacArthur that Hirohito was not necessarily immune from prosecution as a war criminal and that SCAP Headquarters was to collate evidence to be forwarded to Washington, to enable officials there to decide whether or not he should stand trial.

In almost any other political context, the supreme ruler of a country which had perpetrated such behaviour would have been tried and perhaps even executed. Indeed, there is a case for saying that many of those tried at Nuremberg were punished for far less; that their responsibilities, though major, nevertheless fell short of Hitler's — and Hitler was dead. There is an even greater case for maintaining that the fate of the Japanese war criminals sentenced in the Philippines in 1945 and at the close of the "Japanese Nuremberg" in 1947 was a travesty of justice — *Hamlet* without the Prince of Denmark.

This view — prevalent at the close of the Second World War — has since become shockingly unfashionable, and even to raise the subject is enough to provoke a storm of indignation, especially in the United States. Nowadays, any hint that Emperor Hirohito may deserve a portion of the blame for the events that led to Pearl Harbor and tens of millions of Western and Asian deaths is regarded as unwarrantable. The only major English-language "revisionist" book to question the accepted view of

Hirohito as a peace-loving, powerless prisoner of his entourage, David Bergamini's *Japan's Imperialist Conspiracy*, was so violently attacked by a cohort of academic experts that its author became a pariah, reviled, ridiculed and driven to an early death by the weight of negative critical abuse. Bergamini's error was to attempt to discover a conspiratorial pattern in Hirohito's behaviour, from his earliest years as Crown Prince, and to try to prove that he deliberately placed a handful of key supporters in top positions in order to plan Japan's militaristic expansionism, ruthlessly suppressing those who disagreed with the "Strike South" option (the conquest by force of South-East Asia) and favoured, instead, the "Strike North" option (a move against the Soviet Union which would have recovered part of Siberia which had once belonged to China). It was a flawed view, compounded by erratic scholarship and an attempt to twist all available facts to prove his theory. Bergamini also had a somewhat paranoid attitude towards Japan in general, perhaps as a result of his own experiences as an adolescent civilian internee in Japanese hands in the Philippines during the war years, his ordeal as searing as that of "Jim" in J. G. Ballard's autobiographical novel *Empire of the Sun*.

I am not a professional historian. Nor do I have an axe to grind. In South-East Asia at the close of World War Two, a teenage subaltern in the Indian Army, I did catch glimpses of Japanese servicemen, but by that time they were co-operative, disciplined prisoners-of-war. As a veteran journalist and witness of the major events that have shaken the world since the early fifties, I have, however, developed something of a "lie detector" flair for anything that smacks of orchestrated propaganda exercises, of the kind even democratic institutions indulge in so freely; and I was struck by the extraordinarily skilled campaign designed to insulate Hirohito from responsibility for all the traumatic events that took place during the first twenty years of his reign. It was not an exclusively Japanese phenomenon: MacArthur's own attitude towards the Emperor was a determining one. He had been quick to come to the conclusion, even before the end of the war, that the Japanese social fabric might well disintegrate were the Emperor's title to be abolished. Joseph E. Grew, a close wartime adviser to Roosevelt and America's Ambassador in Tokyo prior to Pearl Harbor, thought the same, and the "cold war" that followed on the heels of Japan's surrender, with the Korean War starting a mere five years later, led him – and other key policy-makers – to the conclusion that, because Japan was a necessary bulwark in Asia against Communism in general and Soviet territorial ambitions in the East in particular, it was fruitless, and counter-productive, to harp too much on the past. What had gone before was to be exorcized by the sentences imposed on Japan's war criminals by the IMTFE. A clean sweep of the past was needed.

This view persisted through the years starting with the Korean War and culminating during the Vietnam War: during both conflicts the United States used Japan as a rear-echelon base. It is, today, a widely-accepted fact that the Emperor was a virtual prisoner of the militarists who, from 1931, effectively seized power and led Japan on its expansionist march towards Pearl Harbor and the invasion of the Philippines and Malaysia. In the minds of most people throughout the world, Emperor Hirohito remains the passive, withdrawn monarch-scientist, the marine biologist who let it all happen, was kept inadequately informed of his governments' decisions and was in any case unable to do anything about his unruly soldiers who, while invoking the Imperial Will, in fact imposed their own.

The meeting with MacArthur, however, that September day in 1945, reveals qualities, and determination, that make nonsense of the "passivity" theory. MacArthur's question to him, asking why a man of such qualities had been unable to prevent the war in the first place, remains astonishingly relevant. As the encounter showed, here was a shrewd and skilful manipulator at work, who knew what was going on. That he was capable of decisive and ruthless action was shown on February 28, 1936, when, almost single-handed, he dealt with a serious army uprising that nearly toppled the regime. In August 1945, again almost single-handedly, he decided to end the war.

Yet at other times, during the "Mukden Incident", and the later "China Incident", and during some of the events leading up to that fateful December 7, 1941, Hirohito's behaviour *was* strangely, uncharacteristically passive, his statements in direct contradiction to the policies that prevailed. There are two possible explanations: either Hirohito was, as his own propagandists have, so far successfully, claimed, a mere stooge of the military (and this is belied by his decisive behaviour in two key events), or else there was, in Hirohito's make-up, an ambivalence towards the military, along with a combination of guile, ruse and a passion for secrecy, that enabled him to "ride the tiger" of militarism when it suited him while at the same time insulating himself from any concomitant blame for the militaristic expansionism that marked the 1931–41 decade.

The "official" Japanese line that Hirohito could not be held responsible for any of the steps that led to World War Two because, for all his status as a "living God", and his total unaccountability, he was unaware of what was going on behind the scenes and was, in any case, lacking any real power, seems to me incredible. On the evidence of what actually happened, it is clear that, for all his occasional verbal disapproval of the militarist expansionists, their aims and goals – if not always their methods – had his wholehearted approval.

He endorsed Japan's full-scale war against China from 1937 onwards, his only complaint to his generals being that they had misled him by promising him quick victories and were not winning them fast enough. He believed, without any apparent reservations, in the Japanese "Monroe Doctrine" (prevalent from 1940 onwards) that gave his country the untrammelled right to hegemony in Asia; and he certainly believed, until events proved him wrong, that the Italian and German Axis powers had similar rights over Europe – the Western hemisphere remaining America's legitimate sphere of interest so long as she respected both the Japanese and the Axis rights to dominate *their* "legitimate" spheres of interest after Germany's final and, in Hirohito's view, inevitable victory in Europe.

It has become fashionable, among historians, to underline the limited nature of his "discretionary" or veto powers. But the plain fact is that no major decision, promotion or troop movement could occur without Hirohito's seal of approval, and that such an approval could be, and sometimes was, withheld – without any one of his army or navy staff either objecting or threatening to rebel. Instilled into every Japanese was the notion of blind obedience to the Emperor, and it is inconceivable that any decision taken by him, or any opinion expressed by him, not even necessarily in forceful terms, would have been ignored. As Tojo – the leading war criminal judged at IMTFE – let drop during the court proceedings, Hirohito was the ultimate arbiter of the situation, for "no Japanese subject would go against the will of His Majesty".

Despite his ineffectual and, almost certainly, deliberately half-hearted verbal reservations, Hirohito allowed the Manchukuo and China "incidents" to happen, promoted those responsible for them, and was fully aware of preparations for World War Two without ever making one concrete move that would have reversed the trend towards confrontation. As diaries of his most intimate staff have revealed, he was not only aware of the key step taken in advance of Pearl Harbor – the establishment of Japanese army and air force bases in what was then French Indochina in 1941 – but also openly questioned whether this should not also be accompanied by an invasion of Thailand. And it is hard to claim, as some apologists still do, that Hirohito had no advance warning of Pearl Harbor when records exist of his debate with his military Chiefs of Staff about December 8 – a Monday in Japan but a Sunday in the USA – and of his being told that Sunday was the best possible day for the attack since US Navy and military personnel generally tended to over-indulge on Saturday nights, and that they would therefore be "tired". Hirohito also openly exulted in the early Japanese victories, and pointed out to his Court that they were the fruit of careful planning – preparations in which he had a hand, with briefings occurring almost daily. After the war, he went so far as to tell a visiting clergyman (himself involved in last-minute attempts to prevent war breaking out) that, had he received Roosevelt's personal letter in time, he would have "called off Pearl Harbor", a statement implying either extreme hypocrisy or that it had been within his powers to do so.

The Emperor, according to substantial rumours, had kept a diary since the age of eleven, and a detailed, hour-by-hour record of his daily activities, compiled by Imperial Household officials, undoubtedly exists within the palace walls. Because evidence contained in those papers would have conclusively proved the extent of Hirohito's guilt – or innocence – investigators on the prosecution staff of IMTFE tried to persuade its Chief Prosecutor to impound and examine them. The request, made while the trial was already in progress, was rejected out of hand. For by this time the fiction had been established that the only individuals responsible for the events leading up to Pearl Harbor were the twenty-seven individuals arraigned at the trial: neither President Truman nor MacArthur wanted to know otherwise.

All this means that Hirohito escaped the consequences of his actions with total impunity. After a decent interval he resumed his State visits to major countries, was greeted with deferential courtesy by Queen Elizabeth and President Ford alike. He was respected by many Japanese as "the man who stopped the war". He became, since 1945, a highly regarded constitutional monarch, and the Japanese monarchy is, with Britain's and Spain's, the only real going concern: the notion that the monarchical system might one day come to an end is regarded not just as *lèse-majesté* but as aberrant nonsense. The official "line" concerning Hirohito's responsibilities in the events leading up to war is accepted not only by the overwhelming majority of Japanese themselves but by the mass of academic expert opinion, at any rate in the United States. Japan's huge post-war wealth, and her new status as a world power, make it ill-advised to question what has come to be accepted as an established fact: with Japanese investments on such a vast scale in the United

States, and with sizeable Japanese funding of major American seats of learning, it would be a very brave American university indeed that would these days commission an impartial study of Hirohito's role in the thirties and forties, for it would almost certainly end up the poorer.

In contrast, other monarchs similarly caught up in wars not always entirely of their own choosing have fared badly: Kaiser Wilhelm II ended his days in exile after the collapse of Germany in 1918, and King Leopold III of the Belgians was compelled to abdicate simply because he chose to remain during the German occupation, instead of fleeing to Britain — even though he scrupulously avoided the taint of collaboration.

Hirohito not only survived, but lived on to become not merely the "last emperor" but also the longest-living monarch in contemporary history. Here is a ruler who became Regent in 1921, and Emperor in 1926. It is as though Winston Churchill were still at the helm in the eighties, or Raymond Poincaré still a power in Mitterand's France. The biography of Emperor Hirohito encompasses so many changes, and so much history, that it makes the life story of any other twentieth-century statesman appear ephemeral in the extreme. Hirohito rode down the Mall in a carriage with King George V in 1921, and in his lifetime became familiar with the France of President Etienne Millerand (1859–1943) as well as with that of President Mitterand. For all his failing health, he was still carrying out formal duties in 1988. On the grounds of longevity alone, Hirohito's story is unique. But even more fascinating than his staying power is the nature of his controversial rule while Japan was on its expansionist, militaristic rampage. Hirohito not only survived defeat, his country's near-total physical destruction and the ignominious end of the "Greater Asian Co-prosperity Scheme", but became a "born again" constitutional emperor, revered by his people, and respected if not admired all over the world. Time has been good to Emperor Hirohito, and in the interests of *realpolitik* everyone has been impressively kind. Too kind, perhaps?

This book may restore the balance.

CHAPTER ONE

Japan at the time of Hirohito's birth in 1901 was a country that had experienced incredible change in the previous fifty years after centuries of isolation in a seventeenth-century time-warp.

As a small child, Hirohito grew up at the Court of Emperor Meiji, his grandfather, and Japan's first modern ruler. It was under Meiji that the "great leap forward" had taken place. Before that, for over 270 years, the Emperors had been mere figureheads, virtual prisoners of the "shoguns", the hereditary overlords and real rulers of Japan. The Emperors did not even reside in Tokyo, or Edo as it was then called, but were confined to the religious capital, Kyoto, where they were respected as religious leaders of Shintoism, but denied any temporal power. The Tokugawas, the family of shoguns who ruled Japan in the nineteenth century, imposed police state techniques and sealed the country off from the outside world to such an extent that ocean-going shipbuilding was banned and those unfortunate Japanese, shipwrecked off Japan's coast and rescued at sea by foreign ships, were not allowed to return to their country.

The end of the Tokugawa shogunate was hastened by the arrival of Commander Matthew Perry's "black ships" in 1853. Initially, the civil wars that terminated their rule were inspired by xenophobia, and the rallying-cry: "Revere the Emperor! Expel the barbarians!" But the uprising was social and economic too: Kyoto silk merchants sided with Emperor Komei, Meiji's father, and so did the "ronin", the disgraced samurai reduced to lawlessness after the shoguns' brutal repression of local feudalism. Two leading noble families, the Choshu and the Satsuma, supported the Emperor. Japan was still in turmoil when Meiji, a mere boy of fifteen, succeeded to the throne.

Under Meiji Japan at last came of age. The first few years of his reign were marked by a series of wars, initially against the last shogun, Keiki, who despite his personal oath of allegiance to the new Emperor was persuaded to attack Kyoto and rid him of "evil advisers". He failed, but the notion that it was morally acceptable to try to eradicate the Emperor's henchmen on the grounds that they were providing him with bad advice was one that would plague Meiji's grandson, Hirohito, throughout the 1930s. Keiki survived, after handing over his Tokyo palace to the young Emperor, and many years later, in 1902, after Meiji's many victories and his fundamental reorganization of Japanese society, he was received in audience, and subsequently granted the title of prince.

From 1868 onwards, Japan underwent the same breathless modernization that characterized Napoleonic France and Kemal Ataturk's Turkey: no sooner had the young Emperor settled in Edo, now renamed Tokyo (the Eastern capital), in 1869 than he realized that he needed the barbarians – or at any rate the skills they brought with them – in order to become, in time, strong enough to expel them. Foreigners were hired to run harbours, railways, schools. The ban on foreign travel for Japanese was eased. Japan was put under modern, centralized rule, with Prefects in each province responsible to a Home Minister. Western dress became fashionable, and sword-carrying was outlawed in 1870. There was a cult of all things foreign, so much so that by 1880 a popular children's song, sung to the accompaniment of a bouncing ball and entitled the "civilization ball song", recorded the ten most worthwhile Western inventions. In order of priority, they were: railway engines, gas lamps, cameras, telegrams, lightning conductors, newspapers, schools, a postal system, steamships and cabs. And, in every domain, the Japanese started to prove they were superlatively good at copying the West – whether in administrative systems, engineering or armaments, especially after compulsory education had been established, early in Emperor Meiji's reign.

With the modernization and increased travel abroad came a growing awareness of life beyond Japan's own frontiers, especially on the mainland closest to it – China. Here, Meiji's advisers soon realized, was a state of affairs to be avoided at all costs: China was becoming a virtual colony of the foreign powers at the very same time that Japan was becoming part of the modern world. Because of her weakness, and ungovernability, she was in the process of surrendering chunks of sovereign territory to Britain, France and Germany. Foreign concessions were springing up all over China, and Japan – after providing half the relief troops that broke the Boxer rebellion in 1901 – was, in time, to ask for her share of these. She was determined, moreover, never to be compelled, as China had been, to accept for any length of time a foreign presence on her soil enjoying extra-territorial rights. There were in fact many similarities between China and Japan – the imperial tradition, ideograms, Confucianism and Buddhism – but there was Japanese dismay at China's lack of patriotism: increasingly, from the Meiji era on, most Japanese were to regard China not as a nation, but more as a culture, a state of mind.

It was an age when navies assumed the importance that nuclear forces have today, when China was the last frontier left for aggressive, industrial Western powers, so dominant on the world scene that Britain, France, Germany, Russia and the United States were known simply as 'the powers' – there were no others – though Japan was beginning to qualify, and soon showed she was determined to become a member of this exclusive club.

The reason why Japan succeeded where China failed was, in part, due to the foresightedness of Japan's leading families, including those who had destroyed the Tokugawa shogunate. During Emperor Meiji's reign from 1868 to 1912 China was destabilized by a series of revolutions and civil wars, a prey to warlords, unable to establish for long a unified, centralized rule of any kind under the discredited, "fin-de-race" Ching dynasty that was finally overthrown in 1912. Japan might well have

suffered the same fate, but her ruling families, after overthrow-
ing the shogun, voluntarily surrendered their power to the
Emperor. "There is no soil within the Empire that does not
belong to Him," their memorial read, recalling that "Imperial
Power had declined, and military classes usurped power in the
recent past. Now that Imperial power is restored, how can we
retain possession of land that belongs to the Emperor and
govern people who are his subjects? We therefore reverently
offer up all our feudal possessions so that a uniform rule may
prevail throughout the Empire. Thus the country will be able to
rank equally with the other nations of the world."

Without this act of allegiance, the "Meiji restoration" would
have been short-lived – and Japan would not have been able to
play an active role on the world scene so soon after emerging
from her isolation. It was fear of becoming another China that
was behind this statesmanlike impulse, along with the determination to deny the Western powers a monopoly role in the
acquisition of Chinese "International Concessions". As a com-
paratively small nation, a cluster of islands close to China, Japan
could not stand by and watch Britain consolidate her enclaves
along the China coast, France move into Cochin-China and
Cambodia, and Russia annex part of Chinese Manchuria, without fearing for her own integrity. The best defence was offence,
which explains why, under Meiji, Japan countered the encroach-
ing Western powers first by extending her influence over Korea,
after a lightning war with China, then by providing a huge
contingent for the relief of Peking during the Boxer rebellion of
1900 (Japanese troops were the only ones who refrained from
looting), and finally by challenging Russia over Manchuria.

Emperor Meiji had taken personal command of his new,
modernized army in the 1894 China war, and his terms were
harsh: Korea became a virtual Japanese Protectorate, Taiwan
became Japanese, China was made to pay a large "indemnity"
and Japan moved into the south-eastern part of Manchuria
known as the Kwangtung peninsula. So dramatic was Japan's
emergence as the rising power in the East that, deeply alarmed,

France, Germany and Russia joined together in a "triple intervention" to put pressure on Japan to be less greedy. Emperor
Meiji reluctantly gave in – the war had left Japan financially
exhausted – but the memory of such "colonialist" behaviour, and
suspicion that the West would always try to prevent Japan from
reaping her just rewards, was to rankle in the Japanese collective
subconscious for generations.

In the late nineteenth century, rail communications were as
important to a nation's prestige as the mastery of space is today,
and Russia's completion of the trans-Siberian railway was, in a
way, as noteworthy a feat as the first launching of Challenger or
permanent orbital stations; the shortest route to Vladivostok was
through Manchuria. The Russians set up the Chinese Eastern
railway with a Chinese nominee, but it was in fact a Russian
railway crossing China. All of a sudden Manchuria became an
area of huge strategic importance, and the Russians, three years
after forcing Emperor Meiji out of the Kwangtung peninsula,
moved in themselves, leasing enclaves, including Port Arthur,
running a railway from Port Arthur to Harbin, gradually
turning the whole of Manchuria into a Russian sphere of influence.

These were the days of Kipling's "great game", with Russia
constantly threatening British hegemony over India through the
buffer-state of Afghanistan – and to Japan the Russian push into
Manchuria was a Japanese version of the "great game", one
Meiji became determined to resist. Britain had refused to be
part of the "triple intervention" powers – her suspicions of
Russia were too great – and it was the new Russian threat to
Japan, through Manchuria, that led first to the British-Japanese
friendship treaty of 1902, then to the Russo-Japanese war of
1904–5.

It was a war that astonished the whole world: before it
started, it was known that Japan had a first-class army and navy,
with 13 divisions, brand-new artillery, and some 76 warships.
But no Western specialists believed she could take on a major
European power and win. Even in Japan, there were doubts: the

Constitutionalists, Japan's first major political party, were against the war, and Emperor Meiji himself insured against a humiliating defeat by secretly obtaining from the United States the assurance that she would prevent Russia from invading Japan.

Though Japan severed diplomatic relations with Russia on February 5, 1904, she did not formally declare war until February 10. On February 8, the Imperial Japanese Navy launched a surprise attack on Russia's Far Eastern fleet near Port Arthur (later renamed Lushun) with devastating results. It was a prefiguration of Pearl Harbor: in the samurai tradition, all was fair in war, and attacking the enemy by stealth, and without warning, was not merely acceptable, but part of the cruel Japanese rules of the game. Admiral Heihachiro Togo scattered the Russian fleet again at the battle of Tsushima, on May 27–28, 1905. "Gallant little Japan", so inferior to Russia in size, was so much the underdog that – in contradiction to world opinion after Pearl Harbor – this subterfuge was condoned. "The Japanese Navy has opened the war by an act of daring which is destined to take a place of honour in naval annals," wrote *The Times*.

The remnants of the Russian fleet sought refuge in Port Arthur, while another Baltic-based fleet set out to relieve them and lift the siege. Loyally implementing the friendship treaty, Britain denied the Tsar's navy the right of passage through the Suez Canal, forcing it to sail round the world, and France compounded its difficulties by denying it bunkering rights in French Indochina.

It was vital for Emperor Meiji to overwhelm the Russian garrison in Port Arthur before the reinforcements arrived, and he ordered his favourite general, Maresuke Nogi, to capture it at all costs. Nogi in turn told his soldiers to be prepared to die for the Emperor. Officers were not expected to survive, and anyone leaving the battlefield without reason was shot out of hand. For five months, wave upon wave of Japanese infantry attempted to break through the Russian defences. Nogi watched through binoculars as his two sons went into battle, waving their samurai swords at the head of their troops. They were both killed, and Nogi, fanatically devoted to the Emperor, made it known he intended to commit suicide. Meiji forbade him to do so. "As long as I am alive," he told Nogi, "you must remain alive also."

General Nogi became a figure in the world press, as did Admiral Togo. *The Times* waxed lyrical about Japan's final victory: "the attitude of the Japanese people in the presence of this epoch-making triumph is a sight for men and gods," it wrote on June 7, 1905. "No noisy and vulgar clamour, no self-laudation, no triumph over a fallen enemy, but deep thankfulness, calm satisfaction, and once more reference of the cause of victory to the illustrious virtues of the Emperor of Japan."

The British press had another reason for being blatantly pro-Japanese: the new Japanese Navy was largely the product of British engineers, naval dockyards and of Royal Navy advisers and instructors. When Admiral Togo, the "Father of the Japanese Navy", virtually wiped out the relieving Russian fleet at Tsuchima in the most decisive naval encounter of modern times, he became, overnight, the leading authority on modern naval warfare, and a hero to the British.

The Treaty of Portsmouth (New Hampshire) gave Japan uncontested rights over Korea, and territorial rights in Manchuria which she was this time determined to preserve. The new South Manchuria Railway Company, soon to become a tentacular industrial and trading corporation along the lines of the old British East India Company, was protected by a permanent force of Japanese troops, stationed in Manchuria, known as the "Kwangtung army".

While Japanese politicians inflamed public opinion, claiming that Japan should have gained more from the war, including a Russian indemnity, Emperor Meiji knew that the war's end, and the providential American peace-making role between Japan and Russia, had come not a moment too soon: once more, Japan was impoverished, almost bankrupted by the costly series of campaigns on land and sea and by the invasion of Manchuria. It was the first time an Asian country had decisively beaten a major Western power, but the cost, in terms of casualties and sheer financial deficit, had been enormous.

It is impossible to over-estimate the impact of the Japanese victory over the Russian giant in the Japanese psyche: the "bushido" qualities of its army and navy, the stories of legendary heroism in the face of overwhelming odds told and retold in the Japanese press and history books, the new self-confidence and pride, and above all the image of the Emperor Meiji himself as a godlike commander, influenced Japanese from all walks of life. Army and navy careers became more sought after than ever, and for the first time began attracting youngsters from the lower middle class and the peasantry; Japan's evident superiority over one of the largest powers on earth, now self-evident, encouraged notions of Japan's "civilizing mission" in the rest of Asia.

Two Japanese officers were, in different ways, indelibly marked by the Russo-Japanese War: aboard the *Nisshin*, one of Admiral Togo's warships, a young naval officer called Isoroku Yamamoto, a tough, humorous runt of a man, had two fingers amputated and was left with scars all over his body when one of the guns aboard his warship misfired, its recoil all but killing him. In later years, Admiral Yamamoto, architect of Pearl Harbor and, for all that, one of the sanest, most level-headed, far-sighted and endearing members of the Japanese armed services oligarchy, was to brag that he had been wounded by a Russian shell. His early experience as an admiring disciple of Admiral Togo made him conscious of the need for surprise in battle and for ultra-modern weaponry – the new Japanese torpedo boats had played a determining role in the Russian defeat.

The war made a similar impact on another young officer, Hideki Tojo, who was too young to see active service in it (when it started he was still a student at the Military Academy) but owed his lightning promotion to the vacancies resulting from Japan's severe casualties. All his life, until he was hanged as a war criminal in 1948, Tojo was to remember the lessons of the Russo-Japanese War, especially the way a smaller power, provided it was bold and unscrupulous and sufficiently organized, could humilate a giant empire.

Hirohito was only five at the time of the Russo-Japanese War, a lonely, introspective boy with none of the normal comforts of a family life. He was already being treated like someone apart, surrounded by adults and formal priests and courtiers inculcating in him the notion that – as a future "living God" – he was different from all others. Most of his childhood companions were older, already highly motivated nationalists, fully aware of the unfolding drama at sea and on the Manchurian battlefields, hero-worshipping the Emperor's victorious generals and admirals, whom they were occasionally able to glimpse at close quarters. Perhaps inevitably, given the jingoistic climate brought about by the war and its aftermath, they too grew up thinking that Japan not only had a special role to play, but was uniquely qualified to lead the Asian world, owing to the superior quality of her armed forces.

Significantly, Hirohito's first public appearance, at Emperor Meiji's side, in 1905, at Tokyo's railway station (to greet Prince Arthur of Connaught, come to invest Emperor Meiji with the Order of the Garter), was in the uniform of a Japanese army officer.

It was in the Imperial tradition for the heir to the throne to be brought up by outsiders. Originally this had been inspired by security reasons, and the custom remained: it was supposed to instil toughness, and guard against excessive sycophancy. At the age of only seventy days, Hirohito was taken away from his mother, and brought up by a series of wet-nurses in the house of a retired admiral, Count Kawamura. The Count took his duties seriously. He consulted an English governess, in the employ of another princely family, who imparted her three basic rules for successful child-rearing: inducing in her charge "an independent spirit, a sympathetic heart and a sentiment of gratitude".

Count Kawamura was seventy at the time, a traditionalist who was determined to impart, also, a "dauntless spirit to withstand all hardships" and to eradicate "traces of arrogance and egotism". Once during dinner the tiny Hirohito threw a tantrum. He flung down his chopsticks and said: "I won't eat that." "You don't have to eat, but you will be served no more food," the Count said sternly. Hirohito quietly sobbed, then said, "in a subdued voice 'I'll eat it, I'll eat it.' " Kanroji wrote that when Kawamura saw him eating the food he had rejected, "with his chubby fingers grasping the chopsticks, he turned his face to one side and wept".

Hirohito was not quite four years old when the Count died (in 1904). He returned to the Akasaka Palace, where his father, the Crown Prince, lived, but not to the bosom of his family. In a separate small house, he was surrounded by chamberlains and courtiers, attending a special "imperial" kindergarten with princely children of his own age. The school was run by a former teacher of the Peers' School who was something of a martinet. Another teacher, Tsuchiya, though also a strict disciplinarian, was deeply interested in marine life and plants, and Hirohito's lifelong passion for marine biology originated with after-school sessions with him. Another kindergarten teacher was Mrs. Takako Suzuki, a naval officer's wife whose husband, many years later, was to become Hirohito's last wartime prime minister.

The tough kindergarten routine, with plenty of homework and calligraphy lessons, included one monthly outing outside the palace. Invariably, Hirohito chose to visit the Ueno Park zoo. But even here he was not allowed to behave like ordinary children, but was endlessly lectured on animal life by the zoo superintendent. A court chamberlain, Osanaga Kanroji, in a portrait of young Hirohito,[1] recalls that the sight of a newly captured badger, trembling with fear in its small cage, depressed the small boy almost to tears. "I don't want to look at it any more," he wailed. "I want to go home."

"Home" was precisely what he lacked: Hirohito and his younger brother, Prince Chichibu, one year his junior, living in a separate compound (where they shared the same room), saw their mother only once a week, their father much less often.

Life was hard for Hirohito, harder than for Chichibu, an athletic extrovert, who rapidly became the natural leader of the kindergarten group. Hirohito was isolated from the other children, partly because of his status as future emperor and "living God", but also because of his physical disabilities: he walked with a slight shuffle, a hereditary defect he had inherited from his grandfather, had poor posture (a curved spine), suffered from myopia (but was denied glasses for several months because "an emperor does not wear spectacles"), and was generally weaker, smaller and less aggressive than other children of his own age. He was also exceedingly clumsy, and Chichibu made fun of him. "When Hiro falls down," he said, "he doesn't know how to get up." Needless to say, Kanroji makes no mention of sibling rivalry (though there is evidence of this in other Court writings), painting instead an idyllic and somewhat false picture of Hirohito "clutching Chichibu's hand or looking at picture books with him". The situation did not improve when a second younger brother, Prince Takamatsu, joined them, for he too was livelier, and more outgoing, than Hirohito. One of Hirohito's few surviving contemporaries, Torahiko Nagazumi, recalls that the Emperor was far more introspective than his two "lively" brothers, but always, in childish war games played out in the Hayama Palace gardens, insisted on being "the commander-in-chief". "Chichibu," he says, "was almost always the commander of Hirohito's advance guard, and the two brothers were always on the same side, for Chichibu never wanted to play at being 'the enemy'." Hirohito was not entirely insulated by his rank from the rough-and-tumble of war games. Nagazumi recalls that his own father told him: "If you wrestle with Hirohito, don't lose on purpose simply because he is going to be the Emperor one day."

But Hirohito was denied small pleasures accessible to others: his tutor saw to it that he did not jump off walls, for fear of breaking a royal leg. At a ridiculously early age, Hirohito was imbued with a sense of gravity – a melancholy recognition of his inherent difference. There were a few minor compensations:

he could assume responsibility for the childish misdemeanours of his companions (like making holes in paper screens) without being punished.

So determined is Kanroji, in his memoirs, to make Hirohito a paragon of all the virtues that, when he admits to the Prince's clumsiness, one infers that Hirohito must have been very clumsy indeed. He also had to submit to grim routines designed to improve his posture and his eyesight. For hours on end, he was made to stare into space. Some trees were cut down so that he could look at the distant Shinagawa coastline – concentrating on distant objects was supposed to cure myopia. He was also made to sit for hours at a time in a specially designed chair, with handles on either side to keep his spine erect and a reading stand fourteen inches from his eyes – all in a vain attempt to improve his posture.

The Imperial Court under "the great Meiji" was a strange place to grow up in: the atmosphere – despite the pace of change outside the Palace – remained medieval, something from an epic Kurosawa film. Meiji himself, a thick-set, commanding figure with a short beard, piercing eyes and, very probably, a club foot, was hardly the epitome of the jolly, indulgent grandfather: though Hirohito saw him more often than he saw his own father, Crown Prince Yoshihito (later Emperor Taisho), Emperor Meiji scarcely lavished any affection on the small boy.

Hirohito, Kanroji wrote, "snuggled up to Emperor Meiji and called him granddaddy", but Meiji, "because of his position as emperor, and because of the nature of his temperament, showed his affection only by smiling at the little prince". Meiji behaved in exactly the same way towards his own son. At the Japanese Court, the notion that children should be seen and not heard was even more prevalent than in upper-class Victorian Britain. Kanroji wrote that Meiji saw his own son, "only on formal occasions", when the Crown Prince would "bow low", while Meiji, "though nodding in acknowledgement, would remain silent throughout the audience". Though Kanroji was Prince Yoshihito's constant childhood companion, the only time, he recalls, Emperor Meiji actually spoke to them was during an archery practice along a palace corridor. Meiji came across the two boys, and, unobserved, watched them. After a particularly good hit, he boomed, "Excellent!" The boys turned, bowed low, and went on with their practice. Emperor Meiji stayed to watch, shouting "Good . . . Excellent" whenever they scored a bull's-eye.

Hirohito did not even get that small measure of encouragement from his own father. In his memoir, Kanroji hardly mentions him, and with good reason: Crown Prince Yoshihito was almost never there, and when he was he was liable to fits of drinking and debauchery, neglecting his family for days on end. He hated Tokyo in the winter, and sought warmth elsewhere. Even by the standards of Japan where husbands tend to live their own lives and wives (especially in those pre-World War I days) were confined to rigid domesticity, Crown Prince Yoshihito behaved exceptionally badly. What Hirohito did see of Court ways left an indelible mark on him: drunkenness was common, and Hirohito, early on, became a teetotaller. Both Emperor Meiji and his own father were promiscuous; Hirohito, from adolescence, was prim, monogamous and puritanical.

Emperor Meiji himself remained, in his habits, a profoundly conservative Japanese noble lord, enjoying vintage claret, the writing of poetry, and beautiful women, in that order. A dozen concubines, euphemistically termed ladies-in-waiting, nightly awaited the drop of the imperial handkerchief at their feet to follow him into his quarters, furnished in the Japanese style and out of bounds to all but a handful of specially chosen page-boys. Meiji slept, however, not on a tatami mat but in a comfortable, Western-style bed. He also mastered the mysteries of capitalism with remarkable ease. Under Meiji, the Mitsuis, Sumitomos and Iwasakis (of Mitsubishi fame) became familiar figures at court, and as these founder-members of the "Zaibatsu", the huge industrial conglomerates that were soon to dominate Japan economically, grew, so did the Imperial fortune.

Kanroji's portrait of Meiji is that of a roistering extrovert with Falstaffian appetites, surrounded by drunken cronies. He describes a marathon drinking bout the Emperor indulged in with his Palace Chamberlains, ending with Meiji ordering a horse to be brought and telling one of his drinking companions to mount it. "No matter how many times the tipsy chamberlain tried, he would invariably slip down from the saddle, causing Emperor Meiji to roar with laughter. Apparently Emperor Meiji too sometimes got so intoxicated that he was unable to return to his palace on horseback."

Drunkenness was as excusable then as it is now in Japanese society, and the impression Kanroji conveys of palace life in the Meiji era is of a perpetual overhanging alcoholic haze. Chamberlains sent on errands by the Emperor would return intoxicated, but "Emperor Meiji would listen to them with a smile on his face, with never a rebuke for their breach of etiquette".

Crown Prince Yoshihito introduced Hirohito to drink at the age of five, with traumatic results: he plied his son with sake, forcing him to drink large quantities and respond to toasts, until the obedient boy keeled over in a drunken stupor. Hirohito never forgot the humiliation, or the prodigious hangover that followed. From that day on, he later told his Court, he never touched alcohol in any form.

Like his contemporary, the Prince of Wales who later became Edward VII, Yoshihito led a futile existence in the shadow of a glorious parent. He developed a passion for uniforms, especially the "Death's Head" German Uhlan variety, waxed his moustache, like Kaiser Wilhelm, and was determined to be "modern", which meant, in practice, collecting Impressionists, and building himself a miniature replica of Versailles, the Akasaka Palace, which was crammed with glittering candelabra and neo-Louis XV brocaded furniture. Meiji found it in atrocious taste, and only went there once.

For all his outward "modernism", Crown Prince Yoshihito had bowed to his father's wishes, obediently marrying the Emperor's choice, a girl from the aristocratic Fujiwara clan, a princely family that had provided brides for the Imperial family for centuries. Princess Sadako was intelligent, beautiful, and had been groomed since childhood for such a marriage. She was only sixteen when Hirohito was born on April 29, 1901 – the first Japanese Emperor since 1758 not to be born of an imperial concubine. In his early childhood, however, she played almost no part, for she was seldom allowed to see him.

Hirohito's father – and mother – substitute was General Nogi, the war hero whom Meiji appointed head of the Peers' School. He became, to all intents and purposes, Hirohito's tutor. Nogi not only epitomized the old-fashioned "samurai" virtues but was also that rare breed in Japan – a soldier who was also an intellectual, a skilled calligraphist, a "bonsai" (miniature tree) expert, and a moralist. It was Nogi who instilled in young Hirohito the notion that there was nothing – neither physical weakness nor inherent clumsiness nor faulty coordination – that could not be overcome through practice and the assertion of will. Because he worshipped Nogi, and desperately sought his approval, Hirohito became, from the age of ten onwards, a competent athlete, a strong swimmer, an above average golfer and sumo wrestler. He also took fencing lessons – a sport that had cost Nogi an eye in his youth – and embarked on a gruelling routine of cold showers, exhausting physical training, and long hours of study. Nogi succeeded in bringing young Hirohito out of his shell, getting rid, as he put it, of his "hunchback mentality".

He also acquired something of Nogi's puritanical contempt for the pleasures of the flesh and his sense of thrift. Nogi's house, still standing in central Tokyo, surrounded on all sides by high-rise offices and apartment houses, is a plain, two-storey wooden building looking very much like a small Japanese farmhouse. Now a shrine and little-known museum, it is one of the few houses in the Aoyama district of Tokyo spared by wartime B-29 bombing; it reflects the General's taste for plain living, its only extravagance being its huge stables, for Nogi was a great horseman, and lavished considerable care on his thoroughbreds. Otherwise his lifestyle was unassuming, almost parsimonious. One of his "house rules" was: be ashamed of torn clothes, never of patched ones. It was a lesson Hirohito was to remember all his life. During his years at the Peers' School, Nogi made him wear coarse cotton underwear and kimonos – he never knew the touch of silk next to his skin. He started hoarding things, using his pencils till they were too small to hold, erasers till they were the size of a pea.

In the normal course of events, Hirohito's younger brother, Prince Chichibu, would have become Nogi's favourite. Handsome, bright, athletic, he was clearly more of a natural leader than Hirohito. But Nogi, as a soldier, believed in emulation, and it was the brothers' almost pathetic desire to please their *de facto* foster-father that caused Hirohito to shed some of his inhibitions, though he remained withdrawn, a listener rather than a speech-maker, a strangely inscrutable child.

In 1911, Emperor Meiji chose Nogi as his representative to attend the coronation, in London, of King George V – itself proof of his "family" closeness to Meiji. Nogi absented himself for several months, and it was during this period that Emperor Meiji's cancer took a fatal turn, leading to his death on July 29, 1912, at the early age of fifty-nine.

The Court diarist Kanroji wrote that Hirohito, in a nightmare, had a premonition of his grandfather's death. He was to experience a far more traumatic experience on the day of his grandfather's funeral, which took place after six weeks of official mourning.

On the eve of the funeral, Hirohito had been summoned to General Nogi's study at the Peers' School. "I am not dissatisfied with your progress while I have been away," he told Hirohito, "but I ask you to study harder. You are now the Crown Prince, the youngest of the officers of the Army and Navy, and the future commander of the nation. I beg you to attend to your military duties, and to take care of your health, no matter how busy you are. Please remember that my physical presence is not necessary for me to be with you in your work. I shall always be watching you and your welfare will always be my concern.

Work hard, for your sake and the sake of Japan." They bowed to each other and Hirohito left the room.

The following morning, while Japanese guns boomed their salute to the dead Emperor, General Nogi and his wife bathed, dressed themselves in white kimonos, and solemnly bowed to an autographed portrait of Emperor Meiji. Countess Nogi died first, cutting her throat with a razor-sharp dagger. Nogi himself then committed ritual "seppuku", or disembowelling, with an equally sharp short sword. In a note, he called on every patriotic Japanese to abide by the ancient Japanese virtues, deploring the current "laissez-faire" in morals. He had fulfilled his pledge to Emperor Meiji, made on the battlefield after his two sons' deaths, in a way that ensured his place in history.

The impact on Hirohito, aged twelve, can only be imagined: Nogi had been the object of his admiration as well as the father-figure he had craved in the absence of his own, despised, father.

Outwardly, he showed an almost frightening composure on learning the news. "Japan has suffered a regrettable loss," he said, with no apparent emotion.

---

[1] Osanaga Kanroji: *Hirohito, an intimate portrait of the Japanese Emperor*, Gateway Publishers, 1975.

CHAPTER TWO

Emperor Meiji's death meant little immediate alteration to Hirohito's daily routine, but considerable change in the attitudes of those around him. He was now officially Crown Prince, with a commission in both the army and navy, and he wore his new uniforms proudly. He now had a room to himself. More important still, his younger brothers were compelled to treat him with the respect due to a future "living God". But he continued to attend the Peers' School for nearly two more years, walking there from the Palace with his brothers every morning unless it rained, when he was allowed to take a carriage. Later, a room in his father's Akasaka Palace was turned into a schoolroom and he acquired a set of private tutors, selected for him by Palace Chamberlains with his father's approbation.

The new overall supervisor of Hirohito's studies was Admiral Togo, the hero of the Russo-Japanese War. But Togo was totally unlike Nogi, and the rapport between the two was very different. The Admiral had been a bold naval strategist and an undoubted leader of men. In everyday life, however, he was surprisingly uninspiring, with none of Nogi's mystical samurai fervour − a run-of-the-mill, pleasure-loving officer whose success had infuriated several navy colleagues. Nogi's lifestyle had been almost obsessively austere. Togo was a prodigious (and messy) eater, something which devalued him in Hirohito's eyes. It was impossible for Hirohito not to contrast his new teacher's ordinariness (and relative lack of interest in Japan's hegemony over Asia) with the dead Nogi's outstanding virtues.

Hirohito's tutors were drawn from the cream of Japan's

academic world. So awed were they by the honour conferred on them that they failed to make the most of their opportunities. Hirohito's French teacher, for example, could never bring himself to correct any of his royal pupil's faults, so Hirohito's knowledge of French would never compare, in later life, with that of Prince Chichibu, who spoke the language almost flawlessly. Hirohito's ethics teacher, Doctor Sugiura, a former chemistry graduate from London University, proved to be a very odd choice indeed. Sugiura's lectures were a hotch-potch of Shintoist superstitions and clichés about Japanese national virtues. A great believer in the superiority of the Aryan race, he viewed the Japanese as the Aryans of Asia, racially far superior to the "degenerate Chinese"; but Japan, he cautioned, should be wary of European ways, even those of "Aryan" nations, for in every way the Japanese way of life was better, even its religion superior to any other. Sugiura also had the disconcerting habit of bursting into occasional song, quoting from classical Noh plays or Chinese opera, to make his point. He sang atrociously, but seemed unaware of this. Hirohito observed patiently but listlessly. It would have been bad form to ask his Chamberlains to replace any of the tutors thay had chosen for him — bad loss of face for them and the tutors alike. But their uninspiring, excessively formal relations with their royal pupil had the effect of inhibiting him even further.

The teachings of Isaburo Wada, a graduate of Johns Hopkins and MIT, provided something of an antidote to Sugiura's. He lectured on mechanics, aerodynamics, chemistry. The sessions would have been even more interesting to Hirohito had they taken place in a workshop or laboratory. But protocol required that teacher and pupil face each other across a tatami mat, rigidly motionless, with frequent bows and expressions of mutual respect.

The teacher who made the greatest impact on Hirohito was Doctor Hattori, who instructed him in natural science and biology. Hirohito did voice the mildest of complaints to his Chamberlains that most of his lecturers were as bland as "jagaimo," the potatoes recently introduced into Japan from the West, but Hattori was different. A believer in teaching by doing, he took Hirohito out to the country on natural history trips, and, when Hirohito objected to the cortège of Chamberlains and palace hangers-on trailing behind him and his teacher wherever they went, Hattori not only reduced the size of the party, but started taking Hirohito on boat trips in fishing vessels too small to accommodate any officials at all. Hirohito was by this time a strong swimmer, and when Hattori hired a couple of pearl-divers to collect underwater specimens Hirohito joined them, insisting on bringing in his share. These excursions mostly took place at Hayama, the seaside resort where the Imperial family owned a secluded house, more cottage than palace. Hattori later became Hirohito's scientific aide, and his entire life was spent in the Emperor's service, looking after his laboratory in later years.

In his own memoirs, Prince Chichibu recalled that Hirohito, even as a small boy, always had a meticulous, collector's approach to things. Whereas Chichibu soon tired of it, Hirohito, from the age of ten, kept a careful record of his own collections of butterflies, insects and wild flowers. They have been preserved, dated and signed in his neat hand, and his contribution to marine biology, though later exaggerated by hagiographers, was real enough: at the age of seventeen, at Numazu, Hirohito wandered down to the beach after a storm to collect shellfish and spotted a red prawn, about eight centimetres long. Back in his villa, he pored over reference books, and was intrigued to discover that his find was not catalogued in any of them. This was the famous *sympathiphae imperialis*, whose identification caused a stir when it was revealed to the academic world in 1919. The discovery filled Hirohito with pride, and turned him into a lifelong marine biologist. A special boat was built for him, and trawling for specimens became not just a hobby but a passion. He never duplicated his early success, though he did find several rare specimens of shellfish, including the *genebis argenteonitens*, off the coast at Hayama.

Hirohito's passion for inanimate, invertebrate specimens may have reflected his introspection, aloofness, and inhibitions. Some of the Court Chamberlains deplored in private the fact that he was not more interested in manlier sports like hunting, and some army generals were bold enough to draw Emperor Taisho's attention to the Crown Prince's outlandish pastime. They could hardly complain, however, about the fact that Hirohito also showed, as an adolescent, an almost equally passionate interest in military history. On one occasion, he satisfied another of Emperor Taisho's requirements. Sexual puritanism plays no part in the "bushido" creed, and Taisho despatched one of his young concubines to Hirohito's quarters, who reported back that the fifteen-year-old Crown Prince had been at first somewhat bewildered, but had displayed a certain scientific curiosity in sex, leading in time to a perfectly normal conclusion. The Emperor was relieved that his eldest son, for all his other curious pleasures, was also capable of indulging in what was, in his own case, an almost full-time occupation. This, Hirohito's first sexual experience, did not stimulate a consuming interest in sex. Instead, in his performance with the gifted geisha, one gets the impression of an obedient adolescent once again bowing to imposed traditions.

While Hirohito listened to boring lectures, trawled for shellfish and learned about the Napoleonic Wars, Japan was experiencing the consequences of her new status as a major power. Emperor Taisho, by temperament, was an interventionalist, with a marked pro-German bias, blissfully unaware of Kaiser Wilhelm's own views about the "yellow peril". The First World War, however, saw Japan side with Britain, France and Russia, with Taisho reluctantly bowing to his advisers' arguments that Japan's interests, strategic and financial, were better served in that way.

The real reason, of course, was China, still neutral, though she too was, later, to enter the war against Germany. Japan, without waiting for Allied approval, invaded the German concession of Tsingtao, on the Chinese coast, and also occupied the tiny Pacific Island of Yap, a German colony. As a commissioned officer in both the army and the navy, and as Crown Prince, Hirohito was regularly briefed on international affairs: Japan's reasons for entering the war were made clear to him.

Japan's actual fighting contribution to the war was negligible: the Japanese Navy patrolled the Mediterranean, "protected" Hong Kong and Britain's Shanghai concession, but exacted a huge price in return. Japan's "twenty-one demands", submitted to China's new President, Yuan Shi-K'ai, in 1915, amounted to formal Japanese overlordship over the whole of China. In addition to increased territorial concessions in Shantung Province and in Manchuria, on 99-year leases, Japan demanded that China should formally pledge she would not give away any more concessions to any other power, and would not only turn to Japan for economic development in Manchuria and Tsingtao, but also make Japan China's exclusive banker for any future loans. A further set of demands, which Japan insisted the Chinese keep secret (though they were immediately and deliberately leaked to the press in Peking by the indignant Chinese President), required Peking to use Japanese technical advisers for all its major industrial and armaments projects, to grant Japan the monopoly to build all railways in China, to buy 50 per cent of its military supplies from Japan, and allow Japanese advisers to play a special role in Chinese political affairs.

Hirohito was only fifteen when these demands were made, and of course had no responsibility for them. His tutors presented them in the most favourable light, arguing that Japan was, geographically and historically, destined to play the part of China's "big brother". China's "strong man", Yuan Shi-K'ai, was obliged to accept them under duress. After the war, thanks largely to British and US pressure at the Versailles Conference, all but the Tsingtao and Manchurian clauses were dropped.

They were, however, a watershed, not only in Sino-Japanese but in US-Japanese relations: as early as 1915, in American eyes, the image of "gallant little Japan" began to be replaced by a perception of Japan as a bullying, predator nation.

The "twenty-one demands" also contributed to Japan's rising

militarism, for they put into concrete form the growing nationalism of the new generation of officers who had been fed on the mystique of the Russo-Japanese War. Of all its clauses, it was the Manchuria issue that mattered most. The Russo-Japanese War had wrested concessions in Manchuria from Russia that most nationalistic Japanese believed had not been sufficient. Among Hirohito's small group of aristocratic "uncles", most of them career officers in the army and navy who endorsed the views of the militarists and briefed him about Japan's new role in Asia, Manchuria was regarded as a legitimate prize – not just the existing concessions, but the entire province. Bound up with the Manchurian issue was the whole question of Communist Russia – for with the 1917 October Revolution Russia's presence in Manchuria, even in a reduced form, took on a completely new dimension and was seen as a completely new threat. Among Hirohito's aristocratic coterie, fear of Communism, and hatred of all left-wing organizations, dominated. The bogy of Communism – and the almost irrational fear that it might spread like a cancerous growth throughout Asia – was a proposition the young Hirohito accepted as unquestioningly as did his companions.

The other major event taking place during Hirohito's adolescence was the growing confrontation between the Choshu and Satsuma clans. Both had helped rid the Imperial Dynasty of the shoguns. Now both were jostling for power, and it was proof of Japan's transformation into a modern nation-state that their quarrel was resolved in a series of political confrontations, rather than, as in the past, open warfare. One clan issue, however – the choice of Hirohito's own bride – was of special interest to Hirohito himself. It was only settled after a series of Court intrigues reminiscent of medieval times, but harnessing the forces of "new" Japan – the media, the political parties and even the underworld – with Hirohito a vitally concerned but passive spectator.

One of the few survivors of the glorious Meiji reign was the former army chief of staff, Genral Arimoto Yamagata. This formidable, brutal but politically astute samurai had been the real founder of the modern Japanese army that had crushed the Russians in 1905. He had become a "genro", a permanent, personal counsellor to Emperor Taisho – and like other "genros", past and present, his aim had been not only to advise the Throne, but also to advance the fortunes of his clan, and put his own nominees in key positions. (Another "genro", Prince Saionji, was to outlast him, providing Hirohito with advice, often neglected, right up to his death in 1940.)

Saionji – a leader of the Satsuma clan – and Yamagata between them manipulated not only prime ministerships (they designated likely candidates to the Emperor, who was in theory bound to abide by their advice) but senior military commands. Yamagata first realized his supremacy was being challenged when a non-Choshu appointee, just before World War One, reduced the size of the army by two divisions, to cut defence expenditure. In the confused in-fighting that followed, the cuts were restored, but transferred to the navy. Yamagata was not pleased, for the Navy was dominated by Satsuma clan appointees.

Premierships continued to change hands almost with the frequency of post-war Italy, with real power in the hands of the "genros", but there were further signs of Yamagata's waning influence: in 1916, following the "twenty-one demands", Japan moved into Southern Manchuria, and Yamagata, a cautious tactician, urged moderation. He was well aware the Western powers saw in Japan an aggressive, bullying nation. But, while Yamagata was establishing cordial relations with the Chinese warlord of the North, the Manchu General Chang Tso-lin, whose "capital" was Mukden, and promising him Japan's support, other Japanese "interventionists", encouraged by Emperor Taisho, were fomenting uprisings in Mongolia, and were determined to crush Chang Tso-lin. The Manchu warlord narrowly escaped a Japanese assassination trap in Mukden, and rallied his troops to fling the Japanese out of Mongolia.

This confused, unedifying episode showed how directionless

Japan's foreign policy had become; the reason, though never openly referred to in the Japanese press, and only discussed in hushed voices elsewhere, was that Emperor Taisho was becoming, by fits and starts, increasingly eccentric, unstable and unfit to rule.

It was a secret shared by the "genro", the Empress and Hirohito himself – though he never mentioned it, even to his closest adolescent friends. It explained the growing contempt shown by Yamagata for the Emperor, contrasting him to his legendary father. On good days, as Saionji remembered later, Taisho was capable of brilliance and "shrewd decision-making at least as remarkable as that of Meiji himself". He was sexually promiscuous, and his Chamberlains had great difficulty keeping track of his liaisons with various concubines (for each sexual encounter was supposed to be recorded in a kind of Imperial stud book so that concubines' pregnancies were properly registered), but this was not regarded as a major flaw in an emperor's character. What was embarrassing was his erratic behaviour, so much so that the "genro" were reluctant to let him appear in public at all. On one occasion, during a military parade, he slashed at soldiers with a riding-crop, then embraced an officer, ordered another soldier to unpack his gear, and then insisted on repacking it himself. At a ceremonial opening of the Diet (the parliamentary system was not yet based on universal suffrage – only some 3 million property-owners could vote) in 1915, he rolled up his prepared speech and peered quizzically at the Diet members, as through a telescope. What might have passed for mild eccentricity in any other country was unacceptable in Japan, where the "divine" Emperor's every gesture was closely observed.

Inevitably, as Emperor Taisho's condition (variously thought to have been due to a stroke or an undiagnosed cerebral haemorrhage, but probably stemming from the after-effects of meningitis in childhood) deteriorated, the "genro" assumed increasing power, and so did the Empress, who, like any loyal Japanese wife, rallied to him in his hour of need, overlooking his scandalous past treatment of her. Such was the climate at Court as Hirohito gradually emerged from adolescence to manhood. It was clear to both the Empress and the "genro" that, with Emperor Taisho unlikely to recover, his eldest son would have to bear the *de facto* burden of office far earlier than expected. This meant that the choice of a wife assumed even more importance than usual. Hirohito was having adulthood thrust on him whether he liked it or not. Not for him the carefree bachelorhood of his princely friends and relatives. It would have been unheard-of to attempt to resist moves to marry him off and, besides, it would have been out of character for Hirohito to do so, for both Emperor Meiji and Taisho had unquestioningly accepted the wedding arrangements made for them, aware they were vital to the continued survival of the dynasty. Their acceptance of their brides was probably conditioned by the awareness that marriage had nothing to do with monogamy. Hirohito's mother, Empress Sadako, who herself had married Taisho without ever setting eyes on him, was a level-headed, "modern" woman, who wanted to let her son have at least a partial say in the matter. The Court, and the "genro", drew up a list of suitable girls, and she invited them to tea ceremonies, with Hirohito observing them unseen, like Polonius behind an arras.

There were some charming, good-looking girls from the leading Choshu, Satsuma and Fushimi families, including one remarkable princess who later was to marry a member of the Korean royal family, and later still devote her twilight years to a charitable foundation for orphans of mixed Korean-Japanese race, but Hirohito, surprisingly, chose none of the prettier ones. Instead, he asked his mother to select Nagako, a bright but certainly not beautiful girl whom he had known since childhood – a short, squat, sturdy fourteen-year-old, of impeccable but impoverished lineage.

She was the daughter of Prince Kuni, not a Choshu but a member of the Fushimi house, whose family had intermarried with emperors for centuries. Prince Kuni's wife was a member of the Satsuma clan, and he had nineteen offspring in all, thirteen of them (but not Nagako) the sons and daughters of concubines. Professor Sugiura, Hirohito's ethics lecturer, who also taught at the girls' wing of the Peers' School, where she was a pupil, had spotted her as a possible candidate, and was delighted with his royal pupil's choice.

It also pleased the Empress, who was finding the elderly "genro" Yamagata increasingly overbearing, but it infuriated the crotchety General, who had been convinced that the new Empress would be a Choshu, and needed a representative of his clan at the very highest pinnacle of the Court, in order to restore its fortunes. At first, he extended his congratulations to Prince Kuni on the imperial choice. In the wings, he started to plot to have the betrothal annulled, and in the process enlisted the support of Baron Nakamura, also a Choshu, and Minister of the Imperial Household.

The suspense lasted six years, and during that time Nagako and Hirohito only met nine times, always very briefly. The first meeting took place shortly after the fateful tea ceremony. The two adolescents were allowed to take a walk in the palace grounds alone, but what might have been a romantic moment was marred by a torrential downpour. The second meeting, three weeks later, was for a formal betrothal photograph duly published in the press. Nagako by this time had been removed from school, subjected to gruelling medical examinations, and set up in a separate pavilion in the grounds of her father's house, where, with seventeen assorted tutors and two adolescent companions, she was to remain until marriage, carefully groomed by them and her solicitous father to fulfil her duties as a future empress. She studied English, French and international relations under special tutors, and there were courses on the history of Japan and her relations with Europe. The betrothal was a long one, as it was intended to be, for only if Emperor Taisho's health took a dramatic turn for the worse would it be necessary for Hirohito to ensure that he could sire an heir to the throne.

Yamagata's offensive, four years later, was both unexpected

and masterly. He was eighty-five by now, but shrewdly used a thoroughly modern medium: the press. In a medical journal, a Japanese doctor and expert on heredity wrote a learned article on the transmission of colour-blindness from one generation to the next, and the need to reform the Conscription Law to exclude such sufferers from military service. But the article also examined colour-blindness from the vantage-point of one of Japan's best-known aristocratic families, the Shimazu. It so happened that, on her mother's side, Nagako herself was a Shimazu.

Hardly coincidentally, the former surgeon-general of the Japanese Army, who happened to be Yamagata's personal physician, drew the General's attention to the article, and to evidence of colour-blindness in the Shimazu family. While on the face of it colour-blindness might not appear to be a serious defect, even in empresses, the issue was an important one — for at the Japanese Court every male member of the Imperial Family was expected to enter the armed forces. Showing every sign of hypocritical distress, and listening only to his soldier's conscience, Yamagata, as the oldest living "genro", found it impossible to ignore this warning, which implied that the Emperor's heirs might themselves be born with such an affliction. He asked a group of leading Japanese specialists to study the article and comment on it. When they decided it was scientifically sound, Yamagata approached his Choshu clansmen, Baron Nakamura, the Imperial Household Minister, and the Prime Minister, Hara, and asked them for their advice.

Hara's reaction was that the matter was to be hushed up at all costs: the Imperial Family could not be shown to have made a mistaken choice, for this in itself was an act of *lèse-majesté*. Precisely, said Yamagata. That was why he proposed confronting Nagako's father with the evidence, to ask him to cancel the engagement.

The aged Prince Fushimi was cajoled into the role of go-between, for the Choshu clansmen believed it would be unthinkable for Prince Kuni to go against the wishes of his eminent father.

They were wrong. The meeting degenerated into a noisy family row. "Do you come from the Empress?" Prince Kuni shouted. "Do *they* want the engagement annulled?" Reminding his father that it was the Empress, and Hirohito himself, who had selected his daughter, he told him it was up to them to break off the match; but, if they did, the affront was such he would kill both his daughter and himself.

He began his own counter-offensive: first, he enlisted the support of Professor Sugiura. Sugiura assured him that breaking off the engagement would be a breach of ethics. As one of Nagako's "discoverers", Sugiura had a vested interest in the match. In turn, he threatened to commit "seppuku" if it was annulled.

Prince Kuni then wrote a personal letter to Emperor Taisho, whose affairs, by this time, were handled by the Empress. This masterly document, eloquent yet restrained, made no direct allusion to Choshu clan intrigue. It enclosed a full report of cases of colour-blindness in his family, together with the findings of another group of specialists, contradicting the findings of the first. It came, like all correspondence for the Emperor, into the hands of Baron Nakamura, who, before forwarding it, sent General Yamagata a copy.

At this stage the General made the fatal mistake of intervening directly. In a letter to Prince Kuni, he clearly revealed his own dynastic ambitions:

Of course Prince Kuni is right in insisting that the engagement should be adhered to once entered into. But it should not be forgotten that the engagement was arranged, so to speak, behind our back. If we had been advised of the negotiations, we would have been able to offer our humble point of view beforehand. We are deeply distressed at the way things have turned out.

After questioning the validity of the dissenting doctors' findings, he called for further medical expertise. "In the last part of your Memorandum," he concluded, you say that if you were convinced that the marriage would be to the detriment of the Imperial Family you would gladly cancel your daughter's engagement to the Crown Prince. That is the best witness to your loyalty to the Imperial Family and the cancellation of the engagement would certainly bring public applause. Your reconsideration is sincerely urged.

At the same time, through intermediaries, he let Prince Kuni know that, if he did the sensible thing, he would not regret it financially. Kuni, in turn, informed the Empress of both the offer and the letter. Yamagata, realizing he was dealing with a wily adversary, put pressure on his clansman, the Imperial Household Minister, to speed up preparations for a long trip Hirohito, as Crown Prince, was due to make abroad, in order to get him out of the way.

This was the opportunity to bring the conflict out into the open. The Black Dragon Society, like other ultra-nationalist associations, was against any such foreign travel, on the grounds that exposure to unfamiliar customs might make the Divine Emperor-to-be look ridiculous, and Professor Sugiura, for all his lifelong devotion to ethics, was on intimate terms with Toyama, the Black Dragon leader, and one of the most influential men in Japan. Ultimately, it was Japan's underworld that was to rout the Choshu clan and enable Hirohito to wed the girl of his choice.

Sugiura gave Toyama a detailed account of the crisis, and the underworld leader bristled with indignation at General Yamagata's "disrespect" for the Emperor. He began mobilizing his considerable forces, planting a story in the Japanese press that "a delicate situation had arisen between the Imperial Family and the Imperial Household Minister".

There were also articles criticizing Hirohito's trip abroad, and such was the fear Toyama inspired that Choshu clansmen now mounted guard on General Yamagata's residence. Toyama's masterstroke was his use of the Tokyo mob on National Foundation Day, February 11 — the anniversary of the founding of the Imperial Dynasty by Emperor Jimmu in 660 BC. It was a national holiday (Empire Day) devoted to visits to shrines and prayers for the continued prosperity of Japan and the Imperial Family. Toyama's men distributed tracts supporting Hirohito's betrothal to Nagako, muscular young men paraded through the streets shouting "Death to Yamagata" and "Nakamura insults the Emperor". Hara, the Prime Minister, and leader of the Constitutionalist Party, panicked: his worst fears had materialized. He told Nakamura to obtain an immediate and unequivocal ruling from the Emperor. Did he intend to allow Hirohito to marry Nagako or not?

As a member of the Imperial Household later revealed, Nakamura bowed deeply towards Taisho and the Empress and apologized for his failure to discover in time that there had been cases of colour-blindness in Princess Nagako's family. "Now it is generally known," he asked, "what is your Imperial Majesty's wish?"

Already briefed by his wife, Taisho said, haltingly: "I hear that even science is fallible." The Empress impatiently motioned Nakamura to rise and leave the room. That night, the engagement was officially confirmed, and Nakamura resigned his post. *The Times* said that "a very remarkable demonstration of the power of public opinion" had been responsible for the betrothal. Nowhere was there a mention of Toyama or his men. The Black Dragon leader was surprisingly quick to call off his agitation against Hirohito's foreign trip. The British Foreign Office was now told that Crown Prince Hirohito would arrive in London a week ahead of schedule, and that his trip would last longer than originally planned; which caused the British Government considerable annoyance, since, then as now, State visits were carefully prepared, and were a ritual brooking no last-minute changes, especially when Buckingham Palace was involved. The haste to get Hirohito out of the country as soon as possible, now that the drama was over, was probably due to anxiety that Toyama might change his mind, and not stay "bought".

Hirohito's behaviour revealed a degree of self-control that was daunting in one so young: he had been kept informed of the crisis, but had refused to intervene, even though his own choice of bride was being criticized, and his entire domestic future was at stake. Not once during the crisis did he contact Nagako, to reassure her or express his confidence in its eventual outcome, nor did he visit her before leaving Japan.

CHAPTER THREE

Hirohito left Yokohama aboard the battleship *Katori* on March 3, 1921, with a handful of aides and officers in attendance. There were no important members of the Choshu clan among them. The escort vessel was the battleship *Kajima*, and both his future father-in-law, Prince Kuni, and Professor Sugiura, the matchmaker, were there to see him off.

For the first time, he was free: protocol was less rigid, since most of his Court attendants had been left behind. There were certain unavoidable rituals: Hirohito bowed in the direction of the coast, to the Emperor and Empress, and towards Mount Fuji, as the convoy left Yokohama Bay; and the ships shuddered to a standstill one afternoon while he performed Shinto rites on a religious anniversary day.

He wrestled, swam, played quoits, watched films, and studied English and French. A first-hand account of the trip exists, written by two Palace secretaries who accompanied Hirohito to Europe. Even in the leisurely annals of the Imperial Court their slow pace was something of a record, for their work did not appear for four years. It was not, however, altogether their fault. The first edition was entirely destroyed in the 1923 Tokyo earthquake.[1]

Their hagiographic prose is involuntarily comic, but this kind of flattery was *de rigueur* at the time:

The subject itself is too great and august for our humble pen. We found him a prince worthy of our profound admiration and whole-hearted devotion. His lofty and noble character, his manliness, his intellectual brilliance, his manifold interests, his sympathetic mentality, his wonderful memory, his fine sportsmanship, his most natural and unassuming character, his peace-loving disposition and charming demeanour, his strength of will; the happy union of all these fine qualities never elsewhere found together was revealed to us in full light. It occurred to us that such a joy and pleasure must by no means be monopolized, and that it was our bounden duty to share it with our fellow-countrymen by putting down in black and white the impressions of the most memorable tour ever recorded in the annals of our country.

Hirohito was also praised for his democratic spirit in ordering crew members to sit closer to him during film shows so they could get a better view. But an explosion aboard the *Kajima*, in which three stokers died, and another engine-room accident aboard Hirohito's own flagship, killing two sailors, are dismissed in the book in a couple of paragraphs, as a mildly irritating contretemps.

Hirohito stopped on his way to London at Hongkong, Singapore, Colombo, Cairo, Malta and Gibraltar, receiving on the way the enthusiastic homage of overseas Japanese. Field-Marshal Allenby threw a huge garden party for him in Cairo, which was disrupted by a violent sandstorm; in Malta he attended an Italian opera company's rendering of Verdi's *Otello*, and his first Western cultural experience left him somewhat baffled; in Gibraltar he went to the races, was asked to bet on a horse, and chose one at random, which won. Everywhere, he visited architectural sites, botanical gardens and natural history museums.

During the 28-day cruise, he rehearsed and memorized phrases in French and English, rehearsed the speeches and toasts he would have to pronounce, and perused the lists of foreign guests whose names he would be expected to recognize. With typical Japanese thoroughness, a diplomat from the Embassy in London joined the Crown Prince in Gibraltar with an updated schedule. This was Shigeru Yoshida, later Japan's durable post-war prime minister. On arrival at Spithead, the Prince of Wales was there to greet Hirohito, and the Royal Navy put on an impressive display for him.

He was amazed by the spontaneous welcome he received in London. "Such a great crowd uncontrolled by the police," he remarked. He was also surprised, and delighted, by the informal cordiality shown by the British Royal Family.

This was the time of privileged Anglo-Japanese relations, and the links between the two navies were still strong. While Hirohito was a guest at Buckingham Palace, King George V entered his bedroom suite one evening, unannounced and half-dressed. Hirohito was amazed that the King of England should wander the corridors of his palace unescorted, tieless, and clap him on the shoulder like an old friend. "I hope, me boy, that everyone is giving you everything you need," said the King. "I'll never forget how your grandfather treated me and me brother when we were in Yokohama. No geishas here, though, I'm afraid. Her Majesty wouldn't allow it."

The member of the British Royal Family he most admired, Hirohito told aides, was the Prince of Wales, for his "casual elegance" and relaxed approach to his duties. What impressed him was his languid, mocking, aristocratic contempt for protocol, and his masterful handling of the more pompous Palace officials.

Hirohito spent three days at Buckingham Palace, eight days in Chesterfield House as a guest of the Government, and a week in Scotland shooting with the Duke of Atholl at Blair Castle. He was astonished to discover that the Duke and Duchess only used their castle for formal occasions, living almost servantless in a nearby cottage, and that the hundreds of servants waiting on them and organizing the shoots were in fact clan locals who had volunteered their services free. He was even more amazed when they joined in the Highland reels, dancing with the Duke and Duchess with affectionate familiarity. Here, Hirohito told an aide, was "genuine democracy without class distinctions".

He spent a further week in England as a private visitor, toured arms factories, shipyards, saw Manchester, Glasgow, the Bank of England, Oxford University and Eton College. There was an embarrassing moment when his aides discovered an irreverent piece of prose about him in the *Eton College Chronicle* and tried to have it suppressed. The only unfavourable article was an ill-informed diatribe against Japan in the *Church Times*. Hirohito watched a performance of Pavlova's *Dying Swan*, had his portrait painted by Augustus John, and entertained European-based diplomats, businessmen and military attachés. Such was the importance of the occasion that some Japanese socialites had travelled all the way to England in the hope of being invited.

In his talks with George V, Hirohito put his knowledge of recent military history to good use: much of their conversations had to do with the Great War, still a vivid, traumatic memory. He amazed one British general by his familiarity with the British Order of Battle, correcting him on a point of detail. Later, visiting Belgian battlefields, he cabled King George that the "impressive and edifying scene reminded me of the words in which Your Majesty explained to me the sanguinary character of the struggle on this field of honour at Ypres".

The recent war was one of the few subjects of interest he and King George had in common, but the King may have had another purpose in mind: to remind Hirohito of the huge losses suffered by the Allies, implicitly contrasting them with Japan's negligible contribution.

With Lloyd George, the Prime Minister, topics of mutual interest were fewer. As the authors of *The Crown Prince's European Tour* somewhat condescendingly put it, "one could only marvel at the coming together of the Heir to the most ancient and historic throne in the world and the nephew of a cobbler from an obscure Welsh village – an incongruity furnishing food for thought to philosophers".

The next leg of the Crown Prince's trip was France, and here too Hirohito's passion for military history was gratified by the grizzled French heroes of "la grande guerre". He went through the immutable routine of any important foreign guest – lunching at the Elysée Palace with President Millerand, laying a wreath at the tomb of the Unknown Soldier, also visiting the Eiffel

Tower and getting lost on the Paris Métro. He took in a brief tour of the Louvre (*Le Temps* noted that it was at a jogger's pace) and a lengthy one of Napoleon's tomb at the Invalides.

From the protocol point of view, his visit was a private one, but he was treated like a sovereign on a state visit. For the first time, he went shopping and handled money, buying an indifferent oil painting (which he later gave his ADC, General Honjo, as a parting gift) and a bust of Napoleon, to put in his study next to those of his other two heroes, Lincoln and Darwin. He also made a generous contribution to the upkeep of the tomb.

He saw Versailles, again briefly, went to the Opéra, and took in a performance of *Macbeth* by an American touring company. He shopped at fashionable stores, ate snails at Lapérouse and, in an exclusive interview with the United Press correspondent in Paris, praised America's "noble ideals and patriotism", expressing the hope and desire to visit the US soon. "I know to what point justice and freedom are valued in America and that no efforts are ever spared by her people in the cause of humanity," he said. "I hope that America and Japan will always be found working hand in hand not only to our mutual benefit but to ensure lasting peace throughout the world."

Marshal Pétain, the victor of Verdun, took him to the grim battlefield. He also attended army manoeuvres in Alsace, visited the French Military Academy at Saint-Cyr, and watched French army manoeuvres at Metz.

So many Japanese officers flocked to Paris to see him that the Sûreté, France's counter-espionage organization, became interested. It was Prince Higashikuni, a member of the Fushimi clan and a close kinsman of Hirohito himself (he had married one of Meiji's daughters), who came under particular suspicion. He was "studying" in Paris, at the advanced age of thirty-five, and the Sûreté was convinced that he ran Japan's intelligence network in Europe.

A "familiarization tour" of Europe, America or Asia, often lasting as long as three years, was the standard reward for all promising young officers, and espionage was required experience for anyone earmarked for promotion to the top. In Asia, as China was shortly to find out to her cost, Japanese intelligence networks would in time establish devastating "fifth column" networks, inventing a new form of warfare later copied by Franco and the Axis powers.

In Europe, Japanese agents stood out like sore thumbs, but worked with enormous diligence: not having actually fought in the Great War, the Japanese armed forces had fallen behind technically, and there was enormous hunger, in army and navy GHQs, for the latest weaponry and tactics. Japanese troops had been sent to Siberia in the wake of the 1917 Russian revolution and had been aghast to find that the Communist troops there had been anything but soft. Higashikuni introduced Hirohito to some of the promising junior officers on missions abroad.

Before returning to Japan, Hirohito toured Belgium (more battlefields) and the Netherlands before taking a private train to Toulon to board his flagship there. On the way back, the fleet anchored at Naples, and Hirohito visited Rome, the Vatican (where he had an audience with Pope Benedict XV) and more arms factories. He also met Czechoslovakia's President Masaryk, himself on a visit to Italy.

Time and again, Hirohito was to refer to this trip as "the happiest time of his life". Court officials noted that it changed him. "He blossomed," one Chamberlain said, "and stood taller on his return."

The crowds greeting him in Japan showed the trip had been a public-relations success at home as well as in Europe, focussing attention on an up-and-coming country and on a young Emperor-to-be, who might be expected to transform the relationship between the Imperial system and the people. He brought back some bagpipes for his future father-in-law, Prince Kuni, and a cask of malt whisky for himself – a gift from the Duke of Atholl. This he stored away for a celebration party.

No sooner was he home than he was immediately plunged into a series of crises. The first was provoked by the expected and relatively unmourned death of General Yamagata, the "genro" who had opposed his choice of his bride. Both Hirohito and his Court came to the conclusion that there was no need to replace him: henceforth, Prince Saionji would be the sole surviving "genro". Another death, far more preoccupying because it renewed the tradition of political violence, was the murder of Emperor Taisho's Prime Minister, Takashi Hara, stabbed by a right-wing extremist. Though the Black Dragon leader Toyama had not been directly involved, the murderer's motives showed how crazily susceptible some Japanese were where military matters were concerned. Hara died because a fanatic felt he had shown disrespect for the Navy, by assuming the vacant Navy Ministry portfolio while the previous incumbent was away in Washington negotiating the terms of a treaty limiting ceilings of US, British and Japanese navy tonnage. His murderer later told his judges in court that he had no regrets, because the dead man had insulted not only the Navy but the Emperor as well. After serving a relatively light twelve-year sentence, the killer would get a pension for life from a rightist group. The court's leniency implied that politically motivated murder carried "extenuating circumstances".

These were interesting times for Japan, but anxious ones for Hirohito, the princely oligarchy and conservatives in general. Largely as a result of the personal liberal and "internationalist" convictions of Prince Saionji, who had headed the Japanese delegation to the Versailles Peace Treaty, Japan had not only adhered to the League of Nations but seemed prepared to play a leading role in it. This was almost entirely Saionji's own doing, for the majority of the Government, in 1920–21, was only mildly in favour of such involvement. Saionji, an exceptional statesman and Francophile, who had spent ten years in France studying law before entering the Foreign Ministry (and spoke perfect French with a curious Marseillais accent, because he had been in the South of France) was, in those heady early twenties, a formidably influential figure at Court. By this time one of the few links with the Meiji past (he had served both Emperors Meiji and Taisho), this witty, urbane aesthete was convinced that Japan's future lay in her close cooperation with the West and in the rejection of her militarist past. In a flowery piece of prose at the time of Versailles, he had outlined his convictions in an article addressed to the favourite paper of his student youth, *Le Petit Marseillais*:

In the age of staggering progress in which we live, it is the duty of men of all walks of life and of all races to help in the destruction of all those elements, like Prussian militarism, that could halt or even delay civilization's progress ... This message cannot lend itself to any ambiguity ... The peace that must emerge from the [Versailles] conference must not be just a European peace, but well and truly world peace and it must be kept for ever. Humanity must be able to draw lessons from the mistakes of the past, if it is to live in happiness in rich and eternal peace.

One of the reasons why Hirohito, as Crown Prince, was regarded as a promising, liberal-minded monarch-to-be was the constant presence at his side of Prince Saionji, who had been, at Emperor Meiji's court, the first nobleman to wear Western dress and cut his hair short, Western-style, had met and be-friended Georges Clemenceau, the Goncourt brothers and Liszt, and had a passion for Houbigant soaps and scents and for Vichy water. Saionji saw in the Versailles Peace Treaty and the establish-ment of the League of Nations Japan's only hope of breaking with her isolationist past. As he wrote to Emperor Taisho in 1920 (a letter actually read by Hirohito because by this time Taisho's illness had robbed him of most of his mental faculties):

the results of the [Versailles] Conference will have a profound effect on the position of Japan in international politics. Japan has joined the ranks of the five great powers and this is the beginning of our participation in European politics. Furthermore, since we occupy an important place in the League of Nations, we have acquired the right to participate in future in all East-West matters.

The note was designed to convince Hirohito that Japan could exert her influence far more efficiently through peaceful diplomacy and close cooperation with the West than through the pursuit of militaristic Asian adventures. Saionji's own reward for his role at Versailles – the title of Prince and the highest-ranking Grand Order of the Chrysanthemum – implied that his was now the message the Palace was hearing most attentively.

The early twenties were years of promise but also of economic hardship and disillusion. World War One prosperity had ended suddenly, and Japan was conscious, as never before, of the cost of her military infrastructure and of her new role as a major power.

It was a time marked by a serious agricultural crisis, leading to an influx of farmers' sons and daughters into the towns, a weakening of family ties, and urban unemployment; by worsening employer-worker relations, and the beginning of a class war; by a proliferation of avant-garde and "leftist" clubs, frequently raided by the police, causing the Palace, and the conservative Right generally, to apprehend a "Communist millennium", of which the Soviet phenomenon had been, in their view, the forerunner. Socialism and Marxism, though virtually outlawed, were spreading from struggling, semi-clandestine trades union leaders to the offspring of prosperous middle-class families, so that "Marx boy" now became part of the Japanese vocabulary. So did "Moga" (modern girl) and "Mobo" (modern boy). Japan had her "flappers" and its "jazz age" enthusiasts. Japanese historians labelled these times the years of "Ero", "Guro" and "Nonsensu" – eroticism, grotesquerie and nonsense.

The avant-garde and leftist clubs, however, were nowhere near as numerous as the mushrooming right-wing "nationalist" clubs and secret societies that formed, re-formed, split up and came together again with bewildering frequency from the early twenties onwards.

According to the authoritative *Brocade Banner* study[2] (carried out by US intelligence experts in the immediate post-war period) such secret societies reached the staggering figure of "between 800 and 900" by 1941. Though these societies differed enormously in importance, their "basic premise was that the Emperor, by virtue of his divine origin, should rule not only Japan but all peoples of the earth". They all had one thing in common: a fanatically professed devotion to the Emperor as the bulwark against lax behaviour of all kinds, political and moral.

Hirohito himself, after observing freer societies at work and play in Europe, was in tune with this new spirit, becoming – briefly – a "mobo" himself. He went to the races in Tokyo for the first time, was seen at night-clubs, ordered tweed plus-fours (of the kind he had seen the Prince of Wales wearing) for golf, and became addicted to bacon-and-egg breakfasts. He reduced the size of the Court, streamlining it, and, determined to be the first truly monogamous Emperor in Japanese history, sent all "Ladies-in-waiting" packing, except those in attendance on his mother the Empress. He told his Chamberlains to remove his traditional kimonos from his wardrobe – never again would he wear them, except for the occasional religious ceremony and after bathing.

He tried to emulate the free and easy spirit he had witnessed when staying with the Atholls – with disastrous results. In December 1921 he threw his first and last informal party in the Akasaka Palace to celebrate his return. There were geishas as well as his princely coterie and childhood friends (males only), jazz records were played, there was dancing and a good deal of drinking. Some of his guests (mostly Peers' School old boys or boyhood friends from his kindergarten days) took literally his command to treat him not as Crown Prince but as a friend. The Duke of Atholl's whisky went to their heads. They became over-familiar, either embarrassingly maudlin or mildly disrespectful. The informality of it all appalled the Chamberlains. Scandalized Court officials informed Prince Saionji who immediately boarded the train for Tokyo from his country retreat. At the palace, he gave Hirohito a stern talking-to. Firmly but deferentially, he told a contrite Crown Prince that the worst aspect of it all had been "the appalling familiarity towards His Royal Highness".

It was not the drinking, or the geishas, to which he objected: Hirohito's illustrious grandfather had been addicted to both, and Prince Saionji was no puritan. What really worried him, for all his liberalism, was the fear that Hirohito might start questioning traditional values which, alone, had ensured the unbroken continuity of the Royal House. Privacy had to be maintained at all costs if Imperial prestige was to survive the hazards of these changing times. Hirohito promised it would not happen again.

In Japan's armed forces, too, a new spirit prevailed. On the face of it, Japan's army and navy were still highly regarded institutions, but, with time, memories of the Russo-Japanese War had faded, and the Chiefs of Staff faced both a recruitment problem and politicians' demands for retrenchment. This only made the career officers of both services more determined than ever not to compromise. On the contrary, their leaders argued, what was required was not less but more expenditure, for Japan's armed forces were now old-fashioned compared to those of countries which had participated in major Great War campaigns.

Its idealogues were two maverick intellectuals who were to play a leading part in the dramatic events on the road to Pearl Harbor. One, Dr. Shumei Okawa, a strong personality in close touch with key Palace officials, was to go on trial for war crimes in Tokyo after the Second World War, only to be released after brilliantly faking temporary insanity; the other, Ikki Kita, his erstwhile friend and guru, was shot by a Japanese firing-squad in 1936. Both men influenced not only the army and navy nationalists, but also Imperial Family members, including Prince Chichibu, who was briefly attracted to socialism in general, and in particular, to Kita's brand of national socialism, which advocated not only ceilings for individual and corporate fortunes, profit-sharing and an eight-hour working day, but also the nationalization of all assets owned by the

Imperial Family. Though this worried some Palace advisers, their alarm was tempered by the knowledge that Prince Chichibu's enthusiasms, though intense, were generally short-lived.

Another prominent aristocrat "infected" in his youth with avant-garde ideas was Prince Fuminaro Konoye, later to become Prime Minister three times in the crucial years leading up to Japan's "great Asian war". Konoye, after graduating from Tokyo Imperial University, wrote a much-discussed article attacking the terms of the Versailles Peace Treaty and the establishment of the League of Nations as mere window-dressing for continuing Western colonialism. Having established himself as a left-wing nationalist, Konoye, whose own father was President of the House of Peers, and whose lineage was almost as aristocratic as that of Hirohito himself, then scandalized Palace officials by hinting that he might emigrate to the United States permanently because he was bored with old-fashioned, conservative Japan and its excessively antiquated Court ritual.

Dr. Okawa, also a brilliant Tokyo University graduate and Chinese linguist who had spent years in China on various secret intelligence assignments, was a protégé both of Count Makino, the Satsuma clansman who had accompanied Hirohito on his European trip (and was soon to become High Chamberlain), and of Hirohito's future father-in-law, Prince Kuni. He also had extremely close relations with the Black Dragon Society, and was Toyama's favourite intellectual. It was to Okawa that Makino turned when Hirohito, shortly after his return, decided to transform the Palace Meteorological Observatory into a privately-subsidized "think tank" variously known as the "Social Problems Research Institute", the "University Lodging House", or the "Daigaku" school (the title was derived from the Confucian analect of that name), with Makino in nominal charge.

Inspired by similar institutions in Europe, Hirohito probably intended it to supplement the more formal Staff College and the school for junior diplomats run by the Foreign Ministry. It became, in the four years of its ephemeral existence, a select and secretive club, where bright young bureaucrats mingled with up-and-coming staff officers and policemen, and heard lectures by Confucian scholars, members of the Imperial Household, and prominent generals and War Ministry officials. "The place," noted *Brocade Banner*, "was frequented by imperialistic young army and navy officers who were later to play a prominent part in the attempted coups d'état of the thirties." Hirohito may have envisaged it as a Japanese Chatham House or Council on Foreign Relations, but with coopted members only. It also acquired the reputation of being an "Intelligence University", providing contingency plans on anything from naval rearmament to undercover operations in China and Manchuria; and its members, long after its demise, stuck together and regarded themselves as part of a privileged, secretive clan in close touch with the Palace and the Emperor – able and ready to do his bidding, clandestinely if need be.

The Lodging House also became the sounding-board for Dr. Okawa's own pet theories, a blend of right-wing national socialism and the kind of ultra-nationalist mysticism embodied in the French poetry of Charles Péguy and the writings of the right-wing nationalist French ideologue Charles Maurras. Since Okawa was a brilliant debater, as well as a formidable operator, it is no wonder that many of the graduates emerged as arrant nationalists.

It is not clear why Hirohito closed it down in 1924. The pretext was that the building had become, after the earthquake, structurally unsound, but this was not the real reason. It may be that Dr. Okawa had turned into a somewhat embarrassing figure. Hirohito, always frugal, may also have baulked at the continued expense. Perhaps he felt that the Lodging House had served its purpose, bringing together the best and the brightest of Japan's military élite and administrative establishment and instilling in them a common sense of purpose. Hirohito cannot have been unaware of the contents of the University Lodging House seminars, for it was out of character for him to take an initiative and then lose interest in it. There was a schoolmasterly side to him: seminars on all sorts of subjects, from Zen philosophy to ancient Chinese history, continued to be staged inside the Palace even during the darkest moments of World War Two.

Dr. Okawa was not the only ideologue to preach the dogma of authoritarian nationalism and the need for territorial expansion. There were, within the Japanese establishment, three conflicting views on Japan's role, and Hirohito, with his interest in strategy and military history, again cannot have been unaware of them: one view was reflected by a powerful lobby which believed that Soviet Russia represented Japan's greatest permanent threat, both because of her physical presence in Manchuria and because her leaders openly preached world revolution. The very Japanese qualities of respect for authority and unquestioning discipline, the argument ran, made the Japanese rank-and-file vulnerable to Communism. Therefore, Japan's long-term aim should be to confront the USSR in Siberia, to gain territory there, ensure that Soviet influence was eradicated in Manchuria and in Asia in general. This concept became known as the "Strike North" theory.

Another school of thought focussed on Japan's need to take the lead in Asia, to help the Chinese overcome their many problems and drive out the Western colonialists there. At its best, and most idealistic, this policy was pro-Chinese, and implied real friendship and equality. Japan was uniquely placed to witness the decay of Chinese institutions, and the predatory nature of Western powers. This "positive attitude" towards China took many forms: it was embodied in the brutal "twenty-one demands", but it also explains why both Sun Yat-sen, and, later, Chiang Kai-chek, potential Japanese allies, were initially given a cordial welcome in Japan. Both Chinese leaders, in their day, embodied change. It was Japan's misfortune that Sun Yat-sen was very quickly removed from power, and shortly afterwards fell ill and died. Chiang Kai-chek was also seen, at first, as a possible ally and collaborator in a Japanese "Grand Design" for Asia.

Finally, there were those who believed that Japan, a

"developed" country on a par with the Western powers, could not afford to limit her sphere of influence to China but must compete, on world terms, with the same Western powers, in China and elsewhere. This meant that Japan must not let Britain, France and the Netherlands assume that their colonial possessions in Asia were secure for ever. This came to be known as the "Strike South" theory.

If Japan was to be a major world power, she had to be treated as an equal. She also had to have the means to defend herself against other world powers. Hence the indignation shown by many Japanese at alleged discrimination over the number of warships Japan was to be allowed to build and the maximum size and range of the naval guns. Hence, too, Japan's anger at the "white races'" refusal, at the Versailles Peace Conference, to agree on a text calling for legal equality among nations "without racial distinctions". This was compounded by a US Supreme Court ruling preventing any Japanese from becoming US citizens, and by the *de facto* immigration ban on the Japanese ruthlessly enforced by Canada, Latin America, Australia, New Zealand and the United States. For all Hirohito's friendly statement in Paris to the United Press, American attitudes towards Japan, some Japanese were already arguing in 1921, were profoundly hypocritical.

All these issues were certainly discussed at the University Lodging House, and at Dr. Okawa's later "school", as was a noted bestseller by a retired lieutenant-general, Kojiro Sato, published in 1921, entitled *If Japan and America fight*. A Russo-Japanese war veteran, Sato reflected in print the anger and resentment felt by Japanese officers who believed that Japan's legitimate claims embodied in the "twenty-one demands" had been unfairly quashed by the major powers at Versailles.

As a British officer, Captain Malcolm Kennedy, who spent some time with the Japanese Army in the early twenties, was to write, Japanese officers felt that "just as Japan was getting really skilful at the game of grab, the other powers, most of whom had all they wanted anyway, suddenly had an access of virtue and called the game off". Their vision of America, he wrote, was of "a selfish meddler, interfering unreasonably with Japan's national aspirations", and they saw Japan as a beleaguered fortress facing a hostile world.[3] They were relatively tolerant, at this time, of both Germany's and Britain's axis of influence, referred to, in the military jargon of the time, as the "three BBBs" (Berlin-Budapest-Baghdad), and the "three CCCs" (Cairo-Capetown-Calcutta). It was the "three AAAs", the America-Alaska-Asia axis, that were seen as the real threat to Japan. Dr. Okawa, in 1924, in a book called *Asia, Europe and Japan* which also considered the possibility of war with the US, wrote: "These two countries, the US and Japan, are destined to fight each other as Greece had to battle Persia and Rome Carthage. O Japan, will that be in a year, 10 years, 30 years? No one can tell. Prepare yourselves for that heavenly call."

Sato claimed that the United States had "insolently" revealed her imperialistic ambitions "while professing the open door". Her anti-immigration policy had "insulted the Japanese race". He advocated lightning raids on strategic American centres by Japanese "special forces" in a blitzkrieg which would terrify the US into submission and a more understanding attitude towards Japan. This, the least credible part of his book, was studded with appeals to the Japanese to remember that, in the past, they had overcome insuperable odds through their "indomitable will", and that, in the long run, it was this almost mystical determination that would be required to challenge, and overcome, an enemy of such a size. He also strongly urged Japan's Education Minister to institute compulsory training in Japan's schools, and a general militarization of Japanese society. If his advice were followed, Japan could win, "for in the point of mentality, the Japanese are rather superior than inferior to the Americans".

Though he was, eventually, to reject the "Strike North" theory in its entirety, show considerable impatience with those who caused Japan to be embroiled in a protracted war with China, and clearly favour the "Strike South" option, Hirohito's mind was not made up on any of these issues when, after a further deterioration in Emperor Taisho's health, he became Regent on November 25, 1921. Memories of his European trip were still vivid, and they were revived by the Prince of Wales's return visit to Japan in 1922. Hirohito played golf with Edward, and showed himself to be in every sense a modern, enlightened monarch-to-be. Japanese newspaper editors, however, were shocked by a photograph showing the Prince of Wales dressed up for fun as a rickshaw-puller.

To the Japanese, the first day of September is traditionally the equivalent of Friday the thirteenth. Superstition was hugely bolstered when, on September 1, 1923, the worst natural calamity in the history of Japan struck. Just before noon, a huge earthquake hit Tokyo, Yokohama and the whole surrounding area known as Kanto. At the Tokyo Seismological Institute, readings went right off the Richter scale. An initial "tidal wave on land" undulated through towns, villages and fields leaving devastation in its wake; concrete blocks and shanty-towns alike were flattened, and only those few buildings specially designed to withstand earthquakes, including Frank Lloyd Wright's Imperial Hotel (one of the Imperial Family's prized pieces of property) and a few other office buildings in the centre of Tokyo, designed by American architects, remained unscathed.

The charcoal hibachi stove was then in use in most Japanese homes, which were mostly built of wood. Since most Japanese housewives were preparing their midday meal at the time, the earthquake was followed by a gigantic series of conflagrations, wiping out most of the Tokyo and Yokohama residential areas. In Yokohama, huge oil storage vats collapsed into the sea, and burst into flames. When the fires finally died out, over half a million homes in the Kanto area had been destroyed, and official casualties ranged from 100,000 to 150,000 dead.

The Emperor and Empress, in the hill resort of Nikko, were unscathed, and so was Princess Nagako. The Imperial Palace buildings suffered only minor damage, and Hirohito, at work in his office, did not leave his desk until urged to do so. Japan was in the grip of another Cabinet crisis, and the incoming Premier, the retired Admiral Yamamoto (unrelated to the man who masterminded the attack on Pearl Harbor), was slightly injured by falling masonry as he was holding a party conference inside the Navy Club. Power cuts were general, and electricity was not restored for days. Most radio communications went dead, and no newspapers could be published.

In Japanese folk history, the earthquakes which had ravaged that part of the coast since time immemorial were the work of giant catfish living at the bottom of the sea, which only stirred when the Japanese race misbehaved. This perhaps explains the otherwise absurd reaction of Japanese officialdom: whereas the natural reaction of almost any government would have been to make its plight public, and appeal for international aid, Japanese officials tried their best to keep the news from leaking out, jamming what few radio communications still functioned and denying, until it was no longer possible to do so, that anything untoward had happened.

A young Royal Navy officer, George C. Ross, was aboard a British warship that entered Yokohama with medicine and blankets shortly after the earthquake. He recalls that survivors complained to him that the captains of Japanese Navy vessels at anchor there behaved with extreme callousness: thousands of survivors tried to escape the fires raging on land by swimming out to sea, "but were generally not allowed to board the ships". The Japanese attempt to keep the calamity secret from the outside world was "incomprehensible", he added.

Some of the Palace grounds in Tokyo were opened to survivors as first-aid stations, and Hirohito set up an improvised command post in the gardens. The investiture of Premier-elect Yamamoto took place inside Akasaka Palace the following day, and a few days later martial law was proclaimed. But neither Hirohito, nor the new Government, took the necessary steps to reassure and comfort the dazed survivors. Though Hirohito was eventually to visit the damaged zones, there was no immediate informal Royal tour of the city. The weight of protocol was such that Palace officials were incapable of reacting to unforeseen situations such as this one, and Hirohito himself seems to have lacked the imagination, or social concern, to insist on making an immediate public appearance, though he did, weeks later, tour the ruined capital on horseback, and contributed 10 million yen to the relief fund.

What followed showed that, however much Japan had moved with the times since the Meiji restoration, its Western veneer was only skin-deep: old atavistic fears and superstitions remained strong. Korean immigrants were Japan's *lumpenproletariat*, and had an execrable reputation. Rumours spread throughout Tokyo and Yokohama that the hated Koreans and the leftists had offended the spirits of Japan's ancestors by their conduct, provoking the earthquake. Instinctively, Tokyo survivors turned on them, blaming them not only for the looting but for the earthquake itself. Thousands were massacred, while police and army units stood by.

The earthquake was not the only calamity of the year: on December 27, in Toramoron, Hirohito was in a carriage, on his way to open the new Diet session, when he was shot at by a disgruntled member of the Shoshu clan, Daisaku Namba. The official version was that Namba was a pro-Communist revolutionary. He was also the son of a well-known politician, and the weapon he used was a pistol concealed in a stick, originally purchased in London by a prominent Choshu dignitary, Hirobumi Ito. This time there were no "extenuating circumstances", and Namba was executed. Police reported that he died shouting Marxist slogans.

A month almost to the day after the assassination attempt, on January 26, 1924, Hirohito was married: there had already been one postponement, because of the earthquake. Some Palace officials wanted the ceremony delayed again so that guests should not be reminded of the recent calamity, but Nagako insisted: she had been engaged for five years, and felt she had waited long enough.

[1] *The Crown Prince's European Tour*, Osaka Mainichi 1925.
[2] *The Brocade Banner, the Story of Japanese Nationalism*, Civil Intelligence Section, GHQ Far Eastern Command, Military Intelligence Section, US General Staff, 1946.
[3] M. D. Kennedy, *The Military Side of Japanese Life*, Houghton Mifflin, 1923.

CHAPTER FOUR

A royal wedding is always a great morale-booster: Hirohito's was no exception. The traumatic events of the previous three months were forgotten in the excitement, and loyal Japanese, already avid newspaper readers thanks to a half-century of compulsory education, were able to enter into the spirit of things. Japanese press coverage almost equalled that of Britain's popular newspapers in its wealth of detail and gossipy, but always deferential, handling of every conceivable aspect of the hugely publicized event.

January was not the ideal month but January 26, 1924, turned out to be a fine, mild day. A national holiday was proclaimed, and there were celebrations all over Japan. Large crowds gathered outside the Palace walls, and along the route taken by the royal couple. Hirohito left the Akasaka Palace for the Imperial Palace grounds, alone and in a closed horse-drawn carriage, wearing lieutenant-colonel's uniform. The bride, in another, similarly closed carriage, arrived at the Imperial Palace in a separate procession. Those who stood patiently for hours outside the grounds and along the route of the procession cheered and shouted "banzai", but all but the boldest continued to avert their gaze in religious awe. It was not wholly unlike a British royal wedding, with all the excitement of watching the distinguished Japanese guests arrive for the religious ceremony, and, later, the diplomatic corps for a separate afternoon reception. But the ceremony itself, from beginning to end, took place within the Palace, and even the most privileged guests caught only a glimpse of the actual rites.

These took place inside the Imperial Family Shrine, a small, secluded temple hidden by a screen of trees and strictly out of bounds to all but the Imperial Family and a handful of Shinto priests. The seven hundred guests, all Japanese — they included the notorious underworld boss, Toyama, who had done so much to make the marriage possible, but not Emperor Taisho, who was "too sick" to attend — waited outside the shrine. Apart from a few priests, Princess Nagako and Hirohito himself, only Prince Kujo, the "Master of the Rites", was present at the actual ceremony.

Preparations had taken several hours, for both Hirohito and his bride had to change into heavy, cumbersome ceremonial dress. Hirohito's was an orange robe and skirt, and he carried a sceptre and wore a black lacquered hat. His part in the proceedings, in addition to the marriage vows themselves, consisted of addressing the spirits of his ancestors in the Court language used only for such rites — a language totally incomprehensible to ordinary Japanese — informing them of his decision to marry Nagako. Then came the relatively simple exchange of vows. Hirohito, then Nagako, in a scarlet and lilac kimono, drank three times from a goblet of sacred wine. A hundred-and-one-gun salute marked the end of the ceremony, after which they emerged from the shrine, and briefly faced the bowing guests. There was no immediate secluded honeymoon: the newly married couple spent the night in Akasaka Palace, and the following day Hirohito and his bride visited Emperor Taisho, in Numazu, to pay their respects.

Loyal subjects eagerly awaited news of Nagako's pregnancy, but were disappointed: not till the spring of 1925 was such an announcement made, and the disappointment, when Nagako finally gave birth to a baby girl, Shigeko, was palpable: only male heirs could ensure the dynasty's continuity. Princess Nagako's pregnancy did, however, put paid to a nationwide rumour that the late General Yamagata had cursed Nagako on his deathbed and vowed that she would be barren. After this first birth, the older Palace Chamberlains, and Prince Saionji, the "genro", felt that Hirohito would be luckier next time. If not, they hinted – but never in his presence – a royal concubine could always be brought into play.

This showed how out of touch they were with Hirohito's state of mind. For all his aloofness, during the engagement years, Hirohito immediately proved to be a model and affectionate, if somewhat formal and predictable, companion. The spectacle of the Meiji Court, and the memories of his own father's excesses, turned him into an uxorious, primly monogamous husband. What had been extreme, almost maniacal orderliness in childhood now manifested itself in rigid routine. There were timetables for everything. Court officials knew precisely when Hirohito was likely to be out riding, or playing golf, or feeding the birds and swans in the Palace gardens, what afternoons he would spend with Dr Hattori, now one of his ADCs, studying marine biology. So methodical was the Imperial routine that there were probably set dates and times for procreation. Princess Nagako very quickly adjusted to her new life and appeared to enjoy it: in the early years of their marriage, Kanroji noted, their "attentive intimacy was a beautiful thing to see".

Hirohito's honeymoon years were also something of a honeymoon for Japan herself. From 1924 to 1927, the country enjoyed an unprecedentedly liberal spell: universal suffrage for all males of twenty-five and over was introduced, the size of the army was slightly reduced, and the Japanese press became more lively, and more openly critical, than at any time in its history. The two main political parties, Minseito and Seiyukai, ruled alternately, as if by tacit agreement. Politically they were practically indistinguishable (Minseito perhaps a shade more liberal) but in both camps supporters were more swayed by personalities than by issues. Both parties were heavily dependent on the large industrial conglomerates, the "Zaibatsu", with Minseito financed by Mitsubishi and Seiyukai by Mitsui. Corruption was widespread, the conglomerates dictated economic policy, and, with a few outstanding exceptions, politicians' reputations were low. For all that, Japan seemed to be moving towards a form of parliamentary democracy. On the diplomatic front, she was a signatory to the "nine power treaty" guaranteeing the independence and integrity of China – and the equal rights of those countries wishing to invest there. Briefly, in the early twenties, it looked as if Japan might after all normalize her relations with China and forget about her dreams of overlordship. For all this "runaway liberal movement of the urban middle class",[1] there remained an undercurrent of intolerance and xenophobia. Tokyo's daily *Nichi-Nichi* published a "strong warning to the undesirable foreign elements in Japan . . . who commit in the dark detestable crimes". Though the first part of Tokyo to be rebuilt, after the earthquake, was its huge brothel area, the Yoshiwara district, it was the "immorality of foreigners" that attracted editorial comment, and, in hotels and restaurants, foreigners' behaviour was monitored, and put on file, by Japan's secret police. At a banquet staged in a Tokyo hotel by the Minseito party, its organizers complained that one of the waiters was a police spy. The manager replied that this particular spy had become such a fixture, listening to foreigners' conversations, that he was regarded as part of the staff. Foreign diplomats in Tokyo were routinely spied on by their Japanese employees and servants, and "espionitis" would eventually reach absurd levels.

A. Morgan Young, a British journalist and editor, resident in Tokyo at the time, later wrote that in 1927 there was "independent civilian thinking which five years later would be inconceivable",[2] for the liberal mood did not outlast the twenties. Liberalism was dealt a huge blow when, in 1927, a series of bank failures sparked off a pre-depression crisis leading to business collapses among the new middle class and extreme poverty among the farmers – still the bulk of Japan's population. The "Zaibatsu", unscathed, bought up everything in sight. The anti-parliament, anti-business wave that followed fuelled the lunatic-fringe nationalists, the militarists, and the authoritarian Secret Society bosses. A new "Maintenance of Public Peace" bill, voted into existence shortly afterwards, drastically curbed civil liberties and freedom of speech; an Imperial Decree, signed by Hirohito without debate in parliament – almost certainly at the request of Prince Konoye, the Emperor's kinsman and friend, now a member of the House of Peers and no longer a radical – increased the maximum penalty for convicted offenders from ten years in jail to a possible death sentence; a huge purge began shortly afterwards in schools and universities, as well as a wave of arrests of Communists, socialists and suspected leftists at all levels of society. By July 1928, said Morgan Young, "every liberal professor had been driven out of the universities".

By now, another of General Sato's demands (put forward in *If America and Japan fight*) had been fulfilled: from 1926 onwards, military drill and education began in preparatory and middle schools, soon to be extended to the entire educational system. The "emperor cult" in schools was given an additional, military fillip, with schoolchildren parading in uniform before photographs of Hirohito – himself invariably in the uniform of commander-in-chief. This had been one way of coping with manpower cuts in the army, for many superannuated or redundant army officers found employment as military instructors in schools throughout the country. The decrease in the size of the army (a reduction of some four infantry divisions) was compensated for by the creation of new tank and anti-tank units, a signals corps, and, later, a chemical and bacteriological warfare centre – these last two were, in part at least, the brainchild of the scientifically minded Prince Kuni, Hirohito's father-in-law, and Hirohito himself, with his passion for science and marine biology, took a keen interest in both centres from their creation.

Emperor Taisho, in seclusion ever since his embarrassing public lapses, died on December 18, 1926 – though the news of his death was only made public on Christmas Day. Hirohito, warned that the end was near, had mounted a bedside vigil in the seaside resort of Hayama, where Taisho had lived for the last five years – but was actually asleep when his father passed away. There was little real grief among his subjects – he had been out of the public eye for so long, and Hirohito, as Regent, had already assumed all his father's powers, with the exception of the actual title. But the event was an important one, even if the formal start to Hirohito's reign was only to begin with his enthronement in Kyoto two years later; and it was marked by a minor, but significant crisis within the media, which showed to what extent secrecy prevailed where Palace decisions were concerned.

Every Japanese emperor has two names, one for his lifetime, the other for posterity. In his lifetime, Emperor Meiji had been known as Emperor Mutsohito, and Taisho as Emperor Yoshihito; only after his death were they referred to as Emperor Meiji and Emperor Taisho, (which meant "great righteousness"). Hirohito now had to choose the name under which he himself would go down in history. The daily *Mainichi* correctly announced that the Hirohito era would be known as "Kobun" – meaning "light and literary attainments", the news having "leaked" from the Imperial Palace several weeks previously, when it was clear that Taisho was dying.

Hirohito was furious, and decided to punish *Mainichi* by changing the name to "Showa", meaning "enlightenment and peace", which is how he would be referred to after his own death. In *Fifty Years of Light and Dark*, a book published on the fiftieth anniversary of Hirohito's reign, *Mainichi* revealed that, at the time, the Emperor's decision caused a huge crisis within the paper's staff, compelling its editor to resign. It added that, in the light of what was to happen later, to call Hirohito's reign the "age of enlightenment and peace" was "a dour irony unmatched in the nation's history".

The title Hirohito now assumed had been transmitted, in more or less unbroken succession, since the year 660 BC – the year his glorious ancestor Jimmu first appears in the earliest annals of Japanese history. In fact Emperor Jimmu may have "reigned" within several hundred years of this somewhat arbitrarily chosen date – and there is even doubt cast on his existence. Jimmu himself, the "divine" son of a whole series of divine, mythological ancestors, or someone like him, was in all probability the first of a series of tribal chiefs to leave his mark on one of the islands of the Japanese archipelago, inhabited at the time by primitive tribes of Chinese-Korean descent who had themselves displaced and eliminated its original Polynesian inhabitants.

The myth of Jimmu, a direct descendant of the sun goddess Amaterasu, herself the issue of a whole series of gods and goddesses whose procreations gave birth to matter, oceans, heat and light and each other (they had lifespans of 500 years and more), became dogma only in Emperor Meiji's time, as a useful underpinning of the newly restored Emperor's authority through Shintoism. The holy attributes of the Emperor – the mirror, the sword and the necklace – were, officially at least, believed to be truly authentic holy relics of this heroic, pre-historic age. The copper mirror was the device one of the gods had used to tempt the goddess Amaterasu out of her cave, where she had fled, condemning the entire world to darkness; handing her the mirror, a relative compelled her to come out of the cave to contemplate her features in the light. The sword was an equally mythic attribute, supposedly plucked from a dragon's tail; the necklace, actually composed of crudely carved stones, was perhaps the only truly authentic relic of the three. The mirror remained in the Japanese Holy of Holies, the shrine of Isé, where Emperors went twice a year to commune with their ancestors; the other relics were kept in the Imperial Family Shrine.

Along with their compulsory schooling under Meiji, young Japanese were taught to believe in these heroic mythological tales in the same way that fundamentalist Christians are taught to believe in the Bible. Needless to say, the "crude and bawdy tales" of the origins of the Japanese gods who became, by stages, human beings, and the rulers of Japan, were regarded by nearly all highly educated Japanese as myths. Hirohito, with his passion for marine biology, and keen interest in Darwinism, refused to take them seriously. In his youth, his refusal to listen patiently to specially appointed professors expounding them as though they were historical truths had led them to complain to Prince Saionji that their royal pupil was remiss in studies concerning his own divinity. Saionji, the French-speaking hedonist, composer and poet who admired Voltaire and erotic French eighteenth- and nineteenth-century literature, a cynic who fully understood Hirohito's reservations, agreed with him privately that the myths were probably nonsense, but happened to be useful nonsense: why deprive believers of their faith, especially when this faith made them implicitly obedient to the Emperor's will, and facilitated, to a considerable degree, the ruler's task? It was a lesson Hirohito immediately understood.

The jurists who drafted the 1889 Constitution, drawing heavily on its Prussian model, maintained the fiction that it had been a "gift from the throne". In theory at least, every Emperor, from Meiji onwards, was an absolute ruler, since the Constitution proclaimed not only that "the Empire shall be reigned over and governed by a line of emperors unbroken for ages eternal", but that the Emperor was "sacred and inviolable . . . combining in Himself the rights and the exercise of sovereignty", as well as supreme command of the armed forces.

As defined in the Japan yearbook 1944–45, "the Emperor . . . cannot be removed from the Throne for any reason, and he is not to be held responsible for over-stepping the limitations of law in the exercise of his sovereignty". All such responsibility "must be assumed by the Ministers of State and other organs. Thus no criticism can be directed against the Emperor but only against the instruments of his sovereignty. Laws are not to be applied to the Emperor as a principle, especially criminal laws, for no court of law can try the Emperor himself and he is not subject to any law."

This doctrine of Imperial infallibility was in practice hedged about with tacit limitations, for both the jurists who drafted the Constitution, and the oligarchs who helped the Emperor run the country, realized that no government could be perfect, that errors would invariably occur, and that the same infallibility doctrine – if it was to be respected as part of the Emperor's religious attributes – required that he should have only indirect responsibility in the day-to-day running of the country. The reason was that only by letting others take the decisions could the Emperor remain unsullied by the possibility of human error. By Emperor Taisho's time, the direct exercise of the Emperor's powers was formalistic: he apposed his seal on government decrees, but the day-to-day decision-making process was the responsibility of the Cabinet. The Privy Council acted as an advisory body, and while the Diet's powers were more illusory than real, the two most powerful figures in Japanese life were neither "Imperial" nor elected: they were the Army and Navy Chiefs of Staff, both, in practice, more powerful even than the Prime Minister. They had the right to consult with the Emperor without the presence of any other minister or Court official; the tacit ruling – nowhere referred to in the Constitution – that army and navy ministers should be drawn from the ranks of serving officers was to give the military powers of veto over the composition of successive ministries.

Hirohito fully understood, from the moment he became Regent, that he was "above politics" and that his "margin of manoeuvre" was limited. But these restrictions did not mean that the Emperor was a puppet in the hands of a series of over-lapping oligarchical institutions: far from it, for the Emperor, in the last resort, wielded the ultimate weapon – limited powers of veto. His seal was needed on any document promulgating any decision of importance; by refusing, or delaying, its apposition he could effectively block any measure he was determined to oppose, from the appointment of a Prime Minister to the des-patch of an army unit abroad. All of these had to have his official sanction.

And, because no decision of even minor importance was implemented without first being scrutinized by the Emperor, his behind-the-scenes influence was huge: there could be no single individual better informed of the state of Japan than a hard-working Japanese Emperor. Hirohito was exceptionally in-dustrious, methodical and almost obsessively concerned with detail. A member of the Imperial Family confirmed, in an interview, that "the Emperor read everything he put his seal to". For all these reasons, he knew, at almost all times, every-thing that was going on, not only within the Privy Council, the Supreme War Command and the Cabinet, but within the army and navy and the many ultra-nationalist clubs and secret societies as well. His personal "kitchen cabinet", consisting of the Im-perial Household Minister, the Lord Privy Seal, the Chief ADC and the Grand Chamberlain, were his privileged "eyes and ears", and the information-gathering resources at their disposal were formidable.

There was another area where the Emperor assumed enor-mous importance: because of his huge wealth, he could under-write ventures which, for one reason or another, could not be charged to official government budgets. The Emperor's private funds, until the end of the Second World War, served in a multi-tude of ways to accomplish what had to be kept secret. In the wartime diaries of some of the Court officials closest to Hirohito, for example, there are tantalizing references to a "special weapons research centre" which was clearly privately-funded, through special Palace nominees.

The extent, and limitation, of Hirohito's powers was well understood by those who were determined to turn Japan into an expansionist, authoritarian power. Such was the weight of tradition, and the aura of infallibility around a supposedly "divine" Emperor, that even to talk of attempting to influence his course of thought was regarded as *lèse-majesté*. This also made the formulation of policy in the Emperor's presence, even when relatively simple matters were concerned, exceedingly difficult. For this reason, much of the real business of govern-ment was conducted, as it were, off-stage and the vocabulary used at Court was circumlocutory, allusive and fully compre-hensible only to a tiny, inside clique.

From time to time, however, when the company was con-sidered reliable enough, protagonists were emboldened to speak their mind directly. One such instance was reported by Ryukishi Tanaka, an intelligence officer who later was to achieve considerable notoriety when he became a prosecution witness at the International Military Tribunal (IMTFE) and a confidential aide to its chief prosecutor, Joseph B. Keenan, the "gangbusting" attorney.

Tanaka was part of a small, select group of officers, all members of the recently closed University Lodging House, who celebrated Hirohito's accession shortly after the news of Emperor Taisho's death. Dr. Okawa, who was also present, and paid for the drinks, drank a toast to the conquest of Manchuria, only to be reminded, by Lieutenant-Colonel Tojo (he was to be the wartime premier) that "we can never move troops unless the Emperor says so".

Later the somewhat tipsy group went past the Imperial Palace, and saw Japanese families, some of them from the country, kneeling in the moonlight to pray to the new Emperor. Tanaka remembered: "We felt relieved by the sight, as if the independence of Manchuria was already assured."

While Hirohito was mounting his round-the-clock watch over his dying father, two very different, but equally colourful, individuals were at the forefront of events in China, a country that would soon play a crucial role in determining Japan's drift into war. Both hoped to use Japan for their own ends. While Hirohito never met either personally, he was well aware of their respective strengths and weaknesses, followed their careers with unflagging interest, and – ultimately – betrayed them both.

One was Chiang Kai-chek, the ambitious, wily ex-broker who was determined to unify China and break the power of the warlords, if possible with Hirohito's active support. The other was General Chang Tso-lin, the "uncrowned king of Manchuria", who had fought with the Japanese against Russia during the 1905 war but had narrowly survived a Japanese assassination attempt in 1916. Under Chang Tso-lin, a Manchu orphan pauper who had become, first, a Robin Hood brigand, then the leader of a private army, Manchuria had been turned into the best-administered province in China. A diminutive wisp of a man with the looks of a slant-eyed Clark Gable and a deceptively soft-spoken manner, Chang Tso-lin was a ruthless, highly intelligent administrator. He had the Queen of Hearts' disconcerting habit of ordering "off with their heads" – beheadings without benefit of prior trial were a regular feature of his rule. But his victims were mostly drug-dealers, corrupt bankers, businessmen and black marketeers, and his summary executions made him popular with the common people. His Mukden palace was guarded by a fanatically loyal praetorian guard of hand-picked Manchus in Hollywood uniforms of his own creation. He was a compelling negotiator and attentive host, extraordinarily attractive to women, with a weakness for expensive furs and teenage concubines. He was also a financially sophisticated planner who early on understood the economic and strategic importance of railways, building his own to compete with the Japanese-owned line; though he still lived by the tough gangster code that had brought him to his current pinnacle of power, and had become rich, he was, in his curious way, a patriot, determined to turn Manchuria into a prosperous, well-ordered province. He had the knack of inspiring loyalty among all who worked for him: an Italian adventurer, Amleto Vespa, who became one of his senior advisers, and later wrote about his experiences in Japanese-occupied Manchuria, considered him one of the greatest men who ever lived.[3]

By treaty, Japanese forces in Manchuria were in 1926 limited to a few thousand men: these were units earmarked for the protection of the Japanese-owned and -operated South Manchurian railway, and the long-established "Kwangtung Army" under General Muto, which had its headquarters in Port Arthur.

For all the presence of Japanese troops on Manchurian soil, Japan's relations with Chang Tso-lin were cordial. The Japanese loaned him military advisers, and assured him of their everlasting support.

Had he confined his sphere of influence to Manchuria and Mongolia, both the Japanese, and Chiang Kai-chek, would have found him a difficult nut to crack. But Chang Tso-lin believed that his was a national destiny: he hinted as much to Henry Pu

Yi, the weak-willed, demoralized ex-Emperor of China, then only twenty-one, who had taken refuge in the Japanese-run part of the Tientsin International Concession; and he made the huge mistake of seizing power in Peking, with only a token force, driving out the "Christian general", then Chiang Kai-chek's ally, whose Communist sympathies were well-known.

Chiang Kai-chek, in 1927, had moved north from his Canton base and also saw himself as China's man of destiny. Though his allies included leftists as well as traditional warlords, Chiang had realized, by this time, that if he wanted to obtain international recognition he would have to break with the Communists. When Chang Tso-lin, acting on a Japanese tip-off, had the Soviet Embassy in Peking raided, and found proof, in documents discovered there, of a Comintern plot to "sovietize" China, Chiang Kai-chek seized on the pretext he had been looking for: on April 12, 1927, "black Tuesday" in the annals of Chinese history-books, he turned on his Communist allies with sudden, ruthless cruelty. Thousands were apprehended and executed. Chou En-lai, formerly one of Chiang Kai-chek's subordinates, who had taught at the Whampoa Academy, the staff college for budding KMT leaders that Chiang Kai-chek had set up in the south with Soviet funds, precipitately fled Shanghai, where he had recently been elected Mayor. Soviet advisers dispersed, returning to Russia in huge haste. A few days later, Chiang Kai-chek established his provisional capital in Nanking, a half-way house on the way to Peking.

On April 20, another general, Giichi Tanaka, became Hirohito's new Prime Minister. As usual, the nomination had come from Prince Saionji, and had been approved by the Privy Council. After resigning from the army in 1925 (he had opposed military budget cuts) Tanaka had moved into politics, and become president of the Seiyukai party. He succeeded an administration discredited by bank failures and corruption. As both an army man, and a member of the Choshu clan, Saionji told Hirohito, Tanaka could speak to the military with authority – and help his disgruntled clansmen forget the past. A bluff, hearty, outgoing soldier, Tanaka had some of the requisite qualities for a prime minister. What he lacked was a statesman's long-term vision, and the subtlety, and capacity for intrigue, of the born courtier.

Like all her top military men, Tanaka believed Japan needed to consolidate her hold on Manchuria and Mongolia, as a buffer state between Communist Russia and a weak, divided China. He was disturbed by Chang Tso-lin's recent march into Peking, and advised him to return to Manchuria, where he belonged — for Chang Tso-lin, a rabid anti-Communist, was the best possible insurance against Russian encroachment in that part of the world. But Chang Tso-lin refused. For all Chiang Kai-chek's new anti-Communism, he was not to be trusted, he argued. "My war [against Chiang Kai-chek] is Japan's war," he told Tanaka, deploring the fact that Japan maintained friendly relations with a man who, until so recently, had had Communist allies.

The situation was a complicated one, too complicated for Tanaka alone. In time-honoured Japanese fashion, a consensus solution, based on extensive study, was required. In the month following Tanaka's appointment, a working party convened to prepare for the Far East Conference, which took place in Tokyo from June 1 to July 7, 1927. The middle-level specialists who sat on this preparatory committee included some of the brightest but also some of the most uncompromising advocates of Japanese expansionism and authoritarian nationalism in the ranks of the military and intelligence establishments. Hirohito was fully aware of the contents of its working papers, and may even have indirectly influenced them, for two of its members were his own ADCs — Viscount Machijiri, a former subordinate of Prince Higashikuni in Paris, and Major Anami, who later became Japan's last wartime Defence Minister, eventually committing suicide on the evening of Hirohito's surrender broadcast of August 14, 1945. Nearly all its participants happened to be "graduates" of the late University Lodging House, and Anami was particularly close to Hirohito.

The Far Eastern Conference is rightly seen as the first clear evidence of Japan's "forward policy" in China under Hirohito's aegis. Attended by senior officers and diplomats (including the Japanese Minister in Peking, Kenkichi Yoshizawa, and that up-and-coming embassy secretary who had boarded Hirohito's warship in Gibraltar and was now Consul in Mukden, Shigeru Yoshida), the conference discussed the various alternatives open to Japan in her determination to increase her influence in Asia. This ranged from the outright conquest of Manchuria – one of the proposals drafted by the preparatory committee – to a mere reinforcement of Japan's economic presence there. Complaints were voiced that the Chinese, in defiance of the 1915 treaty with Japan (the famous twenty-one demands), were refusing to lease land to the Japanese. If they continued to do so, outright ownership was the only answer, the conference decided, also suggesting that Koreans, not viewed as first-class Japanese citizens by the Chinese, should be brought in as convenient stalking-horses for Japanese entrepreneurs.

Years later, Chiang Kai-chek's propagandists were to publicize the conclusions of the Far Eastern Conference in a booklet, *The Tanaka Memorial*, which, they claimed, was the text of a formal document submitted by Tanaka to Hirohito as an "address to the throne", and was accepted by the latter as Japan's future "master plan" for Japan's domination of Asia.

This document – nothing less than a blueprint for the military conquest of Manchuria and the whole of China, to be followed by the annexation of all of Asia and armed confrontation with the United States – was almost certainly a fake, though it was undoubtedly based on the preliminary papers submitted by the preparatory committee. Annexation of the whole of Asia – what came to be known later as the "Strike South" doctrine – was discussed at the conference. Though this was indeed what, in time, occurred, the claim that every twist and turn in Japanese policy that followed was based on this Nipponese *Mein Kampf* does not stand up: on the contrary, Tanaka (who had assumed the Foreign Ministry portfolio as well as the Premiership) and the Kwangtung army's Commander-in-Chief, General Muto, were well aware that any open military intervention in Manchuria might lead to reprisals on the part of the Western powers that could prove devastating to Japan in her current economic state. Also, *The Tanaka Memorial* was far too long: rigid protocol required that any formal "address to the Throne" not exceed two pages. For all that, most experts, including A. M. Young, in Tokyo at the time, agree that the tone of the conference's deliberations corresponded to the substance of *The Tanaka Memorial*, even if the latter was not presented to Hirohito exactly in that form.

Shortly after the conference ended, Yoshizawa, at a rare press conference back in Peking, affirmed that "Japan has no intention whatever of adopting a decisive positive policy towards Manchuria, nor does she plan anything like invasion". But all the signs were that he was lying.

Chiang Kai-chek himself arrived in Japan on the heels of the Far Eastern Conference. It was not just a private visit – though he was courting May-ling Soong, the daughter of the Chinese banker C. J. Soong, in Japan at the time, and married her on December 1, 1927. After minor policy differences with his own colleagues, Chiang had temporarily relinquished the KMT leadership, though it remained his for the asking.

His other purpose, in coming to Japan, was to sound out Japanese policy-makers on their attitudes towards a KMT-ruled China, with himself at its head. Though it was out of the question for him to have an audience with Hirohito himself, he did (on November 5, 1927) meet Premier Tanaka privately. Tanaka, who wished to keep both Chiang Kai-chek and Chang Tso-lin in play, warned him against becoming entangled in "warlord politics" in the north. Japan, he said, was only too happy to assist him in his efforts, but not at the expense of such a proven anti-Communist as Chang Tso-lin. Chiang Kai-chek argued that his drive north was essential, and appealed for help to counteract the impression that the Japanese were Chang Tso-lin's allies.

It was an inconclusive, and, for Chiang Kai-chek, unsatisfactory session, but he also met other powerful behind-the-scenes establishment figures, including the Black Dragon leader Toyama, and it is likely that he also urged them to use their influence to topple Chang Tso-lin. Toyama, despite his age (he was not to die until 1945), was still enormously powerful – still with unrivalled access not just to diehard nationalist officers and intelligence specialists whose vocation was to destabilize Manchuria, but also to men close to Hirohito, like Prince Konoye, who had just founded the Tuesday Club, an informal working party of members of the House of Peers which advocated friendly relations with Chiang Kai-chek as a means of achieving a united Asia under Japanese leadership. It is inconceivable for Hirohito not to have been kept abreast of Chiang Kai-chek's "secret" talks in Japan: through his "kitchen cabinet", and close friends like Konoye, Chiang Kai-chek's wishes were certainly relayed to him. It is also probable that Chiang Kai-chek intended to let Hirohito know that – should Japan deal with Chang Tso-lin – he himself would not grieve too much if Japan extended her sphere of influence to Manchuria and Mongolia – provided this did not extend south of the Great Wall.

Hardly coincidentally, in December 1927, an army activist, Colonel Daisaku Komoto, a Manchurian-based staff officer of the Kwangtung army, dynamited a bridge on a Manchurian railway line: the damage was attributed to "bandits". He repeated the experience several times, increasing the explosive charge, over the next few months, and each time "bandits" were blamed. It is not known whether the upper echelons of the Japanese General Staff knew for sure who the real protagonist was, or whether the news ever reached Hirohito's ears. But it is likely that Toyama, and perhaps some of his artistocratic cronies with Palace connections, were aware of the purpose of these experiments. Prime Minister Tanaka certainly was not: he was to try, repeatedly, to save Chang Tso-lin's reputation, and his life, by urging him to give up Peking and return to Manchuria.

For in the spring and early summer of 1928 Chiang Kai-chek

was on the march northwards, and Chang Tso-lin's army was both outnumbered and outgunned. The progress of Chiang Kai-chek's troops was checked, briefly, south of Peking. Here, in Tsinan, Chiang Kai-chek's KMT troops and Japanese army units from the Tientsin International Concession sent to protect Japanese civilians clashed violently in a series of sporadic skirmishes which commanders, on both sides, claimed were the fault of inexperienced junior officers acting without orders. These clashes escalated into a full-scale battle, with a massive attack on Tsinan by Japanese troops on May 8 in which atrocities were committed and at least 1,000 Chinese soldiers and civilians were killed. Chiang Kai-chek requested investigation by the League of Nations, which took no action. The Tsinan "incident" certainly cooled Chiang Kai-chek's ardour for a rapprochement with Japan – for the first time he saw how viscerally anti-Chinese Japanese troops were – but his chief concern was to crush Chang Tso-lin, and he deliberately took no action to further provoke the Japanese.

Ten days later, after meeting Hirohito, Tanaka informed British, French, Italian and US diplomats in Tokyo that he intended to deliver a memorandum to Chang Tso-lin the following day asking him to "withdraw quietly" from Peking. "If he fights on the way," said Tanaka, "we will prevent him from passing into Manchuria . . . I look forward to Peking being evacuated and passing quietly into the hands of the Southerners [the KMT]."

Japan's most senior diplomat in Peking, Yoshizawa, duly delivered the note, assuring Chang Tso-lin that Japan could save him if he agreed to leave. The Manchu warlord was trapped, though at first he refused to admit it. He had counted on Western support, failing to realize that the sole concern of the Western powers was the safety of European and American families in Peking and the Tsientsin International Concession. On no account must any Western lives be lost in this remote, complicated mini-civil war. Chang Tso-lin's own officers knew the battle for Peking had been lost, and some of his troops began their withdrawal to Manchuria of their own volition. On June 1 Chang Tso-lin turned the city over to a "Peace Preservation Committee" and, in a farewell address, announced his return to Manchuria "in order to spare further bloodshed".

The same Japanese officer who had watched crowds outside the Palace pray to the new Emperor just after Taisho's death, Ryukishi Tanaka, was now an intelligence agent in China, keeping a close watch on Chang Tso-lin's comings and goings. As Manchuria's uncrowned king, Chang had private trains at his disposal, and the first of these, a seven-wagon decoy with some of his staff, and his favourite concubine, aboard, left Peking on the evening of June 2. Chang Tso-lin himself followed in another train, departing after midnight. Despite worsening relations with Japan, Chang Tso-lin still had a few Japanese liaison officers with him. Two left the train in Tientsin. The one remaining officer aboard, Major Nobuya Giga, kept him company, playing mah-jong and drinking beer with him throughout the night. Chang Tso-lin felt that he was safe so long as even one Japanese officer stayed on the train.

Tanaka, the spy, had reported the departure of both trains to his superiors in Mukden. The first arrived there without mishap. About a couple of miles south of Mukden station, as Chang Tso-lin's journey was nearing its end, Major Giga casually retired to his own compartment on the pretext of collecting his belongings. What he did was to rush to the train's rear platform, curl up and pray he would be spared. As the train entered the last underpass, a Japanese team trained by Major Komoto triggered the explosive device. There was a huge roar. Chang Tso-lin's compartment reared up in the air. He died instantly, along with eighteen other travellers (Major Giga survived). The outrage, the Japanese army staff in Mukden blandly reported, was undoubtedly the work of "bandits". Two bodies were conveniently put on show, allegedly caught by Japanese army railway troops. These were of course decoys, sacrificed for the occasion, but a third "bandit" managed to escape, and broke the news of what had really happened to Chang Tso-lin's son.

The "bandit's" version of Chang Tso-lin's death remained, of course, the official version for years to come – and it was the only version dutifully reported in the Japanese press. Not until after the Second World War, when IMTFE prosecutors began investigating suspected Japanese war criminals' pre-war careers, did some of the details actually come to light.

Premier Tanaka, of course, immediately suspected that Chang Tso-lin's convenient demise was the work of Japanese officers: indeed some activists later claimed, in sessions with the US interrogators,[4] that Tanaka himself had been perfectly aware, all along, of the plot to blow up the train. He certainly knew that a full investigation might have embarrassing consequences for people in high places.

Hirohito blandly advised him to make a full, no-holds-barred enquiry, probably aware that he was putting Tanaka in an impossible situation. For either Tanaka made only a token enquiry, in which case he was transgressing his Emperor's orders while protecting individuals in key places, or else he went ahead – and risked making public a major scandal, with possible ramifications too embarrassing to contemplate.

When rumours in Japan began to spread, hinting that Chang Tso-lin had died in an elaborately planned Japanese army plot, Tanaka asked the head of the Japanese secret police, General Komatsu Mine, to initiate a full, personal, on-the-spot enquiry. Inevitably, Mine's report turned out to be a risible travesty of the facts: bandits had been at work; the Japanese army unit responsible for patrolling the line had been guilty of negligence. He suggested Major Komoto be reprimanded. In the event, two officers took the blame: a general (later reinstated) and Komoto himself were removed from the active list "for failing to place guards along the line".

Had Tanaka had the gall to accept the Mine report at its face value, he might have ensured his own political survival. But he was himself in an increasingly precarious position: heavily criticized for allowing Japan to become a party to the Briand–Kellogg Pact against war, he was also under fire in the Diet, where an opposition proposal for another probe of the Chang Tso-lin affair was defeated, but only by 220 to 198; Tanaka eventually sent Mine back to Manchuria, and this time Mine, assuming that Tanaka knew what he was doing, produced a report which told most of the story. Tanaka, shocked, again went to the Emperor for advice. After receiving assurances, once more, from Palace Chamberlains, that Hirohito did indeed want the unvarnished truth, Tanaka was reassured. But the Japanese were about to celebrate their new Emperor's formal enthronement ceremony, and all government business ground to a halt. It was only in 1929 that the saga resumed, with Saionji hinting that, if the second report was ever released, the Emperor's "august face would be muddy".

As it happened, Hirohito had already been briefed on the contents of the second Mine report by his War Minister, though Tanaka was unaware of this. His nerve, in the last resort, failed him. He backtracked, telling the Emperor that there were no sensational new revelations to come, after all. Hirohito immediately exploited this volte-face.

"Does this not completely contradict what you told me previously?" he asked Tanaka. To his Grand Chamberlain, he said: "I cannot understand Tanaka. I do not ever want to see him again."

Tanaka had no choice but to submit his resignation. He died three months later. There were reports he had committed suicide as a protest against the slur on his good name. But the Tokyo grapevine had it that he died in a geisha's arms after a drinking bout.

Four years later, Hirohito told his chief ADC, General Honjo, that he had dismissed Tanaka not so much because he had lied but because he had gone about his lying in such a clumsy way. As Honjo recorded the conversation, in his diaries,[5] Hirohito said that "had he [Tanaka] made such a statement [i.e. a cover-up] on his own authority, then explained it had been necessary for political reasons, and *then* submitted his resignation" the Emperor's view was that "as a politician he probably had no other choice ... But he asked me to approve the statement beforehand; if I had given my approval it would have meant telling my people a falsehood." This was why Hirohito had found it necessary not only to get rid of Tanaka, but also to disgrace him.

Even now there are grey areas in the Chang Tso-lin assassination plot. It can never be proved that Hirohito was aware of the detailed ramifications of the "army plot" to get rid of Chang Tso-lin until he received a version of the second Mine report. On the other hand many of the protagonists were personally known to him; and, in the aftermath of the war, several piquant details emerged. General Mine, whose investigation first whitewashed the army then put it on the spot, was himself implicated in the plot up to the hilt. Colonel Kanjo Ishiwara, another top-level intelligence officer involved in the Chang Tso-lin assassination plot, was questioned by IMTFE prosecutors in May 1947. Completely unrepentant for any of Japan's war crimes, Ishiwara, whose career came to a sudden end in 1941 owing to his personal hostility to Tojo and his later conviction that a protracted war with China was a mistake, affirmed that, contrary to general belief, Tanaka had indeed already told the Emperor the truth about the circumstances of the Chang Tso-lin murder by the time he came before him, that final time, with the "cover-up" version.

If Ishiwara's version is correct, then Tanaka's utter confusion, on being dismissed, is readily explained: the bluff soldier was only casting around for a version of events which, he felt, was the one Hirohito wanted to hear. Completely out of his depth, he floundered – and Hirohito brilliantly extricated himself from a personally embarrassing situation by taking a high moral stance and rebuking Tanaka for attempting to dissemble the truth. Scarcely coincidentally, Tanaka's disgrace was also that of the Choshu clan as a whole.

Ishiwara also told IMTFE investigators that Tanaka had given the Emperor the names of the three key "plotters" – Major Doihara, Colonel Itagaki and Ishiwara himself – who had masterminded the Chang-Tso-lin murder. Had his moral indignation been as genuine as he made it out to be to the unfortunate Tanaka, Hirohito could, then and there, have put a stop to their careers. But Major Komoto, the explosives expert, was the only scapegoat, and was made to resign his commission. Very soon afterwards, he became a leading businessman in Manchuria, amassing a considerable fortune. None of the others found their careers impeded. On the contrary, they remained in close touch with those Palace officials and ADCs in daily contact with the Emperor. Itagaki, later War Minister, was to visit the Palace in 1932, and was almost certainly received in person by Hirohito, who showed, for the first but by no means last time, his formidable skill at spinning a spider's web of intrigue, letting others carry the burden of responsibility while insulating himself from all its adverse consequences.

[1] Edwin O. Reishauer, *Japan's Past and Present*, Duckworth, 1947.
[2] A. Morgan Young, *Imperial Japan*, W. Morrow, 1938.
[3] Amleto Vespa, *Secret Agent of Japan*, Little Brown and Co., 1938.
[4] *Brocade Banner*, ib.
[5] *The Honjo Diary*, 1933–36, University of Tokyo Press.

CHAPTER FIVE

While the Chang Tso-lin murder investigation was still marking time, Hirohito was formally enthroned as the 124th Emperor in direct line of succession, in a number of ceremonies symbolizing the temporal and spiritual links between the age-old Imperial Dynasty and the Emperor himself as titular head of Shintoism, Japan's state religion.

Some of the rites surrounding this, the most important event in Hirohito's life, actually began months in advance, with the symbolic planting of high-quality rice at specially chosen sites; this was the "Great New Food Festival", and, since the quality and lushness of the newly-planted rice would determine the prosperity and general quality of his reign, special care was taken to ensure its glorious maturing. Various other religious ceremonies took place throughout the year, leading up to his actual November enthronement, in the ancient city of Kyoto, the capital of his forebears, in a series of pageants, banquets and Shinto rites.

There was an unprecedented effort, beforehand, to personalize the ceremony and present Hirohito to the public as a modern, forward-looking Emperor. Exceptionally, there were press kits and detailed explanations of the significance of the various rites involved, for the benefit of both the Japanese and the foreign press, and though their language was still, by modern Western standards, absurdly reverent and formal, this aspect of the ceremony was a marked departure from what had gone before. For the hallmark of everything involving the Emperor and the Imperial Family generally was secrecy: as anyone who has visited the Shinto Holy of Holies in Isé knows, the actual shrine where the supremely sacred (if fake) Amaterasu mirror is housed is completely hidden from view, and never seen by anyone except the Emperor himself. After a long walk up a hill through spotlessly tended gardens, with rivers full of startlingly-coloured carp, one comes to a small proscenium, an open-air stage setting for an avant-garde Japanese play. The entrance to the shrine is entirely shrouded by an opaque white curtain. What lies right, left and beyond is out of bounds, and even as late as the nineteenth century the penalty for trying to glimpse beyond this curtain was death. In the same way, the actual Palace grounds, occupying a huge area in the centre of Tokyo, are protected from prying eyes by deliberate, man-made landscaping which screens all but the green copper roofs of a few buildings. The Akasaka Palace, that miniature Versailles, is fully visible from the street, but the rest of the 123-acre site, where the Emperor's closest relatives live, walled in (and these days subject to wrap-around electronic surveillance from TV cameras), is not. The Imperial buildings must be among the most discreetly secure homes anywhere in the world.

On November 6, 1928, the Emperor and Empress, in separate horse-drawn carriages, left the Palace for Tokyo railway station, then still a provincial-looking redbrick building, along a route lined with soldiers and cheering crowds. The journey to Kyoto took two days: the royal train proceeded at a deliberately slow pace and crowds of villagers and schoolchildren, all officially convened, lined the track. The royal couple rested that first night in Nagoya.

In Kyoto, several thousand participants – princely relatives, government members, priests, dignitaries both Japanese and foreign – had already gathered. They included a glittering couple: dashing Prince Chichibu and his bride, the glamorous Setsuko, daughter of Japan's former Ambassador in Washington, Baron Matsudaira. In many respects Chichibu and his beautiful bride were far more typical of the new, "smart" Japan than the reigning couple. Chichibu was just down from Oxford, and had a near-perfect command of English. He had met his bride while staying at the Japanese Embassy Residence in Washington, during his Oxford undergraduate days. She was far more sophisticated and worldly-wise than the Empress. Both Chichibu and Setsuko were avid American film and jazz fans, in touch with all the latest Western fads and fashions. By this time, Empress Nagako had given birth to two daughters and both she, and the Palace advisers around her, impatiently hoped her next child would be male. If not, they told each other, something would have to be done.

The ceremonies were preceded by three days of intense rehearsals. As usual, the actual proceedings were witnessed only by a handful of participants within the Secret Purple Hall, the court buildings in the centre of a huge park: the mass of privileged guests saw next to nothing, though, for the first time, some journalists were allowed to be present in the outer chamber. There was no actual crowning, but a series of purificatory rites, which took place behind an opaque white curtain. The royal couple's regalia made it difficult for them to move. Hirohito's costume, deliberately patterned on the earliest records of such rites, dating back at least a thousand years, consisted of a saffron silk robe illuminated with emblems and omens; with this he wore platform shoes and brocaded trousers, both red, and his headpiece was stiffened by black lacquer. He carried his personal emblem, a plain wooden sceptre, in his right hand.

Empress Nagako's dress was even more complicatedly elaborate, a set of five stiffened, embroidered superimposed kimonos, weighing at least seventy-five pounds. Her face was chalk-white, her hair elaborately coiffed in a huge set-piece surmounted by a golden crown. Their "thrones" were miniature temples, set on high platforms.

It was here that Hirohito issued his proclamation, invoking the spirits of his ancestors and the "wish to preserve world peace and benefit the welfare of the human race", to which Prime Minister Tanaka replied with a short congratulatory homily, ending with "Tenno Heika, Banzai!" (May the Lord Emperor live ten thousand years.) With remarkable coordination in this pre-electronics age, the cry was taken up all over the country at that very minute, followed by the nationwide rendering of Japan's national anthem, "Kimigayo".

This was only the first of a series of celebrations lasting nearly two weeks, including banquets, further purification rites, ritual river immersion, contemplation ("Soul Quieting") and the mystical "Daijo-sai", the offering of symbolic food to the Shinto gods in an interminably complicated ritual lasting several nights. One of them Hirohito spent alone under a sacred quilt, in symbolic communion with his ancestor, the sun-goddess Amaterasu, being "reborn". In all these rites, Hirohito was both the object and performing high priest, anointer and anointee. The sacred nature of the proceedings can be gauged from the fact that, after the whole thing was all over, all the artefacts involved, as well as the building in which the ceremonies had taken place, were ceremonially burnt.

Twenty days later, Hirohito and the Empress returned to the Imperial Palace in Tokyo, to the accompaniment of the same crowds, troops and formal welcomes. A 101-gun salute boomed out as they entered the palace, and that night the city was lit up by fireworks as the people rejoiced.

Only now, with the ceremonies completed, was Hirohito considered by the Shinto priesthood to be fully qualified, as their supreme religious leader, to act as the sole intermediary between the world of the living and the world of the spirits.

After his return, with all the ceremonies behind him, Hirohito became even more protocol-bound, but the routine he had already introduced, shortly after his father's death, changed only slightly. His public appearances became less frequent: from 1929 onwards, he was restricted to garden parties, Diet openings, and inspections of his armed forces, including military manoeuvres on land and sea. He was present at the occasional march-past of students and notables, and he regularly received ambassadors – but the informal part of his life now took place, more than ever, far from the public gaze. A nine-hole golf course was laid out within the Palace grounds, and the Imperial Household laboratory built so that Hirohito could indulge in his favourite pastime without leaving the palace enclosure.

Inside his father's palace, Hirohito made a number of significant changes. He furnished his office in the Western style, displaying photographs of distinguished personalities he had met on his European tour – Marshal Pétain, King Albert of the Belgians, the Prince of Wales. There were the busts of Lincoln, Darwin and Napoleon – and a couch, should he be required, in an emergency, to spend the night there. He had a personal telephone line installed, in August 1928, which gave him far freer access to subordinates, ministers and chiefs of staff: he never identified himself on the telephone – those he called were sufficiently intimate to recognize his voice. The Imperial Library was put to more active use, for the more formal receptions. One of his first decisions, after Taisho's death, was to put an end to the habit of being presented on momentous occasions with gifts of dead fish. As a naturalist, he felt the only place for such creatures was the sea. He also cut down on the amount of clothes handed down to courtiers. His forebears – taking their cue from the Chinese Ming and Ching Dynasties – wore their robes only a few times. Hirohito, remembering General Nogi's thrifty precepts, changed all that. Some time-honoured rites and taboos were retained: protocol required that the Emperor's body was not to be touched, not even by doctors or tailors. (Doctors wore silk gloves, but tailors had to guess the Emperor's measurements, which perhaps explains why, in photographs, his suits and uniforms look either too big or too small.) There were still food-tasters, two separate sets of meals, to guard against poison, regular examination of the royal faeces. But, otherwise, his daily life was that of any busy, hard-working twentieth-century statesman.

He rose early, at six, prayed, exercised (on horseback if the weather permitted) and breakfasted with the Empress. He read the papers, including the English-language *Japan Times and*

Advertiser, the Foreign Ministry's influential mouthpiece, and followed this with a brief informal conference with his Grand Chamberlain, reviewing the major appointments and activities of the day to come, or with his chief ADC, if there were meetings later with the military. From 10 a.m. to 2 p.m. he was almost always at his desk, reading, reviewing and ordering the imposition of the Imperial Seal. This was also the time he received visitors, either in his office or in the Library. After a light, Japanese-style lunch, he exercised again, usually playing golf. Most of his Court ministers were or became ardent golfers, especially Kido and Prince Konoye – since proficiency was almost a requisite for a senior Palace post.

Afterwards, he bathed. The Palace was equipped with both European-style baths and the Japanese kind, and Hirohito used both, as the fancy took him. Later there was more office work, followed by private pursuits, reading, conversations with the Empress, relaxation with his growing family, perhaps a spell in his marine biology laboratory. He went to bed early, in a Western-style bed, and no one, not even his most trusted palace servants, was allowed inside the Imperial bedchamber unless specially summoned.

Four personally-selected high officials, in effect staff officers with enormous but somewhat loosely-defined, overlapping powers, helped Hirohito run his private, his Palace and his public life. First in importance, at any rate in salary terms, was the Imperial Household Minister, with responsibility for all public functions and official engagements; next in importance came two men, the Lord Privy Seal and the Emperor's chief Aide-de-Camp, with similar duties, one civilian, the other military. The Lord Privy Seal (like the Imperial Household Minister, he had the rank of Minister of State) was the Emperor's political liaison officer, engaged in a two-way exchange of information not just with cabinet ministers and politicians but with the Japanese establishment as a whole. The chief ADC was his military equivalent, with his own staff of eight more junior ADCs drawn from the navy as well as the army. Finally, the

Grand Chamberlain handled Palace staff administration and supervised the Emperor's own vast fortune, in jewellery, land, bank and business holdings.

Because the Grand Chamberlain knew all about the Emperor's personal wealth, he was also the unofficial link between the Emperor and the Zaibatsu, the large industrial conglomerates. Much of the Imperial Family's assets were in fact invested in the Zaibatsu, or kept in "Zaibatsu"-controlled banks. The Grand Chamberlain was also the official "appointments secretary", and – like all those controlling access – immensely powerful for that reason alone.

Over the years, the relative influence of these four men, all of whom saw the Emperor several times a day, varied with circumstances. As the last surviving "genro", Saionji, became older, and less active, so his political advice tended to count less – and, as a result, that of the Lord Privy Seal increased. The chief ADC should by rights have become more powerful than any of the other three as the armed forces began playing an ever-increasingly important part in the life of Japan, but in fact he never assumed, in military affairs, quite the status a trusted, sophisticated Lord Privy Seal enjoyed, for one very simple reason: both the Army and the Navy Chiefs of Staff had privileged access to the Emperor, alone if they so requested, provided the Grand Chamberlain found them a gap in the Emperor's daily schedule.

There were special tasks for special days. Wednesdays were Privy Council days, when treaties, imperial ordinances and broad lines of both domestic and foreign policy were discussed. Since these were substantive meetings, Hirohito liked to leave the next day free, so that he could mull over the proceedings without being disturbed. Fridays were set aside for formal meetings with ambassadors, foreign guests and award-winning athletes or academics; Saturday mornings for his beloved marine biology. Twice a month he saw the Vice-Chiefs of Staff, and several times a year the routine was shattered: Hirohito had to officiate in Shinto ceremonies, dressed in heavy white silk robes

– the only time, apart from his enthronement ceremony, when he wore formal Japanese dress.

There were tacit regulations where both civilian and military audiences were concerned: it was a house rule, dating back to Emperor Meiji's times, that, when postings were being discussed, no ADC or other outsider should be present. Meiji had heard that, in Imperial Russia, ADCs listening in on such conversations would later claim that they had been responsible for intervening in favour of those promoted or nominated to new commands, and thus exert undue influence. Hirohito was always more at ease with military men than he was with civilians, for the military were less likely to spring unwelcome, unexpected petitions on him. The Lord Privy Seal invariably attended audiences with civilians. Hirohito reduced their frequency after a high official once had the temerity to raise an issue with him not on the official agenda. On occasion, even Chiefs of Staff had their audiences postponed if the Grand Chamberlain felt this was in line with the Emperor's policies: after the Treaty of London regulating the tonnage of Japanese warships, the Naval Chief of Staff attempted to see Hirohito to protest against such limitations, but the Grand Chamberlain (Kantaro Suzuki, an admiral and lifelong courtier, later to become the last wartime Premier) found no place for him on the Emperor's schedule. In this indirect way were the Emperor's preferences known.

All four individuals held such key positions that the Emperor had to be utterly convinced of their loyalty and discretion. Ever since the Choshu "plot" to try and prevent him from marrying the girl of his choice, Hirohito saw to it that he was surrounded by people he had known for years, and trusted implicitly: in 1928 his Grand Chamberlain was Sutemi Chinda, an experienced, sophisticated diplomat who had accompanied him on his European tour, as had his chief ADC, General Nara. Later, he was to draw on people who were either kinsmen or had been lifelong servants of the Court, like Admiral Suzuki, whose wife had taught him in the Palace kindergarten at the age of five. Whenever any situation became threatening,

Hirohito would close ranks and rely, ever more heavily, on Princely relatives or those who had known him since boyhood.

Since several of the most senior palace officials were to keep detailed records of their conversations with Hirohito, and record his day-to-day timetable, it is surprising there are so few glimpses of his informal, "human" behaviour. Even his poetry has a curiously formal, predictable stamp to it, if Kanroji's selections are typical. His first "waka", in 1921, went:

> The day has begun
> with the twittering of birds
> calmly at dawn, gradually disclosing
> the shrine of Yoyogi.

Another, much quoted poem, written on his return home after his European trip, read:

> Would that all the world
> were as tranquil
> as this expanse of sea,
> flooded brightly
> with the warm sunshine at morn.

There are a few – very few – instances of Imperial humour: on one occasion, Kanroji fell heavily on a ski-slope, and started swearing like a trooper. The Emperor glided up to him, and said, with the ghost of a smile, "I wish I knew some of those words." Most of Hirohito's fun was at his staff's expense: he was amused by their falls when skiing, but, Kanroji adds, "His Majesty never laughed." His one recorded practical joke illustrates his naturalist's bent: knowing Kanroji's weakness for watermelon, he presented him with a pumpkin that looked just like one, and asked him repeatedly if he had tasted it. But he rarely, if ever, allowed others to see him behaving like an ordinary human being, and was almost completely devoid of small talk, except of the most stilted, banal kind. (The Empress, foreign diplomats noted, was far more skilful in this respect.) A French diplomat recalls the excruciatingly formal exchanges between the French Ambassador and the Emperor on those rare occasions when they met formally, on National Day or its equivalent. The Emperor invariably said: "And how is the health of my good brother, the distinguished French President of the Republic?" The Ambassador would assure him that he was well. In that case, Hirohito invariably answered, please congratulate him on his good health and also convey my best wishes to the people of France. As the Ambassador left the Imperial presence, he could hear the Emperor ask the Ambassador behind him: "And how is the health of my good brother, the distinguished King of the Belgians?"

Kanroji gives endless examples illustrating his conscientiousness as a monarch, never shirking his official duties, however boring, tiring or repetitive (there is a whole chapter headed "Thinking ever of the people"). Like de Gaulle, Hirohito never allowed his aides to shield him from the rain when reviewing troops or saluting crowds; he seems to have had an infinite capacity for taking the salute for hours on end, and even, on one occasion, bowed to crowds he could not see when told they were massed on the shoreline to greet his flagship.

As an example of his presence of mind, Kanroji cites Hirohito's neatly phrased refusal after he had been offered a ride in a fighter plane, during his visit to Britain as Crown Prince: "I'm sure it would be an interesting experience, but unfortunately it's impossible on today's tight itinerary." Kanroji's tone shows he regarded the off-the-cuff British proposal as an enormous protocol blunder.

Though the gulf between Emperor and people remained huge, Hirohito's enthronement had been an excellent public-relations operation, for him and for Japan. There was a remarkable consensus, among Western governments and Tokyo-based diplomats, that this young Emperor – the only one ever to have travelled outside Japan – would usher in a new, progressive, "moderate" era. The choice of "Showa" as a hallmark of his reign – "peace and enlightenment" – was not yet perceived as ironic. His top four Court officials and ministers were regarded by foreign observers as responsible, sophisticated moderates who would surely be able to restrain the military adventurists among the junior ranks of the services. The details of the Chang Tso-lin murder were still not generally known. The outside world was prepared not only to live with Japan as a major power but to look sympathetically on her coming of age.

Despite the purge of university liberals and the growing militarization of Japan's educational system, foreign observers were not unduly worried, in 1928, by the growth of military influence. Diplomats could not fail to notice that all official portraits of Hirohito invariably showed him in uniform, but saw nothing sinister in this.

What worried observers far more was the economic crisis brought about by worldwide depression following the crash of 1929. Half Japan's farmers relied on raw silk as a cottage industry to eke out their inadequate income, with America by far the biggest importer. Sales of this luxury commodity to the US dropped catastrophically from 1930 on, causing real hardship. Japan was still a predominantly agricultural country, and there was overpopulation in agriculture – simply not enough land to go round. Some of the new military radicalism resulted from first-hand knowledge of the peasants' plight, for many army men now came from poor lower-middle-class or farming families. But Hirohito was not much concerned by his people's plight. Inevitably, perhaps, it was difficult for someone living on such a rarefied plane to grasp the nature of dire poverty. In his conversations, later, with his chief ADC Honjo, there was a naïve element in his apologia for the simple, rural life – the kind of life Hirohito claimed he would willingly have led had he not been born into the Imperial family. Even Honjo, in a guarded, indirect sort of way, expressed some concern, in his diaries, at the Emperor's apparent indifference.

Army officers, and Japan's top technocrats, were fully aware of the crisis. The chief executive of the South Manchurian

Railway Company openly campaigned for government-sponsored emigration by Japanese farmers to the Manchurian countryside as the only solution to Japan's economic and agricultural plight. (One officially-sponsored plan called for emigration quotas of Japanese farmers to Manchuria on a yearly basis right up to 1956.) The widely-believed, popular (and, needless to say, unsubstantiated) myth was that Manchuria, a kind of El Dorado, could accommodate millions of new settlers without displacing the native population, or causing any hardship of any kind. Part of the Japanese expansionist push that came soon after the enthronement was in response to the cry for *lebensraum*. Advocates of colonization of Manchuria regarded such an operation not only as a sound economic proposition but also as a neat military solution. Trained ex-servicemen were to be given preference over civilian farmers, and local officials (doctors, nurses, harbourmasters, railway officials) were also to be drawn from the ranks of the reservists, able, in an emergency, to assume their army role. In politicians' and generals' speeches, at this time, Japan was constantly referred to as a small potted tree struggling to extend its roots – and dying in the process.

Still, in contrast to both her Chinese and her Russian neighbours, Japan appeared immeasurably more stable. In Soviet Russia (recognized by Japan in 1928) these were the early Stalinist years, with forcible collectivization, widespread famine and the elimination of the kulaks; China was still far from united, with Chiang Kai-chek only beginning his struggle against the Communists, facing unrest and subversion in cities and provinces not fully under his control. The Manchurian situation remained volatile: Chang Tso-lin's son, "Young Marshal" Chang Hsueh-lang, had disappointed the Japanese plotters of his father's murder, proclaiming his allegiance to Chiang Kai-chek instead of becoming, as they had hoped, a docile Japanese puppet. Japan had not yet given up hope in him and, as a wry token of esteem, a Japanese dignitary had been sent to attend his father's funeral ceremonies. The Order of the Rising Sun was conferred on the "Young Marshal" in an attempt at ingratiation. This occurred despite a particularly dramatic blood-letting, which showed that Chang Tso-lin's son, for all his reputation as an opium-addict, was a chip off the old block. He invited a Manchu general, and the head of the Chinese Railways in Manchuria, to a game of mah-jong in his Mukden palace. Both men, he had discovered, were plotting with the Japanese to turn Manchuria into a Japanese-controlled puppet province. As they entered the room, the "Young Marshal" had them gunned down, as an example to others.

The choice of the next Prime Minister after Tanaka had been another reassuring factor, to foreign observers and liberal Japanese alike. Hirohito, again after consulting with Saionji, chose Osachi Hamaguchi, a highly-respected leader of the Minseito party who looked a little like a tiny Oriental Einstein. The nomination of Baron Shidehara, a man known for his moderation where China was concerned, as Foreign Minister was also seen as a victory for the liberals.

The only fire-eater in Hamaguchi's Cabinet was Kenzo Adachi, the Home Minister, a man with a sinister past and a reputation for winning elections by knocking heads. In his early days, he had masterminded a particularly horrible crime – the murder of the Korean Queen, deliberately instigated by Japan's intelligence services, backed by Black Dragon extremists, to facilitate Japan's increased hold on the country. That Hamagushi should find the need to include such a monster in his otherwise impressive Cabinet was a sad commentary on the state of Japanese political parties, with their excessive reliance on bully-boys and Tammany Hall-type bosses.

The issue most debated in 1929–30 was not the economy, but Japan's role as a naval power. After preparatory talks in Washington, the leading naval powers met in London to decide on the respective sizes of their navies. The purpose was to avoid an arms race but, in Japan, the conference was regarded as a deliberate, racist slur. What right, nationalists asked, did the Western powers have to interfere in what was Japan's sovereign right to build what warships she needed?

Both in Washington and in London, the brunt of the work fell on a relatively junior naval officer, Rear-Admiral Yamamoto, the man who had lost two fingers of his left hand during the 1905 Russo-Japanese War. Yamamoto did not share the jingoistic views of some of his colleagues. In advance of his time, he believed that to measure a navy's strength solely by tonnage was hopelessly old-fashioned. He believed in a force of speedy, highly manoeuvrable pocket battleships, in submarines and − above all − in a strike force of carrier-based naval aircraft. Privately, he felt a 10–10–6 ratio (six tons for Japan for every ten tons for US or UK navy vessels) more than adequate. Hirohito, military history enthusiast and sound amateur strategist himself, agreed. For bargaining purposes, however, Hirohito felt, like his Navy Chief of Staff, that Japan should press for a 10–10–7 ratio.

In the event, after talks first in Washington, then in London in 1930, Japan won a surprising victory. The final figure (6.9945 tons to Japan for every 10 tons to the US and UK) was far more than Hirohito or his naval experts had expected. Moreover, America agreed to allow Japan 73 per cent parity till 1936, and also announced she would delay the construction of three heavy cruisers. More important still, naval aircraft were not even mentioned in the deal.

Rear-Admiral Yamamoto returned to Japan via the USSR and Manchuria. There he met discreetly with Prince Konoye, the head of the Tuesday Club, and one of the few Japanese able to see Hirohito informally at almost all times, regardless of the Emperor's schedule. Konoye told Yamamoto that his performance had taken everyone by surprise. He congratulated him, assured him of a brilliant future, but warned him not to be surprised if some diehards, back in Tokyo, expressed their disappointment at the outcome. The parity issue had become a symbol for the lunatic fringe nationalists. Nevertheless, both Yamamoto and his Navy Minister got an enthusiastic reception on their arrival. Hirohito received them in audience and formally thanked them for their work. But a Black Dragon activist presented another of the conference delegates with a wrapped dagger – a Mafia-like hint that he should commit suicide "for endangering national defence".

Hirohito shared Yamamoto's view that technical innovation, rather than tonnage, really determined naval power. What concerned him now, far more than international tonnage ratios, was the amount of money needed to make the Japanese Navy one of the best in the world. With considerable in-fighting skill, he refused to sign the Naval Limitations Treaty until his Prime Minister came up with a sufficiently large figure. This in turn sparked off an inter-services quarrel, for the army was not at all pleased to see the navy get the lion's share of the military budget. The generals' eyes were on Manchuria, and a showdown there would be expensive. It would take place on land, not on sea. General Ugaki, the War Minister, took to his bed for months with an alleged ear infection. It was, Prince Chichibu inferred, with his newly acquired Oxford wit, really a "sick-down strike", a mute protest against excessive spending on the navy.

Though both Ugaki, the Army Chief of Staff, and Prime Minister Hamaguchi eventually gave in to navy spending demands, there was some discreet intra-service politicking too: one of the trade-offs was a more tolerant attitude towards nationalist army "clubs" and secret societies of all kinds in return for acceptance of the navy's construction budget. The most important of these groups, founded in 1927, was the Cherry Blossom Society, with restricted membership (150 officers from captain to colonel), which not only became a breeding-ground for military jingoists of all kinds but also played a leading role in the army putsch that was to put Manchuria under effective Japanese control through the Mukden Incident of September 1931. The new tolerance for this, and other, societies of the same kind turned out to be disastrous, since the Cherry Blossom Society – and its imitators – became the focal point for every kind of ideological military extremism, gaining strength, and winning over new recruits, year by year, until the very hierarchical principle of the army seemed at times in jeopardy. The time would soon come when a well-connected colonel, backed by the right kind of secret society or army "club", wielded far more real power than his actual superior.

The Army General Staff also recognized that – with so much money going to the navy – any military operation involving Manchuria would now necessarily have to be carried out on the cheap. It began re-examining a plan, submitted by Lieutenant-Colonel Ishiwara, one of the plotters of Chang Tso-lin's murder, which took this crucial cost factor into account, even turning it into an advantage. Hirohito, who, almost certainly, studied this document, was already taking an almost paternal interest in Ishiwara and his aide, Itagaki, both of them brilliant, unconventional staff officers of immense promise.

In October 1930, with some of the navy budget problems behind him, Hirohito attended naval manoeuvres on a flagship in the inland sea. He was particularly impressed by Yamamoto's display of naval air power: his carrier-based planes wiped out the conventional battleships in the realistic war games laid on for the Emperor. As early as 1921, George C. Ross, the young Royal Navy officer who later helped in the earthquake relief operations, had written home:

Unless we start a naval construction programme soon, we will be left a long way behind Japan as a naval power. They work day and night in their dockyards ... What's more, they are right up to date in everything. It is alarming as it seems they only started a few years ago.

Since then, Japan had become the most up-to-date naval air power in the world, and Yamamoto's secret naval air base, out of bounds to all but a handful of specialists, made the most of a lean budget: the take-off and landing decks of imaginary aircraft-carriers (Japan possessed only four aircraft-carriers, though more were on the way) were simulated on the ground, and a special corps of naval air pilots, hand-picked by Yamamoto, was becoming the most sought-after unit in the service.

To be "top-gun" in the new naval air corps was to ensure entry into top families through marriage, and into the most exclusive geisha houses too: the socially-conscious madames were well aware that the more these dashing, glamorous officers used their establishments, the more "face" they earned, and the more the reputation of their houses soared. For this reason, these prohibitively expensive places – clubs rather than brothels, where discretion was assured – often gave substantial discounts to élite army and navy officers on low salaries. Admiral Yamamoto, with no private means, spent practically all his leisure time in the company of geishas, or gambling in geisha houses. He could not have done so on his salary, despite his frequent winning streaks. But in his case, as in others, the madames were shrewd enough to waive their usual fees, while the doors remained inexorably closed to those lacking the right social, financial or political connections. Word-of-mouth throughout the military, Zaibatsu and government "establishments", to say nothing of the discreet but tentacular surveillance of Japan's secret police, ensured that those in the know were well aware of the off-duty geisha proclivities of "top people". Admiral Ross, himself Britain's Assistant Naval Attaché in Tokyo from 1933 to 1936, was a frequent patron of some of these establishments. He recalls seeing Admiral Yamamoto surrounded by geisha girls in one of the more exclusive houses. The Admiral was suddenly summoned to the phone. He came smartly to attention and began speaking softly into the mouthpiece, with courtly deference, before leaving in haste. From the Admiral's excessively respectful tone and form of address on the telephone, there was no doubt in the minds of anyone present, Ross recalled, that the voice on the other end of the line had been the Emperor's.

On his departure for navy manoeuvres, Hirohito still had no government consensus on the exact amount to be earmarked for navy spending. The navy asked for 500 million yen. Both the Finance and Prime Ministers pleaded with Hirohito to reduce it to 300 million yen. Finally, Hamaguchi obtained the compromise figure of 374 million yen.

But by this time Hamaguchi himself, like Hara nine years previously, was a marked man. By agreeing to the arms limitation treaty, and cutting back on the navy's estimates, he had become identified, by the lunatic fringe rightist movements, as one of the Emperor's "evil advisers" who had to be eliminated as a patriotic duty. Rumours that there was a price on his head reached several people, including Saionji himself, now eighty and feeble, and Saionji's confidential secretary, Harada, passed the word on to Hamaguchi himself. The "old lion", as the fiery politician was nicknamed, dismissed these threats with contempt.

The press never mentioned that the Prime Minister's life was in danger, but the leading figures in the police and Palace establishments knew the threats were real. Hamaguchi continued to receive "routine" protection from his police guards, but the fact that the Home Minister Adachi was a charter member of the Black Dragon Society was hardly reassuring. The news that a gunman was stalking Hamaguchi must have reached the Palace: the editor of a Japanese right-wing defence periodical, *Japan and the Japanese*, with close Black Dragon and Cherry Blossom connections, told Prince Konoye in early November 1930 that "things may start to happen from now on". Through his extreme right-wing underworld connections, the same editor had had prior warning of the murder of Japan's earlier Prime Minister, Hara, nine years previously.

Hirohito, meanwhile, had gone straight from navy to army manoeuvres, taking along with him the Home Minister. Hamaguchi was due to join them. On the morning of November 14, as he was about to board a train, Hamaguchi was shot in the stomach by a near-illiterate rightist, Tomeo Sagoya, who was immediately arrested.

The Emperor heard the news in the field, 300 miles south of Tokyo. He did not find it necessary to return to Tokyo to keep in touch with the situation, but carried on with the exercises. Instead, he appointed the Foreign Minister Shidehara as interim Premier and conveyed his "regrets" for this "mishap" to Hamaguchi himself, through an aide.

At first the doctors who incompetently fussed over Hamaguchi at the Tokyo Imperial University's infirmary thought he would survive. They operated, gave him blood transfusions, and announced he had a 60 to 70 per cent chance of recovery. Hamaguchi, in great pain, was stoical but pessimistic. With extraordinary will-power, he managed to attend some of his essential duties in later weeks. In excruciating pain, he addressed the Diet on navy estimates in an almost inaudible voice. But, five months after the attempt on his life, he died, of complications following a bungled operation.

Though Hirohito did not interrupt his army inspection, the Home Minister Adachi did bow out: he found it necessary, he told the Emperor with some embarrassment a few days later, to return to Tokyo forthwith for pressing police business. It was against all protocol rules to leave the Emperor's presence when one was his guest, and Hirohito was deeply offended. He knew that Adachi's reason for returning to Tokyo was not to enquire into the Hamaguchi murder attempt, but to start planning his own campaign for the premiership, gathering around him his bullyboys and underworld cronies to discuss their election strategy. It proved to be a fatal mistake. After the Hamaguchi murder, Adachi's political career never lived up to its earlier promise: Hirohito saw to that, excluding him from top office thereafter, whenever his name came up for consideration.

What happened to Hamaguchi's murderer, Sagoya, was equally instructive: he spent the next three years on bail, before his death sentence on November 6, 1933. Three months later, he was given an amnesty. Like Hara's assassin, he thereafter lived comfortably on a pension, occasionally taking part in gatherings of extremist nationalists. As late as 1956 he was still active in right-wing circles, staging a mock funeral service for the Prime Minister Hatoyama in Tokyo's Shinbashi Station to protest against his "treacherous" decision to conclude a formal peace with the USSR.

This further example of the extraordinary Japanese leniency towards crimes of violence, provided they were politically motivated, baffled even some of the members of Hirohito's own Court. The Emperor could certainly have advised against an amnesty in Sagoya's case, had he so wished, and been obeyed. The thought that such leniency might raise doubts about the nature of Japanese justice and encourage future politically motivated assassination attempts never even seems to have crossed his mind. The virtually unpunished Hamaguchi murder marked the end of Hirohito's "liberal" first few years: the age of innocence was over. That of the assassins was soon to begin.

CHAPTER SIX

The police, without the benefit of a prolonged investigation of Hamaguchi's murderer's links with the far right, hastily concluded he had acted alone. But, as the stricken Prime Minister lingered on (finally dying in April 1931), a series of conspiracies all invoking the Emperor's name, was being hatched. The first, the 1931 "March Plot", made nonsense of Marx's aphorism that history repeats itself, first as tragedy, then as farce, for this event, at least, had distinctly comic overtones.

What happened was that some key staff officers, including Colonel Hashimoto, the leading light of the Cherry Blossom Society (and the new Russian Affairs desk officer at Staff HQ after a spell in Turkey where he had become a fervent admirer of Kemal Ataturk), hinted to the War Minister Ugaki, early in 1931, that the Emperor, tired of dealing with corrupt, bickering politicians, would look with favour on a military "coup" which would restore the integrity of the Imperial nation. Ugaki, who had loyally served the Emperor as War Minister as far back as 1924, presiding over army budget cuts in the teeth of opposition from within the military, was, they hinted, a natural choice as the Emperor's chosen instrument, his new military "genro".

Ugaki was vain enough to express interest, but cautious enough to seek out more proof of the Emperor's tacit involvement. He was subsequently wined and dined by several senior Palace officials, but the more he was entertained, in their homes and in expensive geisha-houses, the more suspicious he became.

The scenario outlined to him was that of a typical Latin-American putsch: a large mob would surround the Minseito and Seiyukai party buildings and the Prime Minister's house while a hand-picked army unit cordoned off Ministry buildings, the radio station and the Diet. A high-ranking officer would persuade members of the Diet to vote in favour of military rule, the abolition of political parties and its own voluntary dissolution. The trouble was that, when approached by General Ugaki directly, the commander of the 1st Guards Division (the unit earmarked for the putsch) denied any knowledge of it, saying he would certainly not take part in anything illegal without written instructions from the Emperor himself, orders that never came. And such was the aura of divinity encircling the Emperor that Ugaki could not even bring himself to ask for a private audience with Hirohito. In any case, the conspirators told him, it was imperative that His Majesty in no way appear involved.

Some of the preparations, however, were real enough: in order to make the crowds besieging the Diet more threatening, they were to be equipped with grenades. Doctor Okawa, the former director of studies of the "University Lodging House" school, was party to the conspiracy: he was to provide the mobs, and the arms. Crates of training grenades, each capable of simulating the blast of four artillery shells, and sending clouds of smoke into the air, duly materialized: Colonel Hashimoto, the Cherry Blossom Society activist, who supplied them, said they had been provided by the Chiba Infantry School. Okawa had them stored first in his home, then in his mistress's house. They were never used.

On March 2 there was a token demonstration, masterminded by Dr. Okawa and the Black Dragon society, but there was no march on the Diet, and the army did not move. The conspirators carried on as if the real plot were still to come, and Ugaki was again lavishly entertained in the company of Okawa and various emissaries linked with Palace officials. By this time, however, the General suspected he was being manipulated, and announced he would have nothing more to do with such a crackpot scheme.

This, perhaps, was what Dr. Okawa was waiting for. Moving the incriminating training grenades to a "safe house", he demanded money from the conspirators – to pay off the Black Dragon bullyboys who had staged the demonstration.

Whether he actually blackmailed them into parting with large sums by threatening to reveal the army's complicity is not clear to this day, despite subsequent lengthy investigations conducted by US prosecutors preparing for the post-war "Tokyo Trials". He was certainly able to pay off his bills in geisha-houses and settle other costs related to the plot, with something to spare. All the while he continued to draw a sizeable salary from the South Manchurian Railway Company, as a "consultant", and even after his involvement in the plot was confirmed his stipend continued to be paid.

If the purpose of the "March Plot" was solely to discredit General Ugaki, however, it failed. Shortly afterwards Hirohito packed him off to Korea, as Governor-General: it was a largely honorific post but certainly not a disgraceful end to a long army career. Nor was this his swansong: later, Ugaki would play a key role as a member of the "peace party", urging Hirohito to end the Second World War. His opposition to military diehards indeed was such that – in retrospect – the whole "March plot" could well have been an elaborate hoax to discredit one of the few senior officers who might have opposed the army's more irresponsible, jingoistic representatives.

What was Hirohito's role, if any? The activists who invoked the Emperor's name never produced any evidence that Hirohito was involved. So strangely did the plot unfold that Ugaki ended up more a victim than a protagonist. One theory is that both the Minseito Party (including the "genro", Prince Saionji) and some members of the Emperor's entourage had become wary of General Ugaki's influence and integrity, and wished to discredit him. Another is that the plot was seen as a necessary preliminary to any direct army intervention in Manchuria. Most machiavellian of all is the notion that the whole preposterous intrigue represented a test of Ugaki's personal loyalty by Hirohito himself – to see how far he and other senior army officers would rise to the bait.

At the time, very little filtered down to foreign observers. It was only after the Second World War that US investigators preparing the IMTFE prosecution's case uncovered some of its odder details. What is certain is that, as Marquis Kido was later to write, it "came out of darkness" to "return to darkness". No one was hurt, or seriously compromised – and that stormy petrel of Japanese right-wing politics, Doctor Okawa, made a lot of money, which was almost certainly one of his chief objectives. The fact remains that it is unlikely that Hirohito was completely unaware of the "March plot's" broad outline: both Marquis Kido, by 1931 confidential secretary to Hirohito's Lord Privy Seal, and Count Makino himself took part in the manipulation of the unfortunate General – and they could not have kept the intrigue from the Emperor without forefeiting his trust. In the light of Kido's later influential role, as Lord Privy Seal and the Emperor's principal aide and adviser, to have remained silent would have been completely out of character. The enigma will remain: though Kido kept lengthy diary accounts of his activities, he refers to the "March plot" as though he had been a disinterested spectator.

While the "March Plot" was amateurish farce, the plot to gain control of Manchuria, triggered six months later, was superbly planned and executed. Here again the degree, and the nature, of Hirohito's involvement is still a controversial issue. Three officers with considerable Chinese experience – Colonels Doihara, Itagaki and Ishiwara – played leading parts, Ishiwara as theoretician and overall planner, Itagaki as staff co-ordinator, and Doihara as political liaison officer with the Manchurian Chinese. But this plot was on such a huge scale, mobilizing such resources and requiring such split-second timing, that it could not have occurred without the tacit consent, and indeed the active support, of most of the Japanese General Staff. Again, it is unlikely, given Hirohito's industriousness, and curiosity, where army matters were concerned, that he should have remained unaware of the plot. He certainly had a broad knowledge of its preparations, for he did finally take half-hearted steps to caution the "Kwangtung

Army" against precipitate action. But, throughout, he was extremely duplicitous in his dealings not only with his generals but with his Cabinet as a whole.

One is reminded of General de Gaulle's attitude, during and after the May 13, 1958 army putsch in Algiers: de Gaulle, we now know, was in close touch with the Algiers-based plotters and, while ostensibly disclaiming any links with them, was privately hinting that he approved their intentions, and was only waiting for them to step in and put an end to the despised Fourth Republic. In the same way, Hirohito, while indirectly distancing himself from the plotters, did nothing to deter them.

The question – one seldom asked – is why, if really opposed to the "Mukden Incident", Hirohito failed to use his discretionary powers, or even to voice his unequivocal disapproval while there was still time to do so. As Richard Storry[1] noted, it was probable that an Imperial proclamation, "restraining the army in Manchuria, or, later, in China, would have been obeyed by the great majority of officers". But the Emperor preferred to remain completely in the background, using his aides as a "front": the word was duly spread, during the Manchurian army take-over, that he was "highly displeased", that the movement of troops from Korea to Manchuria was in "disregard of Imperial orders"; and Saionji, repeatedly, was to say that the army's attitude was "unreasonable".[2] But further than that he did not go. On later occasions, in particular during the February 26, 1936 putsch, (Japanese refer to this later traumatic event simply as "2/26") he was to show impressive qualities of determination and leadership, conspicuously lacking in 1931.

The inference is that, over Manchuria, Hirohito prevaricated, either deliberately or because of indecision. And the behaviour of some of those generals closely involved in preparing and masterminding the complicated operation known as the "Mukden Incident" only makes sense if one assumes that their inner conviction was that, for all the Emperor's and the Cabinet's public refutations, they did in fact have Hirohito's tacit consent throughout – though the responsibility had to appear to be theirs alone, especially if anything went wrong.

The "Mukden Incident" was based on Colonel Ishiwara's blueprint prepared several years previously, implemented with the assistance of several members of the Cherry Blossom Society. It was remarkable for several reasons. In the first place, it was relatively inexpensive: Ishiwara knew thrift was, in Hirohito's eyes, a major virtue. The plan was to take over Southern Manchuria from the inside, relying almost exclusively on the "Kwangtung Army" and Japanese Railway guards already permanently stationed there in accordance with long-standing agreements with China. Though troops in Japanese-run Korea could later be called on as reinforcements, Ishiwara saw the initial move as a short, sharp blitzkrieg using only those Japanese troops already legally stationed in Southern Manchuria.

The plan's other advantage was that it was conceived not just as a military operation, but as part of a relatively bloodless "revolution" setting up a puppet administration sympathetic and subordinate to Japan. A Chinese Fifth Column had to be on hand to take over the overt running of the country – real power resting at all times, of course, with the Japanese military. Two months before the actual "Mukden Incident" (September 18, 1931), Doihara and his staff were at work, cultivating potential allies among Manchuria's more venal officials and businessmen. It was fertile ground: there were diehard supporters of the dispossessed Manchu Ching dynasty who had never considered themselves fully Chinese in the first place, as well as local landlords and minor noblemen who felt they had a better future under Japan than under Chiang Kai-chek. And in the Japanese-run part of Tientsin's International Concession was Henry Pu Yi, the last Emperor of China, already being assiduously courted by Japanese officers and who was to prove the most prominent Manchu Quisling of all.

The risk, however, was great, for Chang Tso-lin's son, the "Young Marshal", had become a popular and effective warlord. His army outnumbered the Japanese garrison twenty to one.

But, when the "coup" came, the "Young Marshal" and the bulk of his experienced troops were all south of the Great Wall, fighting the Communists, and most of the Chinese soldiers left in Southern Manchuria were raw recruits.

Two military objectives in Mukden – the Chinese Gendarmerie and the "Young Marshal's" tiny air force – had to be neutralized if Ishiwara's plan was to succeed. Months before the September coup, "Kwangtung Army" engineers started building an officers' swimming pool conveniently close to both the Gendarmerie barracks and the airfield. Chinese labourers were brought in to work on its foundations, then the army took over. The site became strictly out of bounds not just to the Chinese, but to most Japanese troops as well: its access was restricted to a hand-picked squad. The concrete "swimming pool", surrounded by a vast wooden enclosure, with gates large enough for trucks to enter, was in fact a gun emplacement, and in due course two 9.5-inch guns were smuggled into the city from the army base in Port Arthur, and secretly installed in the "swimming pool" bunker. Elite Japanese artillerymen practised training the concealed guns on the Gendarmerie barracks and the airfield.

In June 1931, a Japanese spy, masquerading as an "agricultural expert", was caught by the Chinese in Eastern Mongolia, and shot. This incident, unforeseen by Ishiwara but not unwelcome, fuelled the anti-Chinese anger of the Kwangtung Army. Finally, Ishiwara took advantage of a riot between Korean immigrants and Chinese farmers (who had been digging ditches on the Koreans' land, perhaps paid to do so by Ishiwara's men) to have troops sent to the Korean–Manchurian border. The stage was set. All that was needed was a detonator. Ishiwara had thought of that too, but by this time so many high-ranking officers knew about the Manchurian plot that the government, now headed by Wakatsuki, a political kinsman of the murdered Hamaguchi, began to get wind of it. On August 4, General Minami, the new War Minister, briefing divisional commanders after a staff exercise in Japan, warned them of a "grave situation" in Manchuria and Mongolia. This was no "passing phase", he said, but was due to "a decline in Japan's prestige and China's mania for recovery of its rights". The speech, noted at the time by A. Morgan Young,[3] was itself a clear indication that the Japanese army expected to be involved in war in Manchuria. Rumours spread throughout Tokyo that something big was soon about to occur there.

Inevitably, the news reached the Emperor himself. Hirohito saw General Minami, the War Minister, and warned him that the "Kwangtung Army" in Manchuria "must proceed with prudence and caution". Saionji advised Wakatsuki to send a trusted officer to Manchuria to find out exactly what was going on, and to deliver a letter from the Prime Minister to the commander of the "Kwangtung Army" telling him to cancel any plans he might have for military action.

The Prime Minister's choice was an odd one. The man he selected for the task, Major-General Tatekawa, was a hard-liner, already compromised in the March 31 plot, who had written a much publicized article[4] advocating Japanese military intervention in Manchuria. In addition, he was himself one of the key plotters on the Tokyo end of the "Mukden Incident" operation. The plotters were immediately advised of the imminent arrival of the letter-bearing Tatekawa by their Tokyo-based co-conspirator, Colonel Hashimoto, who urged them to go ahead without delay. Instead of flying immediately to Port Arthur, Tatekawa took a leisurely route, by train via Korea, and on arrival in Mukden on September 18, three days later, allowed himself to be spirited away to a geisha-house without delivering the crucial letter. The new Kwangtung Army Commander, General Honjo, was in any case out of town.

That night, while Tatekawa was "resting", Ishiwara pulled the trigger: a Japanese army officer laid some small quantities of dynamite along the embankment of the South Manchuria Railway track north of Mukden, designed to explode with the maximum of noise and the minimum of damage. The detonation took place around 10.20 p.m. Later, the Japanese Government was to claim that this had been a "warlike act" on the part of Chinese troops, removing parts of the track and seriously disrupting traffic. It was at a loss to explain how, a few minutes after the explosion, a train-load of passengers bound for Mukden passed over that same track without mishap, indeed without anyone aboard realizing anything was amiss.

The explosion was, however, heard by a Chinese patrol, which attempted to investigate, and immediately came under Japanese fire. The "incident" was under way: Colonel Itagaki gave the order to attack. The guns from the "swimming pool" went into action, with devastating effect, and all over Southern Manchuria Japanese troops, on alert for days, began their surprise attack on Chinese garrisons. In a few hours it was all over and Mukden was under Japanese control, with the initial loss of only a few Japanese lives (Chinese casualties numbered 400).

That night, Colonel Doihara had been on another kind of mission: at a banquet attended by prominent Chinese, already sympathetic to the Japanese, he asked their views on the new administration. They agreed Doihara should be Mukden's new Mayor.

From the start, the decisions in Manchuria had been made by colonels, not generals, principally by Doihara, Ishigawa, and Itagaki, but the commander of the Kwangtung Army, General Honjo, who had only assumed command in August, agreed to take overall responsibility for military operations which had been initiated without his prior approval. He too was an "old China hand", in favour of direct military intervention in Manchuria, identified, in fact, with the most authoritarian clique in the army, the "Kodo-ha" or "Imperial Way" faction – generals like Araki, Mazaki and Matsui who were anathema to Japanese liberals. He knew, and liked, the trio of colonels: Itagaki had been his deputy during his spell as military attaché in Peking in 1924, and he had worked with Doihara in China as far back as 1918. "Honjo's actions when the crisis finally broke appear to confirm assumptions that he was in sympathy with his subordinates but short on facts about their specific plans," says Mark R.

Peatie, a leading historian of modern Japan, who quotes Itagaki as saying, during the fateful September 18 night: "Never mind Honjo, it's Ishiwara's war." [5] When the Japanese Consul in Mukden suggested the conflict be settled through diplomatic negotiations with the Chinese and cast doubt on the Japanese army's version of what had happened earlier that night, Itagaki rudely reminded him that the military command had precedence over civilians, and, after he refused to go, one of Itagaki's staff officers threatened him with a drawn sword. Soon afterwards, Japanese correspondents were taken to the site of the "damaged" railway track: a length of the track, and three Chinese army corpses, were exhibited as evidence. How the track itself had been so speedily repaired was not explained. Needless to say, the army's version of events was headlined, without question, in all important Japanese newspapers.

Japanese forces took over Changchun, north of Mukden, on September 19, and Kirin on September 21. Incredibly (or was the delay cynically calculated?) it was only late on September 19 that Major-General Tatekawa handed over the Prime Minister's letter to General Honjo, by which time it was of course too late: except for mopping-up operations, the Japanese military operation was as good as over. The generals continued to act on their own initiative: Korean-based Japanese planes were used from September 19 to bomb pockets of Chinese troops, and on September 22 a Japanese Brigade based in Korea moved into Southern Manchuria – all of this without orders from the Japanese Government. The intervention of Japanese planes from Korea, Tatekawa's ready acceptance of geisha hospitality on arrival, together with General Honjo's elusiveness in the first few hours of the "Mukden Incident", all give credibility to the notion that they considered the Prime Minister's missive, inspired by Hirohito's cautionary warnings, to be a huge private joke.

Back in Tokyo, the Japanese Government, faced with a fait accompli, was powerless – and Hirohito did nothing to provide his ministers with a clear mandate. The Prime Minister, Tatekawa, reported to the Emperor that he had ordered the "Kwangtung Army" to return to its bases, and to "localize" the conflict. Hirohito replied that the Government's action was "perfectly appropriate". At the League of Nations Headquarters in Geneva, Japanese diplomats informed their colleagues that the "unfortunate incident" had been "provoked" by "Chinese provocateurs", but that Japanese troops would soon be returning to barracks. In a typical hand-wringing exercise, the League of Nations Council urged the Chinese and Japanese governments "to refrain from action that might aggravate the situation".

The Prime Minister told Minami that the Japanese Government's watchword was "non-aggravation of the incident", but Minami informed his subordinates that "non-aggravation did not necessarily mean non-enlargement", and a mere twelve days after the Japanese attack (September 30) a Japanese emissary from the "Kwangtung Army" arrived in Tientsin with a highly important message for Henry Pu Yi: if he was prepared to come to Manchuria, Japan was prepared to restore the Manchu Dynasty there.

This, more than anything else, suggests that Emperor Hirohito was not as removed from the "Mukden Incident" as is sometimes claimed, for even the most swashbuckling, activist general would think twice before proposing a throne to a puppet emperor – policy that almost certainly must have required Hirohito's consent. Indeed, the Japanese Government – and Hirohito himself – were soon to view the new state of affairs in Manchuria with surprising equanimity. The northern half of Manchuria passed under Japanese military control in November and, soon afterwards, a leading official body, the Economic National Policy Investigation Society, acknowledged that, "even though Manchuria may take on the structure of an independent country, she will be no more than a small, weak nation whose fate is controlled absolutely by an advanced nation. Furthermore, she will not be easily granted an opportunity to get out of this situation. Manchuria . . . would become a territory with no international significance in the same manner as Korea."

And, less than three months after the Manchurian take-over, Colonel Itagaki himself came to the Imperial Palace in Tokyo to report on progress in Manchuria. Marquis Kido, who mentioned Itagaki's visit in his diaries (the entry is dated January 11, 1932), recorded that he "and persons close to the Emperor" (which, in Court jargon, almost certainly meant the Emperor himself was present unofficially) heard Itagaki outline Manchuria's new status, with the imminent arrival of the new puppet ruler, Pu Yi, the formal Japanese commitment to "defend Manchuria from its enemies", and the simple but ingenious means of controlling the new puppet administration without contravening international law: "Japanese officials would assume Manchurian nationality." [6]

Nor is it possible that Hirohito was unaware of the details of the establishment of the new Japanese-controlled puppet state. Kido, in a rare direct critical outburst, deplored, two days later (January 14), that the Emperor was becoming excessively involved in detail. "I am afraid," the diary entry read, "that the Emperor seems too nervous . . . His Majesty attends to small matters. It is desirable that the Emperor should sit 'as a large mountain'."

Hirohito's reactions to the behaviour of his War Minister and his generals were in marked contrast to the decisiveness he was to show later in the wake of the collapse of the "2/26" putsch. Then he would insist on a clean sweep of senior generals, and would replace almost his entire Imperial "Cabinet" (Chief ADC, Lord Privy Seal and Imperial Household Minister).

There is no doubt that the disobedience shown by Honjo, Tatekawa, and the Commander of Japanese troops in Korea could have cost them their careers. Had Hirohito felt strongly about their behaviour, he had the discretionary power to act, either then or later, as he was to act against those who he considered had let him down during the 1936 putsch, by ordering forcible retirements, withholding promotions or suggesting postings to unimportant jobs. But nothing happened that might imply that the Emperor was displeased. On the contrary: Hirohito gave Honjo the strongest possible proof of his esteem, making him his Chief ADC (and hence one of the most powerful officers in the Imperial Army) in 1933. Colonel Itagaki was promoted to general, and became Hirohito's War Minister in 1939. The Commander of the Japanese troops in Korea, General Hayashi, later became first War Minister, then, briefly, Prime Minister. Doihara also rose high in the military hierarchy, becoming the head of Army Aviation and in due course one of Japan's most notorious generals. Only Ishiwara, who fell foul of the mean, vindictive Tojo, ended his wartime army career as a mere major-general in charge of the 16th training division, forcibly retired by 1942. He boasted after the war: "Tojo didn't have the guts to retire me, so he got the Emperor to do it instead."

The hallmark of the "Mukden Incident" was deceit, not only on the part of the trio of colonels who masterminded the plot, but of almost all those in positions of responsibility. The Prime Minister, Tatekawa, and his liberal Foreign Minister were doubtless privately appalled, but tacitly acknowledged its inevitability. As A. Morgan Young put it, "Japan tried to accredit the thesis that, in Manchuria, the army had acted without orders. Certainly there had been no orders from the Foreign Ministry but the notion was untenable: the whole procedure for the seizure of Manchuria was timed so beautifully and carried out so perfectly that the Staff orders must have been very perfect indeed." The excuse that the army had acted without orders, he added, was "an old Japanese diplomatic gambit" though in this case "perhaps the officials themselves did not realize how completely the initiative had passed out of civilian control". Once it was clear that the Japanese occupation of Manchuria was proceeding at an irreversible pace, Japanese diplomats – once "doves" – started using language almost as aggressive as that of the military. Ishizawa, the same Japanese minister in Peking who had blandly denied any Japanese territorial ambitions over Manchuria a few weeks previously, now defended the army's action, caused, he said, "by deep-rooted anti-Japanese feelings in China . . . which had compelled Japan to act in self-defence". As an example of Chinese "bad faith" he cited the boycott of Japanese goods in China – a measure imposed only *after* Mukden. Once the fighting had subsided in Manchuria, the War Minister, Minami, no longer bothered to conceal his feelings: at a banquet (on October 23) attended by generals and high officials of the South Manchurian Railway Company, he made a bombastic speech asserting that what had just happened in Manchuria "sets a precedent for future relations with China". Neither the Prime Minister, Tatekawa, nor the Foreign Minister, Shidehara, made any move to resign – a gesture which might have drawn world-wide attention to the domestic drama being played out in Tokyo.

The official Japanese "line" remains that the Emperor was completely taken in by the behaviour of the "Kwangtung Army", had insufficient prior knowledge of the "Mukden Incident" to act in time, and did his best to restrain his officers and "localize" the conflict, once it had begun. It is also the version accepted by most academics and historians. In the light of Hirohito's behaviour, then and later, his promotion of Honjo and Itagaki, and his assiduous courting of the puppet Manchukuo "Emperor" Pu Yi, it is untenable.

The fact is that a "forward policy" in China, and the establishment of a Japanese-controlled puppet state in Manchuria, were popular not only with "lunatic-fringe" army groups but with a wide cross-section of Japanese. Businessmen and entrepreneurs of all kinds were very well aware of the opportunities in store, especially if – as was to happen – they were to be allowed to operate without any other competition, squeezing out all competitors, Western and Chinese; the army, needless to say, favoured the establishment of a Manchurian puppet state, as proof of Japan's might as Asia's "Number One" power; economists, demographers and university academics also saw in long-term Japanese emigration to Manchuria the only answer to the problem of overpopulation. In short, except for a small minority of liberals, like Prince Saionji, the "Mukden Incident" and its aftermath were highly popular. In a conversation with his confidential secretary Harada,

Saionji, shortly after the "Mukden incident" (in Harada's memoirs, the date is given as September 1932) already saw the writing on the wall, speaking, significantly, in the past tense:

In the past, when we thought about Japan's future, we never thought in terms of anything so narrow as: "Japan, leader of the East", or an "Asian Monroe Doctrine". The problem of the Far East can be better resolved through cooperation with Britain and America than through the mouthing of "Asianism" or an "Asian Monroe Doctrine".

The only logical explanation of Hirohito's behaviour during and after the "Mukden Incident" was that he faced a dilemma: while tacitly recognizing the overwhelming strength of the coalition of vested interests in favour of this "forward policy", he was reluctant to alienate the more cautious, "liberal" elements in his Cabinet, whose members were well aware of the international consequences of Japan's brutal, aggressive action in Manchuria, and of the domestic consequences in allowing the army a free hand in determining policy. Nor did he want to fall into the trap of becoming an overt, military emperor-dictator, in essence a prisoner of the military extremists. By choosing the path of ambiguity, he placated those elements in Japan who were wary of the military without alienating the activists themselves, all the while following the precept, in force since the Meiji restoration, of not appearing to take any day-to-day decisions himself. He also reassured the Tokyo-based diplomatic corps that "his heart was in the right place", allowing the army to shoulder full responsibility for the origins of the controversial new puppet state of "Manchukuo".

At times, efforts to "sanitize" Japan's take-over of Manchuria reached absurd lengths. The League of Nations' Lytton Report effectively proved that the "Mukden Incident" had been naked Japanese aggression, and that the supposed destruction of the railway track which had provoked the intervention in the first place was a carefully planned provocation. But, even today, there are those who – against all evidence – believe the Chinese initiated the "Mukden Incident".

General Honjo, who committed suicide in 1945 rather than face the possibility of standing trial as a suspected war criminal, maintained to the last the official Japanese version of the "Mukden Incident" long after it had been proved to be a pack of lies. In his 1945 suicide note, he insisted the track really had been blown up by Chinese troops and that subsequent Japanese "peace-keeping operations became necessary to protect Japanese and Korean lives".

Such a pattern of deception, on an almost childish scale, was to be repeated: the same imperial prevarications and contradictions would be a feature of events leading up to Pearl Harbor. It would be difficult, at times, to differentiate between Hirohito's talent for ambiguity and the grosser Japanese predilection, in some quarters, for the "big lie".

General Honjo's suicide note, however, had nothing to do with Eastern versus Western conceptions of the truth: it was simply his ultimate, spectacular way of demonstrating, even in death, his mystical loyalty to his Emperor.

[1] Richard Storry, *A History of Modern Japan*, Pelican, 1960.
[2] *Brocade Banner*, ib.
[3] A. Morgan Young, *Imperial Japan*, W. Morrow, 1938.
[4] Tatekawa, *General principles concerning the solution of the Mongolian problem.*
[5] Mark R. Peatie, *Ishiwara Kanji and Japan's confrontation with the West*, Princeton U.P., 1957.
[6] IMTFE Prosecution Documents.

CHAPTER SEVEN

The "Mukden Incident" and its aftermath did not entirely destroy Hirohito's credibility abroad as a peace-loving young "moderate" – he had played his cards too shrewdly for that – but it did seriously call into question the aims of the "Showa" era as he had defined them in his accession "rescript" or imperial proclamation. In 1926, he had stated, "The world is now in a process of evolution. A new chapter is being opened in the history of human civilization. This nation's settled policy always stands for progress and improvement. Simplicity instead of vain display, originality instead of blind imitation, progress in view of this period of evolution, improvement to keep pace with the advancement of civilization, national harmony in purpose and action, beneficence to all classes of people, and friendship to all the nations of earth: these are the cardinal aims to which Our most profound and abiding solicitude is directed."

Admirable, and probably unattainable at the best of times, these pledges became – after the birth of Manchukuo – an ironic reminder of what might have been. "Friendship to all nations" was already, and would increasingly be, friendship on Japan's terms, the friendship of an arrogant master extended to submissive client nations; "beneficence to all classes of people" turned out to mean unprecedented belt-tightening to pay for Japan's mushrooming arms costs; and "national harmony" now floundered in a welter of plots, the conspirators becoming ever bolder in the knowledge that "patriotic motive" was a catch-all excuse guaranteeing judicial leniency.

The years 1932 and 1933 were grim ones for Hirohito, now in his early thirties and in the prime of life, for they coincided with a nagging domestic and dynastic problem: after six years of married life, he still had no male heir. The plots that succeeded each other from 1931 onwards were linked, in part, to this failure. Though the issue was far too sensitive to be raised in the Japanese press, the Emperor's inability to produce a male heir led to tensions throughout the Court, uneasiness in successive governments and in the armed forces. It also explained why some plotters brought Hirohito's younger brother, Prince Chichibu, into play as a possible alternative. In the past, the free-and-easy morals of the Imperial Court had ensured a permanent supply of potential male heirs, sons of Imperial concubines. There was no stigma attached to them, even the great Meiji himself had been technically illegitimate. But Hirohito was finding it difficult to justify his monogamy in the face of discreet, but persistent, reminders that he was expected to father a son, in the interests of dynastic stability.

Before the wedding, Princess Nagako had received, among her many presents, elaborate "pillow books" – including one from Hirohito's own mother. These beautifully illustrated, classic works of art contained advice not only on sex techniques but on ways of ensuring a male heir. Hirohito's mother, Empress Sadako, at intervals, gave her son's bride "herbal infusions" which were supposed to guarantee fertility – and male babies.

Nagako had given birth only to girls: Terunomiya (Little Sunshine), in November 1926; another daughter (who died two years later) in 1927; a third daughter in 1929; yet another daughter in 1931. Even such a Western-oriented Palace courtier as Prince Saionji, was urging Hirohito, by 1930-1, though always in deferential, oblique terms, to consider reviving the time-honoured custom of taking a concubine to bed. Nagako would surely understand, he told the Emperor. Lists of suitable young women were prepared, and photographs submitted to Hirohito.

His apparent inability to father a male heir was almost certainly a factor in the 1931 "October Plot" which implicated, for the first time, Prince Chichibu: the plotters drew up plans for a coup on the lines of the "March Plot" but with a far grimmer modus operandi, for this time they intended not only to dissolve parliament and compel Hirohito to accept a military government, but to murder Hirohito's entire Cabinet as well. Dr. Okawa, the perennial plotter, was deeply involved, as was the Cherry Blossom Society activist, Colonel Hashimoto. Both saw themselves as future members of a new "strong-arm" government, Okawa as Finance Minister and Hashimi as Home Minister; they were arrested, and briefly held in custody by the Japanese Military Police on October 17, but almost immediately released. "There was a rumour," said the post-war *Brocade Banner* study (using archives from Japanese police files) that the (civilian) police "had prior knowledge of the conspiracy but had felt they could not interfere because they knew Prince Chichibu was involved". The Emperor's younger brother had, by this time, shed his earlier, "socialist" views and was increasingly sympathetic to the army nationalists. Another feature of the plot was that its organizers intended bringing the retired Admiral Togo (the Russo-Japanese war hero and subsequent Imperial tutor) out of retirement to "persuade" the Emperor to countenance it. Police testimony also included reports of the plotters falling out: they quarrelled bitterly, accusing Dr. Okawa of tipping off his patron, Count Makino, the Lord Privy Seal, and presumably reaping a cash reward. Reviewing the whole affair, the War Minister, Minami, himself an unashamed nationalist, told his civilian Cabinet associates that it was imperative for the "October plot" to be hushed up "for ever".

The rest of the Government obeyed: none of the plotters was tried. Okawa was held the longest – twenty days in a comfortable cell. General Minami's warning was heeded, for though the plot was widely discussed within the Japanese "establishment", and by foreign diplomats in Tokyo, nothing at all transpired at the time in the Japanese press. The "October plot" even proved useful to Hirohito, for the League of Nations postponed its expected condemnation of Japan for its behaviour in Manchuria, on the grounds that the League did not want to irritate the military firebrands while they were already embarrassing the Emperor.

Manchuria's take-over, and the March and October plots, had destroyed the Cabinet's prestige. Its loss of face was compounded by the treachery of the Home Minister, Adachi, who refused to attend Cabinet meetings, urging a coalition government with the rival Seiyukai party, with himself as its head. Hirohito dismissed that out of hand. Instead, on Saionji's advice, he summoned the seventy-five-year-old Seiyukai leader, Tsuyoshi Inukai, and appointed him as the new premier. Inukai was an old friend of Chiang Kai-chek, and here was an opportunity to heal the rift brought about by the "Mukden Incident". Hirohito gave Inukai a formal mandate to establish lasting peace with China, and curb the powers of the military. In their first meeting with him, the Emperor castigated the army: its interference in domestic and foreign policies, he told Inukai, "and its wilfulness, constitute a state of affairs which, for the good of the nation, we must view with apprehension".

These words are often quoted to prove that Hirohito genuinely meant to crush the army activists and "normalize" relations with China, and Inukai took them at their face value. He was wrong, and within a year he paid for the mistake with his life. For not only did pro-army informers within his own ministry invariably tip off the militarists, but Hirohito himself ensured that any peace plan with China would fail, and that the pendulum swing towards moderation would be "corrected" by a move in the opposite direction.

The man he chose as the new Army Chief of Staff was a leading prince, a close relative of Empress Nagako and Hirohito's own influential, intimate friend. Prince Kanin, trained at the French military school of Saint-Cyr, was a "grand-uncle", a scion of the Fushimi family whose aristocratic credentials were second only to Hirohito's. Since Kanin was "family", he could have worked hand-in-hand with Hirohito to curb the already dangerous power of certain army hotheads, had the Emperor given any kind of lead. But Hirohito instituted no such sweeping reforms: the Cherry Blossom Society activists were left free to plot. Worse still, any chance of a lasting deal with China collapsed with the Japanese-engineered "Shanghai Incident" of March 1932.

The Shanghai affair was on a pattern with the "Mukden Incident", a deliberate provocation engineered by Japanese civilians and sailors in Shanghai, and designed to lead to Japanese military intervention. For several weeks, Japanese sailors and marines fought the KMT armies in the Shanghai suburbs. Japanese planes bombed Chinese civilians, causing several thousand deaths. Earlier, on January 8, 1932, a Korean separatist had tossed a bomb under what he thought was the Emperor's carriage while Hirohito was on his way to attend a military review. Some Chinese newspapers wrote that "unfortunately the Korean attacked the wrong carriage". Hirohito himself joked with his Palace officials about the clumsy Korean's mistake, but wherever there were Japanese enclaves in China Japanese troops went berserk, venting their rage on Chinese civilians. And, while Chinese and Japanese forces were still embattled in Shanghai, Japan was rocked by another plot that was to have catastrophic repercussions abroad.

The secret society known as "Ketsumeidan" (Blood Brotherhood) was so preposterously fanatical that it made Dr. Okawa's bullyboys and the Cherry Blossom Society activists look like innocent Rotarians. Its founder, Nisho Inoue, a former Japanese spy in China who had become a "born-again" Shinto Revivalist, believed that all Japan's ills could be solved if only she turned her back on the twentieth century and reverted to a rural economy under her "divine" Emperor, in direct touch with his people. "Friar" Inoue was against the bureaucracy, the "Zaibatsu", Parliament, and anything that smacked of Western modernism or culture; his mystical idealism went hand-in-hand with a bloodthirsty reliance on selective assassination to bring about his aims. All the members of his tiny sect swore secret "blood oaths" to murder whoever the mad friar designated. They met regularly in a house in the Tokyo suburbs for prayer, meditation and rites of Inoue's own devising.

Crazy Inoue may have been, but he was also singularly well-connected: his brother Fumio was a senior test pilot–instructor in the Japanese Naval Air service, on first-name terms with Prince Higashikuni (whom he had taught to fly) and Marquis Kido. Through this brother, a small number of naval officers attached to the ultra-secret "Misty Lagoon" naval air base became converts to the "brotherhood" as did some impressionable cadets at the Military Academy. Dr. Okawa, always on the fringe of any extremist movement, supplied Friar Inoue with pistols and ammunition. The family of the Black Dragon Society leader, Toyama, also took him under its wing. All in all, the Blood Brotherhood acquired considerable support, including army and naval officers advocating the "Showa restoration", in other words a military dictatorship under the supreme command of Hirohito himself. Friar Inoue's "hit list" included Japan's top "establishment" figures, in banking, government and even within the Palace itself.

On February 7, 1932, the Blood Brotherhood struck for the first time: one of its members, a student, gunned down Hirohito's Finance Minister, who had made no secret of his opposition to increased arms spending. Following the established practice of political assassins, the murderer did not seek to escape, but surrendered to the police. A week later, however, Friar Inoue took refuge in a house belonging to Hidezo Toyama, a son of the Black Dragon leader. Hirohito was shocked by the murder, but regarded it as an isolated phenomenon.

Next to die, almost a month later (on March 5), was Baron Takuma Dan, an elderly US-educated banker and prominent supporter of the League of Nations, shot outside his office in downtown Tokyo. This murder was a personal blow for Hirohito, appalling "loss of face", for it coincided with the arrival, in Tokyo, of the League of Nations committee, headed by Lord Lytton, which was investigating the circumstances of the "Mukden Incident". Baron Dan had given a dinner for the visitors the night before his murder. It was known that the Prime

Minister, Inukai, had chosen him to present the Japanese case over Manchuria to influential Americans. Again, the murderer made no attempt to escape.

This assassination led to the first serious crack-down on terrorism: most of the Blood Brotherhood members were rounded up, and their targets given protection. But police action came too late, and failed to prevent another, even more calamitous outbreak of terrorism, which put an end to party government and left the military in an impregnable position: on May 15, 1932, Hirohito's own Prime Minister, Inukai, was murdered by members of another "back-to-the-land" terrorist brotherhood calling itself the "Love of native village Academy" (Aikyo Juko). The background to the "May 15 Incident" was disturbing: there is a strong case for deducing that high Palace officials, and perhaps even Hirohito himself, were aware of Inukai's impending fate. Light was only thrown on the affair during the post-war Occupation, but even then it was only partial: the *Brocade Banner* investigators were themselves inhibited by understandable police reluctance to go on record and openly implicate close members of Hirohito's Court.

The circumstances of the "May 15 Incident" were these: shortly before, Dr. Okawa, free as air once more (and busy setting up yet another extremist club, the "Jimmu society"), accompanied a group of officer-cadets, specially selected for their good marks, to Manchuria, ostensibly to see for themselves the benefits of Japanese colonization. With the cadets went the commandant of the Military Academy. The group received a pep talk from the Kwangtung Army commandant, General Honjo, who also had private discussions with Okawa. On his return, the Doctor met the five leading "May 15" plotters in a country inn; one of them was a cadet who had gone on the Manchuria trip.

On May 15, 1932, four groups, all belonging to the "Love of native village Academy", struck, in downtown Tokyo: three of them bungled their assignments, only slightly damaging a power-station and failing to occupy banks and ministries as planned. But the fourth squad, composed of civilians, naval officers and military cadets, after first taking a solemn oath before the altar of the Yakusuni shrine, the famous Shinto monument to Japan's war dead, bundled into taxis and headed for the Prime Minister Inukai's residence. There, they asked a receptionist for an audience with the premier. A bodyguard tried to warn Inukai, and was gunned down.

Brandishing revolvers, the terrorists swept through the house, and on the floor above came across the diminutive Inukai, wearing a kimono and chatting with his doctor and daughter-in-law. With extraordinary composure, Inukai suggested the intruders, whatever their intentions, first follow Japanese custom and remove their shoes. One of the cadets excitedly called on Inukai to explain how cheques and confidential notes from him to the Chinese "Young Marshal" had been found in the war-lord's mansion in Mukden – a fact he could only have learnt from the recent cadets' visit to Manchukuo. "I can explain," said Inukai calmly. He was not given time. A naval officer shouted, "No more talking," and shot him in the face. Immediately afterwards, the killers surrendered to the Japanese military police.

Inukai did not die for some hours. Hirohito, who immediately learnt of the outrage, told aides to contact Prince Saionji to prepare for a successor, appointing the Finance Minister as interim Premier. Saionji angrily replied that Inukai "wasn't dead yet". He knew that, long before Inukai's assassination, the topic of his replacement had become Palace gossip. Many years later, the unimpeachable *Brocade Banner* report contained the ominous phrase that there was "no doubt in the public mind that the [May 15] conspiring was by no means limited to the little men who fired the guns". It named an influential army colonel, Shigeto Chiaki (never officially implicated or brought to trial), as one of the main conspirators, and more ominously still noted that among papers removed from Dr. Okawa's home by the police after Inukai's murder were "compromising documents" belonging to Hirohito's Lord Privy Seal, Count Makino, and to the former War Minister, General Ugaki. This, said *Brocade Banner*, "was why there was such pressure put on the court, during the later trial, to save Okawa's neck". In Manchuria, General Honjo wrote, cryptically, in his diary, that "military men of action *under the gaze of their ruler* [author's italics] today defied authority in a negative deed of daring".

The protracted court case that followed turned into farce: the accused were allowed unlimited opportunities for incendiary speeches; judges and prosecutors permitted them to turn the courtroom into an activist forum, with ample time for impassioned oratory and full press coverage. The verdicts, in 1934, were staggeringly lenient: all the killers were free by 1940, and Dr. Okawa's fifteen-year sentence, reduced on appeal to five, led to his almost immediate release: he and all but six of the fifty-four sentenced were out of jail by 1935.

The "May 15 Incident" marked the end of Japan's attempt at party government: from then on, prime ministers would all be non-party men – and this meant in practice that Hirohito chose them from the ranks of the army or navy. Inukai's immediate successor was a retired admiral, the eighty-one-year-old Makono Saito, but this time Hirohito's injunctions to Saionji had a hollow ring: "His Majesty desires that the genro select as the next premier one who has no fascist leanings and about whom there has been no unsavoury rumour, who is moderate in thought and who is not militaristic." Irreparable harm had already been done. With proper backing for Inukai, and with Prince Kanin's co-operation, Hirohito might well have brought the military into line, had he been determined to do so. The inference is that he either refused to see the military as a genuine threat or else was too preoccupied by his domestic problems to make a stand while there was still time.

There is also the possibility that he was genuinely intimidated by the weight of the militarist movement, and its embarrassing ramifications. He made no attempt to remove Count Makino from his crucial post, despite his past connections with Dr. Okawa. And he cannot have been unaware of his brother's intrigues. Chichibu was Hirohito's opposite in many repects; his beautiful wife and he were frequent guests at Western diplomatic gatherings (he loved going to American Embassy parties best of all, because they were invariably followed by private showings of the latest Hollywood films). But Chichibu's cosmopolitanism implied no commitment to democratic principles, and did not prevent him from flirting with fellow-officers who were activists and devotees of a "Showa restoration".

The plots followed thick and fast: in August 1932 police nipped in the bud a conspiracy to murder the new Prime Minister, Admiral Saito. The chief instigator, a close friend of Dr. Okawa's, got off with a suspended sentence. In September police uncovered a plot to kill the former Premier, Wakatsuki; in November they discovered a plot to kill Count Makino, though this may well have been designed to draw attention away from his links with Dr. Okawa. In July 1933 came an aborted repetition of the "May 15 incident": forty-four terrorists from two little-known secret societies, the "Love country labor party" and the "Great Japan production society", were rounded up as they prepared to wipe out the Cabinet, politicians and "villains of the Imperial entourage". All were acquitted on the grounds that their intentions had been "patriotically motivated", but what probably inhibited judicial action even more was official police recognition (again revealed in the post-war *Brocade Banner* report) that the army group behind the plotters intended placing Chichibu on the throne, with Prince Higashikuni as his prime minister. Whether Chichibu actually knew his name was being invoked is not known.

The army's effrontery became boundless, as illustrated by the absurd "go–stop" controversy of June 1933. An off-duty soldier was rebuked by a policeman for crossing the street against the traffic lights. He then proceeded to defy the policeman by crossing and recrossing the road no less than seven times against the light, until he was arrested. In the ensuing "cause célèbre", his Osaka district commander demanded the charge be dropped, and the policeman punished, on the grounds that "no police has the right to check the advance made by a soldier of the Supreme Being". "Are we not," police officials asked, "His Majesty's police too?"

The "stop–go crisis" was finally solved by Hirohito, who, Solomon-like, ordered the Osaka military commander to pay the soldier's fine, and the local police chief to apologize in writing to the commander. The army's arrogance was displayed more ominously in the Chinese "occupied territories", where all Chinese were now compelled to bow to Japanese uniforms, and swaggering Japanese soldiers treated the Chinese as serfs.

After the Lytton report's unequivocal condemnation of the Japanese "putsch" in Manchuria, Japan left the League of Nations in March 1933, despite Hirohito's half-hearted reservations. As Kido noted in his diaries, the Emperor instructed his government to note that, despite her enforced, but unavoidable, "very regrettable" withdrawal, Japan would "continue its policy of co-operation and intimate international relations with other powers". He also appears to have believed that limited, calculated gestures might prove sufficient to avert isolation. Japanese troops had by this time advanced close to China's Great Wall, occupying Jehol province, and then retreated. Hirohito asked Kido in confidence whether "the need to withdraw from the League still held in view of the favourable settlement of the Jehol problem". Cosmetic concessions in return for major diplomatic gains were to be a later feature of Hirohito's diplomacy too. Kido replied it was too late for Japan to appear to be changing her mind. Shortly after Japan's departure at Geneva, her troops overran Jehol province.

By the end of 1933 Japan's isolation was complete, and there was a grim contrast between Hirohito's blueprint for Japan at the start of the "Showa era" and reality – so much so that the Emperor even hinted to Kido, in 1933, that he was thinking of resigning. But, nine months later, he was in a far better mood, and never mentioned the possibility again: for, in December 1933, Empress Nagato finally gave birth to a male heir.

Hirohito's Grand Chamberlain rushed to the Emperor's study to bring him the news. "It's a boy," he said. "I saw the honourable signs of manhood myself." Hirohito ordered champagne to be served to all his staff and any visitors. As Marquis Kido wrote that day in his diary: "Now, at last, the biggest problem has been solved."

CHAPTER EIGHT

From 1932 onwards, Joseph C. Grew, a shrewd, experienced American diplomat with close family ties with the "old Japan" became US Ambassador in Tokyo. At first highly sympathetic towards Hirohito and Japan generally (his wife was a granddaughter of Commander Perry), Grew kept a diary for the next ten years (later published in book form) [1] and saw more of Hirohito, and his Court, than any other ambassador. As time went on, he was to become increasingly shaken by the contrast between the cordial attitude shown towards him personally by most influential Japanese and the growing hostility and double-dealing encountered on policy matters. He analysed this contradiction dispassionately and – to the last – with equability and balance, reluctantly coming to the conclusion that Japanese "mental processes are different. A Westerner believes that because a Japanese has adopted Western dress, language and customs, he must think like a Westerner. No greater error can ever be made." It was because of this difference that "treaty commitments between East and West will always be open to misinterpretation and subject to controversy . . . When obligations run counter to [Japanese] interests he will interpret the obligation to suit himself." Though he refrained from criticizing Hirohito personally, he clearly had him in mind when he contrasted the Emperor's privately conveyed comments about the need to face up to Japanese chauvinism and the growing evidence of rampant nationalism in all walks of life, noting, for instance, that for all Hirohito's reassuring remarks, maps of the Far East, in Japanese primary schools, as early as 1933, showed French Cochin-China (South Vietnam), Siam, the Straits Settlements, the Philippines and the Dutch East Indies all under the Japanese flag.

Grew was very deaf and, while this affliction did not affect his work in general, it did lead to one embarrassing moment: after the new Ambassador presented his credentials to the Emperor at the Imperial Palace, Hirohito made a short welcoming speech. Grew had no idea what he was talking about, for the interpreter was not allowed to raise his voice in the Imperial presence. Hirohito, he wrote, "has a small mustache and glasses and smiles pleasantly while talking". The Empress "looks more like a charming Japanese doll than any of the other women. She is not so pretty as the really lovely-looking Princess Chichibu but she has a nice expression and she does smile delightfully." Attending an Imperial banquet Hirohito gave to celebrate the birth of his son, Grew noted that the over-ornate Palace dining-room had "too much rather unattractive woodwork and heavy draperies". But he was enchanted by the gold screens, the stunted pinetrees, the artistic flower arrangements – and the friendly reception. During the dinner party, "the Empress extracted nearly the whole story of our lives". Early on in his assignment, Grew noted how strange it was "to live in a country where individually everyone is thoroughly friendly but where collectively one is constantly aware of distrust and animosity against one's own nation".

It was clear to Grew that even top-level Japanese had a distorted view of the world. An American League of Nations official reported to him that Prince Chichibu had asked (in 1933): "Tell me, is it true that the United States is actively preparing for war against Japan?" The Chichibus were Grew's frequent guests and with some Palace officials and veteran politicians he developed a relationship of mutual trust and real friendship. They, and other privileged sources in contact with the Palace never failed to stress that Hirohito disapproved of his country's move towards extreme, expansionist nationalism. "The Emperor," Grew wrote in 1933, "is a man of mild and peaceful character . . . there is no reason to believe he approved of the Manchurian venture, for the matter did not lie in his decision." Later, his references to Hirohito become fewer and fewer: the impression is that, having been charmed by him at first, he later regretted falling under his spell.

For Hirohito, despite his remoteness, was, when it suited him, capable of masterly public relations touches, at least where foreigners were concerned: early in Grew's ambassadorship, his dog, Sambo, fell into the Palace moat, and its rescue was featured in all the Tokyo papers. At the banquet held to celebrate the birth of Crown Prince Akihito, Hirohito's first words to Grew were: "How's Sambo?"

With inside information about the Palace at a premium, friendly ambassadors regularly exchanged information, and Grew was quick to pounce on any visiting journalist who managed to get close to a senior Hirohito adviser. The *Le Temps* editor, Dubosc, told Grew (after a session with the Lord Privy Seal, Makino) that he was wrong to infer that "Japan was going through dangerous times". "Cut out the word 'danger'," Makino told him. "We have a unique safeguard, namely, the Imperial Household. There will never be 'danger' from military fascism or communism or from any other kind of 'ism' simply because the Emperor is Supreme and will *always* have the last word." The impression Hirohito gave to resident journalists was somewhat different. The *New York Times* correspondent, Hugh Byas, wrote, around this time, that the Emperor was "a divine person, a symbol of the eternity of the State; he is an automaton who accepts advice without demur when it is offered by the right person; he is a high priest, but he is not a king ruling a country." The whole issue of Hirohito's role in the Japanese body politic would soon come out into the open: a controversy over the nature and origins of Hirohito's powers that would divide Japan almost as dramatically as the Dreyfus case had divided France. It broke shortly after Grew settled down to report on Japan's troubled, plot-ridden state.

The crisis had been brewing since Grew's arrival but got almost no mention in the Japanese press until 1934. That year an ultra-conservative intellectual agitator, Koki Minoda, made a virulent attack on Dr. Tatsukichi Minobe, Japan's best known, most distinguished constitutional law expert, who held the Chair of Constitutional Law at Tokyo Imperial University, and whose academic distinctions had won him a seat in the House of Peers. He had been writing and teaching since 1903, and his courses had been attended by the elite of Japan's civil servants, diplomats and politicians at the most exclusive university in the land.

In a pamphlet entitled *Dr. Minobe the Anarchist*, also attacking other distinguished professors from Tokyo and Kyoto Imperial Universities for their interpretation of Japanese constitutional law, Minoda, the fanatical rightist, described their work as a "violation of the Imperial constitution" and "a danger to the nation", and criticized the Home Minister for not banning their books. The response was immediate: Hirohito's cabinet dismissed one of the law professors after the President of Kyoto University refused to do so. Hirohito's Education Minister, an arrant fundamentalist, responded with contempt to students' and teachers' protests. "Let all the professors resign if that is how they feel," he said. "We do not mind closing the universities altogether."

In February 1935, a politician with strong right-wing connections, Major-General Genkuro Eto, resumed the attack, actually in the Diet, and another right-winger, Baron Kikuchi, followed up with a further speech in the House of Peers, in Minobe's presence. A second target of Kikuchi's was President of the Privy Council (and former Imperial Household Minister), Kitokuro Ikki, whom the speaker identified as a "follower" of Minobe.

Minobe's crime was that, in books, articles and lecture notes, he had defined the Emperor's place in relation to the Japanese state as a whole, arguing that Hirohito, like his forebears, was "an organ of the state". The passage in one of his law books which had particularly infuriated the rightists ran as follows:

There is an idea current that the Imperial prerogative is sacred and inviolable, that because it is executed by Imperial Will there can be no discussion of it, nor can anyone debate its merits in any particular instance of its exercise . . . This is a gross error contrary to the spirit of the constitution.

Minobe's first reference to the Emperor as "an organ of the state dated back 31 years – but he had never aroused this kind of controversy in the past. The professor was certainly no radical, criticizing again and again, the "inadmissible error" of those constitutional law experts who claimed "the Emperor is the subject of government power". In his view, "the state alone is the subject of government power, and the monarch is an organ of the state . . . in present-day legal terms, Japan's national unity does not differ in pattern from the constitutional monarchies of Europe", and the Emperor was "like a brain in the human body".

In fact, as Saionji's biographer, Lesley Connors, has pointed out, the "organ" theory was a pretext: "it was Minobe's untiring academic support of the liberal group's efforts to restrict the role of the military in politics by means of constitutional inter-pretation which ensured military support for any move to undermine his position."[2]

Minobe rose in the House of Peers to refute allegations of treason, using irony as his weapon: "For a Japanese," he said, to considerable applause,

there is nothing more shameful than to be called treasonous . . . We may question whether the dignity of this House has not been violated . . . If an academician trained in law as I am should meddle in a military school and criticise the sayings and writings of military specialists, it could only be a laughing matter.

While the "organ" controversy was raging, Hirohito greeted Henry Pu Yi, on his state visit to Japan – the "puppet emperor's" payment for four years of docile behaviour as the loyal collabor-ator of Japan in Manchukuo, a country run by Japan, but enjoying a fictitious existence as an "independent" state. Prince

Chichibu had been Hirohito's representative at Pu Yi's coronation the year before in Changchun, the railway town selected by the Japanese as Manchukuo's new capital.

Advance arrangements for Pu Yi's visit revealed the extraordinarily ritualistic nature of the Japanese Army's Emperor-worship: while the ceremonies were being discussed, the War Ministry made the unusual request that Hirohito not attend the military review organized in Pu Yi's honour. As Chief ADC Honjo, acting as go-between, noted, "The army authorities explained that the Army's reverence for the Japanese Emperor makes it incapable of saluting a foreign emperor and not the Japanese Emperor when he is also present." Hirohito's Imperial Household Minister, after consulting the Emperor, rejected this demand out of hand, as both a violation of protocol and an unfriendly gesture towards the Emperor's distinguished foreign guest – himself an emperor, albeit a puppet one. The army and the palace then worked out a compromise: Hirohito would attend but would get a special salute from the army on his arrival and departure. Pu Yi would not.

The crisis seemed over, but the army now requested, through Honjo, that regimental colours should not be dipped on this occasion. Honjo agreed with his colleagues on the grounds that this was an occasion honouring a foreigner, and that colours were not to be dipped to foreigners. Hirohito was irritated by such insistence on protocol but decided to think the matter over. Two days later his mind was made up. He intended to stand firm. As Honjo noted in his diaries, the Emperor "pointed out that he returns the salute of even a single soldier. 'If the regimental flags are not to be dipped in honour of the person that I am honouring, does it mean that the regimental flags are held in higher esteem than me?'" Honjo, carefully briefed by his army friends, replied that for the Emperor to return a soldier's salute was "a voluntary act based on his magnanimity and benevolence", but the regimental colours were to be dipped for Hirohito alone. "They are not used to return the salutations of even the Empress or the Empress Dowager ... I implored

His Majesty not to permit any action that might in the least diminish the men's faith in the regimental flags. His Majesty accepted my explanation." Hirohito gave in. The dipping of the flags would not occur after all.

The army authorities came up with a new demand; it had been agreed that Hirohito would meet Pu Yi at Tokyo railway station. As Honjo put it, the army "contended that it would demean His Majesty's dignity if when in exchanging positions His Majesty were to proceed behind the Manchurian emperor while the troops were in formation in front of them". Hirohito rejected this as "an unreasonble request" but Honjo privately told the guard commander to see to it that "this particular operation be conducted in an inconspicuous manner".

The overall impression is of protocol-obsessed generals testing the ground to see how far they could go. In the event, Pu Yi, who had been appallingly seasick aboard the antiquated Japanese warship that brought him to Yokohama, was unaware that he had been at the centre of any such controversy. The absurd quarrel over precedence and military rites is a precious insight not only into the army's psychological state of mind at this time but also into Hirohito's ability to face the growing jingoism. For it was not just Hirohito's ceremonial presence that was being debated, or the propriety of his playing second fiddle to a State guest. What had been at stake was a minor, but symbolic, battle of wills, and when the chips were down Hirohito shied away from a head-on clash with the army over an absurdly simple, straightforward issue. It was the kind of vacillation already displayed over Manchuria, and it would be repeated again and again on the road to Pearl Harbor. Admittedly the haggling over where the Emperor should stand at the station in Tokyo may have seemed petty enough, but the army's behaviour was all part of the same campaign, by extremists, to erode what remained of Japan's liberalism.

Everyone in the Japanese "establishment" realized that the "organ" issue transcended arguments over the interpretation of Japan's constitutional law. The challenge to Minobe, and to

Ikki, was but the latest example of pressure being exerted by the nationalists to undermine the position of those "moderates' – in politics and in the Palace – who opposed Japan's aggressive policies in Asia and her excessive arms spending. It was, in its way, the intellectual equivalent of the "October" and "May 15" plots and it came at a time when Japan's "will to power" was suddenly revealed as a real threat to stability and peace in Asia: in Manchuria, in September 1934, a reorganization of the local administration, approved by Hirohito without a murmur, put Manchukuo under the overall supervision of the brutal Japanese Military Police; shortly afterwards, a document widely distributed by the military, and entitled "the true meaning of national strength and proposals for building it", (it began with the Mussolinian premise that "war is the father of creation and the mother of culture") advocated "national defence for total war", the wholesale regimentation of the Japanese people and an end to "Western individualism". In December 1934, Hirohito approved a policy declaration on China that represented a final break with Chiang Kai-chek, stating that "for the time being it is desirable to reduce to a minimum the influence of the Nanking [i.e. KMT] government". Finally, just before the 1935 New Year, after protracted discussions with American and British admirals and officials in London, Japan abrogated the Naval Arms Limitation Treaty.

At the time of the "Emperor-organ" controversy, Hirohito revealed the same indecision and spirit of compromise that marked his climb-down over the ceremonial parade. His intentions were clearly honourable: in Honjo's first mention of the affair, he records in his diary that Hirohito told him that "although there might be a difference in status between the two of us, he did not believe that physically there was any difference whatsoever. In light of this the Emperor found it highly upsetting both mentally and physically that in order to attack the organ theory he was being turned into an entity without any freedom whatsoever. I responded that this was not the case at all. His remarks filled me with deep sorrow."

Proof of Hirohito's concern came later in the day. Honjo was again summoned, and told that the Emperor was aware that the attack on the "organ" theory was in fact an attack on his former Imperial Household Minister, Ichiki Ikki, who had written in the same vein as Minobe on the Emperor's role in state affairs. "Ichiki," said Hirohito, "is a loyal subject and there is no justification whatever for the kind of public criticisms being directed against him." As for Minobe, the Emperor said, "I think Minobe could never be disloyal. Is there anyone in Japan his equal today? Minobe may have gone too far in some respects but I can never think ill of him."

The "Emperor-organ" debate continued in the Supreme War Council, an advisory body of senior generals and admirals, and once more Honjo, the go-between, behaved more like an activist spokesman than a palace official. To Hirohito's remark that, in international relations, labour agreements, loans, etcetera, "it seems that the organ theory is more important", Honjo replied that "the military worships His Majesty as divinity incarnate, and if His Majesty were to be treated just like any other person, it would create grave difficulties in the areas of military education and the supreme command". The whole issue was clearly causing Hirohito considerable irritation. He summoned Honjo later that same day (March 29, 1935) to point out that article 4 of Japan's Constitution "states that the Emperor is head of the state. This shows that the constitution is based on the organ theory, so if the organ theory is revised, the constitution also will have to be revised." That same day, the Cabinet met to discuss the "organ" issue, with the War, Education, Justice and Home Ministers demanding that the "organ" theory be "rectified".

Later, Hirohito returned to the attack. "If the Emperor is viewed as the head controlling the entire life of the state," he told Honjo, "then, if a disaster strikes the Emperor, the state would lose its life also . . . To hold that sovereignty resides not in the state but in the monarch is to court charges of despotism. And difficulties would arise in concluding treaties and borrowing money from foreign nations ... I, too," he continued with disarming candour, "would gladly accept the theory of imperial sovereignty if it did not lead to the bane of despotism, the disapproval of foreign nations and if it did not conflict with our national polity and history. Unfortunately, I have yet to encounter an explanation of this theory that is worthy of respect."

Ever the loyal subject and unquestioning believer in Hirohito's "divine" right, Honjo replied that the military "were not concerned about academic theories" but about principles of religious faith. Distorting Minobe's theories, in a way that showed that this blunt, bluff soldier, ill at ease in the field of academic abstractions, had nevertheless been well briefed by his army colleagues, he added that "theories holding that the Diet is the core of the government, that imperial edicts may be criticized, and that Diet members may not heed the Emperor's commands, are totally incompatible with the army's faith and convictions". Needless to say, Minobe had never gone that far.

Given Hirohito's powers, and the role the army wished him to play as a "divine" sovereign, it would have been relatively easy for him to turn the tables on the critics of the "organ" theory by proclaiming, in some public form, his support of Minobe and his contempt for the latter's critics. An imperial proclamation would have been too drastic a means of spreading his views, but he could have reduced the nationalists to silence merely by summoning Minobe to the Palace for an informal audience – or even allowing his Court "Cabinet" to divulge, to the press and to the public generally, the views he expressed in private to Honjo. Hirohito's passivity, and his tendency to test the pros and cons of his every move, allowed the "Emperor-organ" issue to grow into a major crisis: the powerful Military Reserve Association entered the fray, as did the Army Officers' Association, which published a pamphlet stating that "state sovereignty" was nothing more than "democracy" – a hated, despised ideology in the eyes of Japanese jingoists.

Honjo finally wearied of his role as go-between: in talks with the War Minister and the fire-eating Inspector General of Education, Mazaki, one of the most vocal opponents of Minobe, Honjo told them to deal direct with Hirohito if they wanted to debate the matter further. They replied that they were "not interested in debating its merits as academic theory. Their main objective was denunciation of the organ theory as an ideology".

Hirohito took the Army Officers' Association pamphlet seriously enough to study it at length. To Honjo, he delivered a point-by-point rebuttal two days later (April 27). State sovereignty, he said, was *not* identical with democracy; it was untrue to say that individualism was at the root of all Western institutions. How could one explain the American Prohibition Act, or the fact that many members of the English aristocracy sacrificed their lives for the country in World War One? It was wrong to assume that, unlike Japanese emperors, "European monarchs are only concerned with political matters. In fact, the King of England devotes much time and energy to cultural affairs".

Hirohito's preoccupation with the "organ" theory also caused him to spell out, to Honjo, in the days that followed, his own intimate convictions and beliefs concerning the nature of government and the lessons drawn from recent history. When Honjo argued that the Allies, in the First World War, had used "anti-Statist propaganda" to bring down Germany, and that this proved the need for the "divine right" theory (which presumably would have given the Kaiser sufficient nationwide support to continue the war), Hirohito displayed his superior knowledge of European history. Germany, he said, had not been defeated by propaganda alone. There had been multiple reasons, among them the fact that none of the German states, except Prussia, had any confidence in the Kaiser; disunity between the army and the civilians; and the Kaiser's misguided flight to Holland. In the same way, he added, the Russian revolution succeeded because, "like the *ancien régime* in France, there were only two classes in Russia: the aristocracy and the lower class. It did not have a moderate, stable middle class" – implying that he saw the growing Japanese middle class precisely as a factor of stability.

As the "Emperor-organ" debate increasingly turned into an army onslaught on "moderates" in general, Hirohito did strike back, but in a limited way: he dismissed his Chief Naval ADC for taking an arrant "anti-organ" stand, and also replaced General Masaki, not only because of his support of right-wing movements attacking the "organ" theory, but because he had repeatedly encouraged junior officers to plot the violent removal of the Cabinet. But the extremists had the last word: Okada's lacklustre government (the Prime Minister was another retired admiral who succeeded Saito in 1935) eventually decided to "stamp out the organ theory" and pay more attention to the ideological contents of works written by university professors. Minobe, who steadfastly refused to resign from Tokyo Imperial University, continued to be hounded by his detractors. He finally gave in to the inevitable, resigning his seat in the House of Peers in September 1935 in order to avoid prosecution in the courts for "lèse-majesté", his reputation as a scholar destroyed. Few if any of Japan's "establishment", among those who deplored the drift towards totalitarianism, had the courage to stand by him, or even acknowledge his existence. He was repeatedly called upon to commit suicide. Despite Hirohito's regard for the soundness of Minobe's theories, and his anger at right-wing exploitation of the "organ" theory, the Emperor never conveyed these feelings to the Minobe family. Professor Minobe himself was given police protection, which he supplemented with bodyguards hired at his own expense, but there were two attempts on his life: on February 20, 1936, he was badly wounded, shot through both knees by a right-wing terrorist who immediately became a hero, while Minobe had to be hidden in the children's ward of a Tokyo hospital to ensure that there would be no further attack.*

The continuing dialogue with Honjo, recorded at length in the latter's diaries, has the historical merit of defining the extent

---

* Minobe's son, a prominent Japanese liberal and Governor of Tokyo, was until his recent death one of Japan's leading campaigners against the post-war trend, in schools and politics, towards nationalism and Emperor-worship.

and the limits of Hirohito's "liberalism". If, on the "organ" issue, he held moderate views, substantially similar to Minobe's own, on social issues he emerges not so much a conservative as someone hopelessly insulated from the realities of life and the plight of many of his countrymen. Because the army rank-and-file (and, increasingly, its officers too) were drawn in the main from families of impoverished farmers and the "new poor" generally, a few generals, Honjo among them, attempted to draw Hirohito's attention to the social unrest that fanned the flames of extremism as advocated by the "Secret brotherhood". General Araki, a former War Minister, discussing the May 15 plot with the Emperor, remarked that "capitalists could perhaps be criticized for building grand mansions to gratify their expensive tastes". Hirohito replied it was "too harsh" to say that capitalists lived like that simply for pleasure. "It is said that Louis XVI of France, despite the fact that he had the splendid palace of Versailles, built in addition a small palace which he loved and used as his residence. It is not necessarily true that people are inclined towards grand, luxurious things. I myself would prefer to live in a simpler place rather than in a huge palace like this where many people are employed. But . . . my place of residence is determined by the fact that this palace was built by my ancestor as well as by other traditions and customs. I have no way of knowing how other people feel, but I believe there must be others who feel as I do and prefer to live a simpler life but because of various circumstances are compelled to live in spacious dwellings built by their ancestors."

When the subject arose again a few days later, Hirohito took a tougher stand. "It was inevitable," he said, that officers, and particularly NCOs and soldiers who had close ties with agrarian life, "would sympathize with and worry about the villagers who are in such dire straits, but if they were to become excessively interested in such problems simply to indulge their own fancy, they would cause harm instead." When Honjo replied that such concern was only natural, Hirohito remarked: "It is, of course, necessary to sympathize with the dire plight of the peasants, but peasants in their own way lead happy lives. One cannot say that members of the aristocracy are always happy. I enjoyed my freedom when I went on a tour of Europe. The only time I feel happy is when I am able to experience a similar feeling of freedom . . . So, peasants should think about the pleasures of nature that are there for them to enjoy and not dwell merely on the unpleasant aspects of their lives. In other words, in guiding the peasants, one should not rely only on legalistic principles but should emphasize moral principles." This, at a time when famine was ravaging Northern Japan, and farming families, to ward off starvation, were selling their daughters as factory-hands, apprentice geishas and prostitutes at a rate unprecedented in the twentieth century, showed an extraordinary lack of sensitivity to the problems facing his less privileged subjects.

There was a growing belief, among superstitious Japanese, that the arrival of 1936, an inauspicious year, would herald some vastly calamitous event. In the army, rumour was rife that it would mark the start of the expected war against the Soviet Union – to such an extent that the War Ministry found it necessary to ban any references, in the press and army publications, to the "crisis of 1936". It was indeed to be a disastrous year, but it was callousness towards the farmers' plight, and growing anger among young army officers at the ostentatious wealth of the Japanese industrialists and other nouveaux riches, that was to provide Hirohito with his most serious challenge – and leave a permanent mark on pre-war Japan.

[1] Joseph C. Grew: "Ten years in Japan", Hammond and Hammond, London.
[2] Lesley Connors: *The Emperor's Adviser, Kinmoshi Saionji*, Croom Helm and Nissan Institute for Japanese Studies, 1987.

CHAPTER NINE

On the eve of February 26, 1936, which was to be the worst day in his life, until Japan's surrender to the Allies nine years and six months later, Hirohito had several reasons to worry about the state of Japan, but one overriding cause for optimism.

This was the strong family bond between himself, Empress Nagako and their five children. Hirohito was a loving father, and though he doted most on his elder son, Akihito, celebrating his third birthday with pomp and dressing him up in a red suit to mark his move away from babyhood and white clothes, he was almost equally affectionate towards the three girls. If ever anything were to happen to the Crown Prince, he now also had a second son (Masahito, born in 1935), so the dynasty was assured, and no plotter, army or otherwise, could possibly use the succession issue as a pretext for replacing him with the dashing Prince Chichibu – who, ironically, remained childless.

There were, however, serious, indeed intractable problems. The "Emperor-organ" affair had stirred up a huge controversy, goading every fundamentalist association and secret society into a concerted attack on "red judges and scarlet professors". Beyond these avowed targets, the fundamentalists' and army hotheads' rage was directed at moderate opinion in general, and at the "moderates" in Hirohito's own court Cabinet and in the Government in particular. Secret police informers reported a continuing spate of assassination plots, and the general outlook seemed grim, but the results of the Diet elections held on February 20, 1936, proved that, for all the bombast and stridency of the ultra-nationalists, Japanese voters were still remarkably clear-headed, and unaffected by jingoistic propaganda. The

elections were a particular success for the small left-wing groups,
and for the more moderate of the two main parties: 205
Minseito Party MPs (out of 296 candidates) were elected, while
the more right-wing Seiyukai suffered a sizeable defeat, with
only 174 members elected out of 336 candidates. Even so,
Hirohito was aware that the discrepancy between nationalistic
fervour and the lukewarm mood of Japan towards foreign
adventurism was likely to lead to further plots and further bloodshed.

In the armed forces and among their rightist sympathizers,
the mood was best reflected in a popular song, written by
Takashi Mikami, himself a Navy lieutenant, entitled "The Song
of Young Japan", which was a clear call to action. It ran:

> Those in power are swollen with pride,
> but have no concern for the nation;
> the wealthy flaunt their riches,
> yet care nothing for the welfare of society.
>
> Brave warriors united in justice
> in spirit a match for a million
> ready like the myriad cherry blossoms to scatter
> in the spring sky of the "Showa restoration".
>
> But let us leave these lamentations
> Gone is the time for idle grieving!
> The day has come when our swords
> shall gleam with the blood of purification!

The consequences of one particularly dramatic political
murder were front-page news. Lieutenant-Colonel Aizawa, a
former fencing instructor, was standing trial for a particularly
gory killing in the War Ministry building – and February 25
had been marked by a particularly dramatic court hearing.
Aizawa, known personally to Prince Higashikuni, was a fanatical
right-wing fundamentalist and a fervent disciple of the recently
ousted Director of Military Education, General Mazaki. Aizawa,

incensed at the dismissal of his hero, had called on General Nagata, the head of the Military Affairs Bureau rightly seen by fanatical junior officers as Hirohito's "éminence grise" in the War Ministry, at his home, and urged him to reinstate Mazaki. Nagata's reaction had been prompt: he had immediately ordered the impetuous Aizawa to be posted to Taiwan.

But Aizawa – perhaps thinking that such action would be condoned by powerful army elements, including even Prince Higashikuni himself – two days later stormed into Nagata's office just outside the Imperial Palace, drew his sword and, after slashing him across the face and chest, ran him through.

Either hoping to provide evidence of insanity or else convinced he was assured of immunity, Aizawa went immediately to the army infirmary to have a cut finger tended to. He mentioned he was in a hurry and needed to buy a new cap to replace the one he had left behind in the struggle in Nagata's office. He also had to pack, he said, he would be leaving soon for Taiwan. Arrested shortly after leaving the building, he hired two nationalist firebrands as defence lawyers, and they succeeded in turning his trial into a festival of jingoistic, "greater Japan" expansionism. On February 25, the courtroom had been packed with off-duty army sympathizers and reporters, for General Mazaki had been summoned to appear as a defence witness. He disappointingly refused to answer any questions, invoking "official secrecy" unless given a personal waiver by the Emperor himself, but the defence had had a field-day nevertheless. "If the court fails to understand the spirit that guided the accused," said one lawyer, "a second Aizawa and even a third will appear."

These were prophetic words, for in two army barracks across the moat from the Palace a score of junior officers were preparing to stage a putsch which, they believed, would rally the entire Japanese officer corps and lead to the much-heralded "Showa Restoration", the establishment of authoritarian army rule under Emperor Hirohito that would also trigger widespread social reforms and the end of capitalist, zaibatsu-dominated politics. An artillery officer, Captain Kawashima, who also happened to be General Honjo's son-in-law, was party to the conspiracy, and had, on February 25, distributed some 200 city road maps to the rebels so as to ensure they would not lose their way.

At the Palace, there was no inkling of an imminent crisis. On the evening of February 25, two of Hirohito's closest advisers, the Grand Chamberlain, Suzuki Kantaro, and the new Lord Privy Seal, the former premier Saito, attended an informal dinner party at the United States Embassy residence. Grew had planned the evening with care: after dinner, there was an MGM movie – *Naughty Marietta*, with Jeannette MacDonald and Nelson Eddy. The guests came with their wives and, though it was known that Suzuki liked to retire to bed early, he stayed on with every sign of enjoying the sentimental love story. Among the Japanese women guests, Grew noted, there was not a dry eye in the house. There was a brief interval to change reels during which refreshments were served. Kantaro could have left then but did not do so. As the Palace officials drove away into the cold midnight air (it was snowing heavily) Grew could congratulate himself on a particularly successful evening, for both the chief guests were immensely sought-after by Tokyo's Diplomatic Corps because of their intimate, daily contacts with Hirohito.

Only a couple of hours later, at 2 a.m., within earshot of the Palace, buglers sounded "reveille" in both the First Division and the Imperial Guards barracks, and the coup was under way. As the sleepy soldiers stood to, fully expecting yet another night exercise, the officers involved in the plot assembled their men and began briefing them about the operation they were about to launch.

Both units had been told two months previously that they would shortly be posted to Manchuria on active service, and, while the news should have been welcomed (neither élite unit had seen action since the Russo-Japanese War), it was greeted instead as an unforgivable slur on their integrity. The officers, knowing that the secret police and the top military hierarchy considered both the Guards and the First Division to be hotbeds of political activism, were convinced that the order to send them to Manchuria had been a deliberate decision taken at the highest level to get them out of harm's way as fast as possible in the wake of Aizawa's trial and amid rumours of further army plotting. It was no coincidence that the men leading the "2/26" uprising were on close terms with several former army officers dismissed for their involvement in previous plots and for their uncompromisingly hostile views towards the military and political hierarchy. One, Captain Koda, later sentenced to death and executed, under interrogation analysed his motivation in detail, revealing his resentment at prevalent social injustice and the huge gulf between rich and poor as well as the irresistible impact of crude, simplistic nationalism.

Introduced into a conspiratorial circle of like-minded officers, Koda helped draft a document called "The Great Purpose", setting out their aims and grievances. "With due reverence," it read, "we consider that the basis of the divinity of our country lies in the fact that the nation is destined to expand under Imperial Rule until it embraces all the world . . . It is now time to expand and develop in all directions." The officers blamed "self-seeking, refractory men" who had "encroached on the Imperial Prerogative, obstructing the true growth of the people, themselves driven to the utmost depths of misery, making our country an object of contempt . . . Words fail to express our anger at such wickedness".

The sacrifices of the "Blood Brotherhood Martyrs" and "Colonel Aizawa's flashing sword" had had no effect on such evil Imperial advisers. "Even after so much bloodshed knaves continue not only to live in ease and selfishness but show no signs of repentance." Meanwhile, "it is clearer than light that our country is on the verge of war with Russia, Britain and America, who wish to crush our ancestral land . . . We are persuaded that it is our duty to remove the villains who surround the Throne".

The rank and file of the First and Third Infantry regiments of the First Division, called on to take part in the plot, dared not refuse. The men of the Imperial Guards Division, however, were not told of its real nature. Significantly, though several officers in both divisions felt that the insurgents were embarking on a mad, doomed adventure, few opposed their colleagues outright or attempted to alert their superiors. The huge majority of the senior officers of both divisions clearly sympathized with the insurgents, who numbered around 1,200 men in all, and procrastinated for as long as they could – until it was clear that the coup would fail.

The insurgents had organized themselves into nine squads, fanning out into the snow-covered streets to occupy their objectives and to set up barricades and road-blocks in front of the buildings they were to move into. Group number one occupied the official residence of the War Minister, Yoshiyuko Kawashima, with surprising ease. There were no casualties. Kawashima, a nondescript figure whose only claim to fame is as adoptive father of the famous spy "Eastern Jewel", the Manchu princess who operated in China for the Japanese secret service, behaved with ignominious indecision. When the insurgent officers asked to see him, he begged to be forgiven. He was ill with a bad cold, he told them. They insisted, finally bursting into his bedroom and reading him their "Great Purpose" memorandum. He showed no indignation, clearly doing his best to stay on the insurgents' right side, for they made no attempt on his life, and – even more surprisingly – allowed senior War Ministry and General Staff officers to come and go freely throughout the next three days, to confer without any constraint.

Group number two stormed the Metropolitan Police Station opposite the Imperial Palace, again encountering no resistance After setting up road-blocks and leaving a token force, the insurgents joined the group that had occupied the War Minister's residence.

Group number three burst into the home of Admiral Kantaro Suzuki, Hirohito's Lord High Chamberlain, who was fast asleep, recovering from the late-night party at the American Embassy residence, but was roused by the noise. He rushed to seize his ceremonial sword, but was too late.

One of the soldiers asked him: "Are you His Excellency?" Suzuki replied: "You must have some reason for doing this? Tell me what it is." There was no reply. An NCO shouted: "No time. We're going to shoot." 'Go ahead and shoot,' said Suzuki. Three officers fired at him with their pistols, wounding him in the head, lung, shoulder and groin. The insurgents wanted to make sure Suzuki was dead, and one of them put his pistol to the Admiral's head. "Todome," (coup de grâce) he said. Suzuki's wife, who had witnessed the shooting, struggled with her captors. "Don't do it, I'll do it," she screamed. The men's leader, Captain Ando, ordered them to leave without firing the fatal shot. But first, in an incongruous homage comprehensible only in the context of Japan's "bushido" culture, they knelt in front of the Admiral's body, then saluted him. Ando turned to Mrs. Suzuki. "I am particularly sorry about this," he said, "but our views differ from His Excellency's, so it had to come to this."

Group number four, 300-strong, surrounded Premier Okada's official residence, killing four policemen at the gate. "They've finally come," said Okada. The Prime Minister's brother-in-law and aide, a retired colonel called Matsuo, looked for a hiding-place. With the help of a loyal policeman, both men (Okada still in his nightgown) were bundled into a disused storeroom. Matsuo then left to get further help. The policeman, mounting guard over the storeroom door, shouted to Okada to stay where he was. Okada's private secretary, Hizatsune Sakomizu, who was also his son-in-law, called the Metropolitan Police Station for help. "The situation is out of control," a policeman replied. "What can we do?" Another voice said: "This is the insurgent unit," and hung up.

Matsuo bravely attempted to escape from the house, but was caught by insurgent troops in the courtyard outside. He was pushed against the wall, the soldiers took aim. There was a brief moment's hesitation, until one of the insurgent officers shouted:

"What's the matter? You'll be fighting in Manchuria soon! Can't you kill a man or two?" As they fired, Matsuo shouted, "Long live the Emperor." An officer gave him the coup de grâce. Another insurgent, who had taken a framed photograph of the Prime Minister from the bedroom, compared it with the dead man's face. "Okada," he said. They took the body indoors and left it in a vacant room near Okada's own hiding-place.

Moments later, the real Okada crept out, stumbled over corpses of more dead and dying policemen, found some clothes, and then caught sight of his dead brother-in-law. He burst into tears, and wandered off. One of the rebel soldiers caught sight of the old man and told his companions: "I've just seen a ghost." Two maids grabbed Okada and hid him in a cupboard, covering him with a pile of laundry.

Group number five – insurgents from the Imperial Guards Division – arrived at the house of the Finance Minister Takahashi. A rebel lieutenant ripped off his bedclothes and shouted: "Tenchu!" (punishment from heaven!) "Idiot!" Takahashi shouted back. "When he opened his eyes," the Lieutenant said later, "I gave it to him three times with my revolver. Someone else slashed him in the side and belly with a sword, and he died instantly." As the insurgents left, their leader told hysterical servants: "Excuse me for the annoyance I have caused."

Group number six took part in an even bloodier killing. About 200 soldiers from the Third Infantry Regiment broke into the house of the ex-Premier and newly-appointed Lord Keeper of the Privy Seal, Admiral Saito, who had also been at the American Embassy party the night before. As the squad's leader later said, "When I approached the bedroom Viscountess Saito opened the door but quickly slammed it shut. She faced us with raised hands and said, 'Please wait.' Saito emerged in his nightgown." The insurgents opened fire, he fell, "but his wife covered him with her body, begging us to shoot her if we had to shoot someone. We had to shove her off, and fired again and again until we were sure there was no more life in the old man. When a soldier entered and asked to be allowed to fire too, we let him have several shots. We wanted to cut Saito's throat, but we gave up the idea because the woman refused to leave the body. Afterwards, we gathered at the front gate and gave three 'banzai' for the Emperor." Saito's body was later found to have forty-seven bullet-holes. His wife was treated for multiple sword cuts.

Another group attacked the residence of General Watanabe, who had taken over as Inspector-General of Military Training from General Masaki. They fired at the lock on the front door, burst in and made for the bedroom. The General's wife calmly asked them which regiment they were from, and was brushed aside. Watanabe was gunned down, and his throat slit.

More insurgents occupied the *Asahi Shimbun* newspaper building, while yet another group, which had set out in cars from Tokyo at midnight, drove to Yugawara, near Artami, where the former Lord Privy Seal, Makino, was on holiday with his twenty-year-old granddaughter, Kazuko. They killed a policeman, and burnt down the hotel, but thanks to Kazuko's courage and presence of mind failed to kill Makino: she led him up a hill, but they were pursued by soldiers. The accepted story is that she stepped in front of the old man, covering him with her body, daring them to shoot, and that they turned back. In an interview in Tokyo recently, the still indomitable Kazuko, now Mrs. Aso, insists things were not quite as dramatic. "Our bodyguard managed to kill their ringleader before being gunned down," she told me. "We hid. They lost heart and didn't search the hill too thoroughly." After hiding all night, they took refuge in a farmhouse. A friend collected them in a car the following day, "and we remained in hiding in Tokyo until it was all over".

Yet another group, which should have left Tokyo during the night to seek out the genro, Saionji, in his country home, failed to do so. After a mysterious telephone call which warned Saionji that he risked being killed that day, he wisely took refuge in the local police superintendent's house, while his home was guarded by sixty armed policemen.

On that dawn of February 26, Hirohito was still asleep, unaware of the mutiny, the carnage, the road-blocks a mere stone's throw from the main gate to the Imperial Palace grounds, or the fact that some of the coup ringleaders had turned the Sanno Hotel into a command post. One of the first outsiders to find out about the situation was General Honjo. "While I was still asleep," he wrote, "a Second Lieutenant Ito arrived in a state of agitation, claiming to be a messenger from my son-in-law, Captain Yamaguchi Ichitaro, who was on duty at the First Infantry Regiment. Wondering what had happened, I agreed to see him. The Lieutenant handed me a hastily written message stating that about 500 officers and men of the regiment, unable to restrain themselves any longer, have decided to take direct action. It was expected there would be continued reinforcements. An extraordinary message!"

Honjo ordered the officer to tell his son-in-law to prevent any such action being taken. The troops had already moved out, Ito said. "I instructed the Lieutenant to tell Yamaguchi in no uncertain terms that the projected action cannot be permitted to take place in the Imperial capital. He must do everything possible to stop it." Honjo could not know that his son-in-law, far from discouraging the rebels, was in the conspiracy up to the hilt, one of its chief logistical planners, in charge of the hit squads' transport (he was later sentenced to life imprisonment, but was released in 1940).

Honjo then telephoned the head of the Military Police, the Palace ADC on night duty, and ordered a car to take him to the Palace. On the way he passed some insurgent troops from the Imperial Guards Division. Arriving at the Palace at 6 a.m., he found the Imperial Household Minister, and the Vice Grand Chamberlain, already waiting to be summoned by the Emperor. He heard the news of Okada's, Takahashi's and Watanabe's deaths – news that Hirohito, too, had just received. Honjo was ushered into his presence. Hirohito, in army uniform, glowered. "His Majesty was extremely upset and said the incident must be quashed as quickly as possible and a way must be found to turn the disaster into a blessing," Honjo noted. "He also recalled I had expressed fears about such an incident breaking out."

By early morning on February 26, Hirohito had a reasonable idea of the extent of the rebellion. In his methodical, school-masterly way, he assessed the damage and the consequences of a possible extension, to the country as a whole, of a mass army revolt. So far, it did not appear to have spread beyond Tokyo.

He reacted with calm, but, as Honjo shows in his diaries, growing irritation as the Generals and the Cabinet, in separate rooms, began their futile discussions. "2/26" was a watershed in Hirohito's life: it was the first time he had been confronted with a truly major, national calamity: the "Mukden Incident", in comparison, had been a side-show; at the time of the 1923 earthquake he had been Crown Prince and Regent but still very dependent on the traditional, protocol-bound palace officials and absurdly deferential Cabinet. This time he realized that his entire future was at stake, and, perhaps, his life. The days of compromise and scheming to keep rival groups at bay and in play were over. He ordered his Navy Minister to mobilize the fleet: if necessary, the Navy would have to be used to crush the Army, though Hirohito was aware that there were Navy die-hards, too, who might spread the mutiny to the senior service.

He behaved not just as the commander-in-chief of a mutinous army but also as clan leader, summoning his family to rally round the throne. The least trustworthy member of the royal family, Prince Chichibu, was ordered to come to the Palace forthwith. Hirohito had a special reason for summoning his brother: as a student of the Military Academy, Chichibu had been friendly with four of the officers now identified as the coup's ringleaders. What was more, he had been, for several years, an officer in the very same mutinous Third Regiment – even if, as the Em-peror's brother, his duties had been light and his leaves of absence frequent. Hirohito knew, from police reports, that Chi-chibu had met the radical right-wing agitator Ikki Kita several times, and that the two men had got on well; it was be-cause of Chichibu's embarrassing friendships and associations that he had been posted away from Tokyo to a different unit (he now commanded a battalion of the 8th Regiment in Hirosaki, where, the Emperor knew, activist officers were few and far between). If the coup succeeded, there was the likelihood that the insurgents would turn to Chichibu as the saviour of Japan. The younger brother had to be kept out of harm's way, if only for his own good.

That first morning, Hirohito's most important visitor was the War Minister, Kawashima, who drove straight from the rebel-held Ministry residence and was immediately ushered into the Imperial presence.

He had never been a favourite of the Emperor's, and his sorry performance, that morning and on subsequent days, was to put an end to his undistinguished career. For, instead of proposing immediate military action against the insurgents unless they surrendered immediately, which Hirohito viewed as the only possible solution, he insisted on reading, in a quavering voice, as he had promised them he would, the rebels' verbose manifesto.

From the moment he first heard news of the uprising, Hirohito realized that to negotiate with the rebels would lead irrevocably to a fatal loss of face. He knew it must soon be front-page news all over the world. Most major embassies were close to the square mile of central Tokyo occupied by the insurgents, and Japanese-speaking diplomats were already out in the streets, wading through the thick snow to talk to the rebels, prior to cabling back the news, and an assessment of the crisis, to their respective governments. The French and German Embassies were so close to the rebel army barricades that they were in the firing-line, should fighting start between mutineers and loyalists. Several correspondents had obtained copies of the rebels' "Great Purpose" manifesto, distributed in pamphlet form in downtown Tokyo by sympathizers, despite attempts by the police to seize them all. Buses had to make considerable detours to avoid the rebel-held area, and soon the whole of Tokyo was aware of the army mutiny, even though radio newscasts referred to it in oblique, almost incomprehensible terms.

Inside the Premier's residence, the insurgents were still unaware the man they had killed was not the Prime Minister. His son-in-law, with commendable courage, re-entered the house, with the rebels' permission, and, guided by loyal maids, whispered a message of encouragement to the demoralized Premier, still hidden under the pile of laundry. A rebel officer told Sakomizu to pick up the telephone. Someone from the Palace wanted to speak to him.

It was a message from the Imperial Household Minister, Yuasa. The Emperor, he said, wanted to convey his regrets to Okada's family for what had happened. Should he send a Palace messenger to the official, or to the family, residence?

It occurred to Sakomizu that the telephone call might have an ulterior motive: Hirohito might be trying, in this roundabout way, to find out what was happening. Here was a chance to tell the whole story of the rebels' mistaken-identity murder, but he cut himself short. He might be overheard by one of the officers and, besides, the telephone might be tapped. He gave a vague reply, suggesting the Palace defer sending a messenger for the time being. He was aware that, at the other end of the line, there was considerable uneasiness, and he even had a nagging suspicion that the official he was talking to was wondering whether he too had not rallied to the rebels' cause. He needed to convey to the Palace without delay the news that the Prime Minister was still alive.

Much time was lost in the endeavour. In the first place, protocol dictated that any civilian official entering the Palace and seeking audience with a member of the Emperor's court cabinet had to be properly dressed. This meant Sakomizu returning to his own home, and donning court dress – morning coat, striped trousers and top hat. Taking a taxi to the Palace gate, he had to talk his way past a rebel checkpoint. They eventually let him through.

By the time he arrived at the palace, however, an unforeseen event had taken place, complicating things still further: Hirohito had just appointed his Home Minister, Fumio Goto, interim Prime Minister – a move he was to regret almost immediately. So by the time Sakomizu finally reached the Imperial Household Ministry office, Hirohito actually had two prime ministers.

Protocol also required that, inside the Palace, everything must proceed at a quiet, leisurely pace. Yuasa did something no Imperial Household Minister had ever done before: as soon as he learnt that the Prime Minister was alive, he actually ran to Hirohito's quarters to break the news, charging in unannounced. Flushed and almost incoherent, he was back, still at a run, a few minutes later. "His Majesty is most pleased," he told Sakomizu. "He said: 'That is excellent,' and he wants Okada brought to safety with all possible speed." It was the first piece of good news Hirohito had received since the start of the mutiny, for he still had no reliable reports on the state of the Army in the rest of the country.

Out of earshot of the Cabinet Ministers and the Generals, Sakomizu quickly conferred with Yuasa. He suggested that perhaps the commander of the First Division might be ordered to escort the Prime Minister from the rebel-held residence. Yuasa rejected this out of hand. Clearly, he felt that none of the Generals, at this point, could be trusted. Some of Yuasa's misgivings infected Sakomizu in turn. Cabinet Ministers, waiting for their new interim Premier to appear, crowded around him, asking for details of Okada's murder. Sakomizu fended them off. There was one member of the Cabinet, however, he felt he *could* tell, Okada's old friend the Navy Minister, a fellow-admiral. Surely *he* could be trusted? Sakomizu asked him for a Navy detachment to bring the Prime Minister's body away from the residence. Out of the question, the Minister said. It would only lead to further bloodshed. In a whisper, Sakomazu then told the Navy Minister that he had vital news to impart. If he could not help, he would like him to forget he had ever spoken. He then informed him that Okada was still alive. The

Navy Minister said: 'I haven't heard a thing,' and promptly left the room.

Hirohito now waited for the Cabinet and the Army commanders to devise a plan to end the mutiny. Every half-hour he sent for his ADC, Honjo — by this time considerably demoralized by the news of his son-in-law's key role in events. "What's going on?" the Emperor kept asking. "What are they doing?"

Not much, it seemed — and none of it to Hirohito's liking. For hours, the Generals failed to agree on any course of action, or even on the terms of any address to the rebels. Finally, at 3 p.m., they issued an absurdly mild "Admonition" and announced that Tokyo had been placed "under the jurisdiction of the First Division". It was a grotesque attempt to conceal the gravity of the situation from the Japanese public, a risible face-saving pretence that the barricades and checkpoints were officially sanctioned — by the Emperor, no less. This subterfuge fooled no one, for by this time city-dwellers and rebel soldiers were huddled together, discussing the situation, the more politically conscious officers justifying their action in the grandiloquent rhetoric of the "Grand Principle" manifesto.

The "Admonition" was also an admission of tensions within the high military "establishment". All the senior commanders could finally agree on was a statement telling the rebels that their purpose had "reached the Emperor's ears. We recognize that your spirit and true motives are based on a sincere desire to clarify the national polity". It added that the Generals were "unbearably awed". Hirohito, through Honjo, expressed his displeasure with both decisions, and was further infuriated when, through a slip of the pen that was almost certainly deliberate, the word meaning "spirit and true motives" (shini'i) was altered to read "your actions" (kodo) — implying that the murder of high-ranking Palace dignitaries and ministers had official approbation. This doctored version of the statement was the one issued to the media, and it naturally convinced the insurgents that Hirohito was on the verge of surrendering to their demands.

Honjo wrote later that he had never seen the Emperor so angry, for his orders to Kawashima had been: "end this incident as quickly as possible" – meaning, by force of arms.

By the end of the day, the Cabinet, in permanent session inside the Palace, finally established a consensus on two points: in a meeting with the Emperor, the new interim Prime Minister announced that martial law would be declared forthwith. The second decision was that, in shame at what had happened, the Cabinet had decided to resign. Hirohito welcomed the imposition of martial law but told the ministers they should remain in office for the time being. His tone was so cold, however, that their days were clearly numbered. Throughout the night, they drafted their letters of resignation, experimenting with different forms of verbal contrition and abasement. It was a measure of his distrust and contempt for the entire group that Hirohito had told none of his ministers or generals – not even Honjo – that Okada was alive and well. After summoning Honjo one last time, around 2 a.m., for an up-to-date report on the situation, Hirohito went to bed. By this time, he knew, ships were converging on Tokyo Bay, and loyal units, including tanks, were being prepared for a possible confrontation. That night, for the first time since he had had it installed, Hirohito, still in his army uniform, slept on a camp bed in his office.

That night, too, one more person came to know that the Prime Minister was alive. A military police sergeant, removing the bodies of dead policemen, stumbled across him – and told a minor official in Okada's service. The official was a close and trusted friend of the Premier's son-in-law Sakomizu. After making sure the sergeant was to be trusted, the three of them got together to plan Okada's escape.

The following morning (February 27), having smuggled Western clothes into Okada's hiding-place, dressed him and put a germ mask on his face, they ushered him into the presence of his dead brother-in-law, along with a group of mourners allowed in, by the rebels, to pay their respects. Half pushing him, half carrying him, they guided him through the crowd and into a waiting car, which whisked him away to the temporary safety of a Buddhist temple. Okada was so shocked by his experience that he was clearly unfit to resume his duties for some time.

Now there was another problem – making sure the mutineers remained unaware that the body inside the Prime Minister's residence was not Okada's. Sakomizu made sure the coffin ordered by the family was a closed one, and, when it was delivered in late afternoon, personally wrapped the corpse in a blanket and closed the lid himself. The rebels saluted as the funeral carriage set off for Okada's private house, where another mourning ceremony was being prepared, complete with visitors' book and black-framed photograph of Okada.

The indefatigable Sakomizu took a taxi back to the Imperial Palace, and broke the news that Okada was alive and unhurt, reminding the Cabinet that Hirohito wanted to see Okada as soon as possible. A fresh obstacle now arose: Goto, the acting Prime Minister, soon to be relegated to oblivion, in a farcical attempt to prolong his own tenure of office claimed that Okada, by allowing the mutiny to occur, had forfeited his job, and should no longer be treated as Prime Minister. Sakomizu appealed to the Generals, and was ignored. Should the rebels discover their error, he was told, they might well in a rage attack the Palace. Once more Sakomizu returned to Okada's private house, to ensure that the funeral ceremonies went ahead in Okada's name after all. He had by this time told the family the truth about the Prime Minister's survival, and Okada's brother-in-law's heroic death. "I am glad," said the latter's widow, "that my husband could be of service." They all agreed to keep up the deception. Sakomizu also telephoned the Buddhist monastery and told his military police sergeant accomplice to keep Okada there for the time being.

While Sakomizu was scurrying back and forth between the Palace and Okada's official and private residences, a Palace escort waited at Tokyo station for Prince Chichibu's arrival from northern Honshu. (In his diaries, Honjo wrongly claims that the Emperor's youngest brother, Prince Takamatsu, was part of the welcoming group. Hirohito had so decreed, but Takamatsu preferred to remain within the Palace walls.) Chichibu was taken directly to see Hirohito because, as Honjo euphemistically put it, "the court attendants feared that if Prince Chichibu returned to his residence first some people might contact him in order to make use of him". Hirohito wanted to find out whether Chichibu was in league with the mutineers (he claimed he was not) and extract from him some pledge of loyalty. Chichibu was being less than candid; one of the mutineers who was later court-martialled assured his family that Chichibu had encouraged them. In a farewell letter, after being sentenced to death, one of the ringleaders wrote that "Prince Chichibu told me that when the coup comes, I want you to head a company and invite me to see you off as you leave the barracks".

News did finally leak of Okada's survival. The Military Police commander, an ailing general so crippled with arthritis he could barely walk, heard from one of his informers, and told the Palace. But the news was still not made public.

Hirohito's impatience was increasing: he summoned Honjo every half-hour to brief him on developments. There were none. Hirohito called in the commander newly appointed to administer martial law in Tokyo, and ordered him to disarm the rebels "by force if necessary", without, however, setting a mandatory deadline. During his frequent meetings with Hirohito, Honjo did not hesitate to put the Army's point of view. Of course the "activists" (he carefully avoided derogatory terms like "rebels" or "insurgents") could not be entirely forgiven, "but from the standpoint of the spirit that moved them to action, because they were thinking of the good of the nation, they should not necessarily be condemned".

Hirohito refuted this view in unusually brutal terms. "How can we not condemn even the spirit of these criminally brutal officers who killed my aged subjects who were my hands and feet?" he asked. "To kill these aged and venerable men whom I trusted the most is akin to gently strangling me with floss-silk."

"In response to this," Honjo wrote, "I reiterated that, needless to say, maiming and killing the aged subjects are most horrible. But even if they were misguided in their motives these officers did so in the belief that this was the best way to serve the state." Hirohito replied that their only excuse was that they had "not acted for selfish reasons". Clearly, in his mind, this was not sufficient to warrant any leniency. Invariably, Hirohito used "rebels", not the milder word "activists". The vocabulary of the War Ministry communiqués, throughout the four days of "2/26", was highly revealing: in the first news bulletin, it had referred to the rebels as "a party which rose to uphold and clarify the national constitution". It was not until two days later, when it was clear there had been no sympathetic upsurge elsewhere in Japan, that they were called "rioters". The term "insurgent army" was not used until the last day – almost certainly at Hirohito's own instigation.

As the hours dragged by, Hirohito again expressed his rage at his generals' inability to act against the insurgents, at their "excessive caution and unnecessary procrastination". If they didn't act soon against the mutineers, he told Honjo, "I will personally lead the Imperial Guard Division and subdue them".

Hirohito, by now, had read the letters of resignation submitted by his Cabinet, and ironically noted that their language was identical. "When the Toranomon incident [the assassination attempt on his life in 1923] occurred, and the entire Cabinet resigned, the minister most responsible, the Interior Minister, wrote a statement of resignation completely different from the others," he told Honjo. "He expressed his profoundest sense of agony. When We refused his resignation, he resubmitted it, explaining in highly emotional terms that he was unable to continue in office." In contrast, he said, the War Minister's letter was "odd". It was Hirohito's way of conveying – through Honjo – not only his extreme displeasure, but his suspicion that the War Minister was in league with the plotters. Late that afternoon, the rebel officers requested a meeting with General Mazaki, whose ousting had sparked off the mutiny. The General had been in and out of the War Ministry residence several times already. The meeting took place. It was inconclusive.

Another meeting occurred behind closed doors inside Hirohito's own office. In the presence of his two brothers, and of several close relatives, Hirohito demanded, and extracted, from all those present an oath of loyalty and allegiance. The assembled Imperial Family also decided that, for the oath to be absolutely watertight, Prince Kanin (bedridden in his house in the country), however ill, had to come to the Palace and make a similar pledge. Hirohito told them to make sure he would be there without fail the following day. For the second night running he slept on his office camp bed.

On the third day of the crisis (February 28), Hirohito had had enough: he issued a dawn edict ordering the rebels to "speedily withdraw" from the occupied zones and return to their units. If they had not done so within twenty-four hours, they would be fired upon. Police began drawing up plans for the evacuation of some key downtown areas, to avoid unnecessary civilian casualties. Foreign Embassy personnel in the sensitive zone next to the barricades were warned to stay indoors.

Two princes who had been absent from the earlier clan meeting appeared: the Army Chief of Staff, Prince Kanin, who swore his absence had been due to illness, and, to prove his claim, immediately took to his bed; and the elderly Prince Nashimoto, a retired field-marshal, who emotionally pledged his allegiance and begged Hirohito's forgiveness for the Army's "crime". Chichibu, who had convinced Hirohito of his loyalty, was allowed to go home, and talk some of the rebel officers whom he knew into surrendering. General Masaki, ever the troublemaker, while convincing the War Minister that he was negotiating with the rebels on the Emperor's behalf, was in fact urging them to stand firm, even arguing with other generals that what was needed was a communiqué approving their aims. But some of the rank-and-file among the rebels were wavering, and started drifting back to their barracks. Confusion was such that, after one of the many meetings between General Masaki and the insurgents, some of the latter tried also to enter the Palace, to talk to Hirohito in person. They were turned back.

That afternoon, Honjo received a call from his son-in-law. The rebel officers in the War Ministry residence, he said, were contemplating suicide as a way out, but would only follow this course of action if an emissary from the Emperor were dispatched to witness their ritual deaths. In any case, he added, the First Division Commander had told him that he would never allow the "loyalists" under his control to fire on the rebels. Honjo dared not relay the second message to Hirohito, but he did broach the theme of collective suicide, in the presence of a Palace official.

He was brutally rebuffed. "If they wish to commit suicide, let them do so as they please," Hirohito told him. "It is out of the question to dispatch a messenger to such men."

"I have never seen His Majesty display such anger," Honjo wrote. "He ordered me to dispatch strict orders that the troops must be subjugated at once."

Honjo received a second call from his son-in-law and told him the suicide offer had been dismissed. At his next meeting that day with Hirohito, Honjo burst into tears. Hirohito left the room, but did not remain silent for long. "He summoned me again and said that I wept while complaining about the slanders against the army, but unless the incident is resolved, there will be serious consequences."

Fearing that Okada, in a terrible state, might himself commit "seppuku", his son-in-law smuggled him into the Palace at dusk, against the advice of all the Cabinet. Palace officials goggled at the old man as they would at a ghost. The Prime Minister, tearful and demoralized, begged to be allowed to resign for causing the Emperor such grief. Hirohito refused permission. "I am very pleased," he said, trying to put some resolve into the old man, handling him with gentle firmness, as one would a hysterical child. Okada was given a room in the Palace, but – clearly on the verge of a nervous breakdown – never again functioned as Premier. The circumstances of his survival were uniquely humiliating, in the Japanese "bushido" context. He had allowed a less distinguished member of his family to make the supreme sacrifice, one he would never be able to repay. He owed his life to humble men, who had saved him only by making him attend his own funeral ceremony – a farcical trick, something that would have made a perfect scene in a Noh play. No wonder, after the event, many Japanese were of the opinion that Okada should indeed have committed ritual "seppuku".

Hirohito woke on February 29 in better spirits, for the army commanders were at last determined to act: when the ultimatum ran out, at 8 a.m., the martial law commander, through a loudspeaker, called on the rebels to surrender. Tanks rumbled through the streets, and planes flew low over downtown Tokyo, dropping leaflets reading:

> Return to your units. It is not yet too late.
> All who resist are rebels. We will shoot them.
> Your families weep to see you becoming traitors.

The drift back to barracks, by NCOs and private soldiers, became a rout. The ultimatum was repeated, again and again, on Tokyo radio. One captain among the ringleaders attempted suicide, but failed; another blew his brains out. But all the remaining mutineers surrendered quietly, and were immediately taken to an army gaol. The reason for their surrender was that they hoped long-drawn-out trials would afford them endless opportunities for speech-making, and that the judiciary would be as lenient in their case as it had been on previous similar occasions. It was a major miscalculation on their part, for Hirohito, acknowledging this "indelible black mark on the history of the sacred Showa reign", was determined to make an example of them. Neither Hirohito nor Japan would ever forget "2/26", nor would pre-war Japan ever be the same again.

CHAPTER TEN

It was only after the collapse of the "2/26" mutiny that Emperor Hirohito realized how far the rot had spread within the Army. "Why did nobody know what was being prepared?" he complained to his Chief ADC. Because of his son-in-law's role in the mutiny, and the Army's lack of resolve in dealing with the mutineers, Honjo knew his days, as Chief ADC, were numbered. Characteristically, Hirohito played a cat-and-mouse game with him. The first inkling he had of the Emperor's determination to replace him was when Hirohito asked Honjo if the Army would take kindly to the next Chief ADC coming from the Navy.

Honjo alone was scarcely to blame, and, as Hirohito acknowledged, had at least told the Emperor that trouble had been brewing. "2/26", in one form or another, had in fact been the talk of Japan's Establishment for months if not years. Secret police archives (brought to light and examined during the postwar US Occupation) showed that Prince Chichibu, Prince Higashikuni and even Marquis Kido had all been aware of certain aspects of the conspiracy – though they had not known that it was planned for February 26.

Other senior officers with prior knowledge of "2/26" were General Masaki, Colonel Ishiwara of Manchurian fame (though he disapproved and played a leading role in suppressing it) and the retired General Araki. Important names found in the notebook of Captain Isobe, one of the "2/26" ringleaders, were those of Yoshiyuko Kawashima, the War Minister, and of Honjo himself.

Hirohito, so decisive in his handling of the mutiny, might

have reversed the trend towards militarism in the months that immediately followed its collapse. His princely relatives now looked up to him with new respect as their uncontested, determined leader, the hot-headed army extremists had been cowed, for the time being at least, and his military commanders whipped into obedient submission. With Hirohito's knowledge and encouragement, a vast purge of unreliable officers began, affecting several thousands.

The scene was set for reform, and the public mood was not yet frenziedly pro-Army and pro-war. Yet, less than eighteen months later, and with Hirohito's approval, Japan was locked in an all-out war against China, and well on the way to becoming a fully-fledged totalitarian state. In the words of Sir Robert Craigie, the new British Ambassador in Tokyo, Japan was "embarked on a policy of aggression no less calculated and methodical than was Hitler's course in Europe after the occupation of the Rhineland". Joseph Grew, the US Ambassador, came to the reluctant conclusion that "thwarted in attempts to seize power at home, military extremists committed Japan to a large-scale war in China". Both assessments were correct, though the two diplomats were inclined to give Hirohito the benefit of the doubt at every twist and turn, blaming his war-hungry advisers instead.

The China War was the decisive step on the road to Pearl Harbor. To further her war effort, Japan needed more raw materials than she could produce domestically or from captive Korea and Manchuria; in particular needed oil for her huge navy. In an attempt to force Japan into a more conciliatory mood, the United States, followed by Britain and Holland, would impose embargoes on oil and severely restrict other raw material exports to Japan. It was these embargoes that finally convinced Japan's military leaders that, unless they overran the whole of South-East Asia to obtain what they needed, Japan would be economically strangled, her huge army and navy reduced to complete impotence. In the long run, Hirohito was to acquiesce in this assessment and give his blessing to Pearl Harbor.

The events that were to lead to Pearl Harbor were set in motion almost immediately after the end of the mutiny – when Hirohito decided that, rather than face the likelihood of continuing plots and Army unrest at home, he preferred to allow military adventures abroad. So, for all his pugnacious attitude towards the mutineers, Hirohito allowed his hands to be tied by the Army as securely as if he had given in to them in the first place.

In a talk with Honjo just after the rebels' surrender, Hirohito recognized "the need to accommodate to the urgent demands of the military to some extent to avoid a repetition of the tragedy". In another indication of the lessons he had drawn from "2/26", he told Honjo, shortly before "letting him go", "that since we fear a repetition of this kind of incident if we do not accede [to the Army's demands] we want to take their view into consideration". "Forming the new Government will be difficult," Hirohito informed Marquis Kido. "The Cabinet that will be welcome in military circles will give rise to anxieties among economic circles. However, we can't consider only the interests of the economic circles."

One Imperial concession that was to have immediate repercussions was the revival of the old custom whereby all Army and Navy Ministers should be drawn from the ranks of serving officers. This gave the Army hierarchy a *de facto* veto over all future governments: whenever the Army Chief of Staff and his acolytes took a dislike to the programme or the personality of the Prime Minister-elect, or to his choice of ministers, they simply refused to allow any serving general to accept the post of War or Navy Minister. The Premier-elect was then forced to report back that he was unable to form a government, and another candidate, more acceptable to the armed forces, was chosen.

The new Prime Minister (May 1936–January 1937) was Koki Hirota, a former Foreign Minister. He was – exceptionally – no aristocrat, but a stonemason's son who, thanks to exceptional academic brilliance and hard work, and the support of the "Black Dragon" leader Toyama, whose enthusiastic supporter he had been in adolescence, had managed to pass the difficult Foreign Ministry entrance exams and worked his way up as a career diplomat. For all his youthful enthusiasm for extreme "Black Dragon" nationalism, Hirota as a diplomat had acquired a reputation for liberalism, so much so that Ambassador Grew, welcoming his appointment, believed Hirota was "a strong, safe man and that while he will have to play ball with the Army to some extent I think he will handle foreign affairs as wisely as they can be handled given the domestic elements he will have to conciliate". All in all, he noted, "I would probably have chosen him myself".

Hirota took on the job reluctantly, convinced he would eventually be murdered by army hotheads. He was not Saionji's first choice: the latter had wanted his protégé, and the Emperor's close friend and kinsman, Fumimaro Konoye. But Konoye, who was to become Prime Minister from 1937 onwards, refused, on grounds of health; he was probably the only man in the whole of Japan able to refuse an emperor's request.

The new War Minister, and the most powerful man by far in Hirota's Cabinet, was General Hisaichi Terauchi, a hardliner, who drafted a new Imperial Defence Policy, setting out Japan's long-term foreign policy goals. Terauchi started with the premise that Japan's overriding aim was to "establish the Japanese Empire's leadership in East Asia" while at the same time maintaining "friendly relations with foreign powers", and compelling the Soviet Union to give up her "positive aspirations" in the Far East. At the same time, the plan was to "dissuade China from depending on European and United States aid", and to "persuade" China to assume a "friendly [i.e. subservient] attitude". For the first time, Britain, because of her influence and enclaves in China, was included on the list of "foremost enemies of the nation".

For all his professed friendship and admiration for the British Royal Family, Hirohito accepted and endorsed this document, which also included a blueprint for huge new Army and Navy expenditure. This could only mean one thing: the military were determined, despite "2/26", to flex their muscles in Asia.

Hirohito summoned his new Prime Minister to the Palace and ordered him to have the huge Army and Navy appropriations approved by the Diet as quickly as possible. "I speak," he told Hirota, who dared not even look at the Emperor but kept his eyes fixed on the low table between them, "in my capacity as Supreme Commander of the Armed Forces." It was Hirota's second major surprise since taking office. His first, on the very day he was appointed Prime Minister, came with the Emperor's summons and his advice to respect the constitution, exercise restraint in foreign affairs, avoid anything that would create an upheaval in the business world and *see that the position of the nobility was not endangered.** Hirota pondered the last injunction for weeks. Did this mean the Emperor felt that a plebeian Premier could not be trusted to do his job impartially? Or did it represent a new attitude on Hirohito's part, a determination, after "2/26", to place members of his Imperial Family increasingly in key posts? This would certainly happen, in the very near future.

Hirota very soon realized that General Terauchi had the upper hand, and that there was little a civilian Prime Minister could do to make his presence felt. He resigned, to become Foreign Minister, remaining a loyal servant of the Emperor but fearful of the Army's growing role.

In a final attempt to thwart the Army's rising influence, Prince Saionji now put forward the name of General Ugaki, the man banished to Korea as Governor-General in 1931 after a plot in his name for which he probably had had little or no responsibility. In the intervening years Ugaki had become extremely wary of the Army's expansionist ideology.

Hirohito accepted Saionji's choice, out of respect for the old man, but did nothing to help Ugaki when, as expected, he encountered Army blackmail tactics. On his way into Tokyo, to see Hirohito, he was stopped by the military police, the dreaded 'kempei'. Their commander, General Kesago Nakajima,

* Author's italics.

boarded Ugaki's car and advised him not to accept the Emperor's offer to form a Cabinet. When this threat failed, the Army simply refused to provide a War Minister to serve under him. Ugaki, in desperation, asked Hirohito to command the Army to endorse the War Minister of his choice or else order a reservist of Ugaki's choice back onto active duty, to fill the post. Hirohito turned down the request, and Ugaki gave up his attempt to form a government.

The next Prime Minister was a former War Minister, General Senjuro Hayashi, far more acceptable to the Army than Ugaki. But his government lasted only a few months, resigning after a massive row in Parliament, caused by General Terauchi's bullying tactics towards Diet members. This time, Prince Konoye, yielding to both Hirohito's and Saionji's pressure, agreed to become Prime Minister.

Prince Fuminaro Konoye was, in 1937, well-known to the Japanese public, and one of the few truly popular politicians, because of his frequent writings in the press and his unusual (for Japan) sense of public relations. Indolent, opinionated, passionate and unpredictable, Konoye was the only man, in Japan, who dispensed with protocol when addressing the Emperor. His predecessor Hirota had been amazed to see Konoye, ten years older than Hirohito, sit in the Emperor's presence, even casually crossing his legs. He treated the Emperor like a younger brother, indulging in gossip and banter. Such behaviour baffled Hirohito, who was not used to informality of any kind: the humourless Emperor could not distinguish between private conversation and official business.

Konoye was a member of the Fujiwara clan, which had married into the Imperial Family since the seventh century, and he regarded himself as the Emperor's equal in lineage, and his superior in intellect. His loyalty, as he was to demonstrate, tragically, in 1945, was beyond reproach. Hirohito liked and admired him. His casual elegance and lifestyle reminded him of that of the Prince of Wales.

Konoye owed his political career to Prince Saionji, whom he

had accompanied to the Versailles Peace Treaty conference as a junior aide. This did not mean that he shared the Prince's patrician, liberal approach. Like Saionji, he despised the run-of-the-mill Japanese politicians but, unlike him, he was, in his youth and up to 1941, when he dramatically altered his views, both a nationalist and a radical. In a famous essay, written when he was a young man just before setting out for Versailles in 1918, he had attacked the League of Nations, then under discussion, as a convenient instrument for British and American domination of the poorer Asian powers. Japan should only join the League, he argued, if the Western powers showed they were prepared to do away with "economic imperialism" and the discriminatory treatment of Asians by Caucasians.

These youthful radical views, and a flirtation with "tatami socialism", went hand in hand with a strong sense of personal privilege and awareness of his princely superiority. His childhood had been a traumatic one: he had experienced sudden poverty after his father's early death, and terrifying perplexity brought about by the knowledge that the woman he worshipped as his mother was in fact his aunt – for his father had secretly married his wife's sister after the former's early death. Though he refused the traditional "arranged marriage" (his was a love match), he almost immediately afterwards took up with a concubine. His active sex life was the topic of constant gossip in aristocratic clubs, and there were persistent rumours of bisexuality. Physically, he was tall, good-looking in a 1930s film-star way, strong, though he claimed to be plagued by ill-health and was a notorious hypochondriac.

Barely a month after Konoye's investiture as Prime Minister, Japanese troops, legally garrisoned in Northern China as part of the limited occupation forces there, deliberately contrived to clash with Chinese troops in what became known as the "Marco Polo Bridge Incident" just north of Peking on July 7, 1937. What began as a limited exchange of gunfire, on a pattern that had occurred on several earlier occasions, quickly escalated into a full-scale war. As with the "Mukden Incident", it had been carefully rehearsed and planned. With Hirohito's consent, Japanese troops immediately poured into Northern China to reinforce the "Kwangtung army", quickly occupied Peking and moved south on Shanghai; amphibious landings on the coast were supported by massive Japanese Navy shelling. Konoye, at this stage of his career at least, fully approved of the incident: his goal was the overthrow of Chiang Kai-chek and his replacement by more docile, pro-Japanese puppets. Hirohito's uncles, Prince Higashikuni and Prince Asaka, were to become senior commanders in this fateful China War. By the end of 1937 Higashikuni commanded Japan's Air Force in China, while Prince Asaka was in charge of ground troops fighting their way past Shanghai.

From the start, the British, French and US governments viewed this latest example of Japanese belligerence as proof that the military had virtually taken over the running of Japan, and that this had happened under a reluctant, and powerless, Hirohito. This assessment ignored two factors: the "Marco Polo Bridge Incident" occurred only two days after the KMT-Communist Chinese Pact whereby these two rivals decided to shelve their differences and regard Japan as their main enemy; and, on July 17, only ten days after the outbreak of war in China, nineteen rebel officers sentenced after "2/26" were executed by firing-squads. Because Japanese newspaper headlines, by this time, were exclusively devoted to the China War, these executions went virtually unnoticed, except among the families concerned. The KMT-Chinese Communist Pact had revived Hirohito's visceral anti-Communist fears; and the "Marco Polo Bridge Incident" neatly consigned the executions to obscurity. Hirohito had worried greatly about the impact of the sentences: the inference is that he was pleased by the way they were handled.

Because he was kept informed of all troop movement and service promotions, the further inference is that Hirohito must have had full advance knowledge of what his commanders were planning in China before the "Marco Polo Bridge Incident" took place. He had audiences with all senior generals before they left with their units for China. His outward behaviour, shortly before the Incident, reveals, however, a considerable capacity for deception: Hirohito had had an unusually friendly chat with Chiang Kai-chek's ambassador in Tokyo, and no occasion was lost to emphasize Hirohito's personal links with the USA and Britain. On his way to America, President Quezon of the Philippines, accompanied by General MacArthur, was received in audience by Hirohito and stayed to lunch. Hirohito oozed cordiality. "I have seldom seen the Emperor so affable," Ambassador Grew noted. Two months after the outbreak of war in China, presenting his credentials to Hirohito on September 11, 1937, Craigie recorded that, in spite of the strain on Anglo-Japanese relations occasioned by the war, "the Emperor was particularly gracious and showed an interest in everything that concerned the members of our Royal Family and the British people generally". Craigie added that his first impression of Hirohito was "of an impassive figure going rather stiffly through the motions of an accustomed ceremonial. But this impression quickly changed when, after a few moments' conversation, His Majesty became interested in the topic and his face assumed an eager, almost anxious expression, indicative of his deep concern with current events. Here was no automaton, but rather a man who felt things deeply and, under the control imposed by a stark military tradition, was genuinely anxious to play a useful and beneficient role in world affairs. Despite a nervous manner, his bearing was dignified and he conveyed an impression of great sincerity". The Empress, he noted, "displayed a good knowledge of affairs and events in England . . . I was told afterwards that both the Emperor and Empress had prolonged their conversation with us beyond the normal time-limit".

Craigie also called on the Dowager Empress, "a little lady of forceful personality, extremely well informed about everything and everyone". After Chichibu's return from England, where he had attended George VI's Coronation, Craigie was at Yokohama to witness the scene. What struck him most was the distance at which the crowd was kept from his special train. Soon after, Prince Arthur of Connaught, who had twice visited Japan, died, and the Chichibus, as well as senior Cabinet figures, attended a memorial service at Tokyo's Anglican St Andrew's Church. Clearly, despite Britain's inclusion on the list of major enemies of the Japanese nation, the world was to be kept in ignorance of Japan's real intentions.

Gestures like these, perhaps the result of Hirohito's fondly-remembered trip to Britain, did much to foster a personal element of goodwill between Craigie and the Palace. While diplomats invariably believe they possess the skills to charm and influence others, they are usually less able to detect when they themselves are being manipulated: in the case of Grew and Craigie, both were very susceptible indeed to the "aura" of royalty. They were, in very different ways, snobs, with an intrinsic respect for the institution of monarchy. What was more, either through privileged contacts with members of the Imperial Household, or subtly influenced by a brilliant Japanese exercise in public relations, they were convinced that, for all the tough, pro-Axis talk of the Japanese military, the Emperor not only meant what he said when he referred to his trip to Europe as the happiest time of his life, but implied that it still conditioned his whole attitude towards the West. The notion was firmly established that − for all his failings or constraints − his "heart was in the right place". But was it?

In Hitler's Germany, anti-Nazis prepared to risk their lives to bring down totalitarianism were a tiny, isolated minority. Among them was an Asian scholar from one of Germany's best-established Army families, Ernst von Reichenau, a Catholic who, from the start, saw Hitlerism as an affront to civilization and was determined to fight it. As early as 1929, while Hitler's Nazi party was still on the road to power, von Reichenau took the crucial step of contacting the French Army Intelligence organization, the "Deuxième Bureau", to warn the French of the dangerous rise of Nazi feeling in Germany. He continued to feed the French with information right up to the outbreak of the Second World War, but also established a good working relationship with British Intelligence, a logical step in view of his Asian connections, and frequent trips to Hongkong and Canton. Ernst's brother Walter happened to be one of Hitler's favourite generals and a rabid Nazi, and for this reason the brothers were no longer on speaking terms. Ernst von Reichenau's British "control" in Hongkong advised him to patch things up with his brother in order to gain access to any confidential information Walter might then pass on. The advice was taken, and Ernst, now professing pro-Nazi views, staged a formal reconciliation with his brother.

On an arms sales promotion tour to both China and Japan, in 1937, General Walter von Reichenau gave his brother Ernst the following detailed account of his meeting with Hirohito (which Ernst von Reichenau later passed on to British Intelligence):

For China it was easy to sell anything in the way of antiquated arms and equipment. It was difficult to sell Japan anything but the best of up-to-date inventions. It must also be recalled that China was merely a customer, but Japan was handled most carefully as a future contemplated and already approached partner of the Axis. The mission of Marshal Walter von Reichenau to the Mikado was to represent as strongly as possible how formidable a future German-Japan pact would figure in the Japanese domination of the Far East. At this time the German-Japan axis was not yet formed. But at this time the idea was presented to the Emperor by one of Hitler's most prominent favourites, my brother.

My brother described in detail the happenings at the audience with the Emperor, which climaxed in his approaching the Emperor privately in order to tell him solemnly:

"Your Majesty, my Führer looks forward – beyond economies – to a greater union between Your Majesty's country and his."

My brother said that the Emperor bade his interpreter to go away and when they were alone the Emperor stared straight into my brother's eyes and answered:

"I have heard and I am pleased."

Then the Emperor turned and left the room while my brother stood to attention with the Hitler salute.

What happened between the end of "2/26" and the start of Japan's full-scale China War has been difficult for Hirohito's apologists to explain away. The Reichenau episode, had they known about it, would have baffled them still further. For, unlike the circumstances of the "Mukden Incident", it was impossible to claim that key decisions were taken behind his back by army commanders facing him with a fait accompli; with the exception of two incidents in Mongolia and on the Soviet Union border – when his troops overstepped their orders, and were promptly ordered back. His stance during the "2/26" mutiny proved that he could act with the utmost toughness when he so willed.

Hirohito's most articulate apologist, the late Leonard Mosley, skirts over this period with some embarrassment. Dedicated to the proposition that the Emperor either knew nothing of events that took place or did his best to stop the drift to totalitarianism and in the last resort lacked the powers to avert it, Mosley puts all the blame on two of Hirohito's "post-2/26" Premiers, Hirota and Prince Konoye, claiming that Hirohito was kept "in total isolation". Lord Privy Seal Yuasa, he says, was "a fusspot with no feelings other than protocol", Kido "was no longer there" to give the Emperor good advice, Baron Matsudaira, the new Imperial Household Minister, "had failed to establish friendly relations with the Emperor", and Prince Chichibu, his son-in-law, who "could have bridged the gap between them" (a doubtful proposition) was away in Hokkaido with his regiment. Prince Saionji was old, infirm and dispirited, and Prince Konoye "was (no doubt) asleep".

This picture does not bear scrutiny: Yuasa, as Imperial Household Minister, had, almost alone among top Palace officials, shown complete loyalty to Hirohito and a healthy distrust of all Army commanders during "2/26"; for all Kido's change in status, he retained his Palace links as director of the Peerage and Heraldry Bureau, saw Hirohito (as his diaries prove) almost as frequently as before, and in any case – before returning to the Palace as Lord Privy Seal – was to remain in close touch with him since he became first his Education and Propaganda, then his Welfare, Minister, brought into the government at the Emperor's request precisely so that he might remain his "eyes and ears" (he was in closer touch with the Emperor than any Education Minister before or since); the notion that Hirohito would ever trust Chichibu (in view of his volatile past) with any sensitive mission involving either the Army or the Palace is too ludicrous to dwell on; Prince Saionji, as an authoritative biography later showed, was more saddened by Hirohito's response to events taking place around him than affected by his physical infirmities and the onset of senility.

Mosley attributed Hirohito's new failure of will to isolation, depression, helpless frustration and "the lack of anyone to galvanize him in this direction . . . he had always been a character who needed a push". But the thesis that Hirohito was cut off from all those who tried to draw his attention to the dangers of a "positive" China policy does not stand up either. Of course Hirohito received disastrously wrong advice from many of those around him, but the notion that he was completely sealed off from any contact with those who held opposite views is simply not true. As the Kido diaries show, there was an unending stream of visitors to the Palace, not all of them committed to aggression in China. One example comes to mind: on August 30, 1939, at a time when war against China was in full swing, General Kanji Ishiwara, the mastermind behind the "Mukden Incident" who, by this time, had become a resolute opponent of war with China, found himself in the same train compartment with a close friend of Admiral Yamamoto – a Navy Ministry official called Norimachi. The two men knew each other. Norimachi asked him where he was going. To the Palace, Ishiwara replied, for an audience with Hirohito before taking up his new post as commander of the 16th training division. "I intend to advise him," said Ishiwara, "that the present war with China should not be allowed to continue. I also intend to tell Princes Chichibu and Takamatsu this. I know the train's loaded with military police in plain clothes and with political police but it won't stop me saying that this business will ruin Japan if we go on with it."

Hirohito's behaviour at the time of the outbreak of the China War, or "China Incident", as it was euphemistically referred to, differed completely from his aloofness and shilly-shallying at the time of the "Mukden Incident". Reinforcements were sent to the new theatre of operations with his full consent. Hirohito's apologists have been quick to point out that he became an increasingly vocal critic of the China War, but have failed to point out that the main basis of his repeated criticism of his generals was *that they were not winning the war fast enough*, and that it was becoming an increasingly futile proposition, especially after 1940, when Japan's military resources were needed elsewhere; Hirohito again and again reminded the generals that they had promised it would all be over in a matter of months. It was the fact that Japanese troops became bogged down in an interminable conflict in China that infuriated Hirohito, not the war itself.

Why, after crushing the "2/26" rebels so thoroughly, did Hirohito allow the "China Incident" to escalate into full-scale war, leading, in time, to Pearl Harbor and "the great Asian war"? There were two reasons: the first is that, for all his show of strength during "2/26", Hirohito believed that the only way of ensuring that there would be no further insurgencies at home was to allow the Army to have its fling abroad. The other is that, despite his eagerness to establish a lasting neutral relationship with the Soviet Union, Hirohito was motivated by a rigidly obsessive anti-Communism − and saw the Communist threat not in terms of a hostile USSR (which could be contained) but of a threatening, increasingly Communist-dominated China.

What makes Emperor Hirohito's views during this crucial period so difficult to pinpoint is their very ambiguity. It would be wrong to assume that they were solidly entrenched, immutable and guided by principle. As the "organ" controversy shows, the Emperor could privately support a view which he failed to defend outright. His powers of dissimulation were, however, considerable, and there is evidence that, as the military consolidated their power, his own foreign policy attitudes oscillated wildly, one day favouring the US and his British connections, flirting with Hitler the next.

The major, tragic casualty of the policy inaugurated as a result of the "Marco Polo Incident" was Prince Saionji, the "genro". He had become a sad, isolated and increasingly irrelevant figure. The uncontested leader of Japan's small liberal intellectual élite, he was witnessing the destruction of all his cherished ideals, the shattering of all his dreams for a modern, internationally-minded Japan. He had been an enthusiastic protagonist of Japan's wholehearted involvement in the League of Nations – and Japan had withdrawn from the League in the wake of the "Mukden Incident". He had condemned Japan's arms race – and watched the Hirota government earmark an unprecedentedly large sum for new divisions, planes and battleships; he had advocated friendship with Chiang Kai-chek, only to see the Emperor accede to the Army's demands for a full-scale war with China and Japan's determination to remove Chiang Kai-chek from the political scene altogether; he had staked his reputation on Japan's need to maintain close relations with Britain and the United States – only to witness Japan's growing links with Fascist Italy and Nazi Germany, as well as the triumph of personal enemies like the right-wing nationalist, Baron Hiranuma, who in 1936, in the wake of "2/26", achieved his lifelong goal, over Saionji's objections, succeeding Prince Konoye as President of the Privy Council. One of the bitterest pills to swallow, for Saionji, was the Emperor's endorsement of the anti-Komintern Pact, which Japan adhered to in 1937, incontrovertible proof that Nazi Germany and nationalist Japan were moving closer to each other. By this time old age (Saionji was eighty-eight), illness and a liberal, patrician hatred for the "ultras" who now had the Emperor's ear brought about a melancholic, lethargic passivity. On hearing of Baron Hiranuma's promotion, Saionji told his confidential secretary, Harada:

"It comes as no surprise . . . that is the trend of the times and there is nothing to be done . . . It is a great pity for the Emperor's sake."

Saionji's greatest sorrow was not just that he had lived long enough to witness the shattering of his dreams; what hurt him at least as much was the Emperor's involvement in an adventure Saionji felt could only end in tragedy, and Hirohito's contempt for the old man's vision of a liberal, open Japan. Without criticizing the Emperor openly, Saionji – with great dignity – told Harada, again and again, that he felt utterly baffled by the disturbing course taken by Japan, not least by the Emperor's refusal to follow his advice. For, though Hirohito still went through the motions of consulting Saionji from time to time, he neither listened nor acted along the lines Saionji advocated. The old genro's comments became ever more bitter, and disillusioned. "What can we do tied to Italy or Germany?" he asked Harada. "It is ridiculous and I am deeply suspicious. To think of Japan with the United States to the East and Britain to the West – that is meaningful. But an alliance with Germany and Italy . . . what possible meaning could that have?"

He was also distressed by Hirohito's increasing aloofness: he deplored the stringent security precautions surrounding the Emperor. "He must go out a little more openly," he told Harada. "If this does not happen, the people will become distant from the throne."

A year before his death (in November 1940, long after he had ceased playing any role at Court) Saionji refused pointblank to advise the Palace any further on the choice of Premier. "If I felt that one would be better than another, I would say so . . . On three occasions, I have received a message from the Emperor saying, 'please advise me on affairs of state.' If I had anything to say which I considered necessary, I would say it *even if the Emperor told me not to speak*.* But at present I have nothing to say . . . ultimately, there is nothing to be done but to hold one's tongue and watch. If I were a little better physically and had a

* Author's italics.

little more energy, I would like to see the Emperor and talk to him about a number of issues, but the way things are, that too is unthinkable."

The implicit rebuke to the Emperor remained unanswered. There would be much to watch, from 1940 onwards. Mercifully, Saionji would not be alive to see his Japan's apocalypse confirmed.

CHAPTER ELEVEN

The July 1937 "Marco Polo Bridge Incident", rapidly leading to full-scale war, did not prevent Hirohito from spending part of the summer, as usual, in the seaside resort of Hayama, fishing for specimens every day. An American neighbour and author, Willard Price, has left a decidedly idyllic account of what it was like to live in close proximity to the Emperor in the late 1930s.

In this fishing village thirty miles from Tokyo, Price noted that Hirohito "has a horseman's balance and a swimmer's suppleness. One would never dream this to see him rigid and unresponsive in his limousine as crowds look on. Then the mantle of divinity rests heavily on him. At home he can forget his Godhood".

His appearance, fishing or wandering along the seashore, said Price, reflected aspirations of "gentle dreams and intellectual delights".

Price must have been taken on at least one tour of the "summer Palace" in the Emperor's absence, for he describes it in detail. "The outer boards of the house are unpainted wood weathered a dull grey. There is lots of dust in the rooms." He noticed there were neither telephones, refrigerators, electric stoves, heating plants, cooling systems nor electric washing machines in evidence, but there were plenty of mosquitoes. "The plainness of the place was a surprise. It was almost shabby. I was ashamed to go back to the luxury of our own home."

Often, Price was woken by Hirohito, wearing "a three dollar chrome Japanese watch", chopping wood in the garden at dawn. On fishing and specimen-gathering expeditions, Hirohito did not entirely escape from the protocol that was a constant feature of his Court. "He handles the spear and the net himself," Price noted, but his "every move is scheduled by the Court, watched by attendants, recorded by scribes . . . fully-clothed attendants and courtiers in morning coats march hip-deep into the water, on either side of his fishing-boat, to bow and then pull it in".

One day, Hirohito left a copy of Aesop's *Fables* (in Japanese) on the seashore. Price came across the book "but a guard snatched it up and conveyed it reverently away". As Price records, ordinary Japanese residents living in the same area were not banned from the beach, "but they never gape". Price may have under-estimated the security precautions in force in Hayama and along the coast wherever the Emperor decided to fish for specimens, for other eyewitnesses tell of whole fishing villages temporarily evacuated before his arrival. The awe Hirohito inspired was extraordinary: according to Price, a Japanese subject who christened his son Hirohito "later killed both the son and himself for his presumption".

The 1937 summer over, Hirohito returned to Tokyo. Inside his Palace War Room, he could follow the progress of his troops in China in minute detail. Civilian Chinese casualties in Shanghai were severe: for the first time, large-scale bombing of civilian urban targets took place in the Shanghai suburbs. Western correspondents followed the progress of the war from the relative security of the international concession, which was barred to Japanese troops. All reported the huge troop build-up, and the impressive Japanese Navy presence. Some were even invited to board the Japanese flagship, and were briefed by Japanese admirals.

The thrust southward from Shanghai to Nanking that took place in November–December 1937 culminated with the "rape of Nanking", the massacre of over 100,000 Chinese army prisoners of war and civilians, the rape of 20,000 Chinese women and the wholesale looting of the town, a stain on Japan's reputation for which the diminutive General Iwane Matsui, the overall commander of ground forces on the Nanking front, eventually paid with his life at the conclusion of the "Tokyo Trials". It is one of the grim ironies of history that the International Military Tribunal handed out the death sentence to the one Japanese general who was appalled by the Nanking atrocities and did his best to prevent them.

As is not the case in Japan, where the subject remains taboo in school history-books, or else is dismissed in a few lines, the Nanking massacres have been well documented by Chinese, American, British and German observers, but two questions remain: why did "the rape of Nanking" occur in the first place, and did the Emperor know? Some of the veterans of the Nanking massacre, filled with guilt for their past behaviour (and determined to atone as good Buddhists before their own deaths), have spoken up about their participation in it. One of them is Shiro Azuma, who beheaded ten Chinese soldiers but returned to China in 1987 to apologize to the Chinese people. He, like his fellow-soldiers, who impaled babies on bayonets, buried prisoners alive and then ran over them in tanks, gang-raped women aged from twelve to eighty and executed them when they were beyond satisfying their sexual needs, did not do so in a sudden fit of uncontrolled, undisciplined rage: all acted on orders handed down from on high. This is the message several veteran Japanese ex-servicemen have courageously and stubbornly imparted recently to tiny audiences of concerned Japanese citizens – mostly peace groups and anti-nuclear lobbies.

The rationale for the savagery was that news of the "rape of Nanking" would put the fear of God into all Chinese and compel them to accept Japanese occupation of their land as a more viable alternative to more Nankings. The corollary was that it would also spell Chiang Kai-chek's doom, for surely the Chinese would begin questioning his leadership after such an appalling débâcle? On both counts, the brutal arguments were wrong: the Chinese will to resist the Japanese increased, and Chiang Kai-chek, though he fled first to Hankow, then to Chungking, did not fall.

Japan's "positive" Chinese policy, inaugurated at Nanking on an unprecedented scale, had a name, used in inner Cabinet and military conclaves but never in the Japanese press – China's "war of punishment". This catchphrase has a far more brutal connotation in Japanese than it does in translation, and it made nonsense of the professed policy of friendship and of the extended hand – the officially-professed view that, if only the Chinese would get rid of Chiang Kai-chek and fall in with Japanese wishes insofar as trade, recognition of Manchukuo and general Japanese hegemony over China were concerned, all would be sweetness and light. One of the hypocritical aspects of Japan's professed "policy of friendship" with China was that – as Ko-A-In, the opium committee report of December 12, 1938, was to prove – Japan had no overriding reason to stop the war since its expense was largely met by officially sanctioned drug-trading, almost all of it in the hands of the Army or police, or licensed by them.

To what extent was Hirohito aware of the various aspects of this "war of punishment"? There is no doubt that he was familiar with its terminology, for it was mentioned in his presence time and time again. But what of the policy itself? Leonard Mosley claims, citing Palace sources, that Hirohito had no inkling of it, only learning about the details of the "rape of Nanking", to his intense grief, years later, after the war. He also argues that there is nothing, either, in the Kido diaries, about the events taking place in Nanking. But the Kido Nikki, invaluable as they are, are personal entries reflecting Marquis Kido's own activities – in no respect are they daily news bulletins: there is no entry, for example, on the start of the China War provoked by the "Marco Polo Bridge Incident", the only reference to it being a somewhat cryptic sentence noting that Prince Konoye failed to come to a dinner party given by Kido because of "events in China".

So it is instructive to turn to Hirota's biographer, Saburo Shiroyama, for a detailed account of the Nanking massacre, as seen from Tokyo, and its impact on Japan's ruling circles.★

★ *"War Criminal, the life and death of Hirota Koki"*, Kodansha, 1974.

As Shiroyama describes it, "the occupation of Nanking provided Hirota with another troublesome and, in the long run, fatal problem". A distinguished Japanese diplomat, Shunrokuro Hidaka, who would become Japanese Consul-General in Nanking, had entered the city in the wake of the troops and cabled back to his Foreign Ministry a vivid, horror-stricken report of what he had witnessed there. A copy of his report was sent to the War Ministry. "When Hirota heard the reports he was violently angry," wrote Shigoyama. "He went to see War Minister Sugiyama to protest and to ask him to take immediate steps to tighten up the discipline in the army. At the same time, Counsellor Hidaka and others in Nanking visited local army leaders in order to urge them to do something. General Matsui, commander-in-chief, admitted that those under him seemed to have behaved outrageously. When Hidaka asked him whether perhaps the ordinary troops had not heard their superiors' orders, he muttered darkly that it seemed the superiors themselves were sometimes to blame."

Matsui's orders had been flagrantly disobeyed: he had wanted only a few hand-picked units to enter the city, and in a special message reminded them that their conduct was to be irreproachable. But several divisions entered Nanking. The most infamous were troops of the 16th Division, under the sadistic Major-General Nakajima, the former "kempei" commander who had boarded General Ugaki's car to warn him not to take up the premiership, but infantry divisions under two other commanders behaved almost as barbarously.

These were Major-General Heisuke Yanagawa, an old rival of Matsui's, and Prince Asaka, Hirohito's uncle by marriage (to one of Emperor Meiji's daughters), a lieutenant-general who had only recently arrived from Japan and taken over command a mere ten days before the "rape of Nanking".

Hidaka, the upright diplomat, also called on Prince Asaka to express his indignation and ask him to discipline his men. Though nothing had appeared in the Japanese press about the troops' behaviour (nor would it), Hidaka knew how damaging the reports of the large foreign community in Nanking would be. Ironically, many Chinese soldiers tortured or executed out of hand by bullet or bayonet had given themselves up after taking refuge in Nanking's International Concession; the foreign community leaders there had assured them that the Japanese would treat them "honourably", and urged them to surrender. Understandably, the leaders of Nanking's foreign community felt searing guilt at subsequent events.

Hidaka's report was the talk not only of the Foreign Ministry (where not all its staff were, as yet, the willing tools of totalitarian Japan) but also of the War Ministry and General Staff. A senior staff officer, Lieutenant-General Masaharu Honma, was sent to Nanking from Tokyo to investigate and two months later eighty staff officers who had been with the Japanese forces in Nanking at the time were discreetly recalled to Japan. Among them was Prince Asaka, who called on the Prime Minister, Hirota, at his office "especially to apologize to him, in the presence of Foreign Under-secretary Horinouchi, for all the trouble that he had caused him".

It is difficult to believe that this – one of the most appalling events of the China War – came and went without Emperor Hirohito becoming aware of it. Even if the General Staff, the War Ministry and the Foreign Ministry had all made a concerted effort to conceal the atrocities from him – and there is no certainty that they did – it is inconceivable that he should have neither read any of the reports on the Nanking atrocity nor wondered why Prince Asaka, whom he had seen just before his departure for China to take up his command, should have returned so soon. Only a few days before the drive towards Nanking, in November 1937, Hirohito had established his Grand Imperial Headquarters inside the palace, an elaborate war room complex from which he was to follow all major subsequent battles, and from which politicians, even the Prime Minister, were rigidly excluded. No major piece of military news failed to reach the

Emperor through this, his latest plaything, and the uproar caused by the Nanking atrocities was the main topic among Japanese diplomats and staff officers throughout January and February 1938. Within a week of his abject apology to Hirota, Prince Asaka resumed his regular game of golf with his kinsman, Hirohito. What did they talk about, one wonders, the weather?

The China War was also one of the first theatres of operations where chemical and bacteriological weapons were used on a vast scale, and in time the Japanese were to become the world's most advanced practitioners of this form of warfare. Buried in the hugely expensive 1936 blueprint for military expenditure which Emperor Hirohito had commanded Hirota to get through the Diet as fast as possible had been allocations for an obscure "Epidemic prevention and water purification supply Unit", established that year by a formal order bearing the Imperial Seal. This unit had in fact existed, on a very small scale, since 1933, but only with the China War – and an epidemic of cholera among the invading Japanese troops – did it become a fully-fledged "Imperial" unit, with sections eventually posted to all Japan's army divisions serving overseas. Veterans of this organization, otherwise known as "Unit 731", are inordinately proud of their "Imperial" origins, pointing out that theirs is the only army unit ever set up by "Imperial decree". Needless to say, the Diet was never aware of the detailed use of the considerable sums earmarked for "Unit 731" (3 million yen for personnel, 200,000 to 300,000 yen per autonomous unit and six million yen for experimentation and research in the first year of its existence).

The story of "Unit 731" is probably the darkest single chapter in Japan's immediate pre-war history – and, as we shall see later, it is an equally dark chapter in American history too, an indelible stain on MacArthur's reputation, adding to the farce of the "Tokyo Trials". For "Unit 731" had a double function: its teams, attached to every single division in the field, did indeed man water-purification plants and provide Japanese soldiers with drinking water, but that was only a tiny part of its activities. The more important, secret role of "Unit 731" was to develop and put into practice biological warfare techniques which, some senior military strategists argued, would probably tilt the war – any war – in Japan's favour. In order to perfect these techniques, detailed scientific data had to be amassed, and this meant experimenting not just on crops and animals but on human beings too: in time, "Unit 731" was to have laboratories and experimental stations as far afield as Singapore, Nanking and even Rangoon, and its huge staff would include most of Japan's brightest civilian scientists, either invited to participate as experts or else, if they refused, drafted and posted to "Unit 731" as conscripts from 1936 onwards.

"Unit 731" was the brainchild of General Shiro Ishii, a gifted scientist whose brilliantly simple mobile water purification plant was exhibited to the Emperor himself during one of his many inspection tours of army units in the immediate pre-war period. Shocked Palace officials saw General Ishii literally turn urine into drinking water in front of a fascinated Hirohito, even inviting him to drink the "perfectly safe" end product (the Emperor refused, but watched as Ishii quaffed a glass). Ishii had other, more sinister scientific goals. As one veteran "Unit 731" member told a British television team at work on an exceptionally disturbing documentary entitled "Did the Emperor know?", in 1985, "I had the impression Ishii saw this [bacteriological warfare] as a means whereby Japan could conquer the world." In the pre-war, pre-Atom bomb era, the impact of bacteriological warfare on the battlefield and on civilian populations was a fraught subject. General Ishii firmly believed Japan, a non-signatory to the 1925 League of Nations protocol outlawing germ warfare, should have that capability.

As early as 1931 Ishii, then only a colonel, had set up a small research laboratory in Tokyo's Army Medical College, without much official encouragement and with only token funds. Then, in 1935, something happened which totally transformed the attitude of Japan's Army General Staff: a huge cholera epidemic broke out in Manchuria, killing 6,000 men of the "Kwangtung Army" there. Japanese security officers claimed this had been no ordinary epidemic, but had been provoked by Chinese spies deliberately spreading it through polluted water. They also claimed to have captured Chinese saboteurs with flea-infected rats bearing typhus, anthrax and smallpox germs. Overnight, Ishii was given a large budget, and told to establish Japan's own bacteriological warfare capacity on a huge scale.

Ishii was promoted to brigadier, and based himself at Ping Fan, forty miles south of Harbin, in Northern Manchuria. By 1939, according to veteran members of "Unit 731", it was a closely guarded, sprawling cluster of laboratories, living quarters and barracks, with a garrison of 3,000 scientists, laboratory technicians and security guards, out of bounds to all Japanese troops save those with the requisite clearance. Huge vats contained bacteria of typhus, tetanus, anthrax, smallpox and salmonella.

General Ishii's attitude to his work was strangely ambivalent: to his army colleagues and superiors, he boasted about the contribution he was making to Japan's defence capability and the interest taken in his work in the highest circles; among his subordinates, he instilled the notion of secrecy, making them swear they would never divulge what they saw at Ping Fan. To make sure of this, he packed his headquarters, and his laboratories, with recruits and volunteers from a small village near Tokyo called Kamo, where he happened to be the biggest landowner. For his work to have scientific value, Ishii needed live human beings to experiment on. Under the brutal "kempei"-run régime of puppet Manchukuo he had no difficulty in obtaining them.

Even the most hardened war criminals prefer to depersonalize their victims. In the case of "Unit 731", the guinea-pigs — convicts, vagrants, suspected spies or saboteurs, Communists, White Russian "stateless" persons with no rights whatever under the "Manchukuo" régime of Henry Pu Yi, and, later, after the start of the China and then the Great Asia War,

Chinese, and possibly British, Australian, Dutch and United States prisoners-of-war as well – were known as "marutas": wooden logs. There were several "holding camps" for them. One of them, in the early years, was the basement of the Japanese Consulate in Harbin. The guinea-pigs were transferred to Ping Fan in the dead of night, and their special entrance was through a tunnel.

Several of "Unit 731's" former members, now old men wracked with guilt, have spoken about their activities. One of them, Naionji Ozono, responsible for the printing and restricted circulation of the unit's top secret documents, estimates the total number of guinea-pigs experimented on and killed in various ways at 3,000. Other Japanese experts on "Unit 731", including Masaki Shimosato, an experienced reporter on the staff of *Akahata*, Japan's Communist daily newspaper, believe the total figure is more like 10,000. Ozono described how the "marutas", allocated numbers on entry, to further depersonalize them, were experimented on in various ways: some were infected with dysentery, or injected with tetanus; others (some wearing gasmasks, others not) were staked out in the open and "bombarded" with cyanide gas; others still exposed to minus 50 degree centigrade "cold rooms", and frozen to death. Since many senior staff officers, in 1936, believed that war with the Soviet Union was only a matter of time, it was important to Japan's Army planners to know what were the human limits to warfare in an excessively cold climate, or in high-altitude flying: one "Unit 731" veteran described how he had seen two Caucasians – White Russians – freezing to death behind glass, hugging each other for warmth, entirely naked except for tubes attached to their bodies monitoring their hearts, lungs and pulse rate. Other experiments were even more frightful: to monitor the limits of human endurance, prisoners were made to carry heavy army packs and march round and round in the cold winter climate of Manchuria, with only minute quantities of food and water, until they died of exhaustion.

There were no survivors among the "marutas": the only way

out, says Shimosato, "was up in smoke through the cremation chimney" – though, again according to Ozono, General Ishii maintained a large collection of pickled specimens, including whole bodies, for scientific study. Some experiments, said Ozono, including dissections of live "marutas", were of doubtful scientific value, and in one "prisoners' revolt" all the "marutas" being held in two cell blocks inside the centre were "put down" with poison gas.

General Ishii's great problem was not the manufacture of bacteria on a huge scale, or the paucity of guinea-pigs, but lack of efficient delivery systems: when the time came to experiment on "offensive delivery methods", it was found that low altitude bombs would – on explosion – destroy the very bacteria they were supposed to spray over the enemy. Eventually, Ishii found a safer, and cheaper, way of diffusion: plague-carrying rats. During the course of Japan's China War, beginning in 1936, such infected-rat "air-raids" became common, and were the subject of reports sent to Roosevelt and successive British Cabinets by Chiang Kai-chek. They were not always believed. Japan's General Staff knew otherwise: during one such "rat raid", the germ strike got out of hand and spread to Japanese troops in the field, killing 1,600 of them.

To what extent was Hirohito aware of all this? Even some of Japan's most outspoken experts on "Unit 731", about which there is now, in Japan itself, a considerable body of work, shy away from even asking this question. On the one hand is the undoubted fact that he put his Seal on the order setting it up in the first place (and, as a member of the Imperial Family told me, "the Emperor read everything he put his Seal to – he would never use his Seal like a stamp machine"). There is also the matter of "Unit 731's" cost: the Emperor always kept a tight rein on expenditure, whether it concerned his own Household or that of the military, and "Unit 731" was expensive, one of its administrators even describing it as "a bottomless pit" (by 1941 the initial yearly 3 million yen grant for research had increased tenfold). Another survivor says that the "Imperial origins" of Unit 731 meant that its budget was indeed virtually unlimited. Furthermore, Hirohito himself was a scientist of no mean stature, even though his own field was far removed from that of General Ishii, whom he knew, promoted, and honoured with the highest grade of the Order of the Rising Sun. There is also his overall legal responsibility to be considered: as Commander-in-Chief, everything done by Japan's Imperial Army was in his name. Finally, it is a fact that, where his beloved armed forces' research and development were concerned, the Emperor's standing orders were that he was to be fully briefed about every scientific experiment: towards the close of the war, for instance, he was kept constantly abreast of Japanese aeronautical engineers' efforts to develop a high-flying experimental plane able to destroy US B-29 bombers in the air.

"Guilt by association" is an unattractive concept, but the involvement in "Unit 731" of immediate members of the Imperial Family cannot be ignored. A "Unit 731" photographer recalls taking a group photograph at Ping Fan of the officers there, with Hirohito's youngest brother, Prince Mikasa, in the place of honour, during an inspection tour. The photographer, Yamashita, was not allowed to accompany Prince Mikasa and his party inside the out of bounds laboratory sections, so he cannot tell whether the Prince "saw everything" or not. He remembers the occasion well, however, because he received a severe dressing-down from General Ishii: reflection from the sun on the Prince's spectacles marred the picture, obscuring Mikasa's eyes. Later, in his memoirs, Prince Mikasa mentioned "Unit 731" – without citing its actual name, noting that he had watched a film about it and talked to a senior medical officer who had given him details of prisoners deliberately infected with cholera.

Prince Chichibu did not visit Ping Fan, but (on February 9, 1939) attended a secret lecture given by Ishii at the War Ministry, and was "awestruck" by the General's findings.

But far and away the most knowledgeable of Hirohito's relatives was a first cousin, Prince Takeda, who became, within the "Kwangtung Army's" HQ, its chief financial officer. Takeda, whose wartime alias was "Colonel Suneyochi Miata", acknowledged in an interview granted in 1983 to the *Observer*'s Peter McGill (but never published) that he had visited "Unit 731" in the course of his army duties. Though reluctant to talk about "Unit 731", Prince Takeda told McGill that he felt no qualms about the principle of biological warfare as such, ("I believe we needed to study all means of waging war") and boasted that Japan had had the wherewithal to develop an A-bomb "earlier than the United States". "Japan could have come first," he said.

It is of course common knowledge that Hirohito became progressively isolated from his brothers and cousins as the "Great Asian War" continued, deliberately restricting his contacts with them on the grounds that, since they had no official policy-making role in the actual running of the war, he did not want them to meddle in affairs that were not their concern. But in the immediate pre-war period such contraints did not apply.

One of the ageing veterans of "Unit 731" has said that "the Emperor must have known because the budget was very large and the people involved were top level". A former "Unit 731" scientist adds that the "reports would have been circulated to all involved in important research. The intermediate termination of the flow is inconceivable," he said. "I believe it's ridiculous to believe that such information was not circulated to the Emperor." The activities of "Unit 731" were known to large numbers of doctors working in the large Military Hospital at Shinjuku, in Tokyo, where hundreds of pickled human specimens were kept (and destroyed in the month following Japan's surrender, before the US Occupation forces became organized).

Paradoxically, Shimosato believes that Hirohito, though he may have been aware of the "broad lines" of "Unit 731" work, was ignorant of its human experiments. "All information was distributed on a need-to-know basis," he says, "and there's no recorded document that shows the Emperor was aware of all that went on." The best-selling novelist, Seichi Morimura, who has written several books on "Unit 731" (leading to death threats from right-wingers), says that Hirohito "might have had a very rough idea of what it was all about". One argument advanced by Morimura is that the Army may have deliberately kept the more gruesome details away from the Emperor, "on the grounds that he was a humanist and might have ordered its dissolution had he been fully aware of what was going on". But all such arguments are based on nothing more than the premise that the Emperor was at all times "humane", "peace-loving" and "fundamentally anti-war"; both Shimosato and Morimura prefer to speculate on who, among Hirohito's entourage, "must have known". Tojo certainly, Konoye and Kido probably, and of course all the senior generals, including successive War Ministers and Army Chiefs of Staff. How such a secret could have been kept for so long, from a sovereign as hard-working and as curious as the Emperor, is never explained. But dwarfing all such speculation, including that concerning Hirohito's knowledge (or not) of "Unit 731's" experiments, is the monstrous fact that neither General Ishii, nor any of his senior staff, some of whom later went on to hold senior hospital, laboratory and university appointments in post-war Japan, were ever prosecuted for what they did – nor is there more than a cursory mention of "Unit 731" in the 30,000 files of IMTFE.

CHAPTER TWELVE

On December 11, 1937, at the height of the siege of Nanking (the massacres were only a few days away), Japanese naval planes bombed the US warship *Panay* on the Yang Tse-kiang, near Shanghai, and Japanese artillery sank the British frigate *Ladybird*. Both ships routinely patrolled the Yang Tse-kiang to protect foreign shipping and reassure Shanghai's international community by "showing the flag", and their sinking, with several fatal casualties, caused a major diplomatic incident. That it did not lead to war, or to a break in diplomatic relations, was largely the result of the deft handling of the situation by Hirohito's Vice-Minister of the Navy, Admiral Isoroku Yamamoto. Rejecting his subordinates' attempts at a cover-up, the frank Navy Ministry communiqué approved by Yamamoto read:

A naval air unit mistakenly bombed three steamboats of the Standard Company, striking the vessels in question together with an American warship which happened to be in the vicinity. This incident, involving as it does the United States Navy, is extremely regrettable.

Yamamoto personally apologized to Ambassador Grew, saying: "The Navy can only hang its head," and promptly sacked the Rear-Admiral responsible. Yamamoto's fury at the *Panay* incident was genuine. Earlier, he had railed against the Imperial Japanese Army's behaviour in China ("it makes me so mad I'm quitting smoking till it's all over") but what infuriated him even more was that the Army failed to discipline the officer responsible for the shelling of the *Ladybird*. He was Colonel Kingoro Hashimoto, a reservist on a spell of duty in China, the same Hashimoto who had been active in plotting right-wing army coups in the 1930s as the leading light of the Cherry Blossom Society.

It was this kind of Army behaviour that gradually led Yamamoto to believe that Japan would never achieve a balanced form of government unless a crackdown on the "rightists" occurred – a move which might lead to a brief confrontation on a far larger scale than "2/26" but would rid Japan of its Army hotheads for good. As late as 1937, Yamamoto was convinced that, in such a confrontation, the Navy would rally around the Emperor along with most of his Army. People like Colonel Hashimoto, he told a friend, deserved to be shot.

This was the same Admiral Yamamoto who was to become the mastermind behind the attack on Pearl Harbor and the man singled out, as a result, by the American press as the incarnation of everything hateful about Japanese militarism. Ironically, Yamamoto could be claimed as one of the very few authentic Japanese heroes in this troubled period. From the start of the China War up to Pearl Harbor, he was in fact not only pro-American and perfectly aware of the Emperor's huge error of judgment in allowing Japan to enter the war; he was also deeply distrustful of most of his colleagues, and himself mistrusted by the jingoists who increasingly called the tune in Army and Navy circles – and would have murdered him had they been given the slightest chance.

This tiny (he was five foot three, and weighed 120 pounds) but imposing man with a head like a billiard-ball and a wickedly irreverent brand of repartee had been singled out since his training at the Naval Academy as a "high flier" and had enjoyed his two spells in the United States – once as a junior attaché seconded to Harvard as a student, the second time as fully-fledged Naval Attaché, getting on splendidly with his American colleagues, who found him entertainingly different from all other Japanese they had ever met. During a leave of absence in the 1920s, he had travelled to Mexico to study her oil industry and report back to his superiors (such semi-clandestine behaviour was routine for all ambitious staff officers posted abroad) and had been picked up by the Mexican police, who informed the FBI that "a man claiming to be Isoroku Yamamoto, a Japanese naval commander, is travelling around the country inspecting the oilwells. He stays in the meanest attics of third-rate hotels, and never eats hotel food, subsisting entirely on bread, water and bananas. Please confirm his identity".

Even judged by the standards of the times, Yamamoto's family life was odd: after playing host to Hirohito aboard his flagship, the *Nagato*, during a Naval review, he decided, for once, to sleep at home, which was such an unusual occurrence that he had to climb over the garden wall and break in as if he were a burglar. His love life was tumultuous: he inspired strong passions in three women of the "water trade", one of whom was only twelve, an apprentice geisha, when they first met. He behaved outrageously at times, openly entertaining his women friends aboard the *Nagato*, and making no secret of his relationships with "ladies of the night". A talented calligrapher, he decorated the geisha-houses of his past and present mistresses, and lived far beyond his means, earning a second income from his phenomenal skill at bridge and poker. A firm believer in the occult, he hired an expert in physiognomy and palmistry to spot outstanding fliers among the recruits to the Japanese Navy's Air Arm; and briefly funded a charlatan who claimed he could turn water into oil.

But this compulsive exhibitionist and gambler who, for a dare, would do perilous handstands on high balconies and ships' railings, and said, after receiving Hirohito's congratulations for Pearl Harbor, "If they really want to please me, why don't they give me a licence to run a casino in Singapore?", was also one of the most original military minds of the century. Just as de Gaulle, after 1918, was among the first to understand how the tank would revolutionize modern warfare, so Yamamoto sensed that the naval battles of the future would be fought and won in the air. Unlike de Gaulle, who remained a prophet without honour in his own country until the Second World War,

Yamamoto was given every encouragement to develop a carrier-based air arm striking force without which Japan could not have fought a major war. As head of the Imperial Navy's aeronautical department, Vice-Minister of the Navy, and finally Commander-in-Chief of the Combined Fleet, Yamamoto was indeed the architect of Pearl Harbor – but the irony was that he drew up plans for the strike on Hawaii with extreme reluctance and even foreboding, fully aware that, in the long run, it would spell Japan's doom.

Yamamoto had been head of the aeronautical research department at the time of "2/26", with an office in the Admiralty, and on the second day of the putsch some young naval officers had burst in on him, clamouring to join the rebel Army officers. Yamamoto ordered them out of his office and, such was the sheer force of his personality, they went back to their desks without a murmur. This stand, and his mercilessly mocking comments on the shortcomings of his colleagues and superiors in the government and armed forces earned him more than his fair share of enemies. As a precautionary measure, during the time when he was Vice-Minister of the Navy, he had an armoured car blocking the entrance to his office building at all times, and, unlike other senior commanders, refused the protection of security guards from the "kempei", whom he regarded as spies for the rightists.

Though he was as fanatically devoted to the Emperor as any of his Navy colleagues, his forthrightness made him something of a maverick. When Prince Takamatsu, Hirohito's younger brother, joined the Navy Ministry in 1937 as a Lieutenant-Commander after graduation from the Navy Staff College, Yamamoto's chief aide drew up plans for an elaborate greeting ceremony, with the entire Ministry staff parading outside the building to receive him. Yamamoto angrily cancelled the ceremony, reminding his colleagues that Takamatsu – inside the Navy Ministry, at least – was not a Prince but a junior staff officer, and should be treated as such.

Later, in 1940, during the elaborate ceremonies that were to mark the 2,600 years since Jimmu, Hirohito's ancestor, had supposedly acceded to the throne, Yamamoto did not attend the rites staged in front of the Palace. He explained his absence as follows: "Japan is at war with China, and if I were Chiang Kai-chek, I would have used all the planes at my disposal to wipe out the Imperial Family and Japan's entire leadership at one fell swoop. So I declined the Imperial invitation and spent two days at sea instead, keeping an eye on the skies." Yamamoto, says his biographer, Hiroyuki Agawa, may have used this unlikely eventuality as an excuse for staying away, for he disliked the way in which Japan's propagandists were increasingly relying on "divine" myths, "the way of the Gods", to induce in the public's mind the notion of the invincible nature of the Japanese armed forces, discouraging any hard-headed, long-term comparisons between Japanese and United States potentials for war.

He made this attitude clear while he was Vice-Minister of the Navy, in a report to the government, which was probably read by Hirohito itself. "A war between Japan and the United States would be a major calamity for the world," he wrote, strongly denouncing moves (finalized in 1940) for a "Tripartite Pact" between Japan, Italy and Nazi Germany. In private he was even more forthright: Saionji's confidential secretary, Harada, also a compulsive diary-keeper, recorded a conversation he had over dinner on October 14, 1940, with Yamamoto, during which the Admiral described the possibility of war between the US and Japan as "outrageous . . . However, with the understanding of the Navy Minister and the Chief of Naval Staff, it is also necessary to make preparations for whatever the Navy is to undertake" (Yamamoto had already begun initial plans for the Pearl Harbor raid). "In my opinion," he went on,

in order to fight the United States, we must fight with the intention of challenging practically the whole world. In short, even if a non-aggression pact is concluded with the Soviets, Russia cannot be entirely relied upon. While we are fighting the US, who can guarantee that they will observe the pact and not attack us from the rear? At any rate, as long as matters have come to this point, I shall extend my utmost efforts and will probably die fighting on the battleship *Nagata*. During that time, Tokyo will probably be burnt to the ground . . .

"Well-informed Japanese might pray for miracles," Harada recalled, "but realistically (in Yamamoto's view) they should be prepared to do and die." Earlier, the Admiral had told an aide: "Japanese cities, made mostly of wood and paper, would burn very easily. The Army talks big, but if war came and there were large-scale air raids, there's no telling what would happen. Have you ever seen the sea on fire when a Navy aircraft crashes and the gasoline starts burning on top of the water? It's hell, I can tell you – and that's on *water!*" He was also astonishingly accurate about future war tactics in the Pacific: "As I see it, naval operations of the future will consist of capturing an island, then building an airfield in as short a time as possible – within a week or so – moving up air units, and using them to gain air and surface control over the next stretch of the ocean." These would be MacArthur's very tactics, but Yamamoto realized they could never be Japan's for, as he put it, "do you think we have the kind of industrial capacity to do that?"

Admiral Yamamoto's tragic dilemma illustrates the extraordinary capacity for "doublethink" shown by leading Japanese statesmen – including the Emperor – during this period: they were intermittently aware of the folly of the appallingly risky policies to which they had committed themselves, including the fact that they were gearing themselves up for war against an immeasurably superior adversary. But, caught up in a thinking process that had its own crazy logic, they became enmeshed, unable to extricate themselves without unacceptable loss of face.

Worse still, they started believing their own propaganda, and their view of the outside world, never profound, became progressively more warped. Even Hirohito, who had read and studied widely, and knew all about the vicissitudes experienced by the Kaiser in the closing stages of the First World War, argued at times like an extra-terrestrial.

What strikes one most about Japan's slide into war is the short-term nature of the thinking involved, and the gullibility shown towards Fascist Italy and Nazi Germany: neither the Emperor, nor his advisers, nor the dogmatic, narrow-minded military leaders seem to have had any real understanding of the forces they unleashed when Pearl Harbor was bombed.

Hirohito himself reflected this curious myopia. He genuinely believed that, even after Pearl Harbor, Japan would quickly be able to negotiate peace terms that would legitimize her hegemony over Asia. There was little realization that the only option open to the Allies would be Japan's total surrender, that her short-term victories were simply not negotiable; and, among the handful of lucid Japanese Cassandras, there was no one brave or powerful enough to say so to the Emperor's face. Not all were taken in by the expansionist rhetoric – Admiral Yamamoto for one was prophetically eloquent, in carefully chosen company, about the terrible future in store for Japan if she went to war. While most of the men around the Emperor lost all sense of reality, he was one of the few who never believed Japan's official propaganda.

There was another, crucial element in Japanese thinking. It is impossible to understand the sequence of events leading up to Pearl Harbor without bearing in mind that Emperor Hirohito, in common with almost all other Japanese decision-makers (with the possible exception of Admiral Yamamoto, who was more of a player than a leader despite his reputation after Pearl Harbor), believed – until the tide of war started going against them – that the late 1930s, in Europe at least, marked the beginning of a "new era" and that Hitler would win the war. Thus, there was no appreciable outcry when in December 1936 Japan signed the Anti-Komintern Pact with Germany – an agreement stating that Hitler would come to Japan's defence if she was attacked by the Soviet Union, in effect guaranteeing Japan from Soviet interference if she were to invade China. Japan's hypocrisy was such that orders went out to her ambassadors abroad that they were to try to persuade other countries to duplicate such a pact with Germany, on the grounds that it was only a defensive measure to prevent the spread of international Communism. Shigeru Yoshida, then ambassador in London, refused point-blank to convey such a notion to the British Foreign Office, knowing full well the ridicule he would experience.

The clash within Japan between "moderates" and "warmongers", from 1937 onwards, was no longer between a liberal minority (epitomized by Prince Saionji), resolutely opposed to war and determined to maintain Japan's traditional friendly links with America and the great democratic European states, on the one hand, and the partisans of military-based Asian Fascism on the other. It was between those who believed in the chances of success of an *immediate* war and those who, like Kido, while approving of war as a long-term goal, believed Japan should hold off from actual fighting for another few years – when her strength would be even more overwhelming. And the situation was further complicated by the fact that some of Japan's leading dramatis personae, including the Emperor himself, were prone to change their views with disconcerting suddenness, at one moment sounding like moderates and the next striking out in all directions, tempted into using the sophisticated military machine within their reach; the hubris of Japanese expansionist nationalism could suddenly overwhelm even the most cautious and timid of rulers.

Marquis Koichi Kido became from 1937 onwards, and remained until the very end of the Second World War, Emperor Hirohito's closest adviser and trusted friend. He was an indefatigable diarist, recording the most banal events in his life as well as the most salient ones. The *Kido Nikki* (Kido Diaries) became a sort of bible for the American prosecution team investigating Japanese war crimes after 1945. In the Japanese bureaucratic tradition, diary-keeping fulfilled a very clear purpose, enabling high officials to keep a record of their day-to-day activities, should subsequent inspectors call their work into question. For this reason, they are seldom self-deprecatory, and tend to reflect the diary-writer's activities in the best possible light. In Kido's case, they proved not only a godsend to IMTFE investigators, but also to Kido himself, who was widely praised by the Americans for voluntarily handing them over. In fact there was considerable debate, inside the Palace, about the advisability of doing so, for while there was much in them that reflected favourably on Emperor Hirohito there were many entries, also, that showed him in a singularly negative light. Not surprisingly, perhaps, in the light of MacArthur's post-war attitude to Hirohito, it is the "positive" aspect of the Kido Diaries concerning Hirohito that has been consistently emphasized.

Kido had been the Lord Privy Seal's confidential secretary at the time of the "2/26" mutiny, earning high praise from Hirohito for his cool-headed zeal and utter loyalty. From October 1937 to August 1939, he was a Cabinet Minister in several governments, at Hirohito's request. In June 1940, he became Lord Privy Seal, the single most influential figure in the Palace, and perhaps in Japan. As his IMTFE assessors noted, Kido "made every office he held more important than it would have been in the hands of other men". He was a born "number two" – loyal, discreet, immensely hard-working. His diaries show that he can have had no private life to speak of, for all his days (and some nights too) were devoted to the Emperor's service.

Yet, in a very important sense, his diaries, for all their extraordinary detail, fail to tell us much about the "real" Kido: we are aware of a superbly competent bureaucrat with an analytical mind and an encyclopaedic knowledge of Japan's civilian and military ruling élite, but are told little about his own feelings, his likes and dislikes, his moral commitments. As the IMTFE assessors noted, "he was not so concerned about the rights and wrongs of any policy as with the risks accompanying it". There is no trace, in the diaries, of the tub-thumping nationalist propaganda that became the leitmotif in everyday life in Japan from 1937, but neither is there any entry that reveals Kido's distaste for it. "From start to finish," said the IMTFE report on him, "it does not appear that he ever drew

Hirohito's attention to the moral aspect either of the initiation of the Pacific War or the manner in which it was conducted. His whole mind was on expediency."

In due course, after the war, Kido would be interrogated at length by US Army Colonel Henry R. Sackett, one of IMTFE's prosecution team. It was the nearest anyone came to questioning Hirohito himself, for the Emperor, like all members of his Imperial Family, had been declared out of bounds by the US Chief Prosecutor Joseph Keenan, relaying General MacArthur's own instructions to that effect.

The lengthy exchanges between Sackett and Kido are a mine of information, since both the investigator and the accused clearly realized that the Emperor was safe, and that nothing Kido said in private about him in these preliminary pre-trial sessions would be used against him or cited in court. But for all the cautionary "hands off the Emperor" warnings issued by Keenan, it is clear from the transcripts that Sackett was curious about the Emperor's actual role and responsibility in those years leading up to the war, and could not entirely inhibit questions Keenan would have preferred to remain unasked.

Early in his questioning of Kido, Colonel Sackett asked him whether he had ever cautioned the Emperor into "curbing" the militarists. Kido replied with the precision of the trained civil servant. He could remember twelve instances, he said, when he had addressed the Emperor on the subject. Of his own accord, he added that he could only remember three instances when the Emperor had followed his advice: at the time of the February and May 15, 1932 plots, and during the 1940–41 French Indo-china crisis.

The implication was clear: during the crucial period from 1936 onwards, Hirohito failed to take steps to curb the military, and it must therefore be assumed that – with the exception of the two occasions when the Japanese Army overstepped the mark by attacking Soviet units across the Manchurian border and in Mongolia and were given an immediate dressing-down – Hirohito approved of his Army's behaviour in China, felt no overriding compunction either to complain about his officers or to discipline them, and was in tune with Japan's increasingly aggressive or, to use the euphemistic Japanese term, "positive" foreign policy.

This was Prince Konoye's policy, too, though, as Japan became increasingly entangled in the China War, he periodically attempted to resign. Cynical, self-deprecating, witty and casually informal, Konoye would have made an admirable Minister of Information, for his persuasive gifts were enormous and he charmed all those he met, but as Prime Minister he was a disaster. Intermittently, he realized he was leading Japan to her doom. His attitude towards the Army was ambivalent: he despised the generals, but was enough of a nationalist to entertain the dream of Imperial Japan ruling indirectly over a docile China, administered by hand-picked pro-Japanese puppets. He further reduced the possibility of cutting Japan's losses in China and coming to terms with Chiang Kai-chek by bringing into his government two virulent nationalists. One was Admiral Nobumasa Suetsugo, a fire-eating, fiercely anti-British officer, whom he appointed Home Minister. The other, even more disastrous appointment at the start of Konoye's second administration, in 1940, was that of Yosuke Matsuoka, a maverick career diplomat who became his Foreign Minister, to the dismay of all those who still hoped to avoid a major confrontation with the United States.

Konoye's rationale for appointing Suetsugo, whose links with the "ultras" were well-known, and who in fact represented only a minority in the Navy, and also General Itagaki (the architect of the 1931 Mukden incident) as War Minister, was that these were men who had a considerable following in the Services, and would therefore be obeyed. Konoye often boasted of his shrewdness in "fighting fire with fire", but was reluctant to recognize his poor choice in subordinates. When Matsuoka started showing signs of megalomania on a scale that called his sanity into question, Hirohito pointed out to Konoye that, since he had personally selected him, he could equally easily replace him; to which Konoye replied that he was responsible for him, and would stick by him, or else resign himself. One of Konoye's most serious flaws was that this highly intelligent, even brilliant man, was fundamentally indecisive: he understood other people's points of view only too well. The army hotheads saw him as one of their own, whereas Prince Saionji, until the mid-1930s, had felt that his nationalism was less important than his popular "persona" and his natural influence as a leading aristocrat. Hirohito was certainly aware of his shortcomings, but treated him with extraordinary indulgence, shrugging off his obvious faults. There was, in Konoye's make-up, a self-assured casualness and contempt for the accepted social conventions of the time that Hirohito found irresistible because they illustrated an individual freedom the protocol-bound Emperor could never hope to enjoy himself. What Hirohito would have regarded in others as inexcusable dereliction of duty was shrugged off with a smile.

With men like Suetsugo and Itagaki around Konoye, no hope of a compromise solution to the China War was possible, nor does Hirohito appear to have pressed for one, beyond repeating, more and more often as the conflict dragged on, that his generals had let him down by promising an early victory within months. Suetsugo argued that any pull-out would lead, at home, to an ugly situation which might easily become uncontrollable. Britain and the United States were, of course, increasingly worried by Japan's determination to pursue the war in China. So, ironically, was Hitler: he already looked forward to the time when Germany and Japan would become allies against Britain, France and the United States, and saw the continuation of Japan's war with China as an irritating diversion, weakening Japan and scattering her forces. For this reason, German ambassadors in Tokyo and with Chiang Kai-chek in Hangkow acted as intermediaries in an attempt to bring about a ceasefire acceptable to both sides. But Japan's terms, including as they did non-negotiable demands that Chiang Kai-chek recognize the puppet régime of Manchukuo, stop collaborating with

Chinese Communists, pay war reparations, accept the presence on Chinese soil of Japanese troops for an indefinite period, and virtually agree to China becoming a Japanese vassal, were clearly unacceptable.

Konoye reacted by announcing he would henceforth cease to deal with Chiang Kai-chek, and, before the Diet, boasted that even if Chiang were to sue for peace he would ignore him. With the precedent of Henry Pu Yi, the puppet Emperor of Manchukuo, in mind, Japan already had her eye on Wang Ching-wei, one of the leaders of Chiang Kai-chek's KMT, as the possible head of a pro-Japanese government in Japanese-occupied Northern China. As Kido noted in his diaries (in an entry dated January 14, 1938), "we expect a lot from the new government of China".

Because Britain was determined to maintain her enclaves within China's international concessions, which she regarded as part of her vital international trading strength, British support of Chiang Kai-chek was strong, even if, after Munich, her overwhelming concern was Nazi Germany. Whereas American help to Chiang Kai-chek was mainly financial, British assistance took the form of allowing the transport of essential equipment to "free" China along the Burma Road. Britain became more unpopular even than the United States in Japanese eyes as a result, and in 1939, just before the outbreak of the Second World War, Japan demanded that this support route be closed.

The official version of the worsening state of Anglo-Japanese relations is that Emperor Hirohito deplored the growing Anglo-Japanese crisis, reflecting as he did on the traditional friendly ties between the two countries and on his excellent personal relations with the British Royal Family – and that he regarded the drift towards confrontation with hand-wringing sorrow and dread. He may indeed have had qualms at times, but an entry in the Kido diaries, dated 21 July, 1940, shows that this was not always the case.

That day, Kido called on Emperor Hirohito at the palace. "He is in his swimming trunks, very relaxed," Kido wrote.

They talked about the Burma Road crisis. The Emperor (Kido noted) remarked: "I imagine Britain will reject our request to end the support route for Chiang. In this case, we will occupy Hongkong, and eventually we will declare war on Britain."

Taken aback, Kido urged caution, and careful preparation of public opinion. But Hirohito was clearly excited, speculating on the possible need to agree to a compromise with China in order to prepare for a confrontation with the Soviet Union.

As it turned out, the Emperor was not put to the test. Because of the outbreak of the Second World War in August, and Britain's commitments in France, China suddenly seemed infinitely remote: to the disgust of Henry Stimson, the United States Secretary of State, Britain, immediately after the Dunkirk débâcle, agreed to interrupt supplies of arms, equipment and food to Chiang Kai-chek along the Burma Road for three months, from July 1940. This coincided with the monsoon period, when the road was frequently impassable, but Hirohito must have regarded such a concession as further proof of the decline of the West, Hitler's irresistible rise, and the validity of Konoye's "Grand Design".

CHAPTER THIRTEEN

From 1937 onwards, and for the next seven years at least, it would be difficult for any Japanese to view his country's unfolding history in perspective: everything seemed to vindicate the attitude of the hard-line right-wingers and militarists who believed that the "new order" in Europe was all part of a Grand Design allowing Japan to assume her predestined role as the most advanced, efficient and racially superior nation in Asia, with a "divine right" to assert her will over the lesser breed of Asian nations and colonies. The notion of *Hakko Ichiu* (eight corners of the world under one roof) was now no longer a mythical Shintoist catchphrase justifying, in the abstract, the Emperor's divine right to dominate the world, but a slogan with very real, practical applications, the religious vindication of Japan's new power and influence. Germany's successful and unopposed aggression in Europe (until the invasion of Poland), and Mussolini's transformation of Italy into an efficient, highly centralized state, were reported in admiring detail by Japan's ambassadors in Berlin and Rome, both unconditional devotees of Fascism, so much so that some wags in the Japanese Foreign Ministry referred to Hiroshi Oshima as "Germany's Ambassador to Berlin".

Even the unexpected 1939 Non-Intervention Pact between Hitler and Stalin failed to shake the German-Japanese alliance: Baron Hiranuma, who had succeeded Konoye as Premier, though only for a few months, did resign, along with his whole Cabinet, "for giving the Emperor bad advice", and Ambassador Oshima was recalled, but not for long. Within little more than a year he was back in Berlin, more influential than ever, and a year after the Non-Intervention Pact (on September 27, 1940) the Tripartite Alliance, between Italy, Germany and Japan, was signed.

The timing was significant – only a few months after Dunkirk, the collapse of France and the entry into the war of Italy on Hitler's side – and its purpose clear: Article Two stated that "Germany and Italy shall recognize and respect the Leadership of Japan in establishing a New Order in East Asia", and the three signatories pledged themselves to go to war against any nation not yet in conflict with Germany which would dare to attack any of them – a deliberate warning to the United States to remain neutral, or face the consequences.

Japan appeared set on an irresistible course: had she not, with impunity, moved troops and aircraft into northern French Indochina in the wake of France's defeat – ostensibly to open a "second front" against Chiang Kai-chek, a pretext no foreign power could take seriously? And had not Britain meekly suspended aid to Chiang along the Burma Road?

By midsummer 1940, as Richard Storry noted,[1] "it argued either staunch pro-British feelings or remarkable prescience in even the wisest Japanese for him to imagine that Germany would lose the war", though a handful of diplomats and statesmen instinctively felt Japan had backed the wrong horse – among them two ambassadors to London, Shigeru Yoshida and his successor, Mamoru Shigemitsu, who both tried to caution Hirohito against believing too much Nazi propaganda about Britain's decline and imminent collapse, and wise old Prince Saionji, who told his faithful secretary, Harada, a few weeks before his death, "In the end I believe Great Britain will be victorious."

In the armed forces, Admiral Yamamoto was not the only commander to express his private misgivings, but this was now the era of "thought control", of the growing influence of the "kempei", and any public criticism of the Tripartite Alliance was treasonable: only General Kanji Ishiwara openly dared defy the military police, and he was a special case: it would have been embarrassing to arrest one of the heroes of the "Mukden Incident".

How did Emperor Hirohito react to these events? Was he, as the official Japanese record would have it, privately appalled by both the rise of Japanese Fascism at home and her expansionist policy abroad? Did he have any influence? Was he, as his many apologists claim, a virtual prisoner, during this whole period, of the militarists and their allies, or did he come to embody Japan's nationalist trend, to the extent of believing in her "divine mission" to rule over half of the world?

It would certainly have required exceptional insight and statesmanship, in his position and in the historical context of the time, to discern the underlying weaknesses of Japan's position; and, at his exalted vantage-point, the notion that Japan was riding the crest of a historical wave must surely have been irresistible to him. It was his trusted kinsman Konoye, after all, who put forward (as early as December 22, 1938), the notion of a "new era" and a "New Order in East Asia". It was Konoye, again, in his public radio address, "Receiving the Imperial mandate", who proclaimed that the old order in Europe was collapsing and that Japan must prepare to cope with a radically different world, and who, a few weeks later (August 1, 1940) in his "Outline of a basic National Policy", called for a strong national "defence state" to face "an unprecedentedly great ordeal"; while his hand-picked new Foreign Minister, Yosuke Matsuoka, asked his fellow countrymen to demonstrate "the Imperial way throughout the world" and first coined the phrase "Great East Asia Coprosperity Scheme" – to include both French Indochina and the Netherlands East Indies. This was heady stuff.

Had Hirohito conceded as much, later, as did his kinsman, Prince Konoye, few would have continued to denigrate him. But Hirohito never once admitted anything of the sort: his attitude was always that he consistently opposed the "war party" at every twist and turn of events, fighting a dogged rearguard action against the warmongers. This is what he told MacArthur (who believed him unreservedly) at their first post-war meeting; it was what he told John Foster Dulles in 1952 and what he hammered home ever since, in his yearly, highly formal "press conferences" with a handful of accredited Japanese "court correspondents". Hirohito's version of events has become the officially-accepted history of Japan, vouched for internationally by historians and diplomats alike. The facts, as we now know them, tell a very different story.

Until Japan's new post-war constitution stripped Hirohito of his "divine" qualities, in 1946, all Japanese were supposed to view the Emperor with "awe and trepidation". These, in retrospect, are the key emotions that seem to have swayed Hirohito himself during the months leading to "the Great Asia War": oscillating between awe at Japan's growing power and trepidation at the possible consequences of her aggressive policies, teetering between elation and doubt, he carefully covered his tracks, making final judgment difficult, encouraging the notion that he was swept into war against his will. That Hirohito restrained his commanders and ministers at times, urging caution and diplomacy, has been amply documented and the record shows that he did indeed, on occasion, deflate their sense of infallibility and sabre-rattling self-confidence. But – as the record also shows – Hirohito not only became infected with their hubris but also behaved, most of the time, during his many sessions with his commanders, less like a doubter than an instructor, coaxing and guiding his pupils through persistent questioning of their aims and tactics.

Japan's war with China is often cited as a conflict over which Hirohito had next to no control, though he did his best to bring it to an end by criticizing his generals to their faces on every possible occasion. But the fact is that Hirohito backed Konoye's hard-line stand in January 1938, withdrawing Japan's recognition of Chiang Kai-chek, against the advice of most of his generals, who were then seeking accommodation with China because they felt that the China War was a "bottomless pit" that would fritter away Japan's military resources and prevent her from

waging a later, far more essential, war against the Soviet Union
– something many senior military men felt was inevitable in the
long run. As the Kido diaries show, Hirohito prevaricated when
Prince Kanin, his Army Chief of Staff, requested a meeting to
discuss the possibility of Japanese forces being pulled out. As the
Emperor told Konoye: "The Chief of Staff wanted to see me
before I met you but I suspect they want to cancel what's
already been decided [non-recognition of the Chiang Kai-chek
régime] so I said I already had an appointment with the Prime
Minister and turned down his request."

When Hirohito did finally agree to meet Kanin, he asked
him: "Why does the Chief of Staff want to stop the war with
China and get ready for war with Russia? Does this mean
Russia is on the move?"

Kanin replied that preparing for conflict with the USSR
was a form of contingency planning, "just like the security precautions for the Emperor's travels. We have to be ready for the
worst scenario". Hirohito later told Konoye about this conversation, adding: "If this is the case then we shouldn't have started
the war with China in the first place, but since we've started it,
we should carry it through to the end."

As Professor Inouye[2] points out, Hirohito was highly skilled
at playing the military off against the Government, and the
Army against the Navy, in order to get his way. Far from
deploring the escalation of the war, after Nanking, the Harada
Memoirs show that the Emperor used his influence to keep it
going. Konoye told Harada (January 15, 1938) that "the chiefs
of staff strongly wished to finish the war with China to get
ready for the war against the Soviet Union", but, Harada
added, "the Emperor kept silent". Hirohito clearly sided with
the hard-liners,who believed that Japan should take no initiative
over a China ceasefire, since this would lead Chiang Kai-chek to
claim that, despite his military defeats, he had ultimately been
victorious. Later still (December 2, 1940), Kido recorded Hirohito's account of his meeting that day with the Army Chief of
Staff, General Hajime Sugiyama – who had recently replaced

Prince Kanin, because by this time Hirohito realized Japan would soon be at war and did not want members of the Imperial Family to be in the limelight "in case events turn against them".

At this meeting the Emperor asked Sugiyama: "Is there any way to hit Chiang Kai-chek once and for all?", to which Sugiyama replied it would be difficult to "destroy him completely".

Hirohito asked: "Can we scale down operations on the China war front?"

Sugiyama replied it would be impossible to "withdraw our troops without a serious loss of morale because then you give the impression you've lost".

Hirohito told Sugiyama to "drastically review the situation" – not because he believed the "war of punishment" was morally wrong, but because, by this time, he had accepted the "strike south" option and realized this would be difficult with his troops bogged down in China.

Another issue about which Hirohito is supposed to have had severe qualms was the Tripartite Alliance, and indeed news was carefully leaked to the Diplomatic Corps in Tokyo that both Hirohito and Konoye disliked the Pact intensely and had agreed to it only under pressure. That Hirohito had initial reservations is certain. But, as he told Kido, "I believe the signing of the German Military Alliance cannot be helped in the present situation. If there are no other means of dealing with the United States it may be the only solution . . ."

His doubts prompted him to tell Konoye, "We're in this together, you and I, for better and for worse," which can be interpreted in various ways – as an appeal for loyalty, a plea for support, even a veiled threat. In the months that followed, Hirohito was to become a staunch convert to his Foreign Minister Matsuoka's thesis that only the Tripartite Pact would stop the United States from attacking Japan.

As usual, the Emperor's statements were leaked so as to present him in the best possible light: as Ambassador Grew wrote, on October 22, 1940:

I was told today on excellent authority that both the Emperor and Prince Konoye were dead against the Tripartite Alliance but that it was brought to the Emperor's attention that he might not survive a refusal and that he said to Konoye: "Well, you and I will have to stand or fall together." *This came indirectly from a member of the Imperial Family.**

The Imperial rescript announcing the Tripartite Alliance to his people is, for all the Emperor's supposedly strong reservations, an exaggeratedly flamboyant piece of prose, and it is surprising, in the light of Hirohito's supposed opposition to it, that he failed to have it toned down. Beginning with:

It has been the great instruction bequeathed by Amaterasu that our grand moral obligation be extended in all directions and the world unified under one roof. This instruction is one we are faithfully observing day and night . . .

it goes on to praise the Agreement as:

. . . a source of great joy . . . We believe that to let all nations seek their proper places and myriad peoples enjoy the piping times of peace are enterprises of unexampled magnitude . . . Our subjects are requested to give clearness and distinction to the concept of polity and to conquer the situation of great moment by deliberation and cooperation, thereby guarding the Imperial Throne coexistive with heaven and earth.

Perhaps tradition required this kind of jargon, perhaps there was nothing Hirohito could have done to modify it or hint as he claimed he did, later, in the rescript declaring war on the United States and Britain, that he was acting reluctantly.

But what, then, is one to make of Kido's September 24, 1940 diary entry? Summoned by Hirohito, and "recording his words with awe", Kido noted that the object of their conversation that day was

* Author's italics.

the Tripartite Alliance and the form of rites that should take place to commemorate it. The Emperor has asked the Imperial Household Minister to consult past records to find out what kind of sacred rituals took place at the time of the signing of the [1904] Anglo-Japanese Friendship Treaty. The Imperial Household Minister has discovered there had been no Shinto religious rites. The Emperor has decided that, dealing with this highly important occurrence ... we should have a special ceremony at the shrine inside the palace, and to ask for the blessing from the Gods on his Tripartite Pact.

It is impossible to underestimate the importance of this decision. Hirohito attached enormous importance to precedent, and for him to have broken with it under any circumstances was exceptional. The Anglo-Japanese Friendship Treaty was the crowning achievement of Emperor Meiji, perhaps the single most important Treaty of the Meiji Restoration period, and to put the Tripartite Alliance on a par with it makes nonsense of the notion that Hirohito accepted it with heart-rending reluctance. Indeed, his decision to opt for solemn religious rites – which had *not* been thought necessary for the Anglo-Japanese Friendship Treaty and which came as a complete surprise to Kido – shows that Hirohito placed it *above* the 1904 Treaty in his order of values.

Another example of Hirohito's "positive guidance" was over French Indochina. Japan was quick to exploit France's reverses and humiliation in the wake of her collapse in June 1940. Two days after Pétain's meeting with Hitler at Montoire, acknowledging the occupation of Paris and France's withdrawal from the war, Japanese inspectors arrived in French Indochina to investigate arms shipments to China. Japanese warships circled Haiphong harbour in a demonstration of gunboat diplomacy, and General Georges Catroux, Indochina's Governor-General (who would slip away to join de Gaulle very soon afterwards), had no alternative but to agree to demands that all arms shipments to Chiang Kai-chek cease forthwith, and the Hanoi–Yunnan railway link to China be severed.

By then, Japanese military thinking had shifted, in the light of France's defeat, to the need for permanent Japanese military bases throughout French Indochina, and on August 2, 1940, as a first step towards that end, Japan sent the new Governor-General of Indochina, Admiral Jean Decoux, an ultimatum demanding transit rights for Japanese troops in Northern Indochina and the use of French airfields there. Decoux prevaricated, but his options were extremely limited, and on August 30 Vichy France allowed Japan "military facilities" in Northern Indochina (Tonkin) and promised to provide large quantities of badly-needed Indochinese rice to Japan in exchange for a pledge, extracted by Decoux, that Japan would continue to recognize French sovereignty over Indochina. Several thousand battle-hardened Japanese troops moved into Tonkin, around Hanoi. The United States retaliated by declaring an embargo on the export of scrap metal to Japan – a measure which many of Roosevelt's advisers felt was an insufficient, as well as tardy, "graduated response" to Japan's growing policy of aggression. Japan, given a clear indication of future probable United States measures, promptly began stockpiling oil and mineral reserves, putting pressure on the beleaguered Dutch Government of the Netherlands East Indies to sell Japan five times as much oil as in the past, for the next five years.

Thailand, who had also taken advantage of France's weakened international position, now demanded the surrender of tracts of Cambodian land she regarded as hers, and Japan, setting herself up as a highly partial, pro-Thai mediator, saw to it that the disputed territories were returned to Thailand.

But this was not enough for Japan. By this time, Japanese territorial ambitions had grown, the "Great East Asia Co-prosperity Sphere" (with both Indochina and the Netherlands East Indies shown on Japanese maps under the Japanese flag) had become a concrete objective, and Japanese military leaders had openly started discussing their "Strike South" strategy with the Emperor. In their new way of thinking, Indochina was important, but now only as part of their overall strategy, as a stepping-stone to Indonesia, Malaya and the Philippines.

It so happens that we know a great deal about Hirohito's conversations with his military leaders and with Konoye during this period, thanks to the famous "Sugiyama Memorandum": an almost verbatim transcript summary of top-secret meetings between the Army Chief of Staff and the Emperor. Sugiyama burnt the original manuscript just before committing seppuku in August 1945, but a copy belonging to his chief aide miraculously escaped destruction, and was preserved in the archives of the Japanese Self-defence Forces GHQ, where it remained until a senior archivist there allowed a Tokyo publishing firm, Hara Shobo, to bring it out in an expensive, de-luxe, two-volume edition in 1967.

Though initially it attracted surprisingly little attention, it remains a unique record of top-secret and frank conversations between the Emperor and his military commanders, almost as immediately evocative as tape-recordings. Since the discussions were often informal, the language used by both the Emperor and his commanders is understated and elliptical, a kind of shorthand: all parties are familiar with the events and conceptions they are discussing, so is there no need to refer to them in full – and in any case there has always been a natural Japanese reluctance to call a spade a spade. The envisaged invasion of Malaya, the Philippines and the Dutch East Indies, for instance, is referred to as "doing the South", or "the Southern problem".

By January 1941 the military were not content with their limited bases in Tonkin. With "Strike South" in mind, they wanted more, and felt that the demoralized French had no alternative but to grant them the run of Cambodia, Laos and southern French Indochina as well.

They wanted bases in Thailand, too, but expected to obtain Thai permission for these as a matter of routine. The stationing of Japanese troops in Tonkin – and the cutting off of all supplies to Chiang Kai-chek from across the Indochina border – were logical steps in Japan's four-year-old struggle against the Chinese leader. The stationing of Japanese troops in southern French Indochina, Cambodia and Thailand, however, could not be explained in terms of Japan's China War strategy. Such bases would, however, be invaluable if, as was the case, Japan intended to invade Malaya, the Philippines and the Dutch East Indies. They could indeed mean only one thing: preparation for an eventual "strike South", to gain a complete hold over East Asia. Sugiyama said as much to Hirohito in a report dated February 1, 1941, using the usual oblique references to "Strike South": Japanese military bases in southern French Indochina, he wrote, were a necessary stepping-stone, "thinking about problems which might arise, if eventually there were problems in the South". In any case, he added, French Indochina was in no condition to resist Japanese armed might.

Hirohito presided over several sessions with his Chiefs of Staff, sometimes alone with them, sometimes with his Premier, Konoye, sitting in during "liaison conferences". As the Sugiyama Memorandum shows, the Emperor was fully aware at all times of what his commanders were planning. On January 23, 1941, he asked his Chiefs of Staff: "Can you keep a military pact with Thailand secret?" Some kind of arrangement was indeed necessary, if Japanese troops were to cross Thailand on their way to invade Malaya. The Army was in favour of a formal military pact, while Matsuoka, the Foreign Minister, felt that Thailand, having obtained a satisfactory "readjustment" of frontiers thanks to Japanese "mediation", was sufficiently beholden to Japan already, and should simply agree to Japanese troops moving through her territory as a matter of course. The following day (January 24) Hirohito returned to the subject. He told Sugiyama that, "since pro-British influence in Thailand is strong", extreme care was needed to bring about a "military pact" with the Thais, for the British were almost bound to get to hear of it.

On the question of military plans to move land, air and sea units into southern Indochina, Hirohito reminded his Chiefs of Staff that same day that negotiations between Japan and Vichy France were currently taking place in Tokyo, so that, if the French acquiesced to Japanese demands, the use of force would be superfluous. Sugiyama readily agreed. A few days later, on February 1, still concerned by world reaction to a large-scale Japanese move into Indochina, Hirohito asked his commanders how Japanese bases in Indochina could be established without "agitating" the United States and British Governments. His commanders reassured him that "there was no warlike atmosphere". At the time they were probably bluffing, but in the event they were accurate enough: though United States opinion was to harden markedly against Japan after the latter's occupation of southern Indochina, in October 1940 Admiral James O. Richardson, then Commander in Chief of the Pacific Fleet, quoted Roosevelt as saying, "If the Japanese attacked Thailand, or the Kra peninsula, or the Dutch East Indies we would not enter the war, [that] even if they attacked the Philippines he doubted whether we would enter the war."

Hirohito asked some highly practical questions: "How much naval force will you need? Where do you intend locating the new air and naval bases in Indochina?"

Admiral Nagano, the Naval Chief of Staff, replied that the Navy intended to occupy Camranh Bay; Sugiyama said that there would be new Army bases in Saigon and Pnom Penh, and air bases in Saigon, Natrang and Tourane (Danang), adding, "*This will be necessary for landing operations, for the Malay peninsula.*" ★

Hirohito accepted this without comment or demur, adding only: "Do you need an air base in Thailand as well?" Sugiyama replied that it was essential to have an air base in Saigon "but we are not at this stage thinking of one in southern Thailand". Hirohito realized, of course, that the Japanese plan to move into French Indochina on a large scale would not have been conceivable without France's collapse in Europe – and he was human enough to have mixed feelings about this ruthless exploitation of an erstwhile friendly nation's misfortunes. He told Kido it was a bit like a thief looting a burnt-out house. "I don't like it," he said, "but I suppose it can't be helped," adding that it was no

★ Author's italics.

good being too soft-hearted. One should not be over-civilized, he went on, or behave like Prince Song, citing the legend of the Chinese prince who was so chivalrous he would never attack an enemy who was unprepared for battle.

The negotiations with Vichy France continued. United States and British reactions to Japan's establishment of bases in Tonkin had been strong, but not overwhelmingly so. Trade restrictions were troublesome, but temporary: by stepping up steel production in Manchuria, Korea and Japan herself, the war planners expected to overcome any shortfalls within a year. High-level talks had at last begun between Japan and the United States on a possible solution to the China War. The Emperor believed this had only been possible because of the deterrent value of the Tripartite Alliance. As he pointed out to Kido, its usefulness was thus proved. "Patience," he told Kido, "patience, endurance and perseverance are everything." Hirohito eagerly agreed that Matsuoka should undertake a long trip to Europe and talk to Hitler, Mussolini and Stalin. His discussions were to stress the importance of the Japanese "Monroe Doctrine" of Japan's superiority in Asia – and he was ordered to try to reach some kind of an understanding with the Soviet Union, possibly to bring that country into some form of association with the Tripartite Alliance signatories.

By this time (March–April 1941) Hitler was already preparing his offensive against the USSR, and, in his megalomania, assumed that he could use Japan like an obedient vassal. His sole concern was to persuade and, if necessary, threaten Japan into seizing Singapore and Malaya, thus bringing Britain to her knees. The argument Ribbentrop and Hitler used on Matsuoka was deliberately crude: Germany had virtually won the war. As the Japanese themselves acknowledged, the old order was crumbling. The Tripartite Pact would effectively keep the United States neutral, even if Japan did move against Singapore. If Japan wanted to be part of the "new order", it must help Germany – or else the Asian spoils of the defeated European nations, including the oil-rich Netherlands East Indies, would pass her by. To Hitler's dismay, Matsuoka talked endlessly, but confusedly – and brought no clear mandate from the Emperor to engage in immediate war against Britain in the Far East. As Herbert Feis put it, in his admirable study,[3] "the invited guest, it had been hoped, would be a man of radiant action; the arrived guest turned out to be a man of excusing talk". On his way home, Matsuoka did conclude a non-intervention agreement with the USSR; he was in blissful ignorance of German preparations for "Operation Barbarossa".

On his return to Japan, just in time for the Emperor's April 29 birthday celebrations, Matsuoka proved that the incessant pressure put on him in Berlin had had its effect: almost daily, he bombarded Hirohito with reports or called on him to express his point of view directly. Japan, he told the Emperor, must attack Britain in the Far East without delay. He had become a total convert to Hitler's viewpoint, so much so that, when – on June 22 – Hitler launched his attack on the Soviet Union, Matsuoka, his own neutrality talks with Stalin and Molotov notwithstanding, now urged Hirohito to take on the Soviet Union as well. Hirohito could no longer tolerate his Foreign Minister's volubility, inconsistency and irresponsibility. Matsuoka, he started telling Kido, would have to go. In typical Japanese fashion, the pressure on him to leave would be exerted indirectly. In due course, Matsuoka would be forced out of the Government not only because of his growing megalomania and undiplomatic behaviour, but because the rest of Japan's ruling élite, including the Emperor, refused to accept his thesis that it was Japan's duty to hit the Soviet Union on its easternmost flank in order to help Germany bring her Russian blitzkrieg to an even speedier culmination.

But, on June 25, 1941, only three days after Hitler's invasion of the Soviet Union, the conference attended by Hirohito, Konoye and his Chiefs of Staff was not concerned with the USSR but with Indochina. The now imminent invasion of that country was discussed in further detail. The military leaders were adamant that there should be no compromise with the procrastinating French, despite Konoye's plea that, since the French were showing goodwill in the Tokyo talks, "is it right to force this matter on them?"

Sugiyama said that it was now more important than ever to carry out the Indochina move as quickly as possible. "The ABCD Powers [America, Britain, China, Dutch East Indies] have been collaborating against Japan to suppress us day by day, we need to establish this sphere as soon as possible. In a very pressing situation like this, with a total ban on exports to Japan and the strengthening strategic structure of the United States and Britain we have to do this very quickly."

Hirohito expressed no reservations at this stage, showing more interest in the overall cost of the operation, and asking: "Is it enough to hit French Indochina alone?" Sugiyama replied that – for the time being – it would be unwise to move troops into Thailand ("we think it'll be better to take care of Thailand afterwards"), not least because to invade both countries simul-taneously could reveal Japan's long-term plans.

Hirohito asked if there was any connection between this plan and the Russo-German War. Sugiyama replied that the Indo-china operation should take place regardless of what was happen-ing on the Russo-German front or indeed in Washington, where negotiations between America and Japan were still pro-gressing.

Hirohito again asked for logistical details. How many troops would be sent to French Indochina, and where would they come from? Again, his Chiefs of Staff provided him with a detailed breakdown of units and proposed Indochina bases. Only now did Hirohito express some guarded misgivings. "I worry greatly about the international repercussions," he said. "Our morality could be called into question. But let it pass." In a strong voice, Hirohito added: "That's fine with me." In his account of the day's proceedings, Sugiyama noted that the Emperor appeared pleased, and "more cheerful than on previous days".

The diplomatic niceties were preserved, but the instructions

Emperor Meiji (1852–1912), Hirohito's grandfather, defeated the Russians and turned Japan into a powerful, modern country.

Emperor Taisho (1879–1926), Hirohito's father, virtually disappeared from public life from 1921 onwards.

Young Hirohito had a solitary
boyhood, plenty of toys but no real
family life.

General Maresuke Nogi, the head of
the Peers' School and a war hero,
became Hirohito's foster-father.

In 1921, Crown Prince Hirohito visited Britain and was charmed by King George V.

He also met Lloyd George.

After his European trip, Hirohito became fond of Western dress and customs.

Empress Sadako and her three sons: *from left to right*, Hirohito, Chichibu and Takamatsu.

Emperor Hirohito and Empress Nagako during the 1928 enthronement ceremony.

Hirohito's family included Akihito (extreme left) and Prince Yoshi (on the Empress's knee). His other children were girls.

In 1935, Hirohito welcomed Pu Yi, 'the Last Emperor', on a state visit.

A year later, two regiments mutinied 'in the Emperor's name' to make Hirohito head of a military regime. He brutally suppressed the uprising.

Prince Asaka, Hirohito's uncle, seen here in China, commanded Japanese troops in Nanking in 1937.

So did another uncle, Prince Higashikuni, who would become Japan's first post-war Prime Minister.

Prince Saïonji, elder statesman and Hirohito adviser, vainly tried to check Japan's expansionism.

Hirohito, fascinated by high-tech inventions, visited these giant sound-detectors designed to forestall enemy air raids.

The *Tatuta Maru*.

December 7, 1941: Pearl Harbor.

Kamikaze plane.

March 1945: Hirohito walks through the ruins of Tokyo.

In this Imperial Palace bunker, Hirohito met his officers and decided to end the war.

Hirohito's first meeting with General Douglas MacArthur at the United States Embassy in Tokyo on September 27, 1945.

Hideki Tojo, wartime Prime Minister (fifth from left) was among the twenty-seven prominent leaders accused of war crimes.

After the war, a civilian Emperor greets a still deferential crowd.

There were six loyal victims: Prince Konoye (1), General Honjo (2) and
General Sugiyama (3) committed suicide; Admiral Yamamoto (4) was shot down.

5

6

Marquis Kido (5) was sentenced to life imprisonment; Tojo (6) was hanged.
General Nakajima (7) and the equally infamous General Ishii (8) were never tried.

7

8

Hirohito and thirteen-year-old Prince Akihito reading the US Army newspaper in 1946.

On his state visit to London in 1971.

The Imperial Family in 1981.

A stroll in the summer residence garden.

The new Emperor and Empress.

that went out by secret code to Japan's diplomats abroad gave an unvarnished version of events. "The Imperial Government," read the cable sent to the Japanese Consul-General in Tokyo on July 16, 1941,

has decided the Imperial Forces are to invade the southern portion of French Indochina with a view to securing military bases. As far as the Imperial Government is concerned, it makes no difference whether this invasion is carried out peacefully or in force.

Because of the possibility of French armed opposition to the "invasion", and to forestall reprisals, the telegram to Hanoi ordered all Japanese nationals to be evacuated to Taiwan and, in order to give them time to embark, a specially-freighted passenger ship was to remain in Haiphong harbour – "so please give out the reason that [its slowness in departing] is due to loading and unloading delays. Please take every precaution not to allow the French authorities to learn of our plans".

The extraordinary veneration shown by his subjects to Hirohito was also illustrated in the cable: a special emissary was to "respectfully carry out the Imperial Portraits and request that on arrival [in Taiwan] they be placed in the custody of the Provincial Office".

Other ambassadors received slightly different versions: to Oshima, in Berlin, the announcement contained a rider pointing out that *this plan is the first step in Japan's southward advance which Germany has been looking forward to for a long time*,* and the cable to Japan's Minister to Vichy France added, ominously, that he should point out that "if the French refuse [the occupation], this will have a bad effect not only on Tokyo-Vichy relations but on Berlin-French relations as well", in other words that Japan would see to it that Hitler cracked the whip in both occupied and unoccupied France if Pétain's government continued to prevaricate.

In the face of such a ruthless exercise of power, Vichy France

* Author's italics.

capitulated. Minor face-saving measures were included in the Franco-Japanese agreement which allowed Japan large numbers of Army, Navy and air bases throughout Indochina, including the fiction that Japan would continue to "respect French sovereignty and the territorial integrity" of French Indochina. On July 21, 1941, Admiral Jean Darlan, Vichy France's Vice-Premier and Foreign Minister, acknowledged that his Government had "no choice but to yield" to Japanese demands and agreed to "cooperate with Japan in the defence of French Indochina".

From Hirohito's exchanges with his Chiefs of Staff, it is clear he knew perfectly well that the Japanese bases in Indochina would be used, not against Chiang Kai-chek, but for another purpose altogether. The IMTFE prosecutors did not know of the existence of the Sugiyama Memorandum, but Colonel Sackett, Kido's interrogator, showed he was well aware of the nature of the Emperor's role in the events leading up to Pearl Harbor. On February 26, 1946, the following exchange took place in Sugamo prison:

SACKETT: The Emperor knew [in July 1941] that the country, through its foreign policy, had become pretty much committed to an expansion into the South, whether by the force of arms or not, and he thought it was an inopportune time to start fighting a war in the North, against the USSR, when you were trying to obtain materials in the South?

KIDO: Yes.

SACKETT: It is a condition precedent to the dispatching of troops to a place like Indochina that the consent of the Emperor must first be obtained?

KIDO: Yes.

SACKETT: In other words, the supreme command would not have despatched troops to French Indochina without first appearing before the Emperor and obtaining his consent?

KIDO: No.

The Japanese planes that sank Britain's warships, the *Repulse* and the *Prince of Wales*, off the Malayan coast shortly after Pearl Harbor came from bases in southern French Indochina.

[1] Richard Storry, *A History of Modern Japan*, Pelican, 1961.
[2] Kyoshi Inouye, *The Emperor's Responsibilities*, Gendai Hyoronsha, Tokyo, 1975.
[3] Herbert Feis, *The Road to Pearl Harbor*, Princeton University Press, 1950.

CHAPTER FOURTEEN

While Japan was busy planning her network of military bases abroad for an eventual "strike South", at home patriotic frenzy reached fever pitch with a growing, officially-sponsored "Emperor cult" of awe-inspiring proportions.

The 2,600th anniversary of the start of the reign of Jimmu, the mythological first Emperor, celebrated with huge pomp and circumstance in 1940 with naval reviews and religious ceremonies, was followed, a year later, by even more spectacular festivities reminding the *New York Times* correspondent Otto Tolischus (who arrived in Tokyo in January 1941 after his expulsion from Berlin) of the many Nazi rallies he had so recently attended. The 2,601st anniversary of the founding of the Japanese Empire was marked by more religious ceremonies, and a parade of over 120,000 factory workers, schoolchildren, "representatives of national organizations" and members of the Industrial National Service Federation, with flags and brass bands, all marching hour after hour past their Emperor, who tirelessly returned their salutes.

The main speaker was Baron Hiranuma, the Japanese Home Minister, former President of the Privy Council and Premier. What made Japan a uniquely superior country, he told the massed crowds, was that "foreign kings, emperors, presidents are all created by man, but Japan has a sacred throne inherited from the Imperial ancestors. Japan's Imperial Rule is therefore an extension of heaven. Man-made dynasties collapse, but the Heaven-created Throne is beyond the power of mere mortals . . ."

Ambassador Grew noted that, according to custom, no Japanese were allowed to "look down" on the Emperor: the rooftops facing the palace in the Marinouchi district remained bare. Tolischus remarked that while, in private, foreign residents irreverently referred to Hirohito as "Charlie", Japanese newspapers constantly harped on the Emperor's divinity, and Japan's totalitarianism so closely resembled the Nazi programme "that I was intrigued to find out who had learnt from whom".

A few years later, there would be a concerted effort by both Japanese and US Occupation authorities to minimize the Emperor's pre-war role, but in April 1941 the Japanese Imperial image-builders were determined to prove the opposite: at a conference of senior provincial officials just before the Emperor's birthday, the Imperial Household Minister told them that "the press of war affairs" on the Imperial time was such that Hirohito had had to abandon his early-morning rides, and that he was "constantly giving decisions on various state papers concerned with politics and military strategy . . . He rises very early and retires very late, receiving reports as late as midnight." It was "beyond the average person's imagination", too, "how deeply the Empress is concerned about the war dead and wounded [the casualties of the 'China Incident'] . . ."

On the Emperor's 40th birthday – April 29 – the *Japan Times and Advertiser*, an English-language paper faithfully reflecting the views of the Foreign Ministry, ran an important editorial on the "new world order" as seen from Tokyo.

This curious document, establishing a rigid hierarchy of "strong" powers, with Germany (and Italy as her junior partner) heading the list in Europe, and Japan in Asia, undoubtedly mirrored the views of Prince Konoye at his nationalistic worst and of the Foreign Minister Matsuoka, who had just returned from a triumphal tour of Berlin and Rome – though he had also been embraced by Stalin after the signing of a neutrality pact with the USSR.

The British Empire, the United States and the Soviet Union were afforded a mention in the proposed "new order", which by and large could have been drawn up by Hitler himself: it

called for the demilitarization of Gibraltar, the eastern Mediterranean, Malta, Aden, the Red Sea, Singapore, Hongkong "and
all United States Pacific bases", the total withdrawal of the
Royal Navy from the Mediterranean, joint British-Axis control
of the Suez Canal, joint German-Italian control of certain
British African colonies and of North Africa "from Gibraltar to
Somaliland", with continental Europe "organized as one state
under the German Reich".

The editorial also demanded German participation in the
Iranian and Iraqi oil industries, the opening up of the Dutch
East Indies to "Japanese advisers", the demilitarization of
Siberia, access to Australia for Japanese immigrants, Indian self-
government and "religious and political liberty for all". Perhaps
the most important aspect was the arbitrary division of the world
into "zones of influence", with Japan the uncontested leader of
Asia. The United States' "sphere of influence" was recognized
over Canada, Central and South America, Newfoundland and
Greenland – provided there were "no US hegemony in Latin
American inamicable to the Axis powers", and no US bases
west of Hawaii.

Wildly hysterical articles, fanning the flames of Japanese
nationalism, were common enough in 1941 – but the *Japan
Times and Advertiser* was no fly-by-night rag but a respectable,
well-produced paper, in lay-out and typography astonishingly
similar to the *New York Times*, and the timing of the editorial –
to coincide with the Emperor's birthday – was deliberate.

For, that same afternoon, as if to underline the importance of
the policy statement, and give it special relevance, the biggest
military parade ever staged in Japan took place: Hirohito,
astride his favourite white charger, Shiranyuki, reviewed a
march-past of 30,000 troops and a hundred tanks, and a fly-past of
five hundred planes. A month later, on "Navy Day" (May 27),
an equally impressive display of force took place, and Japanese
spokesmen took this opportunity to announce that Japan had
500 warships and 4,000 Navy planes in combat readiness – more
than the United States could muster. On June 18, in a deliberate

snub to the Allied countries supporting Chiang Kai-chek, Hirohito attended a state banquet for the China "quisling", Wang Ching-wei, a former KMT leader whose Japan-supported puppet "Nanking Government" included most of coastal central China – a privilege never granted to the "puppet" Manchukuo Emperor Pu Yi, who in 1935 had had to be content with a banquet at which the Prime Minister was host.

Three months after the *Japan Times and Advertiser* editorial, another "philosophical" exposé of Japan's beliefs, goals and policies, of much wider import, was made compulsory reading in Japan. This was *The Way of the Subjects*, which made considerable use of Hirohito's own rescripts or Imperial proclamations, and was distributed throughout the country to schools, adult groups and associations of all kinds, including, of course, the "Imperial Rule Assistance Association" (IRAA). This had been established in 1940 with Konoye's initial blessing, was in the process of replacing political parties and was organized along compulsory, totalitarian lines in offices and factories, with "street committees" monitoring the behaviour of adherents.

The Way of the Subjects deserves close study, if only because it said out loud what Japan's leaders were reluctant to tell foreign diplomats to their faces. It is also important as a statement of totalitarian aims through the use of Hirohito's own proclamations, and as a general re-interpretation of Japan's history along militaristic lines, a posthumous vindication of the ideals of the dead "2/26" rebels. Significantly, this was no polemical pamphlet put out by hotheads in the IRAA, but an official document written by Government officials and distributed by the Education Ministry.

It began with a withering condemnation of European and American culture, and its debilitating ways. "Individualism, liberalism, utilitarianism and materialism" were the evils that had been brought to Japan. Countries outside Europe, "in their sound sleep", had allowed this to happen, but "now the old order is crumbling", and the Western world's economic and political domination was on the wane.

The Manchurian affair had been "a violent outburst of Japanese national life long suppressed", and Japanese intervention had occurred because China "had started to trample over Japan's position in Manchuria, resulting in heavy sacrifices in Japanese lives, menacing Japan's lifeline". With the "Mukden Incident", "world history began its new pages", for "Manchukuo has the Kingly way, as a land of bliss and racial concord ... and has marked a quick and sound growth year by year, thereby consolidating the foundations of the structure of Japan-Manchukuo oneness". Quoting extensively from Hirohito's rescript at the time of Japan's withdrawal from the League of Nations, *The Way of the Subjects* maintained that Europe and America "felt greatly menaced" by the founding of Manchukuo and had tried to sabotage it through the "so-called Lytton report".

The Naval Arms Limitation Talks were a further example of evil foreign intervention, "designed to hamper the advance of Japan as the stabilizing factor in East Asia". As for China, whose "wholehearted rapprochement and co-ordination are sorely needed for the construction of a new order over the whole of Asia", *The Way of the Subjects* again quoted the Imperial rescript on the first anniversary of the "China Incident" ("We believe that unless the evil causes existing for many years are eradicated, the stabilization of East Asia cannot ever be hoped for ... The solidification of a Sino-Japanese coalition and realization of their co-prosperity will contribute to the establishment of world peace") as well as the rescript celebrating the Tripartite Treaty: "Japan's mission of world historical significance," it said, was embodied in that text.

But the China affair "would not and should not end with the mere downfall of Chiang Kai-chek. Until the elimination of the evils of European and United States influences in East Asia that have led China astray is realized, until Japan's co-operation with China yields satisfactory results, and East Asia and the rest of the world are united as one on the basis of moral principles, Japan's indefatigable efforts are sorely needed", for Japan "has a political mission to help various regions in the East Asian co-prosperity scheme so as to rescue them from the control of the colonial powers". Culturally, too, Japan had a mission to "fashion East Asian nations into changing their following of European and American culture and to develop oriental culture to contribute to the creation of a just world".

Japan's concrete objective was now "the perfecting of a highly geared and centralized defence state and the strengthening of a total national war framework". Embodied in *The Way of the Subjects* was the concept of total war: "military action now means diplomatic and economic thought and scientific warfare blended into one harmonious whole". There was a divine precedent, for "Japan's mission of constructing the world on a moral basis originated in the empire-founding itself". The fundamental character of Japan, the document concluded, "is based on this theocracy: the Emperor rules and reigns his state with a solemn mind of serving the Gods. The Emperor loves his subjects with a paternal heart, and the subjects love the Emperor with a spirit as of bowing to their great father. There is no country of this sort in any other part of the world . . . Japan's fountain source is the Yamato [Japanese] race, Manchukuo its reservoir, East Asia its paddyfield."

With growing restrictions and shortages, and industry on a centrally planned basis, Tolischus's first impressions were that Tokyo "was already at war" when he first arrived in Japan. Reporting restrictions were phenomenal: the military Secrets Protection and the National Defence Secrets Acts meant that "nearly everything a correspondent did was a crime".[1] This was compounded by restrictions on cable languages (limited to Japanese, English and German), on international telephone calls (limited to Japanese and English) and ("this really screws things up") on domestic telephone calls, which could only be made in Japanese, so that the police could listen in. For all that, as Tolischus noted, war and raw materials required by the China War amounted to only 10 per cent of Japan's productive capacity, and the "guns before butter" economy seemed to be working.

Japan was clearly on the brink of war, and the *Japan Times and Advertiser*, for all its reassuring social reporting, read at times like an English-language version of a Nazi daily paper, full of news items about the war in Europe written from a strictly Axis point of view and, in its American coverage, giving huge prominence to the isolationist lobby and to its one American hero, Charles Lindbergh. On April 26, 1941, a front-page picture of the devastated City of London illustrated a story carrying the headline: "British capital feels the full force of German strength."

In such circumstances, negotiations to reduce tension between the United States and Japan must have seemed futile, but were taken seriously by both sides: in Washington, Roosevelt was guided by Grew's belief that it was best to continue talks in the hope that saner councils would eventually prevail, for was not the Emperor a man of peace? The truth is that both sides were playing for time: the United States and Japan wanted to wait and see how the war in Europe would go, especially after Hitler's attack on the Soviet Union on June 22, 1941.

It is necessary to take a brief step backwards, at this juncture, to analyse a vitally important Imperial Conference, or "Gozen Kaigi", that took place on July 2, a few days after Hirohito's detailed cross-examination of his Chiefs of Staff (June 25) and shortly before the Japanese occupation of Saigon, Camranh Bay and Tourane (Danang). This meeting, a turning point in Hirohito's attitude towards the coming war, showed that the thinking behind *The Way of the Subjects* (then being drafted inside the Education Ministry) was no mere propaganda exercise.

The decisions of a "Gozen Kaigi", which took place in the presence of the Emperor, key Cabinet Ministers (Prime, War, Navy, Foreign Affairs), the President of the Privy Council, and the two Chiefs of Staff, were sacred and inviolable. Because of its vital importance, and because a remarkably concise summary of its resolutions exists, it is worth quoting them in full:

Policy Outline

1: The Imperial Government is determined to follow a policy which will result in the establishment of the Greater East Asia Co-Prosperity Sphere and world peace, no matter what international developments take place.

2: The Imperial Government will continue its efforts to effect a settlement of the China Incident and seek to establish a solid basis for the security and preservation of the nation. This will involve an advance into Southern regions . . . and, depending on future developments, a settlement of the Soviet Question as well.

3: The Imperial Government will carry out all the above programme no matter what obstacles may be encountered.

Implementation

1: Steps will be taken to bring pressure on the Chiang régime from the Southern approaches in order to bring about its surrender. Whenever demanded by future developments the rights of a belligerent will be resorted to against Chungking* and hostile concessions taken over.

2: In order to guarantee national security and preservation, the Imperial Government will continue all necessary diplomatic negotiations with reference to the Southern regions and also carry out various other plans as may be necessary. In case the diplomatic negotiations break down, *preparations for a war with England and America will also be carried forward.*† First of all, the plans which have been laid with reference to French Indochina and Thai will be prosecuted, with a view to consolidating our position in the southern territories.

In carrying out the plans outlined in the foregoing article, we will not be deterred by the possibility of being involved in a war with England and America.

* Chiang Kai-chek's HQ and the capital of non-occupied China.
† Author's italics throughout.

3: Our attitude with reference to the German-Soviet war will be based on the spirit of the Tripartite Alliance. However, we will not enter the conflict for some time but will steadily proceed with military preparations against the Soviet and decide our final attitude independently. At the same time, we will continue carefully correlated activities in the diplomatic field. In case the German-Soviet war should develop to our advantage, we will make use of our military strength, settle the Soviet question and guarantee the safety of our Northern borders.

4: *In carrying out the preceding article all plans, especially the use of armed forces, will be carried out in such a way as to place no serious obstacles in the path of our basic military preparations for a war with England and America.*

5: In case all diplomatic means fail to prevent the entrance of America into the European war, we will proceed in harmony with our obligations under the Tripartite Pact. However, with reference to the time and method of employing our armed forces, we will take independent action.

6: We will immediately turn our attention to placing the nation on a war basis and will take special measures to strengthen the defence of the nation.

7: Concrete plans covering this programme will be drawn up separately.

"The Emperor," Sugiyama wrote afterwards, "very satisfied, gave his assent to all this at 13.30 immediately after lunch."

Hirohito had several reasons to be pleased: in his report on the state of the war in Europe, Sugiyama told the Emperor that it was clear that Germany was winning, and, consequently, it was virtually certain that the United States would not intervene, and risk war with both Japan and a victorious Germany, by trying to prevent even the forcible establishment of Japanese bases throughout Indochina. Another reason for relief was that the War Minister, Tojo, who had a reputation for speaking his mind and never concealing awkward facts from the Emperor, stated at the "Gozen Kaigi" that the level of discipline among the officers was satisfactory and that the possibility of a young officers' revolt was nil. Finally, the "Gozen Kaigi" – by rejecting Matsuoka's demand for an immediate attack on the Soviet Union – put him in an impossible position: Hirohito now knew the unpredictable and increasingly embarrassing Foreign Minister would soon be dismissed by Konoye if he did not resign of his own accord.

But the Emperor clearly had second thoughts about the meeting, and summoned the Chiefs of Staff to the Palace for more informal talks on July 22. Hirohito wanted to hear more about the chances of successful diplomatic negotiations with the United States – and the attitudes of the Chiefs of Staff towards such negotiations; he also wanted formal assurances from both Chiefs of Staff that – if war did break out – it would quickly lead to a decisive Japanese victory. What they had to tell him was scarcely reassuring.

In the morning session, General Sugiyama explained that the outbreak of the Second World War had completely altered Japan's strategic plans. "Before [the outbreak of war in Europe] we could only think about the 'China Incident'. After the start of the war and Hitler's attack on Russia, the situation moved towards total world war." Chiang Kai-chek's forces were on the defensive, weak and demoralized, only sustained by United States, British and Soviet aid. For this reason, "the only way of solving the 'China Incident'," he said, "is to defeat Britain and the United States."

In the afternoon, the Emperor asked both men several probing questions. In the light of what they had said in the morning, was armed force the only way? Since they had painted such a bleak picture of the armed forces in China, "can we realize our purpose by using force?"

Sugiyama's reply, taken up by the Navy Chief of Staff, Nagano, was that the Emperor was quite right to make this point, but that "if we let things slide further, Japan will not only be unable to solve the 'China Incident' but will get into other difficulties as well – so we have to take action at the right moment".

Hirohito objected that "you say you don't have enough equipment". Sugiyama said he could not speak for the Navy, "but the Army can manage for about a year".

"You say so," said Hirohito, "but is a year enough to win?"

Sugiyama replied that he could not guarantee a year would be enough, "but we have to grab the right moment and take measures to expand [the war]. For example, we should carefully watch the Russo-German fighting and pick the right moment and stabilize our Northern border. It is necessary to decide whether we move North or South. For both the Army and the Navy, the more time we waste the more difficult it will be."

"I wonder if you're right," said Hirohito. "Is there any way to avoid using force? If things are carried out as planned in Indochina, that's fine. However, I've heard that Britain has put some of its troops in Thailand."

Not so, said Sugiyama, who went on to brief Hirohito on British dispositions in Asia: 30,000 men in Burma and between 40,000 and 50,000 in Malaya, "but only a quarter of these are British, the rest are locals or natives, mostly dissatisfied with British oppressive rule . . . They cannot move aggressively,' he said, adding that Japanese military attachés in the area "had submitted the same opinion". "However financially or economically dominant [Britain might be] suppressing Britain will be the right judgement." In case British troops entered Thailand, "we will make the right judgement on how to cope with that and will seek your approval". Hirohito, still worried about the consequences of the Indochina move, said: "You won't have to use force in French Indochina, will you?" Again, he was reassured that the French would not give Japan any trouble. In a note which Sugiyama insisted should remain top secret, he added that the Emperor "seems determined not to use force" and "we must make him change his mind". Hirohito must also, Sugiyama added, make his final decision: did he want to go for a "Strike North" (war with the Soviet Union on Germany's side) or a "Strike South"?

On July 30, Hirohito had further talks with his Chiefs of Staff, and again felt profoundly uneasy at what his Naval Chief of Staff told him. According to the Kido Diaries, Hirohito, almost thinking aloud, told Admiral Nagano: "Of course we will be victorious against the United States and Great Britain, but it will surely not be the kind of total victory we scored against Russia in 1905, will it?"

Nagano replied that such a total victory was indeed out of the question. "Indeed, we're not even sure of winning."

This unexpected reply filled Hirohito with gloom.

Talking to Kido about this meeting afterwards, Hirohito said that, while he was not "in principle" against the option of war with the United States and Britain, "one shouldn't make war without foreseeing victory" for this would mean embarking on a "war of desperation".

But the count-down had, in effect, already started: Admiral Yamamoto had handed over his blueprint of Pacific operations (including a rough draft of the Pearl Harbor attack) to the Naval Chief of Staff, and a mock-up of Pearl Harbor was under construction in the Naval Staff College (where Prince Taka-matsu, in and out of the building in 1941, must almost certainly have seen it).

The War Minister, Tojo, upright as always, reassured the Emperor about the state of morale of the armed forces, but he had not been completely frank: the officers were getting restive, demanding the implementation of the measures submitted to the Emperor at the July 2 Imperial Conference without further delay, the speedy occupation of Indochina, and an assurance that the continuing negotiations with the United States should "main-tain the orientation already decided on, and not go against the spirit of the Axis powers".

In effect, Hirohito's position at this stage was ambiguous: he was now thoroughly apprehensive about the option of war with the United States, not on moral grounds, but because his Chiefs of Staff had informed him that the odds were longer than he had at first been led to expect; at the same time, he was reluctant either to scale down the "Strike South" plans, or to make any real concessions to the United States on China.

In retrospect, one's impression of Hirohito during these months is of a sovereign trapped into an irrevocable course of action through a series of intermediate measures none of which can be annulled, unwilling to accept the consequences of his past decisions, unable to put his war machine into reverse, or to lose face by accepting a compromise solution on China. The United States' response to the occupation of Southern Indochina – the total embargo on oil sales to Japan and the freezing of her assets in the United States from July 29 onwards – only reinforced the arguments of Nagano and Sugiyama that there was no time to lose, and that the sooner Japan waged war the better.

Colonel Sackett, in his cross-examination of Kido, in 1946, was to show an almost intuitive understanding of the Emperor's dilemmas – and Kido's answers, for once, were less than bland.

SACKETT: Isn't it true that the Emperor wasn't so much opposed to Japan acquiring bases in French Indochina as he was fearful of the trouble it might cause in the negotiations with the United States?

KIDO: Yes, that was the prime concern.

SACKETT: So we can say that the Emperor wasn't really opposed to the expansion of Japan in the South if it could be accomplished without incurring the illwill and bad feelings of nations like Britain and the United States?

KIDO: Because the military said they would conclude the Chinese Incident and the Emperor naturally wanted this to happen as quickly as possible, he was in a difficult position.

SACKETT: In fact, there wasn't anyone in high office opposed to the expansion of Japanese influence into the South if it could be done without bringing war with the United States and Britain? Is that correct?

KIDO: Yes.

SACKETT: But when it was decided at the Imperial Conference that Japan would not tolerate interference on the part of the United States, it was then known that the United States might well resent the sending of troops to French Indochina and in spite of that fact, it was decided as the foreign policy that Japan would fight the United States, if necessary, to maintain her programme of landing the troops?

KIDO: Yes.

SACKETT: On July 26, you make some references to air raid defences in the Palace grounds. Why was it that the Palace grounds were being armed for the defence of air raids? Who was it that Japan feared might attack the Palace grounds by air?

KIDO: With the negotiations between Japan and America becoming critical, the construction of air raid shelters was discussed with the Emperor.

SACKETT: In other words, that was just one of the plans that Japan started to make in anticipation of a possible clash with the United States, is that right?

KIDO: Yes.

Later, Sackett was to return to the informal July 28 meeting.

SACKETT: Was the Emperor disappointed in the point of view that Nagano took when he said that the Navy couldn't win a war with the United States and really desired him to express more enthusiasm for really being able to win the war?

KIDO: The Emperor upon hearing the report of the Chief of Staff said that more consideration must be given to this problem. We must not try to overdo [sic].

SACKETT: Who did the Emperor side with? The navy group as a whole or with Nagano? Whom did he believe or whom was he inclined to believe?

KIDO: The Emperor in the first place did not want war with the United States. He had to have more assurance of victory before he was willing to place the nation into war.

SACKETT: The Emperor was very much concerned about the fact that the Navy said they could win the war while the Chief of Staff himself said they couldn't. Isn't that correct?

KIDO: Since the positive success of the plan presented by Nagano was so dubious, the Emperor was greatly worried.

SACKETT: In other words, the Emperor wanted the Navy to take a stand one way or another. He didn't want two views as to whether they could win or not?

KIDO: The fact that Nagano presented the plan of which the outcome was victory and professed dubious doubts in his mind regarding that victory, the Emperor was very perplexed.

Sackett left this line of questioning for a moment and turned to another item in Kido's diaries.

SACKETT: The Emperor requested you make some investigation as to the amounts of rubber and tin the United States had and sources of supply in Latin America. Why did he want to know this?

KIDO: I believe it was as a result of a newspaper article.

SACKETT: Why? Wasn't it from the standpoint of whether or not Japan was capable of fighting a war with the United States successfully?

KIDO: I don't believe he had such a deep interest as that, because the Emperor is quite a scientist, he has made such requests on a great number of previous occasions.

SACKETT: The Emperor was trying to get this information in order to make up his mind as to whether Japan could fight the war with the United States, was he not?

KIDO: Perhaps his thought may have some relation to that respect, correlated to the situation.

As both Kido and the Sugiyama memorandum show, Hirohito may have tiptoed into war but he clearly knew what was about to happen. He had detailed blueprints of the "Strike South" Order of Battle in his possession for several months before Pearl Harbor, and his questions to his Chiefs of Staff showed he was fully aware of all operational details. At every stage of its preparation, he was actively concerned with points of detail, and there would be further sessions of question and answer in September and October, up to the final count-down. For all Hirohito's reservations, the July 2 "Gozen Kaigi" text was not rewritten – though it would later become more explicit.

The most surprising aspect of Hirohito's continuing debate with his Chiefs of Staff is its cold, dispassionate tone. There are no moral qualms, no mental reservations about casualties and the potential sufferings and sacrifices of the Japanese people.

Nor does there seem to have been any awareness of the monstrous size of the Japanese challenge – or of its inevitable consequences: clearly, Hirohito believed that a brief, successful "blitzkrieg" could lead to early negotiations, with Japan retaining at least part of her gains, preserving her ill-gotten hegemony over Asia, with no thought of the enemy's own "face". As members of a US Bombing Evaluation Committee were to note with amazement after the war, nobody, in 1941, seemed to have had any clear idea of how it would all end, or seemed to care. And Hirohito's own brief recommendations – that the Vatican should be cultivated as a mediator, that Hitler and Churchill, and Hitler and Stalin, should be prevented, at all costs, from making separate peace with each other – reveal an abysmal ignorance, or Imperial indifference, about the way of the world outside Japan. Hirohito simply could not grasp that, having provoked a war, he would not be able to end it at will.

Nor can it be said that he remained unwarned: for all his deference, Kido could speak his mind to the Emperor, and he, perhaps alone among the Imperial advisers, was intuitively aware of the dangers ahead. On the very eve of Pearl Harbor, he noted in his diaries that he intended to tell the Emperor that:

Once the final decision is made, it will be truly the last and irrevocably final one. Thus if there should be any doubt in Your Majesty's mind I pray that Your Majesty should be pleased to elucidate the same without the least reserve and take appropriate steps which Your Majesty might not repent of afterwards . . .

and, after seeing him, he noted (November 30, 1941), that:

. . . His Majesty's decision is of such gravity that, once decided, it would not later be retracted. Hence it is felt [by me] that if there is the least uncertainty, every possible precaution should be taken to do that to which His Majesty can give assent.

But Hirohito's mind, by August 1941, was made up: as the events leading to the final count-down show, the cautious Emperor was to show, not for the first time, a considerable capacity for ruthlessness and guile.

[1] Otto D. Tolischus, *Tokyo Record*, Reynal and Hitchcock, New York, 1943.

CHAPTER FIFTEEN

With Emperor Hirohito's approval, Japanese troops and naval air squadrons started moving into their new Southern Indochina bases by ship from Hainan island on July 29, 1941. By August 1, both the United States and Britain had retaliated by freezing Japanese assets, declaring an oil embargo and virtually cutting off all trade to Japan. Konoye, who had not expected such a response, was furious, blaming the military for providing him with inaccurate information about America's reactions. The new restrictions encouraged the more *engagé* Japanese die-hards to step up their cry of "encirclement", and to use the total oil embargo as an additional argument for immediate war. Even so, diplomatic negotiations between Japan and the United States did not come to an abrupt end, lingering on for another four months. In retrospect, it is clear they continued because, at this stage, both countries were still eyeing each other warily, not yet ready for the final, irrevocable, head-on clash.

There were several unusual aspects to these negotiations. The new Japanese Ambassador to Washington, Admiral Kishisaburo Nomura, was inexperienced, and had only reluctantly accepted what he knew would be a thankless task. The talks began as "private" contacts among non-governmental groups, and this state of affairs virtually guaranteed that there would be, at some stage, charges on both sides of duplicity and bad faith. Finally, there was the immense advantage of "Magic": during this whole period, both Roosevelt and his Secretary of State (but only a handful of other senior decision-makers in the Administration) were extraordinarily well-briefed about Japan's real, as opposed to her publicly proclaimed, intentions, because the

United States had broken Japan's top-secret code, and was able to decipher her most confidential cables to her representatives abroad.

The implications of "Magic", as the code-breaking operation was known, were vast, and would later have a huge impact on the course of the war. In the immediate, pre-Pearl Harbor months, "Magic" allowed United States negotiators to contrast Japan's true intentions with her declarations specially concocted for American consumption. In any negotiation, knowledge of one's opponent's reserve position is of the greatest value. Because of "Magic", Americans not only had this capability, but were also fully aware that, while Japan was talking resasuringly about peace, she was actively preparing for war on the basis of the July 2 "Gozen Kaigi".

Some historians, and a handful of diplomats, have argued that it was the strength of the Washington-based "China Lobby" that accounted for United States "intransigence" and the final deadlock between Japan and the US. Sir Robert Craigie, British Ambassador in Tokyo from 1937 to December 1941, would later accuse the Americans of ineptitude, and claim that a modus vivendi might well have been worked out had the talks been allowed to continue. But, if the American attitude was firm, this was less due to Washington's "China Lobby", powerful though it may have been, than to knowledge provided by the "Magic" intercepts: on an almost daily basis, the handful of American policy-makers dealing with Japan at the highest level were confronted with the huge gulf between professed Japanese intentions and the stark implications of Japan's unswerving dedication to a "New Order" within the "Greater East Asia Co-prosperity Scheme", and her readiness to use force to bring it about. By early August 1941, for instance, the US Secretary of State, Cordell Hull, had the gist of the decisions taken at the July 2 "Gozen Kaigi". "Magic" also allowed Americans to know what really lay behind the establishment of Japanese military bases in southern Indochina – for the cables from Japan's Foreign Ministry to her embassies abroad, whether in Berlin or Vichy France, had also been decrypted.

There was, however, some basis to Japanese charges of American bad faith – though this was mostly due to the behaviour of Nomura, a bluff, somewhat pompous man more at ease with American naval officers than with diplomats, who spoke little English, and found it extremely difficult to deal with his Foreign Minister. He was not alone in this respect. One of Matsuoka's odder characteristics was his highly idiosyncratic, and highly un-Japanese, tendency to ramble on, at interminable length, about anything that came into his head. He alternated between moods of elation and anger, professing feelings of deep friendship for Americans one day, regarding them as hateful enemies the next. Even the long-suffering Grew was non-plussed when Matsuoka, after his return from his 1941 visit to Hitler, Mussolini and Stalin, started ranting at him that the "manly, decent and reasonable" thing for the United States to do would be to declare war on Germany "since America's attitude to Germany is so provocative", and Hitler "so very patient and generous". "On my taking exception to the Minister's remarks," Grew wrote in his diary, "he withdraws the implication that the United States is guilty of 'unmanly, indecent and unreasonable conduct', and later writes me that owing to his inadequate knowledge of English he inadvertently used the word 'indecent' whereas he meant 'discreet'." Later, in a personal letter to Grew, Matsuoka said that he was speaking not as Foreign Minister but as one "indulging in thought in terms of one thousand or two or even three thousand years, and if this strikes you as a sign of insanity, I cannot help it as I am made that way." Shortly afterwards, Matsuoka complained to Grew that he should never have reported his "highly personal" remarks to Washington in the first place.

In another age, Matsuoka's violent changes of mood could be attributable to drugs. As it was, his unpredictability led to charges, among those close to him, that he was mentally unstable, an additional "wild card" in an already highly complicated, indeed explosive situation. Grew himself recognized Matsuoka's intermittent capacity for charm, when he was in a good mood, and Matsuoka himself could be inexhaustibly eloquent about his early years as a poor schoolboy in Washington State, the kindness of a little old American lady who had raised him as her son in Seattle, and how, in 1933, he had had a monument erected on her grave. But the last characteristic to look for in Matsuoka, professional diplomats knew, was any element of consistency.

Strangers, however, were more easily taken in, as they often are in casual encounters with the mentally unbalanced, and among those charmed by Matsuoka were two American clergymen, Bishop James E. Walsh and Father James M. Drought, both of the Catholic Foreign Mission Society of America in Maryknoll, who returned from a trip to Japan in March 1941 determined to bring about a better relationship between the United States and Japan. They approached a prominent Catholic, Roosevelt's Postmaster-General, Frank C. Walker, suggesting an attempt at "parallel diplomacy" with selected Japanese contacts – and Roosevelt gave his grudging, distracted approval.

The delighted American priests got in touch with their Japanese contacts, among them a banker friend of Konoye's, Tadao Ikawa, and an army colonel close to Tojo, but professing strong personal feelings of friendship towards America, Hideo Iwakuro. With the Postmaster-General's blessing (and funds) they rented room 1802 in Manhattan's Berkshire Hotel as a discreet office.

Shortly afterwards, on April 19, this odd group submitted to Cordell Hull its "Proposal Presented to the Department of State Through the Medium of Private American and Japanese Individuals". Whether Roosevelt and Hull between them saw this merely as an exercise to test the depths of Japanese duplicity, or whether they took it seriously, will probably never be known. Both men were sufficiently experienced, and wily, to "play it straight". What is beyond doubt is that Colonel Iwakuro's credentials were, to say the least, mixed, since he was also one of the founders of the famous "Nakano Spy School", an Army establishment that selected highly motivated officers and NCOs for training not just in intelligence and espionage but in "special forces" and survival techniques as well. Iwakuro made several trips to the US, ostensibly on "draft understanding" business, but this could also have been ideal cover for his intelligence activities.

Though the text of that initial draft was on the whole quite unacceptable to Hull, it did contain two "positive" clauses: one was the assertion that Japan would only take peaceful measures in the Pacific, the other the promise that Japan would not enter the war on Germany's side unless she succumbed to an "aggressive attack" from the US. Other than these points, the draft proposal was a series of familiar Japanese requests: in return for the two somewhat vague pledges, Japan demanded an end to all trade restrictions, US help in making Chiang Kai-chek agree to peace on Japanese terms, and a cessation of US aid to China if he refused either to recognize Manchukuo or to amalgamate his own Chungking government with that of the Nanking government puppet Wang Ching-wei. Finally, the United States was to give Japan assistance "for the removal of Hongkong and Singapore as doorways to further political encroachment by Britain on the Far East".

Cordell Hull promptly rewrote the "draft understanding" and asked Nomura whether Japan was prepared to present this amended text as an official Japanese "first draft" which could be the foundation for substantive talks. Nomura understood him to mean that the United States regarded this text as an acceptable basis for negotiations – a completely false assessment of the US position.

To make matters worse, Cordell Hull then submitted four points to Japan as "paramount preliminaries" which, he said, Japan had to agree to before any such talks could take place. These "points of principle" begged the question: they ensured that, if accepted, no further negotiations would be needed, since they involved Japan's "respect for the territorial integrity and sovereignty of all nations, support for the principle of non-interference in international affairs, respect for equality of commercial opportunity" and a pledge that there would be "no disturbance in the status quo of any Pacific territory except by peaceful means".

Nomura compounded his initial semantic error by failing even to transmit these "points of principle" to Tokyo for some time. Perhaps, carried away by his own optimism, he felt that what mattered above all was to get official negotiations started, at almost any cost, and realized that, if he forwarded these additional demands, the initiative would be aborted then and there. Hirohito was informed, erroneously, that the United States was willing to accept the amended Hull text as a "basis for negotiations", but thought the draft was one composed by the State Department itself: he was not told until later that it was the outcome of a private initiative in which the State Department had had so far no role.

But, in any event, by this time Matsuoka was no longer interested in the private peace initiative he had so airily encouraged a few weeks previously, for his mind was elsewhere: just back from his "victorious" visit to Berlin, Rome, and Moscow, and completely in thrall to Hitler, he was now convinced that Japan must enter the war on Germany's side as soon as possible; and his ego was such that he was determined to sabotage any initiative elaborated in detail by others. On May 8 he told Hirohito that this dubious peace initiative, clearly a US plot, would come to nothing. A week later, he requested, much as Cordell Hull had demanded a Japanese "declaration of principle", that the United States, before any negotiations started, sign a "neutrality pact" which would have left Japan free to act in any capacity without any possibility of US retaliation. Cordell Hull countered (on June 21) by requesting that Japan abandon the Tripartite Alliance, declare Indochina a "neutral" zone and remove all Japanese troops from Northern China.

An impasse had been reached even before serious talks had begun, but Hirohito was alarmed by Matsuoka's eagerness to do Hitler's bidding prematurely, and wanted the negotiations to continue. On June 21 Hull saw Nomura again, and told him that one of the main obstacles to progress was the influence of "some individuals in high places [Matsuoka]" committed to the unwavering support of Nazi Germany. In a written submission, he noted that the continued presence of Japanese troops on China's soil irrespective of a peaceful Chinese settlement was unacceptable, and this, again, the over-optimistic Nomura seized on as evidence of progress: could it be, he wondered, that this was the sole American objection to what Japan now saw as a possible "peace package"?

Germany's invasion of the Soviet Union the following day paradoxically gave US–Japanese talks another lease of life. For one thing, they spelled Matsuoka's doom, for even the most ardent militarist was unwilling to commit Japan's admittedly large forces to simultaneous war with the US, Britain, the Netherlands *and* the Soviet Union, as Matsuoka now advocated. For another, Germany's move provoked a change of attitude in Konoye himself: he had always, misguidedly, hoped that Stalin might in time become an additional member of the "Tripartite Alliance", and now he saw the invasion as "an act of betrayal" on Germany's part. From that moment onwards, Konoye began to have doubts about Japan's policies in general. He was too shocked, or listless, to speak up when, a few days later, the July 2 "Gozen Kaigi" set Japan firmly on the course of war – but he was determined to try his best to stave it off if he could: after all, even the "Gozen Kaigi" had stated that Japan would only go to war if negotiations broke down – and Japan and the United States were still talking. This, he felt, was also Hirohito's view, and, as a last, romantic resort, he suggested (in August) a personal "summit meeting" with Roosevelt.

It was a typical Konoye volte-face, even though it was seen in Washington as yet another example of Japanese duplicity. In retrospect, Cordell Hull was possibly wrong to deny it any validity, for there was, undoubtedly, an element of irrationality in Japan's foreign policy, and Konoye may have been sincere. It is difficult to be certain, however, for in his eagerness to resort to "summit diplomacy" Konoye suddenly became all things to all men: he told Tojo he would be uncompromising towards Roosevelt about the need for a "Greater New Asia Co-prosperity Sphere". As a result Tojo, though unconvinced, agreed not to veto such a "summit" but wrote to tell Konoye that, if it failed, he was not to resign but should assume leadership in the war against the United States; in his later memoirs Konoye made no mention of this but said he was ready to extricate Japan from the Tripartite Pact.

If Roosevelt and he did meet, and came to an understanding, he intended, he later wrote, to cable the text of their agreement directly to the Emperor. Hirohito would then issue an Imperial proclamation along the lines dictated by Konoye — and the Army would then be compelled to respect the Imperial order.

There is no evidence that Konoye actually talked to Hirohito about removing Japan from the Tripartite Pact, or intended making any other substantive concessions that would have made nonsense of the July 2 "Gozen Kaigi". But, in the last week of July, the Emperor was still reeling from the disappointment of learning that the Navy was not convinced that it could win the war against the United States. When Konoye asked Hirohito for permission to meet Roosevelt, the latter simply replied: "I am in receipt of intelligence from the Navy pertaining to a general oil embargo against Japan by America. In view of this, the meeting with the President should take place as soon as possible.'

In any case, the Emperor could have no objection to Konoye's "summit" proposal because it fulfilled the July 2 "Gozen Kaigi" clauses on "continuing diplomatic negotiations"; even if it ended in failure, it would have been a spectacular propaganda coup.

So now Konoye, the usually indolent patrician, who took to his bed whenever faced with a difficult course of action, threw himself into preparations for a summit meeting with unaccustomed energy, and as a first step proceeded to remove Matsuoka with considerable dexterity — resigning, with his Cabinet, on July 26, and becoming Prime Minister again two days later, with the same Cabinet, except for a new Foreign Minister, the more moderate, and certainly saner, Admiral Teijiro Toyoda.

For summit diplomacy to succeed, however, considerable mutual trust is essential – and, to Roosevelt and Cordell Hull, Konoye remained a warmonger, the advocate of a single-party system, one of the architects of the "New Order", the man who had given his blessing to the start of the war with China and done his best to destroy Chiang Kai-chek. Unfamiliar with the Japanese mind, or with Japan's ancient myths, they could not adjust to such sudden changes. To Roosevelt, Churchill and Cordell Hull, the sudden Japanese interest in a face-to-face encounter was a sinister reminder of Hitler's meeting with Chamberlain: all that would ensue, they believed, was another Munich. The continuing stream of "Magic" transcripts only underlined the extent of Japanese equivocation. To Hull, Nomura insisted that the Tripartite Alliance remained a strictly defensive device and that Japan would not automatically go to war against the US in the event of a clash between the German and American navies in the Atlantic – a possibility that haunted Roosevelt night and day. To Oshima, Japan's pro-Nazi Ambassador, the new Foreign Minister insisted that Japan would indeed declare war if this happened. It was hardly surprising that Hull refused to believe anything any Japanese said. As he put it to an aide, "Nothing will stop them except force . . . The point is how long we can manoeuver the situation, until the military matter in Europe is brought to a conclusion. I don't want us to take for granted a single word they say, but appear to do so, to whatever extent it may satisfy our purpose to delay further action by them." In short, if Japan was duplicitous, America should be too.

So both Hull and Roosevelt were prepared to explore the Konoye proposal for a summit meeting, if only to find out, from "Magic" intercepts, what he really meant by it. Nomura in Washington, in mid-August, met an unusually cordial Roosevelt, and made the by-now well-worn point that Japan's decision to move into southern Indochina had been strictly defensive, and that this was as far as Japan would go in Asia. "Magic" told a different story. Churchill, warned by his own intelligence sources that Japan was planning the invasion of both Singapore and Thailand, was pressing Roosevelt to agree to a Tripartite Alliance in reverse, with America pledged to go to war against Japan if she attacked British or Dutch possessions in Asia. So Roosevelt, full of sympathy for his British ally, but still fearful of the isolationist lobby and the reluctance of Congress to agree to any such decision, smiled and smiled, and listened with feigned interest as Nomura told him that a specially equipped liner, the *Nitta Maru*, packed with sophisticated radio equipment, was ready to steam from Yokohama to any point of the globe to act as Konoye's communications headquarters for the summit, and even proposed a venue – Juneau, Alaska. Then, having raised Konoye's hopes, he dashed them, as though wanting to inflict on him the same kind of emotions Hull experienced whenever he contrasted Nomura's bland promises with the evidence of "Magic".

On September 3, when Roosevelt next met Nomura, he backed off from the summit proposal and said he needed a clearer idea of what was at stake, and what he and Konoye would talk about; this would have to be resolved by traditional diplomatic means *before* their summit meeting could take place. It was a restatement of the "four principles", and now not only Konoye, but the Emperor himself, realized that Japan was being duped.

Hull wrote later, in his memoirs, that "Japan's insistence on holding the meeting and leaving 'details' to be worked out later was in itself significant. It seemed to us that Japan was striving to push us into a conference from which general statements would issue – and Japan could then interpret and apply these statements to suit her own purposes, as she had always done in the past. Moreover, she could then say she had the President's endorsement of her actions . . . Unless the President were willing to agree to vague generalities that would all be to Japan's advantage, there was every likelihood that the meeting would end in failure. In that event Japan's military officials could declare to the Japanese that the United States was responsible for the failure and then proceed to prepare public opinion for war in the Pacific."

Japanese patience was exhausted and, the very day Nomura met Roosevelt and was told indirectly that there could be no summit meeting, a "liaison conference" of inner Cabinet and military leaders took place in Tokyo to prepare for a final diplomatic ultimatum, whose failure was of course a foregone conclusion – and for another, even more historic "Gozen Kaigi" three days later (September 6), committing Japan even more irrevocably to war. The Japanese demands, this time, were still to be obtained if possible by diplomatic means, but with a cut-off date: after October 31, Japan "would not avoid war with the United States, Britain and the Netherlands". The "minimum" diplomatic demands were as unacceptable as ever: no American or British "meddling" in Japan's dealings with China, an end to all US and British aid to Chiang Kai-chek, a restoration of normal trade with Japan, and British and American "friendly co-operation" with Japan's trade ties with Thailand and the Dutch East Indies. This time the only "positive" element in the list of demands was a vague pledge that Japan would be ready to evacuate her troops from Indochina "after conclusion of a just peace treaty in the Far East".

On September 5, a demoralized Konoye called on Hirohito to ask him to preside over a "Gozen Kaigi" the following day. After reading its agenda, Hirohito said he had questions of substance to ask his military commanders. Rather than put them at the formal meeting, Konoye suggested an immediate meeting with the Chiefs of Staff. Hirohito agreed. They were summoned, and faced their most stringent cross-examination yet.

'You mustn't simultaneously prepare for war and for diplomacy," he told them sternly. Then he started on a series of detailed, practical questions: did the Chiefs of Staff think that they could "do the South" as outlined in their operational plans? Sugiyama, as ever vacillating, did not answer directly, but wasted much time, to Hirohito's ill-concealed irritation, running through the detailed operational plans for the invasion of Malaya and the Philippines.

Hirohito asked him: "Are you sure all this will go according to plan? Nothing ever does, exactly. You say it will all be over in five months. You said you would get rid of Chiang Kai-chek within a year and he's still there. Surely one must make allowances for the unexpected?"

Sugiyama replied that the operational plans "had been studied very closely, and we think they will take place as planned".

Hirohito wondered whether the landing operations would be quite so easy. Sugiyama said they were feasible.

Showing considerable detailed knowledge of recent manoeuvres, Hirohito pointed out that, during the simulated invasion exercise held off Kyushu island, a number of ships had been declared sunk by enemy aircraft. "If the same thing happens in real life, what will you do?"

Sugiyama said that was what manoeuvres were for: the fleet had made its move before the air cover was ready. That mistake would not be repeated.

Hirohito asked what would happen if the weather was bad.

Sugiyama said that would complicate matters, but not fatally.

How could he be so confident? "When you were War Minister, you said the 'China Incident' would be over in five months – and it's not over yet."

Sugiyama blamed "special circumstances" in China. Konoye noted, in his diary, that Sugiyama told the Emperor: 'I can't give you an absolute 100 per cent guarantee of victory, but I do say there are good chances of winning." What Japan wanted, and must be prepared to gamble for, was a permanent settlement. "Even if we get peace in six months or a year, it would not be satisfactory to face the same difficulties later on. We must look for peace for twenty, fifty years."

The argument struck home. In a strong voice, Hirohito said:

"I understand." Admiral Nagano chipped in with an illustration from seventeenth-century Japanese history, making the point that Japan should not agree to delay war if, in so doing, the delay only benefited the enemy. This too, Sugiyama noted, had a considerable effect on Hirohito.

The following day, Hirohito returned to the issue of diplomacy versus war. In a pre-arranged question, the President of the Privy Council, Hara, speaking in Hirohito's name, asked for a firm assurance that the former would take precedence over the latter. The Navy Minister assured him this would be the case, but the Chiefs of Staff remained silent. Hirohito intervened directly from the elevated throne at the end of the room. Why had they not said anything? "Hara has spoken well, but you did not answer. Why? This is an extremely serious matter."

Hirohito referred to a scribbled note before him, and read a poem composed by his grandfather, Emperor Meiji.

> Throughout the world
> Everywhere we are all brothers.
> Why then do the winds and waves
> Rage so turbulently?

He often thought of this poem, he said, in his own effort to uphold his dedication to peace.

Both Chiefs of Staff protested they had not meant to ignore the Emperor's remarks. They simply had nothing to add to the Navy Minister's apt remarks. The "Gozen Kaigi", Konoye noted, broke up in a state of great tension.

This incident, and the quoting of the Meiji haiku, are often quoted as proof of Hirohito's desperate striving for a peaceful solution. But, if he did feel so strongly, why were his remarks so totally vague? Now, if ever, was the moment for him to give a guidance to his government and military commanders that would enable them to meet some of the United States requirements without losing face. Konoye was desperately apprehensive, though he still clung to the notion of a summit conference. The Navy Minister, and most of his senior officers, would have welcomed any statement from Hirohito that would have enabled them to postpone actual war. True, it was impossible, in a formal "Gozen Kaigi", for Hirohito to speak his mind informally, but, as the Kido Diaries show again and again, whenever the Emperor wished to convey his point of view to others, all he had to do was summon Kido, and use him as a sounding-board: Kido would invariably relay the message, and, such was his intuitive understanding of the way Hirohito's mind worked, that he never erred, always faithfully reflecting the Emperor's finer shades of meaning.

There is another possible explanation for the Maiji haiku quotation. As Michael Montgomery points out, in *Imperialist Japan*,[1] "peace", in the context of the great Meiji Restoration, did not possess quite the same meaning it had in the rest of the world, being more synonymous with "paradise", that idyllic state of affairs symbolized by *Hakko Ichiu*, "eight corners of the world under one roof" – and Meiji himself, who had wanted to lead his armies into battle in Korea and had destroyed the Russian fleet without a formal declaration of war, could hardly in any case be regarded as a paragon of peace. What Hirohito may have been expressing, Montgomery wrote, was frustration rather than apprehension, for the haiku could also be construed as meaning: since the world is destined to lie under the divine protection of Japan, why is it that some other nations so obstinately refuse to accept this state of affairs, decreed by nature?

In retrospect, Hirohito seems to have behaved as though he was fully aware of what was about to happen, but was determined to provide himself with an alibi, to shift the blame for war on others. At no point, in discussions with any of his advisers, or in hints dropped to Kido, did the Emperor attempt to examine, one by one, the many irreconcilable differences between Japan's and the United States' points of view and see where, if at all, Japan could possibly give ground. He was still, almost obsessively, concerned to obtain from his military leaders formal assurances of victory; and, had they been less honest and forthright in their views, the inference is that he would have raised no objections at all. What Hirohito seems to have required from them was a miraculous ability to bring the United States to heel without having to resort to war, but also without making any concessions whatever. For all the drama of the September 6 "Gozen Kaigi", Hirohito did not attempt to postpone what all concerned must have known was inevitable: after this meeting, war was a virtual certainty from November 1 onwards.

The updated operational blueprints for "Strike South" were handed over to Hirohito on September 9. By this time, it was clear that Hirohito understood, deep down, that all talk of diplomacy was so much window–dressing, asking Sugiyama: "What will you do if there's pressure from the North [i.e. if the Soviets attack] while we are attacking the South?'

Sugiyama said he could cope with such an eventuality. "Your answer reassures me," Hirohito replied. The following day, mobilization plans were given the Emperor's express consent. A few days later, the executive director of the single authorized party, the IRAA, boasted that "heaven did not create superior races only to starve them to death". On September 18, the tenth anniversary of the "Mukden Incident" was celebrated with huge pomp. In the presence of Prince Takamatsu, Tojo called it "the heavensent tocsin signalling at home and abroad the epoch-making dawn of East Asia". And, that same September, the Imperial Mint began printing Japanese "military occupation yen" for future use in the "Greater East Asian Co-prosperity Sphere".

[1] Michael Montgomery, *Imperialist Japan*, Christopher Helm, London, 1988.

CHAPTER SIXTEEN

The September 6 "Gozen Kaigi" should have convinced Prince Konoye that his chances of preventing war, or of meeting Roosevelt, were now non-existent. Instead, he redoubled his efforts. That very evening, he had a three-hour meeting with Grew. They met like conspirators: apart from Konoye and his personal aide, and Grew with his interpreter, the only people who knew of the meeting were Prince Ito, in whose house they met, and Ito's daughter, who prepared their meal. All servants were assumed by diplomats and politicians alike to be unreliable, possible spies bribed or blackmailed into working for the secret or military police, and Ito's had been given the evening off. Both Konoye and Grew arrived in cars with ordinary Tokyo numberplates, instead of their official vehicles.

For Konoye, knowledge of the latest decisions taken earlier in the day in the Emperor's presence must have given him an added sense of urgency. He knew he had less than a month to bring off a summit meeting, and he still could not accept that it was forever beyond his grasp. Now he was determined to do everything he could to persuade Grew of his good faith, even subscribing to the "four principles" Hull had insisted on as a necessary preliminary to all talks, admitting Japan's responsibility for the deteriorating situation.

It was not true, he conveyed to Grew, with almost pathetic frankness, that he was isolated and no longer had any influence, that the military alone had powers of decision. If the "summit" was staged, he would be taking with him a senior general designated by Tojo, as well as the Vice-Chiefs of Staff. Japan, he implied, had turned over a new leaf, and now wanted a complete reconstruction of US-Japan relations. Of course it will take time, he said in essence, of course my record is a dubious one, but trust me, I am your only chance of avoiding war.

Grew was impressed, convinced of Konoye's sincerity, and in favor of "constructive conciliation". Hull was not. The presence, at the proposed summit, of generals at Konoye's side, he felt, was simply further proof that the Japanese wanted a "Munich", and the Japanese counter-proposals (reaching him on September 6 and 25) did not help. Instead of reflecting Konoye's new approach, as reported by Grew, they were merely a restatement of Japan's earlier China demands, couched in admittedly more reassuring language.

On October 2, Hull replied to them, in words that effectively put an end to any hopes Konoye might have had of meeting Roosevelt. But Konoye would not give up. Despite "Magic", no one on the American side knew about the countdown, but Konoye for one was aware he had even less than a month left, for by this time the fatal date was no longer October 31 but October 15, the military having arbitrarily decided they needed an extra fortnight to put their plans into practice. Konoye asked Tojo to give him more time to arrange for a summit. Tojo replied that to tamper with the holy decisions of a "Gozen Kaigi" would be to behave disloyally to the Emperor.

On October 12, Konoye's fiftieth birthday, he made one final effort to convince Tojo. He was both frank and pathetically grave. He told Tojo he had been responsible for one conflict – in China – and he could not take the responsibility of leading Japan into another war. The only way was to yield, "temporarily", to certain American demands, and accept the withdrawal of some Japanese troops from China. In any case, it was an unwinnable war, as Japan would be forced to recognize sooner or later.

Tojo was adamant. To yield anything would be to tamper with the Army's morale, and how, then, could one expect it to fight properly? "I think you are too pessimistic," Tojo said, "probably because you know our weaknesses too well. Doesn't America have weaknesses of its own?" The prim War Minister's irritation was palpable, and, from his viewpoint, reasoned: in the none-too-distant past, Konoye, more than any other civilian, had insisted on Chiang Kai-chek's removal and had been the driving force behind the establishment of the Wang Ching-wei puppet "Nanking Government". Now, in emotional turmoil, he was trying to compel the Army to move in a completely different direction and sacrifice the efforts and casualties of the past four years. After this meeting, Konoye realized that there was nothing further to be done.

A day later, Hirohito came to much the same conclusion, but his mood was very different from Konoye's. For the Emperor now accepted the inevitability of war with apparent equanimity. "In the present circumstances," he told Kido, "I think US-Japan negotiations have little hope of succeeding." If war broke out, he said, he would have to issue an Imperial Proclamation – and he set about telling Kido (who would draft it) what it should contain. Unlike Konoye, with his intuitive sense of foreboding about the immediate future, Hirohito was looking ahead, beyond war, to negotiations from strength.

If it came to war with the United States and Britain, he told Kido, the European situation should be well under control. Germany would have to be watched very closely, for any attempt by Hitler to make a separate peace with either Churchill or Stalin would be a devastating blow to Japan's war effort, so "we need to have good diplomatic contacts to see to it that Germany maintains her co-operation in Japan's war against the United States". It was also necessary, Hirohito went on, to start thinking, even before war started, of the means of ending it, and to look for a suitable mediator. The Vatican would be ideal, and Japan should begin by establishing top-level diplomatic relations with Pope Pius XII.

On October 14, at a Cabinet meeting, Konoye's last, the decision was taken to let the final preparations take their course. That evening, Konoye was a guest at a working dinner organized by some aides to decide on the next President of the North China Development Company. He arrived at six, in a kimono, and said: "Our discussion is no longer necessary. My Cabinet is about to fall." The Army Minister had refused to delay any further, he told his hosts, and the Navy Minister would not voice in public his service's reservations about fighting a war with the United States. Konoye smiled wanly, and said: "Tonight I am here only to enjoy your hospitality." After dinner, his hosts recalled, he picked up a brush and drew in bold strokes the ideogram for "dream". "Two thousand six hundred years," he said. "It's been a long dream."

Later still, that same night, a messenger arrived at Konoye's residence with a message from Tojo. Belatedly, he had discovered what Konoye knew all along: that, within the upper echelons of the Navy, there was serious disagreement about Japan's chances of winning. If the Navy was refusing to go to war while refusing at the same time to voice such a refusal, there must have been grave dereliction of duty somewhere, Tojo's messenger said. The news he had just received called the decisions of the September 6 "Gozen Kaigi" into question, and this in turn meant that all those who had attended it had failed in their duty to the Emperor. There was only one solution: Konoye's entire Cabinet should resign, and Prince Higashikuni should take over as Premier: only he had the necessary prestige to conduct a policy review and bring the two services together.

Konoye got little sleep that night: weighing his few remaining options, he even considered the possibility of secretly leaving Japan on his own authority, making his way unofficially to Washington and forcing a face-to-face meeting on Roosevelt. The following day (October 15), he dismissed this plan. It might not succeed, and it would be a terrible affront to his Emperor. Instead, rallying to Tojo's arguments, he called on Hirohito, urging him to appoint Prince Higashikuni as Premier. The next day he resigned, explaining his reasons in a lengthy note to the "Council of Elders", that informal body of former Premiers which met only at the Emperor's request, when grave issues were at stake. Konoye's letter was addressed to them, but it was really meant for the Emperor himself.

Professor Inouye sees this letter as Konoye's final ultimatum: a plea to Hirohito to choose between negotiations or war. Had the Emperor refused Konoye's resignation, as he had several times in the past, Konoye would then have known that the Emperor was on his side, and that there was a glimmering of hope for peace.

But Hirohito did nothing of the kind. And, despite Tojo's and Konoye's advice, Hirohito also declined to appoint Higashi-kuni, a tough, able officer who was known to be less enthusiastically inclined to war than Tojo. Kido, with the interests of the Imperial Family as usual foremost in mind, argued that if an Imperial prince became Premier and declared war, this might bring "the wrath of the people" down on the Imperial Family. So, instead of Higashikuni, Kido proposed that Tojo should be made Prime Minister, and Hirohito enthusiastically endorsed this proposal.

Many years later, in an interview with Yoshio Ando of *Ekonomisuto*, Prince Higashikuni himself threw additional light on what actually happened during those fateful October days. "Konoye asked me to form a government," Higashikuni said. "The Emperor agreed and so did Kido. I didn't want to be the next Premier. I said to Konoye: 'If Tojo doesn't listen to you, why don't you form the fourth Konoye Government and then sack him? There are some people in the Army who want to avoid war.' Konoye said: 'I'll suggest this to the Emperor.' While we were talking along these lines, General Abe [No-buruku Abe, briefly Premier in August 1939 after Konoye's first government and that of Hiranuma] and Kido were together and they proposed Tojo as Premier, and the Emperor accepted. So Konoye (who had left the room to find out what was going on) rushed back to me and said: 'Tojo is going to be the next Prime Minister and I can't do anything about it any more.'" Harada (Saionji's confidential secretary) commented: "this is the end of Japan."

Kido's championship of Tojo was, on the face of it, odd: but the sophisticated aristocrat and the puritanical, narrow-minded soldier got on well together, and had more in common than was apparent. Both were highly competent bureaucrats, with a strong practical bent, and both were selflessly devoted to Hirohito. Of all the generals in the limelight, Tojo appeared to be the most reliable. Hirohito liked him, Kido noted later, because he never held anything back. He was also intensely hard-working and impeccably honest. Whereas other military police chiefs in Manchukuo had become rich men, Tojo remained poor, and still distributed part of his salary to destitute members of his former regiment.

There is another possible reason for Kido putting his name forward: the astute Lord Privy Seal, so close to the Emperor that he could unfailingly detect his slightest change of mood, must have realized by this time that Hirohito had resigned himself to the inevitability of what he thought would be a short, sharp war with the United States, Britain and the Netherlands, to be followed by a peace treaty that would officially underwrite Japan's hegemony over East Asia for all time.

On October 20, three days later, Hirohito praised Kido's choice. Basking in the Emperor's praise, Kido explained that Japan had been in danger of going to war on a pre-established calendar without adequate preparations, but that Tojo, known for his organizational ability, would correct this. Hirohito had clearly recovered from his earlier gloom, caused by Nagano's remarks about the Navy's doubts about the war, for at the very end of his conversation with Kido he made an extraordinary remark: "We are now in a very difficult situation, very close to war," he told him. "But you can't capture the baby tiger without going into the mother tiger's lair." ("I was very awed," Kido wrote afterwards.)

This is a much stronger Japanese equivalent of "nothing venture, nothing gain". Its only possible interpretation, in the context of the rest of Hirohito's talk with Kido that day, and of his remarks three days earlier on the need to keep Germany in the war on Japan's side, is that the Emperor, convinced of the imminence of war, and no longer doubting its outcome, regarded Tojo as the best possible wartime Premier. Significantly, in his new Cabinet, Tojo retained the War and Home Ministry portfolios, the first Japanese Prime Minister to do so. It was a clear indication that war was at hand. Tojo's insistence on becoming Home Minister was understandable: now he controlled both the secret and the military police.

Many years later (in 1958), Konoye's faithful aide, Tomita, would record his patron's distress, during those crucial weeks. Why, Tomita asked Konoye (during the war years), given his unique access to Hirohito, and the family and friendship bonds that united them, had he not appealed directly to the Emperor, to point out how calamitous Tojo's premiership would be?

Konoye implied, sadly, that the Emperor had vacillated during those crucial days, did not really know his mind and, in any case, by October 16, had already come down on the pro-war side. He told Tomita: "When [in the final days of his premiership] I used to tell the Emperor that it would be a bad thing to start the war, he would agree with me, but then he would listen to others and afterwards tell me I shouldn't worry so much. He was slightly in favour of war and later on he became more war-inclined. Eventually, he started believing that I was no expert on strategy or military matters generally. As Prime Minister, I had no authority over the Army and there was only one person I could appeal to: the Emperor. But the Emperor became so much under the influence of the military that I couldn't do anything about it."

From the tone of Kido's diary after October 16, it is clear that he and Tojo co-operated closely – and that Tojo unburdened himself about the Navy's last-minute doubts. Kido noted that the first priority was to restore harmony between the two services and re-open discussions on the September 6 "Gozen Kaigi". He must have been Tojo's efficient intermediary, for very soon afterwards the Emperor, through Kido, asked Tojo to bring this about, and also told Tojo that the "automatic countdown" decided on at the September 6 "Gozen Kaigi" ought to be reviewed. There should be more thought given to Japan's domestic and foreign policies before an irrevocable decision was made. This, Kido told Tojo, was "an Imperial order". But it was also a highly ambiguous one, for Hirohito never once indicated how the "harmonization" should take place. Should the Navy swallow its fears, and align itself to the Army's bellicose position? Or should the Army reflect on the Navy's doubts, and consider the implications of the Navy's reluctance to fight a war, and its pessimistic projections, on the "Strike South" operation as a whole? With Tojo as Premier, Home and War Minister, the final realignment could hardly be in doubt, unless the Emperor made his preference felt – which he did not. What happened was that the Navy agreed to muzzle its negative views, and Admiral Nagano cravenly aligned himself to his fellow Chief of Staff Sugiyama, with the Navy Minister, equally cravenly, continuing to voice his doubts privately, but refusing to repeat them in policy-making committee meetings.

Between October 23 and November 1, eight top-level meetings took place to amend and refine the decisions taken at the last "Gozen Kaigi", and at these meetings eleven separate questions were tabled. Ten of these agenda items dealt with "strike South" and the probable course of the war, only one concerned talks with the United States. By November 1, naval doubts had been dissipated, for the decisions of September 6 were re-em-phasized, though the calendar was put back, and "X Day" was now brought forward to December – the last possible delay, for the weather was fast deteriorating and, if the December deadline was ignored, everything would have to be rescheduled for March 1942. The Navy was now to be fully operational by December, negotiations with the United States were to continue, but this was sheer window-dressing – for another crucial "countdown" decision was taken: that military relations with Thailand would be established "just before the start of war" to enable Japanese troops to use Thailand as a base from which to invade northern Malaya with maximum surprise. However, if negotiations with the United States succeeded – in other words in the unlikely event that the United States, after resisting unacceptable Japanese demands for several years, abruptly caved in and virtually surrendered to Japanese requests that she abandon Chiang Kai-chek, thus giving Japan an entirely free hand in Asia – then all "Strike South" plans would be scrapped.

Interestingly, in the light of Hirohito's "tiger's lair" remark to Kido, highly-placed Palace sources were still providing Ambassador Grew with reassuring "leaks": in a diary entry for October 25, Grew mentions an "anonymous informant" who claimed to have talked with the Emperor. According to Grew, the Emperor "is said to have asked leading members of the Privy Council and the armed forces to enquire if they were prepared to pursue a policy which would guarantee that there would be no war with the United States. When the Emperor failed to get a satisfactory reply, he quoted Meiji and ordered the assembled individuals to obey his wishes". It was a curious amalgam of half-truths, subtly and probably deliberately concocted.

In fact, conferences between Hirohito and his Chiefs of Staff were now taking on the aspect of an operational checklist. On November 2, Hirohito asked them what was their estimate of initial losses. Their answer was, in retrospect, too pessimistic: one battleship, two heavy cruisers, four light cruisers and 1,800 planes. Hirohito told them they should also take ground casualties into consideration. "I hope you are also remembering the damage to [sea] transport," he said. "Is Air defence satisfactory? What do you do if the enemy destroys Korean dams?"

Sugiyama reassured him on all counts.

Hirohito then turned to the operational calendar in the China-Hongkong zone. "I understand," he said, "that you will 'do' Hongkong after securing Malaya" (this had been decided so as to enable the attack on Malaya to take place with maximum surprise) "but what about the foreign concessions in China?" At what stage, he asked, would Japan launch her attacks there? If Japan moved too soon, Hirohito warned them, surprise would be lost and "the Malaya attack will fail"; so he assumed this, too, would happen after the initial surprise attacks.

Sugiyama assured him this was indeed the plan.

Hirohito returned to the possibility of bad weather. The rainy season was fast approaching. How would this affect landing operations?

It was because of fear of prolonged rain over Malaya, Sugiyama replied, that he had finally decided against a massive initial air strike. In the Philippines sector, he added, such weather problems were not expected.

Then, addressing Admiral Nagano, Hirohito made his sole reference to Pearl Harbor. The cryptic exchange that followed revealed that he was thoroughly aware of its details.

Hirohito asked: What is the Navy's target date?

Nagano replied: December 8.

Hirohito said: Isn't that a Monday?

Nagano pointed out the time difference between Hawaii and Tokyo, (December 8 in Tokyo was December 7 in Hawaii) and reminded the Emperor that the Sunday had been chosen "because everyone will be tired after their holiday". For months spies had been at work in Hawaii, and they had early on pointed out that weekends were taken seriously by the US Navy, and that bibulous Saturday nights were followed by lethargic Sunday mornings.

The Emperor asked whether everything would be planned in such a way as to occur simultaneously. Nagano replied that, because of the great distances involved, this would be difficult. As he pointed out, again referring to Pearl Harbor without, however, mentioning the plan in detail: "The outcome of the war depends greatly on the outcome of the first stage, and the outcome of the first stage depends on the outcome of the surprise attack. We must hide our war intentions at all costs." In the context of the talks that day, it was clear that Hirohito understood what was meant by the "surprise attack".

Nagano added that the initial stages of the war would be more hazardous than anything experienced in China because of the presence of enemy planes and submarines, but "once we land successfully, we're quite sure we'll win. We'll try to end the war quickly," he added, "but we must be prepared for a prolonged war." The United States had to be prevented from using Soviet bases.

Still on Navy matters, Hirohito asked Nagano to remember the possible threat posed by submarines based in Australian ports and the damage they could do to Japanese oil tankers.

On November 4, Hirohito provided Kido with a detailed account of what had taken place. He also gave Kido the specific task of preparing an official brief to be used "when we invade Thailand". Hirohito, in his earlier discussions, had told his Chiefs of Staff there were two alternatives, in dealing with this traditionally friendly, pro-Japanese country: one was to prepare a military treaty in advance, so that Japanese troops moving through Thailand on their way to Malaya would do so quite legally; the alternative was to invade Thailand, and then force the Thais to sign a document agreeing to the Japanese military right-of-way. Hirohito had finally opted for the latter option because it made military sense, since a pact drawn up shortly before the invasion would have given the game away.

That same day (November 4), a top-ranking Japanese diplomat, Saburo Kurusu, left Tokyo to join Nomura in Washington to "strengthen" Japan's negotiating team in Washington. Kurusu's wife was American, and his new appointment was given exceptional prominence in Japanese newspapers. Kurusu, a former Ambassador to Berlin, was aware of the overall operational plans for war, though the secret of Pearl Harbor had been kept from him (Tojo testified as much after the war). Ambassador Nomura knew nothing. Indeed, it was he who had asked for Kurusu to join him in Washington, because, as he put it to his Minister in Tokyo, "I cannot tell you how much in the dark I am. I am now, so to speak, a mere skeleton of a dead horse, and I do not want to continue this hypocritical existence, deceiving myself and other people. I am unable to perceive the delicate shades of the policy of the government and am quite at a loss what to do". Kurusu's brief was to keep the Washington negotiations going for as long as possible. As will be seen later, it was all part of a cleverly orchestrated plan to further lull the United States into believing that, for all the inevitability of an eventual war, it would not happen yet, or in the form already planned so minutely.

Three days later, on November 5, another formal "Gozen Kaigi" ratified the earlier decisions of November 2. The Emperor showed he was familiar with all the points under review, and took the formal decision immediately, Sugiyama reported. Then came some informal questions on the practical aspect of the plan. Hirohito asked at what stage field commanders would be finally briefed, and sent to join their units? What was the optimum date, given the need to maintain total secrecy?

Sugiyama replied that the detailed briefings would begin on November 7. How long, Hirohito asked, could they be kept secret? Since the scale of the operations was so vast, Sugiyama told him, it was very difficult to say. Once more, Hirohito urged Sugiyama not to fight on too many fronts: "don't disturb the North," he said. A Soviet "spoiling operation" – an in-cursion across the Manchurian border to aid the United States – was clearly feared, and Sugiyama told the Emperor it might be necessary to reinforce the units along China's border with the Soviet Union, though he was unwilling to transfer troops from the Shanghai area. In no uncertain terms, Hirohito told him: "It's best to transfer the soldiers from Senshow" (the main Japanese military base on the Yang Tse-Kiang).

A minor crisis within Army Headquarters further revealed Hirohito's overall grasp of "strike South" operational plans and his minute attention to detail: it concerned one of the units earmarked for the invasion of Malaya, the 5th division, recruited from the Hiroshima area. In the original overall Malayan in-vasion plan, it was to join the invasion force directly from its Chinese operational base. Because of their Hiroshima Prefecture origins, most of the men knew how to swim, and this was regarded, by GHQ, as an advantage for the Malayan theatre of operations. Since all troop movements had to be approved by Hirohito, a formal request went to the Palace for the 5th division's transfer from China. To the Army's surprise, the Emperor failed to acknowledge this troop movement request. Eventually, as "X-Day" neared, Army commanders began to worry, and a general Staff letter respectfully asked the Emperor whether he had any objections to the 5th division's role.

Hirohito replied that he did not believe moving the 5th division directly from China to Malaya was a good idea. This particular division had been involved in heavy fighting in China, he noted, and the nature of operations in Malaya would be different from those in China. (By this, the Emperor meant that he was well aware that troops of the 5th division had killed civilians and committed atrocities in China; if they behaved in a similar fashion in Malaya it could be embarrassing, for the divisions involved in "South" operations had to be on their best behaviour at all times.) So, Hirohito went on, he could not agree to a direct shift. Instead, as he ordered, the entire division was given a week's leave in Shanghai (to "decompress") and then returned to Japan prior to the Malaya invasion.[1]

On November 7 Nomura and Kurusu called on Cordell Hull for the first time since Tojo had taken over as Premier. Hull immediately took a strong dislike to Kurusu (he looked "deceitful", he wrote later) but continued to discuss the possibility of a US-Japan settlement. Three days later, Nomura was received by Roosevelt. On that same day, in Tokyo, the "Striking Force Operations Order Number One" was issued, ordering all Japanese warships to complete preparations for battle by November 20 and for the Pearl Harbor strike force to assemble off the Kuriles.

Even though Roosevelt and Hull were certain by now that Kurusu was merely in Washington to distract American attention away from Japan's battle plans, a last attempt at a compromise now took place. The two Japanese ambassadors laid their final proposals before the American President. These were pale variations of earlier proposals: Japan and the United States were not to move in any areas of South-East Asia (but Japanese troops were to remain in French Indochina); all Japanese concessions (eventual troop withdrawals from Indochina and from China) were to be predicated on the basis of "equitable peace" in the Pacific, and in the meantime the United States was to lift her embargo on oil and trade, and "refrain from actions prejudicial to peace between China and Japan".

It was the old story Hull knew so well: in return for vague promises belied by Japan's past behaviour, the United States was being asked, in advance of "peace" in China and any troop withdrawals, to consent to the lifting of trade and oil embargoes, and to Japan remaining a member of the Tripartite Alliance, pledged to attack the US if Germany attacked US shipping in the Atlantic. For Hull, this last series of proposals was as "clearly unacceptable" as previous ones. "The commitments we should have to make were virtually a surrender," he wrote later. On November 22, he met Nomura and Kurusu once again, hoping they might have last-minute concessions to offer. By this time, "Magic" had decrypted a vital cable to Nomura from Tojo's new Foreign Minister, Shigenori Togo. No change in any deadline could be considered, it said, "for reasons beyond your ability to guess", but "if you can bring about the signing of the pertinent notes [i.e. a draft agreement on the latest proposals] we will wait until November 29. After that things are automatically going to happen."

It was now Roosevelt's turn to stage his own "Gozen Kaigi" with his top civilian and military commanders – Hull, Henry Stimson, the Secretary for War, Frank Knox, Navy Secretary, Admiral Harold R. Stark, Chief of Naval Operations, and the Army Chief of Staff, General George C. Marshall. The talk was less about pursuing diplomatic negotiations with Japan than about what to do after Japan had begun the war. According to Stimson, Roosevelt told them: "We were likely to be attacked as early as next Monday [December 1], for the Japanese are notorious for making an attack without warning." From more conventional intelligence sources, Roosevelt now knew that large concentrations of Japanese ships were converging on Shanghai and embarking large numbers of troops. On November 26, Hull completed his final reply to Kurusu and Nomura – a reply he knew would be interpreted as a "fin de non-recevoir". It proposed a non-aggression pact among all countries in South-East Asia and Japan's withdrawal from both China and Indochina. Hull knew it would be regarded as an unacceptable ultimatum, but he had had enough. As he told Stimson, "I have washed my hands of it". American troops abroad were put on full alert, and Admiral Kimmel in Pearl Harbor was given a "war warning". But Roosevelt, and his War Council, at this stage felt that the war would begin with attacks on Malaya and the Dutch East Indies. There seems to have been no inkling that Japan had the capability to conduct a land, sea and air blitzkrieg on several fronts simultaneously.

Nomura had been bitterly disappointed by Hull's note, but still urged Tojo to keep the talks going. Tojo refused. On November 29, the day "things automatically began to happen", a council of former Prime Ministers met the Emperor. Hirohito asked each one of them to speak his mind. The military ex-Premiers were all unreservedly for immediate war; others, without openly voicing their opposition to an immediate war, countered by asking questions: could Japan withstand a long war? Would the food and supply situation enable Japan to carry on beyond the first few months? One former Premier, Yonai, an ex-admiral, was the most forthright: we must be careful, he told Hirohito, "in trying to avoid poverty, not to become bankrupt". But, if the Emperor was looking for a clear, dissenting voice, he was disappointed.

It was Prince Takamatsu, the career naval officer, who nearly succeeded in making Hirohito change his mind at the very last minute: the Navy's doubts, Takamatsu told Hirohito on November 30, had been stifled, but not eradicated. "The Navy," he told his older brother, "will be very pleased if a war can be avoided."

Hirohito immediately summoned Kido and asked him for

advice. "What's going on?" he said. "Are they hiding something from me?"

Kido replied that, if the Emperor had the slightest doubt, he should once more summon his Navy Minister and Naval Chief of Staff and cross-examine them.

That afternoon, Hirohito duly summoned Tojo, then the Navy Minister, then Nagano. His fears must have been allayed, for he told Tojo to carry on. There was no problem in the Navy, the Emperor told Kido later. From that day on, Hirohito's relations with Prince Takamatsu cooled considerably.

The following day (December 1), at a final "Gozen Kaigi", the decision for war was taken, and December 8 (Tokyo time) confirmed as "X-day". Tojo did all the talking. The Emperor did not intervene, nor did he ask any questions afterwards. Things – including a final, brilliantly-executed disinformation campaign – had "automatically started to happen".

[1] Private testimony from one of those involved.

CHAPTER SEVENTEEN

In Tokyo, diplomats and foreign correspondents alike were aware, after Cordell Hull's last note and its brutal Japanese rejection, that war was now only weeks, and perhaps days, away. President Roosevelt's main preoccupation, in the week beginning December 1, had shifted away from negotiations with Japan to thoughts of countering Japanese armed aggression in Asia, but he felt there was little he could do. He toyed with, and dismissed, the notion of a six-month truce; he also considered giving both Britain and the Netherlands Government-in-exile formal assurances that, if and when Japan attacked their Asian territories, the United States would enter the war on their side against Japan. But, because he could not be sure of massive Congressional support for such a decision, even with the US and Japan so clearly on the brink of war, he held back, despite repeated cables from Churchill urging him to declare publicly that "any further act of aggression by Japan will lead immediately to the gravest consequences".

In this curious lull, during that last week of peace in America, correspondents could not know that the die was already cast. Admiral Yamamoto had received his coded message ("Ascend Mount Nitaka! 1208") meaning he should attack Pearl Harbor at dawn (Tokyo time) on December 8. The Japanese fleet had already left the Kuriles (leaving behind a tiny "smokescreen" of communications vessels simulating the cable traffic of the entire fleet) and was already making full speed ahead, to reach the Hawaiian coast just out of range of American reconnaissance planes, with orders to sink any ship that spotted them on their way, Japanese or foreign; the *New York Times* correspondent

Otto Tolischus found Ambassador Grew unusually aloof and unhelpful, unwilling to say anything that might lead to a further deterioration in US-Japanese relations; like his Japanese counterpart, Nomura, the American Ambassador felt out of things, conscious that, in the decisions being taken elsewhere, his advice no longer counted; as he told his staff, he wondered whether his superiors were still bothering to read his cables.

With war so near, and so inevitable, observers clutched at straws — and the principal straw, for both Tolischus in Tokyo and Matsuo Kato, the "Domei" (Japanese news agency) correspondent in Washington, was the *Tatuta Maru,* Japan's finest passenger liner.

For several weeks, the *Tatuta Maru* had been about to sail for the United States, but each departure date had been postponed, and each postponement was interpreted as a further drop in the barometer of US-Japanese relations. The liner was the pride of Japan's merchant shipping, a fast, ultra-modern passenger vessel not nearly as big, or as luxurious, as the *Normandie* or the *Queen Mary* but a tribute, nevertheless, to Japanese naval architecture and engineering. It made sense for the Japanese authorities to prevent its departure, for, if war broke out while it was in American territorial waters or in an American port, it would become an exceptionally valuable war prize, easily convertible into a troopship. So, when the *Japan Times and Advertiser* announced, on December 1, that the *Tatuta Maru* would leave for Balboa (Panama) and Los Angeles on December 2, correspondents and diplomats alike breathed easier. They reckoned that war would not break out for another two or three weeks at least, time for the *Tatuta Maru* to get to Los Angeles, pick up its Tokyo-bound passengers there, and start back to Yokohama. In its cables to the Japanese Embassy in Washington, the Foreign Ministry advised on those Japanese groups in America to be repatriated on the *Tatuta Maru.*

On the basis of the liner's schedule, diplomats and correspondents (and, of course, British and American military intelligence specialists as well) calculated that there would probably be no actual declaration of war on Japan's part until December 14 at least, and probably not until after Christmas. Up to the very last moment, uncertainty prevailed. Would the *Tatuta Maru* leave or not? On December 2, it *did* sail, with 151 passengers, including 23 US passengers and scores of first-generation Japanese immigrants to the United States, mostly from the West Coast, who had not yet acquired US nationality, but had made the trip to Japan to visit relatives they sensed they would not be seeing again for a long time.

The unfortunate passengers aboard the *Tatuta Maru*, who also included some British subjects, were to become the passive victims of a brilliant stratagem. For the *Tatuta Maru* never *did* arrive at Los Angeles, but, instead, on leaving Japan, circled the Pacific for thirteen days. On December 14, it returned to its point of departure, Yokohama, where its passengers disembarked and the British and Americans among them headed for internment.

Alerted by the ship's course in relation to the stars, the passengers must have realized at some stage of their journey that they were not heading in the right direction. How did the captain, pursers and crew explain this? Did they maintain the fiction that they were on the proper course to Los Angeles? How did the passengers get the news of Pearl Harbor? What was the fate of the unfortunate Japanese, compelled to return to Japan, and, in all probability, to serve in the ensuing war?

The *Tatuta Maru* affair was a minor example of Japanese deception, of interest because of the human element involved and because it revealed the degree of preparation and the large numbers of people involved in "X-day". A far more important game, lulling Roosevelt himself into believing that war would not come for maybe a couple of weeks at least, was played out in Washington itself: the main protagonist was Hidenori Terasaki, a brilliant Japanese diplomat who, at the time of Pearl Harbor, was Nomura's personal assistant (and number three in the Embassy, at any rate in terms of his salary) and has gone down in history as the one Japanese who genuinely tried to save the peace single-handed, at considerable personal risk.

Gwen Terasaki, his American wife, in her book, *A Bridge to the Sun*, has left a moving testimony of this humane, cultured, pro-Western aristocrat (later to become one of Hirohito's post-war interpreters) who entered the Japanese diplomatic service in the 1920s, and whose elder brother, a former Consul in New York, was head of the Japanese Foreign Ministry's "America desk" but resigned his post on October 18, 1941, the day after Tojo became Premier.

Hers is an eloquent, under-stated story of an American girl falling head over heels in love with a handsome Japanese diplomat, marrying him in 1930, and devoting the rest of her life to him, overcoming the cultural differences between her own background and that of a traditional upper-class Japanese family and becoming a superbly efficient and "loyal" embassy wife in Shanghai, Havana and, eventually Washington, without ever forgetting that she was, by birth and culture, American.

As related by Gwen, Terasaki approached Kurusu on November 29 and said: "Ambassador, why don't you become a 'national traitor'? Why not go ahead and tell the Americans we will get out of China? We can't remain there for long anyway, and the war party knows that."

Kurusu shrewdly turned the offer round. "How about being one yourself?" he asked. "I think we should approach the President through an intermediary, someone who has his ear, and suggest that he send a cable directly to the Emperor appealing for peace. I warn you that I have already cabled Tojo for permission to do this and been refused. Such a cable will have to be sent over Tojo's head directly to the Emperor. Of course, if your part is discovered, it may mean your death and the death of your family too. But you thought I should take such a risk and now it's your turn."

Terasaki agreed to go ahead, and arranged for a secret meeting with Chiang Kai-chek's Ambassador in Washington, Dr Hu Shih, and the man Terasaki hoped to use as intermediary –

E. Stanley Jones, a well-known Methodist preacher who was a personal friend of Roosevelt.

In a private room at the Purple Iris restaurant, they discussed the best approach to take, and decided that Jones should deliver an oral message to the President. He was to say that – with the tacit blessing of the Chinese Ambassador – Kurusu and Terasaki believed Roosevelt should send the Emperor a personal message, as a last-minute effort to stave off an otherwise inevitable war. As Terasaki told Jones at the restaurant meeting, "if the Emperor interfered, it was known the Japanese would comply, including the military" – another reminder that, despite his constitutional limitations, the Emperor's powers were not quite as diluted as later experts have implied.

Jones wrote to Roosevelt, asking for a meeting, and on December 3 went to the White House to see him. Jones spoke of the secret meeting in the Purple Iris. Roosevelt told Jones he had been thinking of sending such an appeal, "but I've hesitated to do so, for I didn't want to hurt the Japanese here in Washington by going over their heads to the Emperor".

Jones said his démarche came as a direct result of Japanese Embassy insistence: "they asked me to ask you to send that cable, but obviously they could not let me write that for there must be no written record since they are going over the heads of their government to the Emperor."

"That wipes my slate clean," Roosevelt replied. "I can send that cable."

Jones then advised him not to send his message through the Japanese Foreign Ministry. A previous personal cable from Roosevelt to the Emperor at the time of the *Panay* incident had never reached the palace. "Send it direct to the Emperor himself," Jones urged the President. "I don't know the mechanics of it but that's what they [Kurusu and Terasaki] suggest."

Roosevelt said: "Well, I'm just thinking out loud. I can't go down to the cable office and say I want to send a cable from the President of the United States to the Emperor of Japan – but I could send it to Grew. As Ambassador he has the right of audience with the Head of State and he can give it to the Emperor direct. If I don't hear for twenty-four hours – I have learnt to do some things – I'll give it to the newspapers and force a reply."

Jones asked Roosevelt never to refer to Terasaki as the instigator of the cable.

'You tell that Japanese," said Roosevelt, "that he is a brave man. No one will ever learn of his part in this from me. His secret is safe."

Terasaki's decision to approach Kurusu rather than Nomura with the proposal to persuade Roosevelt to send Hirohito a personal message could be explained on the grounds that the "special envoy" had more influence than the actual ambassador. It was also understandable that he should tell his wife, for they were very close, and Terasaki, at home, behaved more like an American than a traditional Japanese husband. Gwen Terasaki knew all about the Roosevelt message, and was proud that her husband was risking his career in the cause of peace. That was why, when the sudden news came of the attack on Pearl Harbor, she was bewildered as well as appalled. Her first thoughts were: what had happened to the Roosevelt message? Had the Emperor actually received it?

Though she was aware of Terasaki's secret plan, there were certain things concerning her husband she did not know and is perhaps still unaware of to this day. For instance, there is no mention, in her book, of Terasaki's active lobbying of the isolationist "America First" group or of his investigation of pro-American sentiment among Argentina's expatriate community. Nor did Terasaki tell his wife that he was on the urgent repatriation list cabled to Washington from the Japanese Foreign Ministry on December 5. As her book makes clear, she kept on hoping against hope, right up to December 7, that war would somehow be averted and that she and her husband would stay in Washington. From her portrayal of Hidenori Terasaki, one gets the feeling that he was himself in two minds about returning to Japan in the event of war, that he was almost tempted, at one stage, to become an early dissident – even if this decision might mean facing treason charges.

Gwen Terasaki's book paints such a sympathetic portrait of this fearless, liberal diplomat torn between his innate patriotism and his love of America that it comes as a considerable shock to learn that Terasaki was not quite what he seemed.

Whether his "liberal" sentiments were real, or a useful cover, we will never know. What is incontrovertible is that, for all his efforts to prevent war between Japan and the United States, he was, in fact, right up to Pearl Harbor, a senior Intelligence operative rather than a straightforward diplomat.

After receiving the list of those members of the Embassy staff required to leave Washington urgently, two days before Pearl Harbor, Kurusu cabled back to Tokyo that he would "*greatly appreciate it if Terasaki, as organizer of our Intelligence set-up*"*, remained in Washington since he was "extremely important in view of the conditions of Japanese-US negotiations".

This secret message, later decoded by "Magic", throws a completely new light not just on Terasaki but on the entire Kurusu–Terasaki version of the origins of the Roosevelt message. As "head of our Intelligence set-up", Terasaki could well have collaborated with Kurusu in concocting the whole plan for very different reasons. Most State Department experts later concurred that Kurusu was specially despatched to Washington not so much to assist Nomura in trying to bring about a US-Japanese solution to outstanding problems as to drag things out and mastermind a "spoiling operation" which Nomura, the honest sailor, was incapable of executing on his own – and would probably have refused to carry out if ordered to do so.

In any event, Roosevelt sent his personal, elegantly penned message to Hirohito via Grew on December 6. It left Washington around 6 p.m. Washington time. "Almost a century ago," it began,

the President of the United States addressed to the Emperor of

* Author's italics.

Japan a message extending an offer of friendship of the people of the United States to the people of Japan. That offer was accepted, and in the long period of unbroken peace and friendship which has followed, our respective nations, through the virtues of their peoples and the wisdom of their rulers, have prospered and have substantially helped humanity. Only in situations of extraordinary importance to our two countries need I address to Your Majesty messages on matters of state. I feel I should now so address you because of the deep and far-reaching emergency which appears to be in formation.

Developments were occurring, Roosevelt went on, "which threaten to deprive each of our nations and all humanity of the beneficial influence of the long peace between our two countries". Americans had hoped for peace, and watched the negotiations between the US and Japan closely. They had witnessed the increase of Japanese forces in Indochina. Now, Roosevelt made a personal plea to Hirohito to bring about a withdrawal of those forces, to allay the fears of those people in Thailand, the Philippines, the Dutch East Indies and Malaya threatened by war. If this happened, there would be no Western interference in Asia. He ended with the reminder that both he and the Emperor "have a sacred duty to restore traditional amity and prevent further death and destruction in the world".

The message, only lightly coded so that it could be dealt with quickly, left Washington just as a much longer cable, from the Japanese Foreign Ministry to the Washington Embassy, began to arrive on the Japanese Embassy telex (transmission started around 6.30 a.m. on December 6, Tokyo time). This was the text of the fourteen-part memorandum ending with a declaration of war on the United States, originally timed – or so Japanese Foreign Ministry officials later claimed – to reach Washington in time to be delivered at least thirty minutes before the actual attack on Pearl Harbor.

As the whole world knows, it was actually delivered *after* the attack on Pearl Harbor (no declaration of war whatever was ever issued to either the British or the Netherlands Governments).

The Japanese explanation has always been that slow decoding (only a handful of diplomats enjoyed the necessary security clearance to work on it) and shortage of staff competent to type the final English version of the memorandum were exclusively to blame. The Emperor, as Kido told IMTFE interrogators later, was "most displeased" at the "sheer idiocy and incompetence" of the Japanese Embassy officials in Washington.

The testimony of the "Domei" agency correspondent, Matsuo Kato, invalidates this version of events. In his book *The Lost War*, Kato recalls that, on December 6, the whole Japanese Embassy staff attended a lengthy farewell luncheon party for one of its officials about to be posted to Rio. The party, at the Mayflower Hotel, went on well into the afternoon, but the diplomats, including those with top security clearance, showed no particular urgency to pursue any kind of work that afternoon. By this time the bulk of the memorandum had already been received.

After the party, Kato noted, "I played table-tennis in the Embassy basement. Katsuko Okamura,* the First Secretary, was watching us . . . He was idle for the moment, although [as Kato learnt later] he had personally been typing the first portion of the Tokyo war declaration."

The atmosphere in the Japanese Embassy was clearly relaxed, and Okamura, who spent most of the afternoon watching the table-tennis, was certainly aware of the minutes ticking by. "We began talking about the likelihood of the *Tatuta Maru* arriving in the United States," Kato wrote. "Okamura said: bet you a dollar it never reaches Los Angeles." Kato took him on. Later, when both were internees, awaiting repatriation to Japan, Okamura admitted he had been one of the few people at the Embassy aware in advance of the Pearl Harbor attack, and had wagered on a certainty, since of course he also knew in advance of the *Tatuta Maru* deception.

Grew did not receive Roosevelt's "triple urgent" message for

* Okamura would become one of Hirohito's interpreters during the US Occupation, and was present at the September 27, 1945 meeting with MacArthur.

another twelve hours, actually learning of the President's move from monitored US radio broadcasts long before getting the actual text. Why there was a delay of some ten hours at the Japanese end of transmission has never been satisfactorily explained, except that Japanese officials later blamed "military censors", though how they could profit by censoring a coded cable is not known. The more likely explanation is that, warned by Intelligence sources in Washington that Roosevelt had decided to communicate directly with Hirohito, they were determined it should reach him too late.

Grew, fuming at the ten-hour delay, immediately called the Foreign Ministry (it was past midnight – 0030, December 8, Tokyo time) to try and arrange an audience with the Emperor. The dapper, moustachioed Shigenori Togo, usually friendly (he had spent nearly four years in the Japanese Embassy in Washington and spoke fluent English) was, this time, coldly formal. Grew insisted the American President's message was so important "I respectfully request the opportunity to deliver it to His Majesty in person at the earliest possible moment".

It was out of the question to disturb the Emperor so late at night, Togo countered. Besides, the Imperial Household Minister would have to be consulted. There was not much likelihood of an early audience. Togo, of course, knew that the attack on Pearl Harbor was only a couple of hours away. He was embarrassed, playing for time, yet unwilling to give Grew a point-blank refusal because this might arouse his suspicions. Grew insisted on reading the message to him. Togo listened patiently, and fobbed Grew off by telling him the matter would be presented to the Throne at the earliest possible opportunity.

Grew returned to the American Embassy, and to bed, still hoping against hope he might see Hirohito in person the following day. Togo immediately drove round to the Prime Minister's office and found General Tojo awake. He showed him the text of the Roosevelt message. Both men knew how futile it now was, but even so diplomatic pretences had to be maintained. The two men decided the note contained nothing new, except, perhaps, a totally insufficient offer of "neutralization" of Indochina. Together, they drafted a rejection in the Emperor's name, simply referring back to an earlier rejection of American proposals, and asking Roosevelt to "kindly refer to this reply". Tojo and Togo between them added a line about "establishment of peace in the Pacific, and consequently of the world," which "has been the cherished desire of His Majesty". While this rapid draft was being prepared, Japanese planes were revving up on the strike force aircraft-carriers 120 miles or so from Pearl Harbor and Japanese submarines were edging nearer.

Togo's night was not over: around the very time (2.45 a.m. Tokyo time) when the air strikes on the American fleet were beginning in Pearl Harbor, Togo was being greeted at the Palace by Kido, and preparing himself for an audience with Hirohito. Kido had been warned of the Roosevelt message, and had driven from his home to the Palace in the middle of the night. In naval uniform, Hirohito received Togo alone, listened to the American President's text, and approved the draft reply – which was never delivered. Togo went back to bed for a couple of hours of badly needed sleep. The Emperor withdrew to his "war room". According to some reports, he listened in to radio traffic with his naval ADCs, to hear, from the *Nagato*, Admiral Yamamoto's flagship commanding operations from its position just off the Hiroshima coastline, the earliest results of the raid.

It was morning in Washington (December 7), and, ironically, the top US Administration and Armed Forces officials with "Magic" clearance by now had most of the fourteen-part Japanese memorandum on their desks, in advance of notification of war, hours before it was to come their way officially. The first thirteen parts were simply lengthy recapitulations of past negotiations. The actual announcement that a state of war existed between the two countries had not yet been transmitted – and the decoding process, resumed at 10 a.m. inside the Japanese Embassy, was still slow, possibly deliberately so. The final, fourteenth part arrived around 10.30, together with an uncoded cable, in English, telling Nomura and Kurusu to deliver the text at 1300 hours. It was this brief message that finally alerted senior US Navy officers, and some of General Marshall's subordinates, that Japan might be preparing for a surprise strike on American military installations immediately after that time. Marshall agreed to send a top priority warning to bases in San Francisco, the Philippines and the Panama Canal to be on the alert. A similar message could not be delivered to Hawaii because of atmospheric conditions.

At 1347 hours the Navy Secretary, Frank Knox, received the first report of the Pearl Harbor attack. Roosevelt was informed almost immediately, and telephoned Cordell Hull at 1405 hours. Nomura and Kurusu had that very moment arrived at the State Department and were waiting to see him, clutching their translated fourteen-part memorandum, which, by this time, thanks to "Magic", Hull had read in its entirety. At 1420 hours they were ushered in. Hull ignored their outstretched hands. The ambassadors remained standing.

Nomura handed over the memorandum, saying he had been instructed to deliver it at 1300 hours.

"Why should it be handed over at one o'clock?" Hull asked. Nomura said he did not know. Hull scanned it, pretending he had not already learnt of its contents, and then told the two envoys he had never read a document "more crowded with infamous falsehoods and distortions". As they left, Hull audibly called them "scoundrels and pissants". After returning to the Japanese Embassy on Massachusetts Avenue, Kurusu and Nomura were told, by the First Secretary, Okamura, that Japanese planes had bombed Pearl Harbor.

Even as the attack was proceeding, elaborate security precautions against the new "enemy aliens" went into effect in Tokyo: the British and American Embassies were sealed off at dawn, British and American reporters were rounded up and taken to police stations, where some of them, including Tolischus, were brutally interrogated for days. The war was announced to selected Japanese journalists at 6 a.m. at a specially convened War Ministry press conference. At a later briefing for foreigners,

at the Foreign Ministry, Robert Guillain, the French correspondent for Havas, noted the absence of all his British and American
friends. He somewhat cheekily asked the spokesman why they
were not present, and whether the attack had taken place before
or after the declaration of war. He was rebuffed.

Inside the sealed-off US Embassy, Robert Fearey, Grew's
personal aide, heard the newspaper sellers' cries outside, daringly
scaled the wall and brought back several copies of the *Japan
Times and Advertiser* announcing war. They became a collector's
item: two hours after going on sale, the military police im-
pounded all remaining copies. The paper, in its inside pages,
carried lengthy stories about the negotiations leading up to war,
and – in the eyes of the now all-powerful military censors –
made too many references to Prince Konoye's role in trying to
avoid the conflict. Since his resignation, Konoye had become
something of a non-person.

Aboard the *Nagato*, Admiral Yamamoto asked an aide to
check the time the declaration of war had been transmitted to
the United States. An honourable man, he had not wanted this
additional deception to take place – and had assumed that the
notification had come thirty minutes before the actual attack.
The Emperor, too, according to many later Palace sources, was
"furious" at the delay.

The Emperor's wrath could be a terrible thing. The thought
inevitably arises: if Hirohito felt such rage at the "idiocy and
incompetence" with which the declaration of war had been
handled in Washington, leaving an indelible stain on Japan's
record as a civilized nation, what reprisals did he order to be
taken against the culprits? Such grave dereliction of duty should,
by rights, have cost those involved their careers at the very least.
The dilatory decoders should have been shaking in their shoes,
all the while they were held in (luxurious) American detention
and later in transit to Japan (ironically, on board the *Tatuta
Maru*). They do not appear to have worried, and Kato, in his
detailed, humorous account of the months ahead, makes no
reference to any apprehension.

Colonel Sackett questioned Kido on this very point, in his pre-trial interrogation.

KIDO: I heard from the Emperor himself that the plans were to transmit the declaration of war first then make the attack.

SACKETT: How was it this was not done?

KIDO: I don't know why there was such a hitch.

SACKETT: Was there any investigation over the hitch? That was most unusual, wasn't it?

KIDO: I haven't heard of any.

In one of the rare IMTFE reports implicating Hirohito by name (document no 3,245 dated November 10, 1947 – "Crimes to which document applicable: question of Emperor's knowledge of Pearl Harbor plans") a report submitted by the immediate post-war Cabinet of Prince Higashikuni made the following points, all designed to protect Hirohito from court proceedings and minimize his personal responsibility.

It read, in part:

1. We believe that the Empire was compelled to start the Great East Asia war in view of the surrounding circumstances.

2. That the Emperor was exceedingly anxious to conclude peacefully the negotiations between Japan and America.

3. That the Emperor, in following the practice established in the application of the Constitution, did not reject matters decided by the Imperial Headquarters and the Government in regard to decisions for the commencement of hostilities and the carrying out of plans for operations.

4. That in order to make every effort to avoid making a surprise attack while negotiations were in progress, efforts

were made to communicate the notifications of the dis-
continuation of negotiations between Japan and America.
(NOTE: that since we exercised our right of self-defence in
the light of the actual circumstances of the economic pressure,
etc., imposed on the Empire, we are of the opinion that the
provisions of the Hague Treaty pertaining to the commencement of hostilities can be nullified.)

5. That the Imperial Rescript for the declaration of war was
of a domestic nature intended chiefly for the people of Japan.

6. That we could not deal with England and other countries
separately in view of the relations existing between America
and these countries at that time.

In a further outline of Hirohito's position, the document
stated that "prior to the attack on Pearl Harbor, although the
Emperor had heard of the outline of military operations in the
initial stages from both the Army and Navy Chiefs of Staff, he
did not receive any reports concerning the details of the operation . . . He understood that when the above plan of operations
was to be carried out, diplomatic measures would be taken
towards the American Government before resorting to arms."
It is interesting, then, to contrast this statement with further
extracts from the pre-trial cross-examination of Kido on this
point. Colonel Sackett asked him how much Kido himself
knew about Pearl Harbor:

KIDO: Generally, the Emperor tells me everything, but on
matters of operation, the Emperor is very reserved and would
not tell me everything.

SACKETT: In other words, when the War or Navy Chiefs of
Staff would discuss operational questions with the Emperor,
they were of such a high degree of secrecy, he normally
would not tell anyone about them?

KIDO: And perhaps the Emperor thought that if he disclosed

these matters to the Lord Privy Seal, I may be encumbered or may be made to regret for it [sic].

SACKETT: The Chiefs of Staff would disclose major operational questions to the Emperor even though you didn't know about them, did they not?

KIDO: There are occasions when he does talk about great problems.

SACKETT: The Emperor, no doubt, knew from the Army and Navy in their private conferences about this plan to attack Pearl Harbor before it took place, did he not?

KIDO: *I believe he did know about the attack on Pearl Harbor.**

And later:

SACKETT: The Emperor, no doubt, knew about these operational plans for attack of Pearl Harbor and the actual plan to attack it long before the attack took place, did he not?

KIDO: *I believe that the Emperor was informed previously because the Naval General Staff submitted directly to the Emperor the general outline of the attack.**

Sackett tried hard, but without success, to induce Kido to give him the earliest probable date of the Emperor's knowledge of Pearl Harbor. Kido prevaricated; he did not know, he said. Sackett replied that he found this hard to believe.

In fact the Higashikuni document submitted to IMTFE set out to prove far too much: while the lack of advance warning was attributed to happenstance ("due to the unexpected length of time required for deciphering and organizing the above telegraphic notification at the Japanese Embassy in America, the notification to the American Government was delayed"), it also advanced the "right of self-defence" – raising "economic

* Author's italics.

pressures" (brought about by Japanese aggression in Indochina) to a kind of economic Pearl Harbor in reverse, thereby "nullifying" the terms of the Hague Treaty.

The explanation of the non-declaration of war on Britain is the least convincing of all. As a further note explained, "the situation was such that in view of the Anglo-American relations existing at that time, it was expected that the final notice to America and the exercise of military forces would be transmitted immediately from the American Government to the British Government and others".

Why was no attempt made to communicate with the British Foreign Secretary, Lord Halifax, in London through the active Japanese Embassy there? An "immediate" notification to the British Embassy in Washington by Cordell Hull would still take minutes, and it would have been hours before the British forces in Malaya were informed, via London, of the impending attack, for radio communication was often hampered by atmospheric conditions, and coding and decoding took time. As it happened, of course, the first inkling of the Japanese intention to wage war on Britain came with Japanese landings at Kota Baru (which occurred over an hour *before* Pearl Harbor) and the land invasion, through Thailand, from the North. The Japanese occupation of the Shanghai International Concession occurred even earlier, several hours before Pearl Harbor.

The real reason was, almost certainly, that by attacking Malaya without any prior notification, just before Japanese planes began strafing Pearl Harbor, Japanese commanders were merely implementing Imperial advice on surprise and secrecy that, as Hirohito himself had remarked earlier, were essential if the complicated, multiple-front operation was to succeed.

In the light of the question–answer sessions transcribed in the Sugiyama Memorandum, Hirohito's detailed knowledge of the multiple plans of attack, his equally detailed questioning and informed comments on the importance of secrecy, timing, and the chronology of events to be followed in Hongkong, Thailand and the Chinese International Concessions, to say nothing of the veiled references to Pearl Harbor itself ("isn't that a Monday?"; "It all depends on the intitial surprise attack."), Kido's candid admission of Hirohito's prior knowledge of Pearl Harbor and the immunity of the Embassy staff in Washington who bungled the transmission of the declaration of war, the Higashikuni report to IMTFE makes ironic reading.

But a new twist was subsequently added: after the war, the Methodist preacher who had been Terasaki's intermediary, E. Stanley Jones, was received in audience by Hirohito. As Gwen Terasaki recorded, Jones told Terasaki afterwards that the Emperor had said that "if he had received the Roosevelt telegram a day sooner he would have stopped Pearl Harbor". Apart from providing further confirmation that Hirohito was no puppet, since he himself claimed he could have called off Pearl Harbor, and was therefore less than candid with MacArthur in claiming his hands were tied from the very beginning, it was also, given Hirohito's behaviour during the lengthy preparations for Pearl Harbor, and his perfunctory interest in the Roosevelt text when it did arrive, the most mendacious allegation of all.

CHAPTER EIGHTEEN

The impression conveyed to the outside world by members of the Imperial Household Ministry, successive Japanese governments, leading scholars and opinion-makers, and, last but not least, Hirohito himself, in his frequently reiterated post-war statements on the subject, is that the war years were a perpetual nightmare and far and away the worst time of his life.

So they may have been, but only from the moment the tide began turning against Japan, as it did, decisively, from 1943 onwards. For the image of an anxious, guilt-racked Emperor, reluctantly forced into war, deploring from the start the death and destruction wrought on innocent people by troops over whom he had no control, is a carefully elaborated fiction, part of a "grand design" to convince the world at large that Hirohito, from first to last, bore no responsibility for the war.

Kido was to note that Hirohito did increasingly speak of his friendship with the British Royal Family, of the kindnesses they had shown him as Crown Prince, and his bitter regret at the state of war between the two nations. With tongue in cheek, perhaps, Kido observed that the more perilous the state of war for Japan, the more nostalgically the Emperor seemed to harp on those blessed days in London and Balmoral. Immediately after promulgating the Imperial Rescript of the declaration of war, on December 8, 1941, Hirohito did mention to Kido how heart-rending it was to have the British King as an enemy, but, after that, recollections of friendship with the Royal Family do not seem to have been uppermost in his mind as long as Japan was on a winning streak. One sentence in the Imperial proclamation of war, eight hours after Pearl Harbor ("it has been truly unavoidable and far from Our Wishes that Our Empire has now been brought to cross swords with America and Britain"), was later cited as proof that he did so reluctantly. But the war Rescript also contained other flowery formulas, including the somewhat untenable claim that Japan's invasion and forcible occupation of Malaya, the Philippines, the Dutch East Indies, Hongkong and the foreign "enclaves" in China, were all in the cause of world peace.

Because he knew that war was a colossal gamble for which, as Head of State, he would be held responsible, Hirohito may well have had inner reservations, despite the elaborate operational planning he had monitored so thoroughly. But in the heady early months of the war, as Robert Guillain observed, the whole of Japan was in a state of euphoria.[1] The occupation of Malaya and the Dutch East Indies resulted, at least for a short while, in more food and consumer goods in the shops, loot in the form of "liberated" cars and radios from Singapore and Batavia, the Dutch East Indies' capital, along with rice and other badly-needed raw materials; nearly all Japanese were both elated and proud. As Kido's diaries show, Hirohito, far from urging caution on his commanders and aides and displaying a Cassandra-like sense of doom, shared in this euphoria, at least at first. One gets the impression, from Kido's day-to-day entries, that he wished the Emperor would at times show more restraint and start asking himself questions about Japan's long-term strategy.

In the circumstances, having opted for war and declared it, Hirohito's relief at the success of the "surprise attack" was understandable, and it was of course his duty, as Commander-in-Chief, to congratulate his troops and his Navy (which he did at regular intervals) on their major victories in the early weeks of the war.

But Hirohito's rejoicing went far beyond such formal responses. It was perhaps normal, in the early flush of the Pearl Harbor report, on December 8, for him to tell Kido and Sugiyama that "when I heard the good news of the surprise attack, I felt the goodwill of the Gods". The Emperor, Kido noted that day, was "poised and serene, and I detected not the slightest anxiety in his behaviour".

When Kido congratulated Hirohito on the fall of Singapore, in mid-February, he found Hirohito in an even more elated mood. "The Emperor," he wrote, was "very cheerful." "My dear Kido," Hirohito said, "I know I harp on this all the time, but as I've said before and will say again, it all shows the importance of advance planning. None of this would have been possible without careful preparation."

Even when Hirohito advised Tojo to draw up possible peace plans, as he did on February 10, 1942, these were conceived more as terms of limited surrender on the part of the Allies: from Japan's point of view, her victories entitled her to negotiate from a position of strength. Having given him these instructions, Hirohito immediately qualified them. "Of course the end of the war does not depend on ourselves alone," Hirohito told Tojo. "It also depends on the United States, Britain and how things turn out on the Eastern Front. One should not give up halfway in order to ensure access to raw materials from the South. You should think about all this and act accordingly." The peace terms Hirohito was urging his commanders to draw up in fact amounted to a virtual Allied surrender to Japanese hegemony in Asia.

The Emperor's "humane" qualities do not seem to have been immediately noticeable at this stage: the end of the war was desirable as soon as possible, Hirohito told Tojo, not, as one might have expected, because the longer it continued, the more loss of life and suffering would ensue, but because, as he put it, "if it goes on for too long the quality of the Army will inevitably be lowered" – a professional soldier's view of war, certainly, but a singularly cold-blooded one.

David Bergamini imputes to Hirohito overall responsibility for the wholesale massacre of Chinese in Malaya and Singapore, on the basis of the Emperor's allusive conversation with General Sugiyama at a "Liaison Conference"; but there is no "smoking gun" in the form of a direct order or reported statement in either the Sugiyama memorandum or the Kido diaries that might prove that Hirohito actually encouraged the atrocities that took place in Malaya and during the Bataan "death march". He did, however, follow the campaigns there closely, dispatching aides from the Imperial Court to both the Singapore and Philippines battlefronts; and, while the infamous orders calling for massacres of wounded personnel and nurses and the systematic ill-treatment of prisoners-of-war stemmed from Colonel Masanobu Tsuji, one of General Sugiyama's principal staff officers, who claimed to have the Emperor's ear, he, like other Japanese military men, may have used his Imperial connections to give orders in the Emperor's name without Hirohito's specific authorization. What is certain is that when, in 1943, a detailed account of the horrors of the Bataan "death march" was released to the world, and brought to Hirohito's attention by Kido, the Emperor changed the subject – and never ordered an investigation into the conduct of those responsible.

Changing the subject or avoiding it altogether was Hirohito's favourite way of indicating his preferences to his generals: on February 23, 1942, he was present at a "Liaison Conference" which should have discussed an enormously important issue: the invasion of Australia. One school of thought, among the military commanders, was that this was the only step that would enable Japan finally to win the war: Admiral Yamamoto held this view, and had also been in favour of a land invasion of Hawaii. Tojo, by nature a cautious and unimaginative general, was opposed. As it happened, the subject was not raised by the Emperor at all. He preferred to ask questions about the possible occupation of Portuguese-owned Timor and Japanese bank guarantees for the "occupation currency" yen. The possibility of an Australian invasion was never raised again in the Emperor's presence.

Whether Japanese "peace", "cease-fire" or "truce" proposals had been made, of course, there was no chance, by this time, of their acceptance by either Roosevelt or Churchill: Hirohito badly underestimated the fighting mood of the United States after the humiliation of – and the indignation caused by – Pearl Harbor; as for Churchill, he was preoccupied, first and foremost, by the war in Europe. After the disastrous British defeats in Malaya and in the Pacific, he was resigned, as the Australian historian David Day has pointed out[2] to see Japan temporarily overrun Asia, and even Australia as well: Japan, he felt, could be dealt with after Hitler had been crushed.

Three weeks after the fall of Singapore (March 9, 1942), Kido was summoned into Hirohito's presence and found him exultant "Kido, do you realize Java has surrendered, that our troops have obtained the complete surrender in the Dutch East Indies, that Burma is ours, that Rangoon has fallen! The series of victories are too much, too fast," he said. The Emperor, Kido wrote, "looked tremendously satisfied. I couldn't find words to congratulate him, I was so moved."

Hirohito's delight extended to his German ally's successes as well. On June 28, 1942, Hirohito told Kido that "the Germans have not only taken Tobruk but are well on the way to Egypt, having captured Sidi Barrani on the way". He wished to send a telegram of congratulation to Hitler on the fall of Tobruk, he added.

Kido said he would talk to the Imperial Household Minister about this. No such telegram was sent, but only because Tsuneo Matsudaira, the Imperial Household Minister, advised against it, on the grounds that Hirohito had never received a congratulatory telegram from Hitler after *his* Asian victories. It is almost certain that Matsudaira, known for his pre-war Anglophilia, deliberately resisted having such a cable sent, for in the event he told the Emperor an innocent lie: Hitler, King Victor Emmanuel of Italy, and, inevitably, the craven Pu Yi, the Manchuko "puppet emperor", had all in fact dutifully cabled their fulsome congratulations to Hirohito after Pearl Harbor and the sinking of the *Repulse* and the *Prince of Wales*.

In one respect, Japan emulated her German ally, without, however, going all the way: in March 1942, at another "Liaison

Conference" in the Emperor's presence, Japan adopted a series of measures concerning Jews on Japanese soil and in the newly-occupied territories that were a pale copy of laws in force in Nazi Germany. Immigration of Jews to China, Manchuria, Japan and all occupied territories was banned; Jews already living in these areas were not arrested, but, "due to the special racial characteristics of the Jews, surveillance of their residence and businesses will be intensive. At some time also their pro-enemy activities will be eliminated and suppressed." Jews "who can be useful to the Emperor (including those who can be useful for Axis nations and those not against the national Polity) will be carefully selected and given appropriate treatment." Sugiyama admitted that such measures stemmed directly from Germany's own restrictive measures ("this has forced us to take special regard for our new relationships with third countries in the treatment of Jews") but that they were in any case necessary: "if immediate and appropriate measures are not taken concerning Jews and their racial characteristics, it cannot be excluded that there will be untoward incidents in occupied areas." German Jews "will be regarded as stateless and will be kept under strict surveillance". But Sugiyama added that "to persecute Jews is not our policy and would make propaganda for the United States and Britain". The new legislation affected very few people – mostly refugees from Europe who had emigrated as far as Japan, Dutch Jews in the Dutch East Indies, Jews in the former International Concessions. White Russian Jews, nearly all living in Manchuria or Northern China, were already subject to appalling discrimination, not as Jews but as stateless White Russians, and potential "wooden logs".

The March 1942 measures are chiefly interesting as an example of Japanese sensitivity to German attitudes. The notion of the "Emperor's Jews" probably stemmed from memories of the Russo-Japanese war of 1904–5: then, the American banking firm of Kuhn, Loeb had been Emperor Meiji's chief financial backer.

The wartime rules concerning Jews are a reminder that Japanese anti-semitism, a phenomenon of the seventies and eighties (illustrated by a series of bestsellers blaming the US "Jewish lobby" for America's alleged anti-Japanese policies), has deep roots. Aristocratic Japanese, including Prince Konoye, often displayed the prejudices of their nineteenth-century British counterparts. The anti-semitism of Konoye, the tolerant aesthete who admired Proust and Oscar Wilde, as his posthumous writings showed, was bound up with his fear of Communism: he saw Marxism as a "Jewish disease".

Not everyone reacted enthusiastically to Japan's victorious advance in Asia. Konoye was despondent, according to his friend Morisada Hosokawa. "At the Peers Club, everyone around him was revelling in excitement over the success of Pearl Harbor. In a voice filled with dread and sadness, he said: 'it is a terrible thing that has happened. I know that a tragic defeat awaits us in the end. I can feel it. Our luck will not last more than two or three months at best.'"

On New Year's Day, 1942, Konoye, in semi-disgrace but in his capacity as close kinsman and ex-Premier, called on Hirohito to present his greetings. He told his aide, Tomita, later, that "everybody at the palace was celebrating the success of Pearl Harbor. Even Admiral Okada [the former Premier, left for dead during 2/26, and later a leading 'peace party' figure] was carrying on, giving toast after toast. A number of other old fellows who understand nothing at all started singing boisterously with Okada. What an unpleasant spectacle! How vulgar they are! At this rate, they will push us all the way to defeat . . ." His outspoken anti-war remarks threatened to get him into serious trouble with the political and secret police. He was already under a cloud for his past friendship with Hotsumi Ozaki, who had been a "closet Communist" for years, and the chief informant of Richard Sorge, the *Frankfurter Zeitung* correspondent in Tokyo and probably the Soviet Union's single most valuable spy.

Another leading figure who refused to join in the jubilation was Admiral Yamamoto himself. Aboard the *Nagato*, just after the attack on Pearl Harbor, there was considerable rejoicing in the messroom. "Yamamoto, alone, apparently, remained sunk in apparent depression." He also replied in subdued, prophetic terms to those fellow-officers who sent him their congratulations. To Mineichi Koga, a fellow-Admiral, he wrote: "The mindless rejoicing at home is really deplorable."[3]

Dowager Empress Sadako was one of the few senior members of the Imperial Family to take a resolutely anti-war stand – and her relations with her son, Hirohito, in the early months of the war, were seriously strained as a result. She moved out of Tokyo, to Numazu, on the coast, where she had lived with Emperor Taisho, during his illness, for a full year. On April 17, 1942, she summoned Kido and asked him pointed questions about the events that had led to Pearl Harbor and the "subsequent expression of brute force". When Kido later related this to Hirohito, during a rare, relaxed country excursion, the Emperor changed the subject and lectured Kido on mushrooms.

Prince Takamatsu, reflecting the fears and unspoken apprehension of many of his fellow naval officers, was, from the start, a "dove", and would, in due course, play an important if little-known role in edging Japan towards peace; but Prince Mikasa was, at least at first, a willing "public relations" figurehead, deputizing for Hirohito on morale-boosting visits to the front: on May 8, in Manila, in a ceremony organized by the victorious Japanese troops, he watched US prisoners-of-war march through the streets on their way to detention. Empress Nagako – for all the later image-building – was, like her husband, a "hawk" in the early days of the war. She did not share Hirohito's once-close relationship with the British Royal Family, and was convinced, even after Hirohito himself had ceased to believe in an Axis victory, that Hitler would win the war. One entry in Kido's diary tells of the former Japanese Ambassador in London being brought specially to the Palace to lecture the Empress on the fortitude of the British people during the Battle of Britain and the bombing that followed, in an effort to convince her that the Axis propaganda then at its peak in Japan had to be treated with circumspection.

The first tell-tale signs that the war would not be the hoped-for quick burst followed by negotiations acceptable to Japan came with the air raid on Tokyo, Yokohama, Nagoya and Kobe by B-25 bombers led by Lieutenant-Colonel James H. Doolittle, on April 18, 1942. This hazardous operation was strictly for badly-needed American morale-raising purposes, for little damage was done, but the impact on Japan's ruling élite was considerable. The planes, originally lifted by cranes onto the *Hornet*, took off in choppy seas 650 miles from their target. The Army fliers had never before operated from an aircraft-carrier, and every successful lift-off was a miracle.

After dropping their bombs, some from treetop level, the sixteen planes were due to land in "friendly", KMT-controlled China, but, some, short of fuel, crash-landed in Japanese-occupied China, and one plane landed in Soviet territory, near Vladivostock, where its crew was temporarily interned. Eight airmen were captured and — to Japan's lasting shame — tried as "terrorists". Though Hirohito commuted five death sentences, he must take responsibility for the three remaining executions: Sugiyama had demanded "severe punishment" and, after a farcical court-martial (preceded by torture), the death penalty for all eight.

Tojo did his best to have the sentences commuted. As he was to tell the IMTFE court after the war, he discussed the case of the airmen with Hirohito, and asked the Emperor to show mercy. The commutation, Tojo told the court, "was the Emperor's because of the fact that the Emperor is invariably benevolent". At the trial, all defendants, at almost all times, did their utmost to protect the Emperor, and no one more so than Tojo, but it was clear, both in his pre-trial cross-examination and at the trial itself, that Tojo had argued against the execution of the airmen, and that the Emperor had not shared his views. Had Hirohito been a little more "benevolent", he could easily have commuted the death sentences of the remaining three Americans without a murmur from Sugiyama. The inference is that he did not wish to do so.

American reactions to the airmen's deaths, and to the news of the Bataan "death march" and other atrocities that followed the 1941–42 Japanese blitzkrieg, were partly responsible for the ensuing stream of Allied anti-Hirohito propaganda, identifying him, along with Hitler and Mussolini, as one of the "three most hated men in the world". Ironically, among those who resented Hirohito's decision to try the American airmen were the Germans, who regarded this as an embarrassing precedent that might affect the morale of their own bomber crews.

The Doolittle raid was a bitter personal defeat for Admiral Yamamoto, but it was also a matter of considerable concern for Tojo himself, proving that the Emperor himself was not immune from possible retribution from the air. An elaborate military parade was about to be staged for Hirohito's forty-second birthday (April 29, 1942) and endless top-level meetings took place to debate whether to cancel it – and what to do if an air raid warning went off while it was in progress. The Generals and Court officials argued endlessly; finally, it was decided that the parade should go ahead as planned ("for if it is known that the Emperor stays away from the parade because of an air raid this would be shameful," Kido wrote) but that if an air raid warning sounded immediately before he was due to leave the Palace he was to remain there.

By the fall of Tobruk, in fact, the tides of war had already changed – for, that same June, Japan lost the battle of Midway, though the implications of this defeat were not understood for some time. Admiral Yamamoto, who had gambled so successfully on Pearl Harbor, wanted to strike a further decisive blow against the United States Navy. This time he lost, partly because his operation was ill-conceived, partly because skilled US cryptanalysts had broken the Japanese naval code, so that the US Navy knew exactly where his fleet was heading, and in what formations. At the Battle of Midway, Japan lost four aircraft-carriers, one heavy cruiser and the pride of her naval air pilots, to the American loss of one aircraft-carrier and one destroyer. The Japanese did land troops on the islands of Attu and Kiska, and still showed their superiority in the air (US dive-bombers were able to destroy the enemy aircraft-carriers only while their planes were on deck, being rearmed) but never again would Japanese ships attempt to score a major "classic" sea victory – henceforth their naval war was to be a war of attrition, or, eventually, of kamikaze strikes on a huge scale. Not the least blow, to Japan, was the loss of one of her famed Zero planes, which crash-landed almost intact on a US-held atoll. United States specialists took it apart and, as a result, American pilots were to fly the Hellcat, superior to the Zero, in the later stages of the war. The fears of the cautious minority within the Japanese Naval Staff were proving correct – but, for many months, the Japanese public was lulled into believing that Midway had in fact been a victory.

Hirohito was aware of the truth, but probably not of its implications, and he reacted like a warrior king faced with a minor, temporary setback. "It's really regrettable, it's a shame," he told Kido, "but I've given orders to the Chiefs of Staff to be careful not to lose our sense of combativity, not to become passive as far as operations are concerned." Hirohito's behaviour on this occasion, Kido noted, was "worthy of that of a great leader . . . I see in His Majesty's reaction the glittering quality of an Emperor and I am overwhelmed by my feeling for the Japanese Empire". Hirohito also showed that he approved of the way in which the Midway defeat was camouflaged for propaganda purposes into a Japanese victory, even asking Kido whether, to give the "official" version more credence, he should not issue an Imperial Rescript praising the Midway "victors". Kido advised him against, and Hirohito followed his advice.

The Midway defeat, followed by United States combined offensives in the Solomon Islands and at Guadalcanal, had immediate repercussions: Army and Navy chiefs started squabbling over available resources, especially planes, and Hirohito found himself increasingly forced to arbitrate between the two services. Congratulatory messages to the Imperial forces became more restrained, and diminished in number. But, as the United States counter-offensive gathered strength in the Pacific, and long after most of the Japanese government and military élite had tired of Tojo's increasingly high-handed ways, Hirohito continued to pin his faith on him.

The strains became personal ones. The Emperor – as in the crucial stages of the China War in 1937–38 – gave up his weekend visits to his palace laboratory, his early-morning riding, and, as food shortages increased, his English breakfasts, reverting to soups and coarse rice to set an example to his people. A year after Pearl Harbor the euphoria was gone, and inter-service rivalry, with bitter quarrels over resources, especially allocations of planes to the Army and Navy, was such that the Emperor had to step in and intervene, the first of many such Imperial arbitrations. Early in 1943 Buna, in New Guinea, was lost, partly because of insufficient sea transport for Japanese reinforcements – or, later, orderly evacuation. Hirohito praised the fighting qualities of the troops defending New Guinea, and noted that the Buna battle "must be rated a failure but if this can be the basis for future success it may turn out to have been a salutary lesson". He showed a considerable grasp of detail about the fighting there. "I understand the enemy used twelve or more tanks. Don't we have any tanks in this area?"

By mid-1943 United States forces had reoccupied the Solomon Islands, and Guadalcanal, after long and bloody battles, was free of Japanese by the end of 1943.

In a letter to Kido in 1943, Admiral Yamamoto aptly compared the war to unequally matched sumo wrestlers. "Instead of waiting for the usual limbering-up ceremonial exercises, the little chap attacked and almost pushed the big fellow out of the ring, while the audience cheered this clean, direct bold approach." But the heavyweight champion had "staggered back from the brink of disaster, planted his feet firmly on the ground and slowly come forward again. Now [in 1943] he faces the small wrestler in mid-ring. From now on we are in a real power struggle when reactions, training and technique will count for everything. The perseverance of the last five minutes will decide the game." Perhaps, knowing Hirohito's passion for sumo wrestling, Yamamoto was trying, through Kido, to convey the hopelessness of the situation.

But Yamamoto never did see the end of the game, for shortly afterwards, as he had predicted, he was killed in battle, though not aboard his beloved *Nagato*. From his land headquarters in Rabaul, he decided to fly to Bougainville on April 18, 1943, to boost the morale of young Navy airmen there who had been making repeated sorties against Allied shipping. United States cryptanalysts decoded his flight plan and detailed itinerary. A sophisticated operation was mounted to blast him out of the skies. Because US field commanders felt this was tantamount to a cold-blooded assassination, and might also lead the Japanese High Command to suspect its codes had been broken, approval was sought at the highest level. Roosevelt gave it without compunction, and a daring long-range P38 raid was organized. At dawn on April 18, eighteen Lightnings converged on the Admiral's plane, with its nine Zero escorts, shortly after take-off, and shot it down. When Yamamoto's body was finally recovered in the depths of the jungle, it was found that he had died instantly from a bullet in the face.

He may have had both a premonition of death and a secret longing for it, for he was known to be saddened beyond belief by the huge losses in his élite corps of Naval Air Arm pilots, all of them hand-picked, man for man probably the very best fliers of World War II. Among his personal effects, in his superb calligraphy, a poem was found, which Kido was later shown, and almost certainly handed over to Hirohito. It read:

> So many are dead.
> I cannot face the Emperor.
> No words for the families.
> But I will drive deep
> Into the enemy camp.
> Wait, young dead soldiers,
> I will fight farewell
> And follow you soon.

Yamamoto's death led to a further drop in Navy morale, though his State funeral, on June 5 (on the ninth anniversary, to the day, of that of Admiral Togo, the hero of the 1905 Russo-Japanese War), became yet another occasion for military page-antry (of the kind Yamamoto hated) and a propaganda exercise on the virtues of self-sacrifice, with senior representatives of the Emperor, Empress and Dowager-Empress Sadako in attendance. (Kido went on the Emperor's behalf: protocol banned the Imperial Family from attending any funeral ceremonies in person, except those of their immediate kith and kin.) Yama-moto's real loves, the three geishas with whom he had kept up a detailed correspondence from the start of the war, were excluded from the official ceremony. They regarded themselves, however, as his real "family", and their grief was in sharp contrast to the dry-eyed self-control displayed by his stern, poker-faced widow.

The fighting on Attu in the Aleutians, in May 1943, ending in a kamikaze-like final sortie of its 2,500-man garrison, all of whom were killed, was transformed by Japanese military propagandists into a heroic episode illustrating the traditional Japanese virtues of courage and self-sacrifice in the Emperor's name, but by now Hirohito was openly blaming his Chiefs of Staff for their failure to bring about a single clear-cut victory. He warned them to be more conscious of the United States military tendency to cut off Japanese lines of retreat. "You should not forget about this."

Three days after Yamamoto's funeral, in a post-mortem on the fighting at Attu, Hirohito told his Chiefs of Staff that such strategy was "regrettable. I wonder whether the Army and the Navy are really cooperating." He came back to the same subject two days later: "You make all sorts of excuses like thick fog and so on, but this should have been taken into consideration beforehand. I wonder if the Army and the Navy talk to each other at all? . . . We can't win with this kind of lack of co-operation. If we go on fighting like this we will only make China rejoice, confuse neutrals, dismay our allies and weaken the Co-Prosperity Sphere. Isn't there any way, somehow, some-where, of closing in on a United States force and destroying it?"

Shortly afterwards, Tojo visited the Solomon Islands, with a personal message from Hirohito to the field commanders. For all the Emperor's understanding of Tojo's difficulties, he spoke to him harshly: "You keep saying the Imperial Army is invincible but whenever the enemy lands, you lose the fight. You have never been able to repulse an enemy landing. If we don't stop them somewhere, where, I ask you, will it all end?"

Two months later, his impatience reached new levels. "When will you start hitting the enemy on all fronts?" he asked his Chiefs of Staff. "Can't we at least have one spectacular success against the United States? We can't go on retreating like this." Hirohito also asked Sugiyama detailed questions on the impact, on Germany, of the Allied landings in Sicily: did this mean Italy would pull out of the war, and out of the Tripartite Alliance? Did Germany have sufficient resources to send reinforcements to Italy? How would the loss of Italy affect German oil supplies from Rumania? On September 8, 1943, the Emperor's worst fears about Italy were realized, for she indeed pulled out of the war. The Tripartite Alliance was reduced to two partners, each in parlous shape.

Hirohito was becoming increasingly irritated by Sugiyama, and alarmed by Admiral Nagano's growing fatalism. But, despite his infrequent outbursts, he still trusted Tojo, who was as determined as ever, and now reassured the Emperor that the inter-service squabbles were "small misunderstandings" that would not seriously affect the outcome of the war. But the problems would not go away: the Chiefs of Staff requested 40,000 planes, then raised the figure to 52,000. After endless arguments, the Army agreed to take 27,000 and the Navy 25,000 – but only after Prince Takamatsu had been specially briefed by senior Navy Staff officers to present the Navy's needs to the Emperor. In the event, they had to settle for far less, for in the next year (1944) only 28,000 planes were built.

To use Japanese manpower more effectively in conquered territories, turn passive garrison troops into fighting units on the Pacific and Burma fronts, and give substance to the "Co-

Prosperity Sphere", some of the Asian colonies occupied by Japan had been granted independent status under suitably docile or pro-Japanese politicians. Dr. Ba Maw became head of State of an independent Burma on August 1, 1943; under José Laurel, the Philippines became an independent Japanese "client" in October of that same year. On November 5, 1943, a gathering of "Co-Prosperity Sphere" leaders met in pomp in Tokyo to discuss further steps towards Asian unity and attend a banquet in Hirohito's presence.

A group photograph of them, with Tojo in the centre, is dismal proof of Japan's growing isolation: Wang Ching-wei, the overweight Chinese "puppet", was to die of cancer a year later; Pu Yi was represented by his Prime Minister, Chang Chung-hui, a shady ex-businessman with narcotics connections; a Thai Prince, President Laurel of the Philippines, Burma's Ba Maw and – as "observer" – the Indian National Army's Subhas Chandra Bhose completed the group.* None of those present could help Japan with her growing difficulties, and most of them were dependent on Japanese generosity for their continued existence. The one credible collaborator, the Indonesian nationalist leader Soekarno, was not invited, because Japanese policies towards the Dutch East Indies were as yet unclear: this rich colony was Japan's lifeline for oil and other raw materials, and Tojo refused to grant the maverick Indonesian nationalist leader independent status, at least not yet.

By January 1944 not only Konoye, but a substantial part of the Imperial General Staff, including most of the Navy, were aware that Japan had lost the war. US troops landed in the Marshall Islands; a massive air attack on Japan's big naval base in Truk further depleted her fighting capacities. Tojo worked round the clock: the military machine was no longer reacting obediently to his commands; but, instead of perceiving the

* The INA was raised by Bhose from Indian prisoners-of-war captured in Malaya. At its peak, it was several hundred thousand strong, but like the BNA (Burmese National Army) was dependent on dwindling Japanese weapons and supplies.

underlying causes for this failure, Tojo reacted by trying to concentrate more and more power in his own hands.

It was scarcely a new phenomenon: as early as September 1942, when Japan was still in full control of the Pacific, Tojo had advocated the establishment of a "Great East Asia Ministry" under Army control to run the newly-occupied territories along standardized military lines. The Foreign Minister, Togo, saw this as a major erosion of his own powers, and objected. Because Hirohito felt Tojo was far more essential to the war effort than Togo, he sided with Tojo in this Cabinet crisis, and, using the Navy Minister Shimada (a protégé of Tojo's) as an intermediary, obtained Togo's resignation. Tojo added the Foreign Ministry to his portfolio (he had, in the meantime, given up the Home Ministry) but this was still not enough to satisfy him. As Prime Minister, War Minister and now Foreign Minister, Tojo was experiencing – from the civilian end – the frustration of dealing with the military who still saw themselves as a separate entity, their bonds with each other far more important than their loyalties to the Government, even a government headed by a lifelong professional soldier.

Tojo's brisk approach to problems was that of a clean-living workaholic whose philosophy was more suited to simple Army life than to complicated diplomatic and political realities. Even when it became clear to others that Japan's war production economy was hopelessly faltering, he continued to believe that longer working hours, leaner rations, and mobilization of women (and later children) would radically change the situation; faced with the problem of the responsiveness of the military, he took the simplistic line that, by assuming the functions of Army Chief of Staff, in addition to his other duties, he would cut through red tape, compel the Army to obey, and institute a new pattern of working relations between the Cabinet and the services. Long after Konoye, Kido, and the Emperor's brother Takamatsu, were convinced that Tojo's leadership and conduct of the war was distastrous, and military defeat inevitable, Hirohito still had faith in him. He was impressed by Tojo's "unflappable" qualities, his spirit of quiet, dogged determination. Also, unlike most senior Army and Navy commanders, Tojo gave the impression of speaking frankly, of taking Hirohito into his confidence. For all these reasons, the Emperor was prepared to allow Tojo to break with tradition and assume this additional burden. He was by now (January 1944) completely disillusioned with Sugiyama – whose forecasts had turned out so wide of the mark – and anticipated no problems.

Sugiyama, however, proved reluctant to leave. "I've heard His Imperial Majesty has already decided to sanction [this] change," he said. "It's a grave matter affecting not only the military but the entire nation. If His Majesty has decided, I have no more to say, but even so, I wish His Majesty would make clear this is a special case for the present circumstances only and will not become routine."

What finally destroyed Tojo, however, was a combination of military disasters and the emergence of a powerful cabal of former politicians and elder statesmen, working hard behind the scenes to extricate Japan from the appalling mess brought about by the war. Kido, a pivotal power-broker, was won round to their cause; by January 1944, they were already looking beyond the end of the war to the new post-war Japan. To some, it was inconceivable that Hirohito should remain on the throne – but all were determined, as their top priority, to preserve the "Emperor System", with or without Hirohito.

[1] Robert Guillain, *Orient Extrême*, Editions Le Seuil, Paris, 1988. Also: *I Saw Tokyo Burning*, John Murray, London, 1981.
[2] David Day, *The Great Betrayal*, Angus and Robertson, London, 1988.
[3] Hiroyuki Agawa, *The Reluctant Admiral*, Kodansha 1982.

CHAPTER NINETEEN

Discreet blueprints for ending the war had been in existence ever since Pearl Harbor. Only six days after the Battle of Midway, Shigeru Yoshida, the former Ambassador to the Court of St James (and, in earlier days, the young diplomat who had boarded Hirohito's flagship in 1921 at Gibraltar to bring him details of his British schedule during his extended trip to Europe) had submitted a brief to Kido proposing that he and Konoye discreetly leave for Europe, establish a base in Switzerland, and sound out belligerents and neutrals alike on the chances of a settlement. Kido felt the time was not yet ripe, and did nothing to encourage Yoshida's proposal: there is no record, in his diaries, of his referring it to the Emperor.

In February 1943, with the situation deteriorating rapidly, Konoye, still in semi-disgrace, met Kido in the home of the Lord Privy Seal's confidential secretary, Yasumasa Matsudaira, and urged him to persuade the Emperor to end the war as soon as possible, arguing that if it continued much longer Japan would become a prey to Communism. The following March Kido saw Yoshida again. The diplomat was still idle, because of his lukewarm sentiments towards the war, and once more Kido and he talked of possible peace negotiations. Once more, there is no evidence that Hirohito was kept informed.

But by 1944, when Japanese naval, air and ground losses were horrendous, a hard core of prominent politicians and military leaders began to try to shape long-term peace policies. Their motivations were various: some, like Princes Fushimi and Higashikuni, were consumed with hatred for the upstart Tojo, who had dared to break with military tradition and concentrate operational military power as well as Cabinet responsibilities in his own hands; others, like Prince Takamatsu, reflected the growing demoralization of the Navy, which had no confidence in the mediocre Shigetaro Shimada, Tojo's crony who combined the posts of Minister and Naval Chief of Staff.

Others, like the ex-Premier Okada and Hiranuma (the latter once a hardliner), had long since abandoned thoughts of victory, and hoped for an honourable peace short of unconditional surrender.

All, especially the Princes, were concerned about the survival of the "Emperor-system", and realized that, with mounting casualties, shortages of all kinds, and the piecemeal loss of all of Japan's conquests, the tide could very well turn against Hirohito himself.

By 1944, the secret police were reporting growing animosity towards Tojo, who, having assumed so many positions of responsibility, was being blamed for everything. But they also noted that the Emperor, who had made Tojo Premier, and allowed him to assume so many posts, was also concerned. Even the cautious Kido noted in his diaries that, if Hirohito continued to trust him, hatred concentrated on Tojo could well extend to the Emperor as well – and this must be avoided at all costs. As early as January 1944, Konoye and Higashikuni, both with a huge stake in the "Emperor-system", met secretly in Tokyo to discuss how to preserve it in the increasingly likely event of Japan losing the war.

The dénouement came with the United States attack on Saipan on June 15, 1944. Saipan was not like the Gilbert Islands, Tarawa, Kwajalein and Eniwetok, all now occupied by the United States after bitter fighting. It was not just another Pacific island conquered by Japanese troops in the wake of Pearl Harbor but the first integral part of Japan to be invaded, a former German colony, part of the territories assigned to Japan after the First World War, with over 10,000 Japanese civilians living there in addition to a large Japanese garrison. Tojo insisted that Saipan was impregnable – the killing zone which would compel the United States to reconsider any further plans for confrontation on land – but, for Japan's small élite, aware of the elimination of so many Japanese ships and planes, and the huge imbalance between dwindling Japanese war production and the huge American production capacity, there was no doubt that Saipan would eventually be overrun. Thereafter, as Prince Konoye was among the first to note, the war would take on a completely different character, for America's B-29 bombers, from Saipan, would be within striking distance of most of Japan's major cities, and the round-the-clock bombing of Japan, as Admiral Yamamoto himself had predicted, would almost certainly begin.

Tojo had put his faith in Saipan's 32,000-strong army garrison and interlocking networks of underground bunkers, immune to shells, as well as the protective screen of what remained of Japan's Combined Fleet. But the US task force included 100,000 men, 7 battleships, 15 aircraft-carriers, 21 cruisers, 69 destroyers and nearly 1,000 aircraft. By the time Saipan fell, three and a half weeks later (July 9), Japanese military deaths totalled nearly 30,000, plus at least 10,000 civilians, all but 35 of its 475 combat aircraft had been shot down, and the Combined Fleet largely destroyed.

Seven days after the start of the battle for Saipan, Imperial approval was given for the development of the first piloted one-way "flying bomb" prototype design, later the standard vehicle for kamikaze pilots. Orders were also drawn up in the Palace to be relayed to the Governor of Saipan, promising that all civilians who died there would achieve the same glorious status as soldiers who died in battle. This ambiguous Imperial message, which could be – and was – interpreted as a call for self-immolation as an alternative to falling into American hands, was not at first relayed to the Saipan authorities, and, as Tojo told IMTFE interrogators later, he tried to have it stopped. But it *was* sent, on whose responsibility no one knows to this day: the Emperor was certainly unaware of its contents, some say. But Imperial messages of this kind were not easily faked, or slipped through the highly efficient, fussy Court bureaucracy against the Emperor's will or even without his knowledge. Whoever was responsible, thousands of civilians, men, women and children, were, as a result, to throw themselves from cliffs into the shark-ridden sea in the closing stages of the battle, rather than surrender. Shocked US Marines filmed the unbelievable mass suicide from afar.

Appalling though they were, casualties on both sides might have been even higher, for Unit 731's commander, General Ishii, intended, for the first time, to launch his plague-ridden fleas on the American attackers. The only reason this did not happen was that the Japanese ship taking the Unit 731 squad and their lethal cargo to Saipan at the start of operations was sunk by an American submarine with the loss of nearly all hands.

While the battle for Saipan was raging, a different kind of contest was taking place in Tokyo, behind Hirohito's back. Prince Higashikuni was the first to receive the news: an emissary came to see him on June 20 to say that Tojo no longer felt he had the Emperor's confidence or that he could lead Japan to victory: he was contemplating resignation. Two days later Konoye and Higashikuni met secretly in the house of a mutual friend, a prominent businessman, and Higashikuni relayed the news. He added that he had advised Tojo to stay on. This had been deliberate, the shrewd Higashikuni explained: the important issue was not Tojo's future but the preservation of the "Emperor-System", and how to prevent Hirohito from taking responsibility for everything that had happened in the last four years. If Tojo were to continue in office, in a worsening war situation, he would become a convenient scapegoat, "like Hitler". If the government were to be reshuffled, responsibilities would be diluted and those of the Imperial family increased.

Konoye may have appreciated Higashikuni's ruthlessness, but made the point that, sooner or later, a new government would have to emerge, and that, to steer Japan out of the war, it was essential for it to be headed by a member of the Imperial Family.

Only a prince closely related to the Emperor would have sufficient authority over both the military and the people. Higashikuni said that, if such a time came (as it did, thirteen months later), he would not shirk such a responsibility.

By this time the views of the cautious Kido were slowly drawing closer to those of the two Princes. Two days later, it was Kido's turn to meet Konoye, this time in Konoye's house, in the presence of his wife, to discuss "family matters", including the forthcoming marriage of Kido's son.

Interestingly, this was one of the rare occasions when Kido failed to note, in his diaries, the details of a conversation, simply recording that "family matters" were discussed. A résumé appears only in Konoye's records. The reason is not hard to seek: the substance of their talk was so out of character, and perfidious, that Kido, in all likelihood, could not bring himself to record it on paper, even in a private diary. In Konoye's version of events, Kido agreed in principle to a "princely" Premier but wondered whether such a new government should not be ushered in *before* the end of the war. He also stated that, when the end of the war came, it would indeed be necessary for Hirohito to assume full responsibility, to avoid humiliating mutual recriminations and buck-passing between Army, Navy and Government leaders. This view was not, at first, shared by either Konoye or Higashikuni: in the months that followed, they were to change their minds several times, before coming to the conclusion that, for the good of the dynasty, the Emperor must at all costs be protected from the consequences of his actions.

Two days later, the plot thickened: Prince Takamatsu, thanks to his senior Navy connections, knew just how desperate things were. A link was established between him and Konoye, again behind Hirohito's back, thanks to a mutual friend and go-between, Morisada Hosokawa, one of Konoye's former aides who also worked, as a political contact, for Takamatsu. Hosokawa relayed to Konoye, on June 26, an alternative plan for ending the war which, he said, had Kido's approval: Tojo should remain as Premier, until the next major military calamity. Then, a new government should be appointed with a completely new policy, and with a princely figure at its head. This government should negotiate the best possible peace terms.

Two other prominent politicians, the ex-Premiers Okada and Hiranuma, also contacted Konoye during the course of the Saipan fighting, both telling him that Tojo must go.

No longer a pariah, Konoye decided to relay the thoughts of this small group to the Emperor, which he did through Kido's private secretary. He also drafted an up-to-date "position paper" destined for Hirohito himself, which he handed over to Kido.

It was an extraordinary document: had Hirohito taken it seriously, the end of the war might have come far earlier, sparing millions of Japanese lives. Konoye began by stating that the war situation was so hopelessly compromised that some form of surrender was necessary, but that no one in the Emperor's circle, or in the Army or Navy, had the courage to say so. The Emperor should extract the truth from his Chiefs of Staff, Tojo and Shimada, and request answers, in writing, to three questions. How bad was the war situation generally? How did the Chiefs of Staff envisage the future conduct of operations? What were their plans?

Cornered in this way, Konoye went on, Tojo would react in one of three ways: he would either resign on the spot, or ask Hirohito to decide for him, or reply in deliberately vague terms. In the third alternative, he should be compelled to resign.

Should Tojo resign, Konoye added, the next Premier ought to be a member of the Imperial Family (Takamatsu, he felt, was the most suitable candidate) and this new government should proclaim the cessation of hostilities.

There were different ways of rationalizing this decision vis-à-vis the outside world, Konoye continued. One was to explain the end of the war on humanitarian grounds; another was to claim that Japan's objectives had been achieved and Western "encirclement" ended; the third alternative was for the Emperor to announce the end of the war on the grounds that he could no longer stand idly by witnessing the pointless sufferings and sacrifices of his people. Since the first two options were too laughable to be believed, only one credible course of action remained. By proclaiming an end to needless suffering, Konoye wrote, the Emperor would re-affirm his links with the people. The earlier this happened the better. Japan should not be forced into unconditional surrender, Konoye added, for the "Emperor-system" had to be protected at all costs. It is noteworthy that in Hirohito's historic radio speech, announcing the end of the war, recorded on August 14, 1945, some of the language and vocabulary of this part of Konoye's report is incorporated almost verbatim in his text.

On July 4, as the Saipan campaign was nearing its end, Kido relayed a message to Konoye. He agreed with most, but not all, of his proposals. On July 8 Kido and Konoye met secretly: Kido told Konoye that it looked as if the Army and Navy were determined to carry on with the war regardless of casualties. It was all the more imperative to remove Tojo. The next government could be a transitional one, headed by a reliable general (Kido suggested Terauchi), then a princely government could take over and end the war. Kido favoured Higashikuni over Takamatsu, for he was aware of the bad blood betweeen Hirohito and his younger brother.

Kido and Konoye then returned to the question of the Emperor's responsibility: as in his earlier "family affairs" meeting, Kido stressed that Hirohito should take full responsibility for everything. It would probably be necessary for him to resign. The Crown Prince could be proclaimed Emperor, with a Regent exercising interim control. (Prince Chichibu by this time was seriously ill with tuberculosis, from which he would die in 1953, and so was excluded.) Kido still had doubts about the suitability of Takamatsu.

During and after the battle for Saipan, prominent princely relatives in the Army and Navy (among them Higashikuni, Asaka, Mikasa, Fushimi and Prince Kaya, an army colonel) all began to debate the best way of ending the war, and Hirohito eventually became aware of their comings and goings, and their frequent, supposedly secret meetings. Possibly his informant was Prince Mikasa, his youngest brother, more bellicose than either Takamatsu or Chichibu, and who had already informed on a group of Army officers plotting the assassination of Tojo.

Hirohito was furious. This was intolerable, "irresponsible behaviour" on the part of relatives who had no call to meddle in affairs of state. Hirohito was particularly incensed by the outspoken views of his younger brother, Prince Takamatsu. According to Colonel Kaya, a cousin of Hirohito's, the Emperor became "very excited" whenever Takamatsu talked to him frankly; so much so, Kaya said, that he could not envisage helping Hirohito if he persisted in this attitude, and threatened to resign his princely status altogether, formally opting out of the Imperial Family to become a commoner. Only Prince Higashikuni's talent as a peacemaker prevented this from happening.

On July 13, after a stormy meeting with Kido, Tojo was compelled to relinquish his post as Army Chief of Staff, and also forced to oust Shimada as both Navy Minister and Naval Chief of Staff. He agreed to broaden his government to bring in prominent ex-ministers who were known to be in favour of negotiations – but these men refused to serve under Tojo.

On July 18, partly as a result of the cabal against him, and his consequent loss of face, partly because of the Saipan disaster, Tojo resigned the Premiership – but attempted to stay on, briefly, as Army Minister. A meeting of former Prime Ministers debated who should succeed him. General Terauchi was their first choice, General Koiso their second, General Hatta the third. Kido pointed out to Hirohito that Terauchi (GOC-in-C, Southern Regions) would need GHQ's permission to return to Tokyo. Hirohito, still apparently under Tojo's spell, even though he was resigned to his stepping down as Premier, consulted him about the advisability of recalling Terauchi from operational duties on a highly sensitive, major front. Tojo said it was out of the question.

This left Koiso, a somewhat colourless personality despite his army nickname of "the tiger of Korea", but Konoye was having second thoughts about him. Why not, Konoye suggested to Kido, have a two-headed government, introducing an admiral, Yonai, in a senior role? Yonai was a "dove", and would be useful to the "peace party". Hirohito agreed. But, though this new government was more inclined to peace than Tojo's, it was unable to start the necessary negotiations, and the Emperor still showed no sign of adopting Konoye's peace strategy. Hard-liners remained in responsible positions: though Tojo was compelled, against his will, also to resign as War Minister, his replacement was none other than the discredited General Sugiyama, the man who, as Chief of Staff, had promised Hirohito victory within a year – and who had requested the execution of all US airmen after the first Doolittle raid. Hirohito clearly would not abandon hope of a dramatic victorious engagement that might be hailed as the turning of the tide. In March 1944, the likeliest place where this might happen was Burma. For this reason, all available Japanese war correspondents were sent to the Burma front to report in suitably glowing terms on the expected fall of beleaguered Kohima and Imphal. But the heroism of British and Indian troops – and decisive British air power and airlift capability – denied Japan this consolation. By July the siege was over. The newsmen were withdrawn.

These were grim but not yet desperate weeks for Hirohito, for the raids over Tokyo did not materialize as fast as Konoye had expected – and, when they did, damage, at first, was slight. As Robert Guillain noted, it was not until November 1, 1944 that the first major B-29s appeared, and then only on photographic reconnaissance. By this time the students and schoolboys, mobilized as civil defence workers, had cut "fire lanes" through Tokyo's jumble of wooden houses. But, despite Admiral Yamamoto's earlier, dire warnings, the Japanese authorities seriously underestimated the threat of incendiary bombs. As Guillain put it, at this time "air raid warnings were obviously still considered devices for controlling the population and stimulating its morale.

No thought seems to have been given to the danger involved". Schoolchildren and old people were evacuated; young Prince Akihito would, later, be among those taken to the safety of the mountains. Those who stayed were ordered to defend their own homes, and dig their own personal shallow shelters. Official Japanese thinking was that Tokyo houses were such tinderboxes that families had to be on the spot so as to extinguish the fires immediately; for this reason construction of public shelters had been discouraged.

Blazing houses were to be a night-time feature of Tokyo from the end of November onwards. Aesthetically-minded Tokyo residents called such fires "the flowers of Edo", and when Guillain took a tram the day after the first major raid he discovered that "a Japanese neighbourhood could vanish without a trace". A mass exodus began soon after, for the rumour spread that B-29s would come in their hundreds on December 8 – the third anniversary of Pearl Harbor.

The shelter inside the Imperial Palace was deep and practically bomb-proof, and Hirohito began to spend an increasing amount of time there, eventually using it as both office and conference room, and, finally, sleeping there as well. Though he heard the drone of the B-29s, and the bombs exploding, it was a long time before he realized the extent of the damage – for by this time he was virtually confined to the Palace, for security reasons, and, initially at least, given sanitized accounts of the impact of the bombing.

There was no way, however, of concealing from him the disastrous course of the Pacific War. In October the US campaign for the liberation of the Philippines began; Japanese training of pilots had been drastically curtailed, because of fuel shortages; and Hirohito vented his spleen, and his frustration, on the unfortunate Koiso, just as he had bullied Sugiyama when – after the first victories – the tide had begun to turn against Japan. Koiso had described the battle for Leyte as "decisive", and that battle had been lost. What did he propose to do now, Hirohito asked. Were Luzon, and the Philippines, definitely lost? If so, what did Koiso have in mind? By this time, the Allies were advancing on a broad front in France, and the Soviet armies were fast regaining lost territory.

Since August, a "superior council of war directives" (including the Premier, Foreign Minister, Army and Navy ministers and the two Chiefs of Staff) had been meeting inside the Palace twice a week, discussing broad strategy. Increasingly, they congregated in the stiflingly hot, airless underground conference room.

Hirohito followed the inexorable United States advance in the Philippines in detail on war room maps, and knew, too, the ever-widening gulf between propaganda and reality: in October he had agreed to the promulgation of an Imperial rescript congratulating the Japanese Navy on its great victories, though he was perfectly aware that his warships had suffered a series of almost mortal blows, including the loss of the *Yamato*, which had replaced the obsolete *Nagato* as the flagship of the Combined Fleet. Finally, after a stormy meeting with Koiso, Hirohito told Kido that the situation in the Philippines was becoming desperate, and that he was anxious to listen to advice from "people close to me". By this time the B-29 raids had begun in earnest, hitting industrial centres like Nagoya – and even damaging the sacred shrine at Isé.

In early January 1945, Kido noted that Hirohito was now fully aware of the situation in the Philippines. On the 4th, Hirohito told Kido: "Now a decisive battle will have to be fought on Luzon as Leyte has been lost . . . We will have to conceal this from the people." Two days later, Kido noted, Hirohito said: "It's reported that the US army intends to land at Luzon. The war situation in the Philippines is extremely grave. So I think it may be necessary to listen to the intentions of the 'jushin' [former Prime Ministers] stemming from the upcoming war situation. What do you think?"

Kido advised him to discuss the overall situation informally, to get the unvarnished truth, then call in key Cabinet ministers, "giving your questions as lucidly as possible", and then summon the former Premiers for advice. Kido knew that it was no use suggesting that Prince Takamatsu talk to Hirohito, but arranged, in early February, for all the surviving Premiers – Hiranuma, Hirota, Wakatsuki, Okada, Konoye and Tojo – to come to the Palace and say their piece.

Whatever their private sense of doom, neither Hiranuma, Hirota, Wakatsuki nor Okada were able to conquer their diffidence and speak honestly. Instead they hid behind a smokescreen of hazy generalities. Only two people spoke out: Tojo, who advised Hirohito to continue with "total war", on the mainland and to the death if necessary, and Prince Konoye.

Konoye advised Hirohito to make peace on almost any terms. But by this time, perhaps out of a sense of personal guilt, or a need to rationalize his past behaviour, the Prince had become obsessed with the fear of Communism, which he had begun to regard as an even greater threat to Japan than defeat itself. He believed that the army "reformists", who he had once courted and admired, had themselves been, consciously or not, the tools of a vast Communist conspiracy. He lectured Hirohito on the evils they had perpetrated (state planning, a centralized economy), and on their shady alliances with unreliable left-wing secret societies eager for reform. His anti-Communist diatribe must have sounded singularly irrelevant to the Emperor, and cast doubt on the soundness of the rest of his analysis.

Hirohito's preoccupations were more down-to-earth: did Konoye believe, as some of his generals told him, that the United States would massacre the Imperial Family?

Konoye replied that he did not think this would happen. "I know Grew and other senior Americans," he said. They would never allow such a thing to occur.

Hirohito said he was inclined to agree. "General Umezu [the Army Chief of Staff] says they will massacre my whole family but I don't entirely believe him." Hirohito added that Umezu was in favour of luring a huge American force into fighting to the finish in Taiwan, which would be so costly in US lives that negotiations might then start with Japan in a position of comparative strength.

Konoye was unable to gather whether Hirohito believed in the Taiwan option or saw it for what it was – an Army excuse to prolong the war and bring it to an apocalyptic ending. A shrewd, lucid observer when he was not trying to rationalize Japan's predicament by blaming everything on a Communist conspiracy, Konoye came away from his meeting with Hirohito downcast. He told Hosakawa that, if Hirohito still took the advice of people like General Umezu seriously, "I am very pessimistic [about the chances of peace]".

B-29 raids were now a daily occurrence, seriously affecting war production, and civilian casualties were mounting. On January 16, 1945, Kido noted the figures communicated to the Emperor since the raids had begun in earnest: 7,600 dead, 5,000 homes destroyed, 55,000 more evacuated and 20 per cent of Tokyo's population (including 200,000 schoolchildren) evacuated. At the same time, there was still an air of unreality about Court life: on the 18th, Kido noted the almost peacetime schedule of Hirohito and Empress Nagako: a lecture on calligraphy by one of Japan's foremost practitioners, followed by a philosophical discussion on the nature of Chinese culture and its emphasis on politeness, followed by a more relevant lecture, by an expert, on "the deployment of electric wave weapons" (i.e. radar). All this took place with complete punctuality between visits to the bomb-proof bunker during raids, and diligent morale-boosting work on the part of Nagako, who was engaged in writing letters of condolence to the families of the war dead: until they became too numerous, and communications deteriorated to such an extent that it was no longer possible, families of all the bereaved received notes bearing the Imperial seal thanking them for their service to the nation.

Meanwhile, Prince Konoye was pursuing his own, increasingly odd contribution to the ending of the war and the preservation of the "Emperor-system". On January 26, 1945, he took the train to Kyoto (a city spared by B-29s because of its profusion of sacred temples) to see Prince Takamatsu, who had moved there, and put before him a breath-taking proposal.

Japan was doomed, Konoye told the Prince. Because of the Emperor's role in events leading up to the war, it was inconceivable that Hirohito should remain on the throne. But resignation was not enough. He must not be subject to arrest – and should devote the rest of his life to prayer for the souls of the departed war heroes who had lost their lives in his service. There was a tradition, in the distant past, of Emperors voluntarily abdicating, and entering monasteries. What Konoye proposed was that Hirohito, in advance of total defeat, should not only resign, appointing his small son, Akihito, as Emperor and Takamatsu as Regent, but then immediately enter the Ninna temple in Kyoto and become its chief abbot.

Konoye's plan had been carefully prepared. He had talked to the incumbent abbot, Okamoto, the thirty-ninth in line since its establishment, and he had agreed to step down and allow Hirohito to take his place. Konoye and Okamoto had even decided on Hirohito's new priestly name: Yu-Nin Ho-Oh (Yu Nin was a different way of pronouncing Hirohito, using the same calligraphy, and Ho-Oh was the terminology for Emperors entering religion). Konoye spent nine hours trying to convince Takamatsu that it was a viable idea – and the only way of preserving the "Emperor-system". "I will join him in the monastery," Konoye said. He added that he had already talked to Admiral Yonai, the Navy Minister, and the ex-Premier, Okada, and that they were in favour.

The following month, Konoye submitted his plan to the Palace, despite the scepticism of both Kido (who had also been brought into the picture) and of Takamatsu himself, who refused to support it. Takamatsu's opposition was commonsensical: how could the Americans and British, who were Christians, understand the motives of an Emperor becoming a Buddhist priest? It was completely outside their frame of reference. Kido, too, was totally opposed. He no longer believed, as he had a year earlier, that the Emperor should resign and appoint a regent. Such an alternative was now too perilous. "If the Emperor abdicates, it will only become more dangerous for him," he told Konoye. The Allies would not see such a move in its proper religious context, but come to the conclusion, instead, that the Emperor regarded himself as a guilty man, and was running away, ostensibly taking refuge in religion.

Diehard army commanders were meanwhile devising a different scheme to protect the Emperor from the rapidly approaching nemesis. At huge expense, engineers started to build a vast fortified underground complex at Matsuchiro, near Mount Fuji, to house the Emperor and his family and ensure their safety while the final battle raged on Japanese soil. They even constructed a special armour-plated caravan to convey the Imperial Family from the Palace to the Matsuchiro bunker. It was because Konoye had got wind of all this activity that he had taken the trip to Kyoto, for he realized that, once the Emperor had been spirited away by the Army, there was no chance of seeing his own plan succeed.

The Dowager-Empress, too, was making her views felt. "The Emperor," Kido noted cryptically on January 29, 1945, "told me of the Empress-Dowager's feeling re the war." Less than a month later (February 25) her house was burnt to the ground during an air raid.

By this time Crown Prince Akihito had been sent to the safety of the mountains. A short letter to him, from Hirohito, exists, dated March 6, 1945: it is no different from the average letter busy fathers might write to their small sons at boarding-school: "Thank you for your letter. I'm very pleased to know you enjoy skiing and are in good health. Our war is in a very difficult phase but I want to go through this by my best efforts and divine power and I appreciate your prayers. Don't worry, I'm all right. I had a walk in the garden with your mother and collected items relating to B-29s – shell fragments."

On March 9 came the truly horrendous night raid on Tokyo that killed over 100,000 people and destroyed most of the city. Three days later, a meeting took place inside the Palace to determine whether Hirohito should tour the devastated areas. Kido told the Grand Chamberlain: "An Imperial trip under heavy guard, as usual, may cause harm. It is all right to do it but this is wartime so use a very simple system so it looks as if the Emperor did it on the spur of the moment." An "informal" tour of the shattered city, with a small retinue, took place on the morning of March 18.

So far, B-29s had been given strict instructions not to aim for the Palace grounds in Tokyo, but a debate was taking place in Washington on whether to bomb the Palace itself, and an Office of Strategic Services report – actually not published until July 1945, when the war was almost over, but in preparation during the peak of the incendiary bomb raids – outlined the official pros and cons.

The report noted that there were a number of cogent arguments in favour of "taking out" the Palace: the possibility that rumours of such an act might cause panic among the people; that "elimination of the Emperor from the political scene might be desirable because of his position as the center of the Japanese nationalistic tradition"; and because "it would afford satisfaction to Americans demanding revenge for the Philippines and Japanese war conduct".

On the other hand, the OSS experts noted, bombing the Palace might, on the contrary, "stimulate the offensive spirit" of the Japanese. Moreover, the authors of the report assumed that the Emperor's bunker was bomb-proof, so his death was unlikely, and in any case "his death would not affect the 'Emperor-concept'". Strategically, there was no point in hitting the Palace since "no vital documents in carrying out the war" were likely to be kept there. But the most telling argument was that "Hirohito might prove a useful influence later". Even the bombing of the Army and Navy Ministries, situated close to the Palace, "might be construed as an unsuccessful attack on the Palace" and were therefore to be discouraged. Summing up, the OSS experts felt the "bombing of the Imperial Palace is considered disadvantageous to the attainment of US military and political objectives", and that the net effect of such an attack "will be to increase the will of the Japanese people to carry on the war".

While preparations for landings on Okinawa were going ahead, and incendiary bomb air strikes on Japan continued, the Prime Minister, Koiso, was attempting to end Japan's involvement in China on almost any terms. His reasoning was that, in the last resort, Japanese forces dispersed throughout China would be required on the Japanese mainland for the final battle. Secret talks, through intermediaries, began, but Hirohito angrily ordered Koiso to put a stop to them. This was the main reason for Koiso's resignation, on April 2, 1945, and his replacement by another retired Admiral, Kantaro Suzuki, a lifelong courtier whose wife had been one of Hirohito's teachers when he was a little boy. And, when Hirohito finally learnt both the Army's and Konoye's proposals to spirit him away, the Army to a bunker and his kinsman to a monastery, he firmly refused to move. When Kido timidly proposed that the three sacred Shinto relics – the mirror, the necklace and the sword – should at least be taken to the Matsuchiro bunker, Hirohito refused permission. "I will stay with my people whatever happens," he told his Grand Chamberlain. To Kido he said: "I will share the fate of the sacred relics." He would eventually show the same flashes of determination, and leadership, that had resulted in the collapse of the "2/26" mutiny, but first Japan would experience appalling suffering, and hundreds of thousands of lives would be lost.

CHAPTER TWENTY

After inspecting parts of bomb-damaged Tokyo on March 18, 1945, Hirohito could no longer harbour any illusions about the outcome of the war. The military, however, still thought in terms of a *Götterdämmerung*, a final sacrificial battle on Japan's sacred soil that would inflict such casualties on the United States invaders that an "honourable" peace would still be possible. If one in ten able-bodied Japanese each managed to kill one invading soldier, their crazed reasoning went, the war might still be won, and, even if they failed, the "honourable death of a hundred million" was preferable to surrender.

The military also believed they still had a few cards up their collective sleeve. "Unit 731's" weapons would never be tested against the Americans (at the start of the battle for Okinawa, in April, General Ishii once more offered his services, but these were turned down on the grounds that bacteriological warfare "wouldn't make any difference") but several high-altitude prototype aircraft were under construction to counter the B-29s. Hirohito was kept abreast of their performances – and their failures – and enquired repeatedly about progress in this field.

There was another secret weapon the Japanese hoped to use against the invading US armada as it approached the Japanese mainland: the atom bomb. As with "unit 731", there is no direct evidence that Hirohito was aware of progress being made in this direction. The only proof of a link between the "father" of the Japanese atom bomb, the distinguished nuclear physicist Yoshio Nishina, and the Palace is a photograph of Nishina, still extant, taken in his office in the company of Prince Chichibu, probably in May 1940, after the Prince's inspection of

Japan's first cyclotron, devised and built by Nishina. The scientist would die in 1951, himself a victim of radiation sickness contracted during his heroic attempt to provide a full report on the effect of the Hiroshima bomb on its surviving population, and, though he was "debriefed" by US interrogators, immediately after the war, he was evasive about Japanese efforts to construct a bomb, and did his best to conceal the truth. It is, however, almost inconceivable that Hirohito, himself a scientist in close touch with Japan's academic community and indefatigably curious about new scientific accomplishments of all kinds, should have been unaware of the desperately urgent work being carried out by the "Rikken", Japan's Institute for Physical and Chemical Research, from 1940 onwards, or of the existence of the huge nuclear installation in Hungnan (North Korea), later dismantled by the Soviets, who may have gained as much information about nuclear fission from this top-secret Japanese base as they did from the Rosenberg and Fuchs reports.

Japan's race to be first with the atom bomb, obliquely confirmed by Prince Takeda years later in his interview with the *Observer* correspondent Peter McGill,* has been chronicled in Robert Wilcox's *Japan's Secret War – Japan's Race Against Time to Build Its Own Atom Bomb*, a brilliantly researched piece of detective work. It contains a reference to the late David Snell's story of a Japanese engineer's eyewitness account of an experimental atom bomb explosion off the Hungnan coast on August 10, 1945, that could not easily have been invented; it also has the fullest account of Japanese efforts to obtain uranium supplies from Germany even in the last days of the war in Europe – which explains why, in the final resort, Japanese military leaders hoped to harness at least one atom bomb to a kamikaze plane or submarine and launch it against a substantial American target.

Despite the incontrovertible evidence of Japanese nuclear expertise provided by Wilcox, there is no reference to a nuclear programme anywhere in any of the diaries of members of

* See Chapter XI.

Hirohito's entourage; but, given the Emperor's close monitoring, right up to the end of the war, of scientific, engineering and technological experiments of all kinds, and of Japanese efforts to introduce new weapons to counter the crushing numerical and industrial advantage of the United States, it is more than likely that he knew about Japan's nuclear war effort.

The facts were these. Increasingly, as the war turned in favour of the Allies in the Pacific, Oshima, the Japanese Ambassador in Berlin, began pestering the Nazi leaders for technological help. In particular, Oshima told them, Japan was interested in rocket technology (the V1s and V2s were beginning to hit Britain) and was in desperate need of uranium. She possessed some, mainly mined in Korea, but not nearly enough. A few German submarines were sufficiently large to carry up to 240 tons of equipment, and Germany did allow some of her precious advanced weapons to be taken to Japan by U-boat: by 1944–45, there was no other way.

The last German submarine to make the highly dangerous and lengthy run between Germany and Japan was the *U-234*, a giant 22,000-tonner, whose captain, Johann Heinrich Fehler, though only thirty-five, was one of the most experienced German Navy commanders, once captain of the decoy ship *Atlantis* that had lured countless Allied vessels to their doom. On March 25, 1945, seven days after Hirohito's inspection of martyred Tokyo, the *U-234* left Kiel, packed with secret devices, badly needed mercury (hidden as ballast), the latest German anti-aircraft shells, parts for jet planes and rockets, and bomb fuses. But the most sensitive cargo was 1,120 pounds of uranium oxide, packed in ten containers, capable of providing the wherewithal for two atom bombs.

The *U-234*'s odyssey had elements of high drama: after sixteen days, desperately dodging the US and Royal Navies which by now had total command of the seas, the *U-234* was in mid-Atlantic. The war in Europe was over, and by May 2 the submarine's signals were no longer being returned. Fehler did not know it, but Germany's Naval headquarters was in Allied hands. Shortly afterwards, Admiral Doenitz transmitted his final order to his remaining U-boats at sea to surrender, and on May 10 this message was picked up by the *U-234*. Fehler was practically equidistant from British, Canadian and American ports. Wisely, he decided not to continue his journey, and headed for the United States' East Coast.

Aboard the *U-234* were two Japanese Imperial Navy officers, one an expert on submarine construction, another a rocket specialist. Rather than surrender, they told Fehler, they would commit suicide. Fehler told them to proceed: out of consideration for the crew, they took sleeping pills instead of committing seppuku with their swords, and on May 11 were buried at sea. On the 14th, still 500 miles from the American East Coast, the *U-234* was boarded by a US Navy crew and shortly afterwards newsmen flocked to Portsmouth, New Hampshire to inspect her.

Reporters covering the *U-234* story sent back graphic descriptions of the U-boat's surrender but understandably concentrated more on the physical appearance of the disembarking crew than on the submarine's contents. US naval authorities later took her apart, bit by bit, and in this way the mercury, used as ballast, was discovered. At the time, of course, the word uranium meant little except to specialists. As Wilcox later discovered, at the US Naval Historical Center's Operational Archives in Washington, the inventory of the *U-234*'s cargo, published in May 1945 by the US Navy (but not released to the press), included "560 kilos of uranium oxide for the Jap army". This information was kept secret at the time of the submarine's surrender; it could only mean that, in some form or another, Japan might have been close to making her own nuclear bomb.

Wilcox tried in vain to find out what use was made of this precious information, and, indeed, what happened to the not inconsiderable amount of uranium oxide. It is almost certain that President Truman was told of the find aboard the *U-234*, and this discovery may have been one of the unspoken additional reasons for his decision to authorize the atom bomb strikes on

Hiroshima and Nagasaki. It is equally probable that Hirohito was aware of the *U-234* venture, even though his own decision to surrender came before she could have reached a Japanese port. He was well aware that German U-boat crews had obeyed Admiral Doenitz's order and surrendered to British and American ships at sea.

From April 1945 on, Kido's daily entries in his diaries become shorter and more elliptical. On April 13, he noted, in only a few lines, that his own house had been burnt to the ground during a raid. "I can't escape from the feeling of regret," he noted, "but on the other hand I feel somewhat cleansed." On April 29, the Emperor's forty-fourth birthday, he wrote the words "no celebrations", and, the following day, "air raid cut short my haircut". That April, the "peace party" éminence grise, Shigeru Yoshida, was arrested by the military police and kept under arrest for a month. Konoye cynically, but with considerable foresight, noted that "this would serve him in good stead in due course".

On May 25, eleven days after the *U-234* was brought into Portsmouth, the Palace was badly damaged during an incendiary bomb night raid. The B-29 raiders had not transgressed the order forbidding them from bombing the Palace, nor had bombs landed in the Palace compound by error: a strong wind swept burning fragments over the walls, and into the Palace grounds, and in the ensuing conflagration twenty-eight members of the Imperial Household, including a dozen firemen, were killed. In that same raid, eighteen square miles of Tokyo were burnt to the ground, and the palaces of Crown Prince Akihito, Prince Kanin, Prince Chichibu and Prince Mikasa destroyed, as were the more modest mansions of Prince Hashimoto, Prince Riken and Prince Rigu, parts of the Navy and War Ministries and the official homes of several Cabinet Ministers.

The Emperor's home was now almost exclusively his swelteringly hot air raid shelter, immediately below the Imperial Library, which contained bedrooms, bathrooms, a kitchen, a

telephone switchboard and conference room. Crown Prince
Akihito was safely away in the mountains, but both Prince
Mikasa and Prince Takamatsu spent some nights in the Imperial
shelter, after May 25. The tension must have been considerable,
for Hirohito had never forgiven Takamatsu for plotting the end
of the war, and relations between the two brothers were still
strained.

On June 11, Kido noted in his diary: "Four kempei came to
guard me." Whether they were actually for Kido's physical
protection, or whether he, too, was close to being arrested for
his behind-the-scenes peace ventures is unclear. Perhaps the
military police feared demonstrations against the man who had
been Hirohito's right-hand man for so long. Two days later
(June 13) Kido recorded that one of the Empress's stewards
called on him to discuss "the honourable movement of the
Emperor's palanquin" and the "headquarters in the Alps". The
army was again urging the Emperor and his family to move to
the secret bunker in the mountains – and the inference is that
the Empress may have been more inclined to flight than Hirohito himself.

Still there was no move on the Premier Suzuki's part to end
the war. It was an absurd situation. By May, Hitler was dead,
and the entire resources of the Allies would soon be free to
concentrate on Japan. The Soviet Union had formally announced that her non-aggression treaty with Japan would not be
renewed. Okinawa was about to fall, and the Allied invasion of
Japan was only a matter of time. Despite the romantic death-
wish theories of the military, defeat was inevitable, for Japan
was running out of food, fuel, planes and raw materials of all
kinds. Her major cities were in ruins, millions of her people
homeless and starving. Tentatively, the Supreme War Guidance
Council began discussing options, not for surrender, but for an
"honourable" end to the war. It was a measure of Japan's
insulation from reality that the Council, Hirohito included,
believed that the Soviet Union might intercede between Japan
and the Allies.

Absurd though this notion might have been, and proof of Japan's desperation, it was not even followed through with any consistency, for the initial meetings of the War Guidance Council, discussing possible Soviet mediation (May 11 to 14), were followed by diehard, fight-to-the-death assurances by Suzuki that made nonsense of the earlier debates.

The concept of surrender was so alien to anyone steeped in the Japanese military tradition (and Suzuki was a career naval officer, though he had spent a number of years at Court) that the seventy-seven-year-old Admiral, confused and exhausted as well as deaf, could not bring himself to adjust to such an eventuality. Every time Kido expected Suzuki to speak out in favour of peace, the Premier made the kind of blood-curdling, no-surrender speech (both to the Diet and to the other members of the Supreme War Guidance Council) that had become the standard conditioned response throughout the armed forces and the country as a whole.

So pervasive was the official "no surrender" line that, barely three weeks after broaching the subject of Soviet mediation, the War Guidance Council actually passed a resolution, in Hirohito's presence, on June 8, calling for "supreme self-sacrifice" and "the honourable death of a hundred million" rather than surrender. The official document, endorsed that day by Hirohito (it was entitled: "Fundamental Policy on the Conduct of the War") had the sacred, irreversible finality of a formal "Gozen Kaigi" decision. Mesmerized by the climate of romantic self-sacrifice prevalent during those doom-laden days, none of the participants at the meeting, least of all the Emperor, said anything to prevent it from becoming official policy. There was not even a reminder, on the part of the less bellicose Foreign Minister, Togo, of the possibility of Soviet mediation.

Immediately after this latest act of folly, Kido sat down and drafted his own report ("Measures for managing the situation"), urging Hirohito to cease hostilities immediately. This required considerable moral courage, and the following day he spoke in person to the Emperor. Thirteen days later, on June 21, the day after the fall of Okinawa, Hirohito was at last galvanized into action, and told Suzuki that he should not be bound by the June 8 "Gozen Kaigi" decision, but should base his policies instead on the Kido report and examine the situation "concretely and speedily". By this time, in addition to military casualties on Okinawa, some 120,000 civilians had died there too, and tens of thousands more in Japan herself, as a result of the bombings.

The Emperor had known Suzuki since he was four years old. "To him," Hirohito told Kido, "I could pour out my heart." The many barriers between Emperor and subject could never be entirely removed, but Suzuki, along with Kido and Konoye, was one of the few people with whom he could have frank and informal discussions. To have waited so long, and done nothing, while the bombings continued at home and carnage abroad (Rangoon fell in June, and Japanese troops were mown down at sea as they fled in makeshift craft), was an aberration that can only be explained in terms of prolonged catatonic shock, brought about by the unrelenting series of disasters, compounded by the bombing and the shattering of the Showa dream, paralysing Hirohito's will. The prospect of surrender, on the part of an Emperor who was also a "living God", the heir to a 2,600-year-old dynasty which had never been defeated by a foreign power, was daunting enough. But his Generals had deliberately made things worse, encouraging him to believe that the Americans intended to destroy the "Emperor-system", to exile or put him on trial, to deport his family, maybe even to take his small son hostage and keep him a prisoner for life in America. These rumours had spread throughout the Armed forces: they would soon lead to one of the most absurdly romantic plots in modern Japanese history. Because he felt there was no alternative, and despite the evidence to the contrary, Hirohito still clung to the belief that Soviet Union mediation was the only way of avoiding unconditional surrender. Togo met the Soviet Ambassador, Jakob Malik, and hinted that the USSR would be suitably rewarded if she agreed to cooperate. He was treated with contempt.

Now, Hirohito turned once more to Konoye, as the man uniquely suited to argue Japan's case with Molotov, and asked him to go to Moscow.

Had Hirohito been aware of what was then taking place in Washington he might have acted sooner, and more decisively – and thus saved the lives of the Hiroshima and Nagasaki victims. For, ten days after Kido's courageous, commonsensical report on the need to bring the war to an end with all possible speed, Truman and his chief aides met to prepare for the Potsdam Conference to be held the following month. Despite polls showing how determined American public opinion was that the Emperor should be punished (30 per cent wanted him executed, 37 per cent felt he should be tried and imprisoned for life, and only 7 per cent believed he should be immune from prosecution or used as a puppet), an influential "Tokyo lobby" headed by Grew and the Assistant Secretary for War, John J. McCloy, argued that Hirohito should remain on the throne as a constitutional monarch, provided Japan renounced militarism. Truman came away convinced that McCloy's suggestion that the US President should send a personal message to Hirohito outlining such an offer was worth consideration, and that only if it was refused or ignored should the atom bombs be dropped.

Konoye agreed to go to Moscow. Privately, he had no illusions about his mission, "but", as he told his secretary, Tomita, "I could say nothing when I saw the Emperor. He had come out of his air raid shelter to the temporary audience-room, with his usually neatly combed hair unkempt, looking pale and terribly haggard". Konoye hoped to revive the plan he had initially devised for the aborted 1941 Roosevelt meeting. To prevent Army obstruction, he suggested that the Emperor should issue an Imperial Order, drafted by Konoye from Moscow, endorsing the peace terms Konoye hoped to work out with Molotov. In that way, the military would be faced with a fait accompli. Again, as in 1941, this proposal demonstrated Konoye's faith in the sacred nature of the Emperor's decisions, and in his unquestioned authority.

The Soviets prevaricated. Sato, Japan's Ambassador in Moscow, found Molotov "too busy" to see him. The victorious Allies were already working out the agenda for the Potsdam Conference, but Stalin in any case had no intention of acting as mediator to obtain favourable peace terms for Japan: for the very good reason that, seven months previously, at Yalta, he had been urged, by Churchill and Roosevelt, to enter the war against Japan as soon as possible after Germany's defeat. At Potsdam (in the company of Churchill and Truman) he knew he would be urged to open a "second front" against Japan – and he was prepared to do so, though delaying as long as he possibly could.

The Allied leaders converged on Potsdam, and on the eve of the first working session (July 16) Truman received the news that a nuclear bomb had been successfully detonated in New Mexico. He told Churchill, whose immediate reaction was that, if Truman did order the atom bombs dropped on Japan (and Churchill was convinced that he should), "then we should not need the Russians". Truman decided not to tell Stalin about the atom bomb as such, but did mention, casually, that America had a powerful new weapon which it intended using on Japan. Stalin expressed only polite interest. But he did introduce the Konoye proposal, which Truman already knew about, thanks to "Magic" interceptions. Stalin then told Truman his armies would launch their attack on Japanese-occupied Manchuria in early August. What therefore should he do about the Konoye peace proposal? Truman replied he should act as he thought best. Stalin said he would continue to prevaricate. So it was Molotov's deputy who finally saw Sato, but only to tell him that Konoye's peace mission was too vague to warrant a visit.

On the final night of the Potsdam Conference, a prodigious number of toasts were exchanged, and Churchill, unaware he would remain in office only for another few hours (Attlee defeated him in the first post-war General Election, on June 26), raised his glass and boomed: "Here's to our next meeting in Tokyo."

The joint US-UK-China ultimatum to Japan, known as the Potsdam Declaration, should by rights have enabled Hirohito to reply immediately and positively, in turn enabling Truman to reconsider his decision to launch atom bomb raids on Hiroshima and Nagasaki. Without outlining any specific concessions, it fell short of the earlier (Cairo summit) request for Japan's unconditional surrender, calling instead for "the unconditional surrender of all Japanese armed forces", a very different proposition. It pledged that, after being disarmed, Japanese troops would be "permitted to return to their homes with the opportunity to lead peaceful and productive lives". It did not mention the Emperor at all, and even, between the lines, implied that the "Emperor-system", purged of militaristic influences, might be retained. The influence of Grew and McCloy on the final text was considerable. "We do not intend that the Japanese shall be enslaved as a race or destroyed as a nation," it said, "but stern justice shall be meted out to war criminals, including those who have visited cruelties upon our prisoners. The Japanese Government shall remove all obstacles to the revival and strengthening of democratic tendencies among the Japanese people. Freedom of speech, of religion, and of thought, as well as respect for the fundamental human rights shall be established."

On July 27 the Supreme War Guidance Council met to examine this text. Togo felt it would be highly unwise to reject it. But the Council, and the Cabinet in a separate meeting that afternoon, disagreed on ways of presenting the Declaration to the Japanese people – and to the Armed forces. The emerging consensus – that an expurgated version of the Potsdam Declaration would be released to the press, without comment, and that Japan should adopt a "wait and see" attitude, while still hoping for a positive Soviet response to Konoye's proposal – in itself virtually guaranteed that an impatient Truman, interpreting such a reaction as sheer delaying tactics, would order the first atom bomb strike. But worse was to come. For Suzuki, at a rare press conference on July 28, summed up the Government's majority view as a mandate to "mokusatsu" the Declaration, that is, to "kill it with silence". The word could also be translated as "treat it with silent contempt". On Government orders, the *Asahi Shimbun* called the Potsdam Declaration "a thing of no great value". Neither the Supreme War Guidance Council, nor the Cabinet, nor the Emperor could know that the fate of the Hiroshima and Nagasaki victims was to be sealed by the use of that unfortunate word, and by the fact that – as Washington was quick to discover – the key phrase in the Potsdam Declaration ("We do not intend that the Japanese shall be enslaved as a race or destroyed as a nation") had been censored in the Japanese version released to the press.

Again, the catatonic state of shock that had paralysed the Emperor's will earlier now spread to the Government as a whole. Hirohito may have believed that a Soviet response was still possible, but very few others did: they may however, have felt they were gaining time, and that more explicit terms, including reassuring statements on the future of the Emperor and the "Emperor-system", might be forthcoming. Truman waited for just over a week. Then, when nothing more seemed likely to emerge from Tokyo, on August 6, at 0815 hours, the *Enola Gay* flew over Hiroshima and dropped its parachute-assisted atom bomb on inhabitants who were so used to B-29 flights that, observing only two planes in the sky and assuming they were on a reconnaissance raid, they did not even bother to take to the shelters.

Not until that afternoon did detailed reports from Hiroshima reach Tokyo, though the Japanese Army headquarters knew straightaway what had happened: Japanese efforts in this field were sufficiently advanced for the Army's knowledge to be both sophisticated and immediate. And Truman, in a statement of questionable taste, confirmed their suspicions. "The source from which the sun draws its power," he proclaimed, "can now totally eclipse the land of the rising sun, on whose throne sits a direct descendant of Amaterasu O-Mikami, the Goddess of the Sun." Hirohito was informed of the nature of the bomb by Togo, and by the Army. Shock, and failure of will, once more engulfed not only Hirohito but the Government as a whole, for a whole day went by, and no move to end the war was made.

Only forty-eight hours later, after Togo had talked to Hirohito in his bunker, urging him to accept the terms of the Potsdam Declaration with all possible speed, did the Emperor react. In a discussion with Kido, he said his own personal safety was unimportant. What mattered was the immediate termination of the war. But so cumbersome and slow was Government machinery that more precious time was lost. A Supreme War Council meeting was not held until August 9. On that day Soviet troops crossed the border and poured into Manchuria, and, that same morning, the second atom bomb was dropped on Nagasaki. Now there was a very real possibility, in the minds of Japan's ruling élite, that a third bomb would fall on Tokyo itself, annihilating the Imperial Family as well as most of the population. When the Supreme War Council met that afternoon in the bunker, Suzuki announced at last that there was no alternative: Japan had to accept the terms of the Potsdam Declaration.

Incredibly, three of the military members of the Council – General Korechika Anami, the War Minister, and the Army and Navy Chiefs of Staff – still believed they could impose their own terms on the Allies. As the authors of the admirable chronicle of surrender, *Japan's Longest Day*, noted, these three were still psychologically unable to accept the *idea* of defeat or surrender – and their proposals were, in fact, a subliminal denial of the *fact* of defeat or surrender. Even now, Anami argued, Japan should insist on a minimal occupation force, the trial of war criminals by Japanese courts, and demobilization carried out without foreign interference. "We cannot pretend to claim that victory is certain, but it is far too early to say the war has been lost," he said. General Umezu agreed. The Supreme War Council was hopelessly divided – three in favour of accepting the Potsdam Declaration in its entirety, and three against.

Now, dispelling his inhibitions, Hirohito decided to act. He summoned Hiroshi Shimomura, the former head of NHK, the national broadcasting company, who was now Director of the

Information Bureau, and remained closeted with him in the bunker for two hours. That evening, Shimomura told an aide: "The Emperor has agreed to make a broadcast telling the nation whether we're to have peace or war." Hirohito talked late into the night to Kido. His mind was made up: at long last he would use his Imperial prerogative.

Later still, that same night, the most dramatic "Gozen Kaigi" of the Showa era took place, in the airless conference room. All those present were drenched in perspiration, especially the civilians, compelled by protocol to wear their obligatory Court dress – black morning coats, starched shirts and striped trousers – but, by the time it ended, tears as well as sweat poured down their faces. The Potsdam Declaration was read. Suzuki formally apologized to Hirohito for requesting his presence before a divided assembly. He then called on those present to speak. Togo urgently recommended, as he had from the start, that it be accepted. The Navy Minister, Yonai, briefly agreed. Anami, as he had the day before, but with more desperate eloquence, urged that guarantees be obtained for the preservation of the "Emperor-system", and that Japan be allowed to conduct her own war trials, disarm her own soldiers, and limit the numbers of the occupation forces. Umezu agreed. Hiranuma, as President of the Privy Council an ex officio member of the "Gozen Kaigi", cross-examined the Army and Navy members present on the chances of an orderly surrender, and obliquely appeared to side with the three diehards. Toyoda then added his voice to that of Umezu and Anami.

Suzuki then rose. Using the habitual ceremonial, circum-locutory forms of speech that were *de rigueur* in the Emperor's presence, particularly on such a solemn occasion, he humbly asked Hirohito to decide for them. The Imperial Command was known as the "Voice of the Crane", for its cry could be heard for miles though it was seldom seen. Now the "Voice of the Crane" was to decide whether Japan was to survive as a nation or continue the war to the bitter, sacrificial end, the "honourable death of a hundred million".

Hirohito spoke quietly. Continuation of the war could only lead to the annihilation of his people and more suffering for all humanity. It was clear to him that Japan could no longer wage war, nor defend her shores. "That is it unbearable for me to see my loyal troops disarmed goes without saying, but the time has come to bear the unbearable. I give my sanction to the proposal to accept the Potsdam Declaration on the basis outlined by the Foreign Minister." As he spoke, he seemed to be addressing one person in the room – Anami. Though no full record exists of the proceedings that day, it was later revealed that, whereas the Emperor referred to the other Ministers and Generals by their titles, as protocol required, he referred to Anami by name, appealing to him personally, almost as though they were brothers. Hirohito knew that it was Anami's acceptance of the Imperial decision that mattered. He was the one who had to be convinced, for he in turn had to convince the Army to obey the Emperor's decision. It so happened that the two men knew each other well: in the 1920s, Anami had been one of Hirohito's ADCs, and Hirohito liked him. Often, he had entrusted him with private errands that had nothing to do with Army matters, such as collecting rare butterfly specimens from Taiwan for the Emperor's collection. Without waiting for an answer from the eleven men in the room, Hirohito rose, and left the conference room.

Suzuki said: "His Majesty's decision should be made the decision of this conference as well." All eyes were on Anami, who remained silent. Silence implied tacit approval by all, and the meeting adjourned, but not for long.

Constitutionally, it was the Cabinet that had to take the formal steps to sue for peace, and now the rest of the Cabinet joined the Ministers who had already participated in the "Gozen Kaigi" at Suzuki's official residence. A communiqué was hammered out, accepting the terms of the Potsdam Declaration, which each Minister signed. The moment came for Anami to add his name to the document: even at this stage, he could have nullified the proceedings by withholding his signature, for the Cabinet decision had to be unanimous. But the Emperor had spoken, and Anami was bound to obey, even if, as he knew, this would cost him his life. There was an almost audible sigh of relief when he did so.

Three hours later, the following cable was sent to the Japanese Embassies in neutral Bern and Stockholm, for onward transmission to Washington, London, Moscow and Chungking:

"The Japanese Government are ready to accept the terms enumerated in the joint declaration issued at Potsdam on July 26, 1945, by the heads of the Governments of the United States, Great Britain, and China, and later subscribed to by the Soviet Government, *with the understanding that the said declaration does not comprise any demand which prejudices the prerogatives of His Majesty as a Sovereign Ruler.*" ⋆

This had been the one condition the military diehards had insisted on to the very end. But all those consulted, including Suzuki and Kido, agreed to its inclusion: it provided Anami with a strong argument in case his own officers refused to lay down their arms for, if the Allies explicitly rejected it, he had extracted from Suzuki the pledge that Japan would continue the war. But it was also the first step in the long, selfless post-war battle on the part of his courtiers to save Hirohito from the consequences of the war, and ensure that – even if the other members of the last "Gozen Kaigi" were to be arraigned as war criminals – the Emperor himself would be immune from prosecution.

⋆ Author' italics.

CHAPTER TWENTY-ONE

It was now for the Allies to determine whether Japan's acceptance of their surrender terms was satisfactory, and, after much transatlantic debate, they decided that it was, though the reference to the "prerogatives of the sovereign ruler" required additional clarification. Their cabled reaction was that "from the moment of surrender the authority of the Emperor and the Japanese Government to rule the state shall be subject to the Supreme Commander of the Allied Powers [General MacArthur] who will take such steps as he deems proper to effectuate the surrender terms". In addition, Truman wanted it put on record that Hirohito in person should take part in the surrender ceremony; but Attlee's new Government, with Churchill's assent, felt this was going too far and suggested instead that "the Emperor shall authorize and ensure the signature by the Government of Japan and the Japanese General Headquarters of the surrender terms". Truman agreed to the new formula, as did Chiang Kai-chek.

Incredibly, in Japan, not even the initial decision to surrender was public knowledge, for no way had yet been found of announcing the Government's decision to its people. The situation was further confused by two completely contradictory communiqués. One, issued by the War Ministry in General Anami's name on August 10, but without his specific authorization (it was drafted by a group of diehard junior staff officers), announced that there was only one choice: "we must fight on until we win the war to preserve our sacred polity . . . even if we have to chew grass and live in fields." The other, approved by the Cabinet, was substantially different, but equally uninformative, only hinting at an epochal decision to come: "the Government will do all it can to defend the homeland and preserve the honour of the country," it read, "but it expects that Japan's hundred million will also rise to the occasion, overcoming whatever obstacles may lie in the path of the preservation of our national polity." For foreign consumption only, the Domei news agency was allowed to broadcast, in morse, the actual text of the Government's response sent to Bern and Stockholm. Debate also raged, among Hirohito's aides, on the meaning of the Allied reply: all, including those most anxious to stop the war, knew it would be difficult for the Army to accept it.

The atmosphere inside the War Ministry resembled that of the heady days of the "2/26" mutiny: excited officers gathered in small groups in crowded back rooms; diehard colonels and captains lobbied Anami and the Privy Council President, Baron Hiranuma; and others even tried to enlist the support of Prince Mikasa in favour of a continued, sacrificial struggle. Plans for a coup, in the pure tradition of "2/26", using the Imperial Guards Division and elements of the Eastern Army Command, were in fact already under way, masterminded by Major Kenji Hatanaka, of the War Ministry's own Military Affairs bureau, with help from Lieutenant-Colonel Masahito Takeshita, Anami's brother-in-law, Tojo's son-in-law and several other influential middle-ranking officers. The Generals suspected that a plot was forming. Approached by some junior staff officers, General Yoshijiro Umezu, the Army Chief of Staff, made it clear he would not join in the conspiracy. Nor would Anami: to do so would mean breaking his word to the Emperor – an even more heinous crime than surrender. Under constant pressure, however, over the next forty-eight hours, from increasingly hysterical officers whose opinions he shared, Anami wavered; and, egged on by groups of junior staff officers, the Army and Navy Chiefs of Staff begged Togo, the Foreign Minister, to change his mind about the surrender terms.

As well as bombs, American B-29s were now dropping

leaflets in Japanese with the text of the latest Allied reply. With the Army in turmoil, the effect could be catastrophic unless the country was told what was actually happening. Kido persuaded Hirohito that the only way to prevent an army coup was to stage yet another "Gozen Kaigi" to bring the wavering military commanders to heel.

This took place in the underground conference room on the morning of August 14. After listening to Admiral Toyoda and General Anami's renewed appeals to carry on with the war, Hirohito, wearing army uniform, and streaming with perspiration, wiped his face with a white handkerchief before he spoke. Gaunt, underweight, exhausted, dizzy with insomnia and apprehensive about his own fate, he nevertheless performed with regal restraint, quiet eloquence and authority. It was, undoubtedly, his finest hour.

"I have listened carefully," he said, "to all the arguments . . . My own opinion has not changed. I shall now re-state it." Continuation of the war would bring nothing but further destruction. The Allied reply was "an acknowledgement of our position. In short, I consider it acceptable. Although some of you are apprehensive about the preservation of the national structure, I believe that the Allied reply is evidence of the good intention of the enemy . . . That is why I favour acceptance of the reply. I fully understand," he went on, "how difficult it will be for the officers and men of the Army and Navy to submit to being disarmed and to see their country occupied . . . I am not concerned with what may happen to me. I want to preserve the lives of my people. I do not want them subjected to further destruction. It is indeed hard for me to see my loyal soldiers disarmed and my faithful Ministers punished as war criminals."

But to continue the war would be to destroy Japan, and, "as things stand now, the nation still has a chance to recover . . . As the people of Japan are unaware of the present situation, I know they will be deeply shocked when they hear of our decision. If it is thought appropriate that I explain the matter to them personally, I am willing to go on the air . . . I am willing to go wherever necessary to explain our action. I desire the Cabinet to prepare as soon as possible an Imperial Rescript announcing the termination of the war." Without waiting for their comments, he left the conference room. Some of the Ministers were on their knees, kowtowing. All were in tears, their sobs audible.

There was nothing more to say. Perhaps the most composed person at this, the last wartime "Gozen Kaigi" was the Emperor himself, who calmly told Kido, shortly afterwards, that he had meant what he said: he was willing to go both to the Army and the Navy Ministries and speak to the rebellious officers in person, if it would serve a purpose. He also told Kido to get in touch with Shimomura, the Director of Information, and tell him that he, the Emperor, would be ready to broadcast later in the day.

It was unthinkable that the Emperor should broadcast "live", so a scratch team was assembled at NHK, the Japanese Broadcasting Company, to cut the record of Hirohito's speech that would later be broadcast. Because of the urgency of the situation, they were told, they would not be required to wear frock coats and striped trousers. The civilians' baggy wartime "austerity" uniform worn by almost all Japanese (called "kokominfuku") would suffice.

After the Emperor's last "Gozen Kaigi", one of the coup leaders, Lieutenant-Colonel Takeshita, took his brother-in-law, General Anami, aside in the Prime Minister's office and made one last attempt to get him to change his mind and lead a coup to neutralize the "traitors" around the Emperor and carry on the fight. They talked just before the Cabinet meeting that would give official approval to an Imperial Rescript ending the war.

Anami refused. "The Emperor has made his decision," he said. "There is nothing I can do. As a Japanese soldier, I must obey my emperor." Takeshita then asked Anami, as one last favour, to resign. Since the Cabinet decision to issue the surrender Rescript had to be unanimous, this would prevent the meeting from taking place, and delay proceedings until a new

War Minister could be found – probably indefinitely. "The war will end even if I resign," Anami replied. "And, if I resign, I would not see the Emperor again." After the Cabinet meeting – again all eyes were on Anami, for some Ministers felt it would be in character for him to resign in the middle of it, and there was widespread relief when it ended without his having uttered a word – the War Minister returned to his own office. He, like his Naval counterpart, had pledged that the Emperor's words were to be obeyed. He drafted a short statement: "The Imperial Forces will act strictly in accordance with the decision of His Imperial Majesty the Emperor", and ensured that all senior officers and officials at the Ministry signed it. He then addressed his staff, explaining the Emperor's decision. "You officers must realize that death cannot absolve you of your duty," he said. "Your duty is to stay alive and to do your best to help your country along the path to recovery – even if it means chewing grass and eating earth and sleeping in the fields." He was asking them not to take the "bushido" path of "seppuku", but he had said "you officers" instead of "we officers"; this meant, some of those present felt, that for Anami at least there was to be no life after surrender.

One of the members of the NHK team ordered to record the Emperor's voice was twenty-three-year-old Shizuto Haruna. He remembers the day well. A Palace car came to fetch him and the rest of the six-man crew at 2 p.m., and they set to work in two rooms of the Imperial Household Ministry, an unattractive neo-Georgian building near the Sakashita Gate. In the room where the Emperor would speak, they erected a large microphone; in the adjoining room, they set up their heavy record-cutting machines. A playback machine was brought over so that the Emperor could listen to his own broadcast. "We waited and waited," he recalls. At six a meal was served, on Imperial Palace china with the chrysanthemum emblem. Then an air raid warning sounded and the lights were dimmed. They heard the all clear, and still the Emperor did not appear. There had been a last-minute hitch: General Anami was to blame.

At the Prime Minister's office, the team of aides and Ministers preparing the Emperor's broadcast text were arguing endlessly over one sentence. Originally it had read: "The war situation grows more unfavourable to us every day." Anami said he could not put his name to such a statement, for it was tantamount to admitting that all the past War Ministry communiqués had been lies. "We have still not lost the war," he insisted. He seemed to have no inkling of the urgency of the situation, and even appeared to be quietly enjoying the irritation he was causing. After hours of discussion, and one interval, the drafting committee agreed to change the phrase to "the war situation has not developed to Japan's advantage".

At the Palace, Hirohito was becoming impatient: he asked his Chamberlains several times whether the text was on its way. Kido briefed Princes Takamatsu and Mikasa on the day's events, and also received Konoye, who called on him to warn him that he had heard talk of a coup. "I don't like it," he told Kido, "I don't like the rumours I've heard about the Imperial Guards Division." The First Imperial Guards Division, whose headquarters was at the rear of the Palace, near the Inui Gate, was under the command of Lieutenant-General Takeshi Mori, known as "the monk" for his devotion to duty – and for his shaven head. It was this Division which was responsible for the Emperor's personal safety, and one of its battalions guarded the Palace at all times. Kido assured Konoye that Anami had the Army under control. But he did pass on the news Konoye had brought to Hirohito's chief ADC, who promptly sought out General Mori, who told him his men were "troubled", but that he knew of no impending coup. Konoye was right, and Mori was misinformed: several Imperial Guards officers had indeed joined Major Hatanaka's conspiracy: these included two men in sensitive posts, Major Koga (who commanded a battalion and happened to be Tojo's son-in-law) and Major Ishihara, a staff officer.

Waiting to broadcast, Hirohito went for his usual evening walk in the Palace gardens. Returning to the Library, he found his Prime Minister, Suzuki, waiting for him – but only to apologize for the delay in preparing the Rescript.

Finally, around 7.30, the text for the surrender broadcast was completed to everyone's satisfaction, though the copy brought to the Palace had been scribbled over with insertions, and would now need to be copied laboriously on special paper in impeccable calligraphy. It was clear the actual broadcast would not take place that day, and a new time was set. The Foreign Minister, Togo, wanted it to go out as soon as possible, and suggested 7 a.m. the following day. Anami objected: he wanted a twenty-four-hour delay so that all Japanese troops overseas would have time to receive it, along with the War Ministry's comments and explanations. As a compromise measure, it was decided that noon on August 15 would be the best possible time. Thereby time would also be allowed for electric power to be restored, temporarily, all over Japan, and for appropriate warning to be given in advance on the radio.

The fair copy of the text to be broadcast was now shown to Hirohito, who read it carefully in the Library, and, in his meticulous, schoolmasterish way, proceeded to fiddle with it. In all he made five corrections, changing yet again the phrase that had held up proceedings – it now read: "the war situation has developed, not necessarily to Japan's advantage." In the process of final revision, a Chamberlain noted a serious grammatical error in the sentence referring to the Hiroshima bomb. Exceptionally, because of the urgent circumstances, it was decided not to rewrite the parchment entirely, but paste over bits of it.

Now the amended text went back to the Prime Minister, who was visibly shaken when he saw that it was not a pristine copy. He returned it to the Emperor, who affixed his Imperial Seal. Then a second copy was taken back to the Prime Minister's office: all the Cabinet ministers had to sign. Anami did so without even bothering to read it, and then went straight to his War Ministry office. Only then did he write his own letter of resignation, and begin clearing his desk.

The Rescript was now official, and Foreign Ministry officials could draft the cable that would announce Japan's surrender to the outside world: "His Majesty the Emperor has issued an

Imperial Rescript regarding Japan's acceptance of the provisions of the Potsdam declaration," it read. "His Majesty the Emperor is prepared to authorize and ensure the signature by his government and the Imperial General Headquarters of the necessary terms for carrying out the provisions of the Potsdam declaration. His Majesty is also prepared to issue his commands to all the military, naval and air authorities of Japan and all the forces under their control, wherever located, to cease operations, to surrender arms and to issue such other orders as may be required by the Supreme Commander of the Allied Forces for the execution of the above-mentioned terms." Like the earlier acceptance, it was sent to the Japanese Embassies in Bern and Stockholm, for transmission to the Governments of the United States, China, Britain and the USSR.

All over Tokyo, indeed throughout Japan, fires began: these were not "flowers of Edo" caused by incendiary bombs, but huge bonfires, inside the Palace, in Ministry and military headquarters' courtyards: all confidential documents and files were being destroyed.

It was now past ten in the evening, and the NHK team was still waiting. Hirohito was ready to make the recording, but his aides suggested he stay in the Library, ready to move down to the shelter, in case B-29s staged one of their raids. If no air raid warning sounded in the next few hours, he could then proceed safely to the nearby Imperial Household Ministry building.

At the Prime Minister's office, Suzuki had called for one last meeting, in order to obtain letters of resignation from his Cabinet and thus pave the way for a new, post-war Government. Afterwards Anami apologized to Suzuki for causing him so many problems. "My chief aim has always been the preservation of our national polity," he said.

Suzuki attempted to reassure him. "The Imperial House will be preserved," he told Anami. "The Emperor is safe. He will soon be praying to the spirits of his ancestors."

"I trust he will be safe," Anami said.

"I am not unduly pessimistic about the future of Japan," said

Suzuki. "If the Emperor and the people are together, Japan will recover."

Anami then handed over a paper-wrapped box of Sumatran cigars, a present from a fellow-General in the Dutch East Indies. "I don't smoke," he said. "The Prime Minister should have them." He saluted and left the Premier's office. Suzuki told an aide: "I think the War Minister came to say goodbye."

It was nearly midnight when Chamberlains, senior NHK officials and the Secretary for Information headed for the improvised studio established on the second floor of the Imperial Household Ministry. The Emperor was not introduced to any of the NHK staff, but said, in a businesslike voice, "How should I speak?" Shimomura said an ordinary conversational tone would be appropriate. "Is this all right?" asked Hirohito.

The cumbersome record-cutting process began. First, the senior engineer started the machine running, and signalled to the Palace official standing in the doorway that proceedings could begin. The palace official bowed to Shimomura, who bowed to Hirohito, who held the text in his hand. The Chamberlain made a short voice test on the Emperor's behalf, and finally Hirohito began to read his text.

"Nobody had ever heard the Emperor's voice," said Haruna. "In the past we had been told that if we ever accidentally recorded his voice at an official function, there would be hell to pay. Because I was very nervous," he said, "I didn't listen to the meaning of his words closely. I had earphones on, and I was more concerned with the level of the voice than its content, but I caught the gist of it. He spoke for about three minutes, and we were cutting two records at a time. We had plenty of blank records – about sixty in all."

After the first record had been cut, Hirohito asked, in a matter-of-face tone of voice, "Shall I do it again?" "We would never have asked him ourselves," Haruna said, "and in fact that first attempt was fine." Shimomura bowed in assent, and Hirohito started reading his speech again. The second recording was not as good as the first, Haruna recalls. It was too high-pitched, and the Emperor fluffed a word. After he had finished, Hirohito said: "I am perfectly prepared to do it again." The two versions were played to him. It was decided that the first one would be used.

Hirohito left immediately afterwards, by car, for the short drive back to the Library. A Palace official told the NHK crew they could sleep in the Imperial Household Ministry dormitory if they wished, but all were eager to get home. In any case, their work was not yet over: the recording gear had to be dismantled and re-packed in heavy containers. As they began, the siren warned that the last B-29 raid over Tokyo was about to begin, and Hirohito prepared for another uneasy, uncomfortable night. The four records were put into metal cases, then into two cotton bags. A junior Chamberlain, Yoshihiro Tokugawa, a descendant of the famous Tokugawa "shogun" clan that had once exercised more power than Hirohito's forebears, locked them in a small safe in one of the Palace offices rather than take the risk of sending them over to the NHK building in the middle of an air raid.

The text of the Emperor's broadcast was released to Domei, and to all major newspapers, with instructions that it not be published until after the actual broadcast had taken place the following day.

While the NHK team were packing up, and the Information Secretary, Shimomura, was enjoying a cup of green tea with one of the Palace Chamberlains, the coup leaders made their last desperate move. Major Hatanaka, and his chief aide, Captain Shigetaro Uehara, of the Air Academy, called on General Mori at the Imperial Guards Headquarters. With the single-minded faith of religious fanatics, they believed they could win him over to their side. Mori was in his office, talking to his brother-in-law, Lieutenant-Colonel Shiraishi. When Mori angrily refused to be part of the coup, Hatanaka shot him with his pistol; then Uehara beheaded him with a sword. With the help of an officer who was party to the conspiracy, they put the General's seal on a Divisional Order, already prepared, calling on the Guards to surround the Palace, cut it off from the outside world, and also to isolate the NHK broadcasting office. The highly-disciplined regimental commanders, with no inkling of what had really happened, and assuming they were obeying Mori's orders, immediately assembled their men. Some of the senior NHK staff, who had not waited for the technical crew to finish work, were rounded up by Imperial Guardsmen as they left the Palace grounds and taken into custody. There were soldiers everywhere, for Major Koga's battalion without official orders had already entered the Imperial enclave. When Haruna and the rest of the NHK recording crew emerged from the Imperial Household Ministry, they too were arrested. As in the "2/26" mutiny, the Palace was isolated from the outside world.

Hatanaka knew the Emperor had already recorded his surrender speech: he also knew, from questioning the NHK staff, that the records must still be inside the Palace, but where? His aim, at this stage, was to prevent the speech from going out over the air. But that was merely the first step. There were also plans, already worked out with friends in the Army Air Force, the Naval Air Service, and other Army units, including the Yokohama Guards, for a last-ditch resistance appeal, and, as at the time of "2/26", for the murder of the "traitors" who had given the Emperor "bad advice". The main targets for assassination were Kido and Suzuki.

The rebel officers cut the Palace telephone lines, and began a search for the records. Imperial Guards officers and NCOs started to ransack the Palace, terrorizing the Palace staff. Kido and the Imperial Household Minister, Ishiwatari, who knew what danger they were in, hid in the Palace "bank vault". The Chamberlain Tokugawa was severely beaten by a Guards officer, for showing him "disrespect". But the rebel soldiers failed to find the records, and, throughout the early hours of the morning, while this upheaval was taking place, palace officials assumed the Emperor was asleep, and unaware that the Imperial Guards were swarming all over the Palace grounds. His Chamberlains gathered at the entrance to the Imperial air raid shelter and debated whether to wake him, and tell him what was going on. They decided against this. As it transpired, the Emperor, insomniac as usual, had been awake when they started whispering to each other about the coup, heard their murmured conversation and wondered what was going on.

While the Imperial Guards were searching the Palace, General Anami was making final preparations for his own, elaborate "seppuku". His brother-in-law, Lieutenant-Colonel Takeshita, had been sent to Anami's home to make one last attempt to persuade him to join the rebels. He found Anami in high spirits, drinking sake, preparing for his death like a true samurai. But he seemed in no hurry to die, and talked dispassionately of the past. By now Takeshita himself knew that the coup would fail. Rather than return to Hatanaka's side, he preferred to stay with Anami, and assist him in the "seppuku" rites if asked. For someone about to kill himself in such a painful way, Anami seemed in great spirits: he joked with Takeshita about having had a vitamin injection that day. 'I could hardly say I didn't want it because I was going to die, could I now?'

It was customary for someone committing "seppuku" to leave a posthumous message behind. Anami had given this considerable thought: first he wrote a poem, in his elegant hand:

After tasting the profound benevolence of the Emperor, I have no words to speak.

On another piece of parchment, he wrote:

For my supreme crime, I beg forgiveness through this act of death.

On the back of this he added, as an afterthought:

I believe in Japan's sacred indestructibility.

He dated both pieces of paper August 14, though August 15 had by now dawned. "The Emperor's broadcast will take place at noon," he told Takeshita. "I couldn't bear to hear it." His "supreme crime", Takeshita understood, was losing the war.

The Imperial Guards officers' coup had so far gone without a hitch, but now one of the regimental commanders, ordered to bring out his men and surround the Palace, found this so unprecedented that, instead of obeying, he decided first to check with the Eastern Army Command headquarters. He did not have far to go: it was housed in the Dai Ichi building across the road from the Palace. Its Chief of Staff, Major-General Tatsuhiko Takashima, quickly determined that something was seriously wrong. He telephoned his superior, General Shizuichi Tanaka, a much-feared martinet, sent his own trusted officers out on a reconnaissance, and also put the military police on alert. By this time some of the rebel Guards officers had begun to wonder whether Major Hatanaka was telling them the truth: he insisted that General Anami had given the coup his blessing, but there was no proof of this. And, when two Eastern Army Command staff officers demanded to see General Mori, and found his body, they knew the coup had gone awry. Minutes later, General Tanaka, the Eastern Army Commander, ordered all the Imperial Guards out of the Palace. Mori, Tanaka told them, had been killed by insubordinate officers. From now on, all the Imperial Guards were to obey the Eastern Army Commander and no one else.

In General Anami's house, Takeshita finally blurted out the news that Mori had been killed in an attempted coup aimed at stopping the Emperor's broadcast. "One last thing to apologize for," Anami said quietly.

Those Palace Chamberlains on duty in the Library above the Emperor's bunker were now convinced that it was only a matter of time before rebel officers tried to break in: they closed the shutters and barricaded themselves inside.

Now, at around four in the morning, the Eastern Army Command's bureaucratic machinery slowly but inexorably went into action: as a first step, General Takashima telephoned the Imperial Guards headquarters and demanded to talk to the leader of the coup, Hatanaka. "Your situation is hopeless," he told him. "You must obey the Emperor."

Hatanaka would not give up. Now he asked for ten minutes of NHK radio time before the Emperor's broadcast went on the air, "to talk to the people and explain our position". Takashima hung up. The ghastly implications of the plot – foisted on the Imperial Guards under false pretences – made Hatanaka an unwelcome guest. He left, as he had arrived, by motorcycle.

But part of his plot was being implemented elsewhere: a squad of Yokohama Guards, along with some civilian youths, had arrived in front of the Prime Minister Suzuki's residence, and opened up on it with machine-guns. Suzuki was not there and, when they found out, the insurgents in their rage tried to burn the house down. They then moved on to Suzuki's private residence: the Prime Minister, forewarned, had time to flee, but this house too was gutted.

Hatanaka now drove as fast as he could to the NHK building and demanded admittance. The Imperial Guards on duty outside, recognizing who he was, allowed him in. Hatanaka announced to the frightened NHK staff that he was going on the air. He was nonplussed when the radio announcer on duty, Morio Tatkeno (he had given the news of the start of the war back on December 8, 1941), told him this would not be possible: "no broadcasts during an alert." In any case, he added, advance warning had to be given for nationwide broadcasts. "It's a technical matter." Coolly assuming that Hatanaka was part of an Army plot to stop the Emperor's broadcast, Tateno was determined not to let this happen. If Hatanaka insisted on speaking into the microphone, he would cut off the power switch. But Hatanaka did not try to use physical force: so authoritative was Tateno's manner that he clearly believed him; and, instead of pushing Tateno out of his chair, he simply stayed in the studio, waiting for the air raid to end.

It was now shortly after five a.m., and outside the Imperial Palace a small procession of Army cars came to a halt. General Tanaka, the Eastern Army commander, emerged, surrounded by hand-picked kempei bodyguards, and immediately started to exercise his authority. He arrested one of the Imperial Guards ringleaders and had him marched away by the kempei. He then entered the Inui Gate: his aim was to order the Imperial Guards regimental commanders to get their men together, march out of the Palace and release all prisoners. His other urgent duty was to apologize to the Emperor for this tragic last-minute coup.

It was around this time that Anami, by now very drunk on sake, but with an unerring hand, took a razor-sharp dagger and drew it across his stomach. Blood spurted, smearing his parchment letters. Anami, kneeling, did not keel over, but watched himself bleed. Transferring the dagger to his left hand, he reached for his carotid artery on the right side of his neck, and made a sudden, deep incision. Blood flowed but still Anami did not die.

The two Chamberlains guarding the entrance to the bunker within the Imperial Library decided they could no longer delay their grim task: they decided to wake the Emperor and break the news to him that he was a virtual prisoner.

Hirohito showed no emotion. "Is it a coup?" he asked. "Tell me what has actually happened." When they had finished, he proposed that he address the assembled Imperial Guards and once more explain his decision. He asked the Chamberlains to find his Chief ADC – but this officer was confined to the Imperial Household Ministry building, with a screen of rebellious Imperial Guards in between.

General Tanaka, having spoken sharply to the Imperial Guards officers, was on his way to the Imperial Library. He passed a Chamberlain trying to slip through into the Ministry to find the ADC. "Is the Grand Chamberlain in the Library?" Tanaka asked.

Not knowing whether the General was on the rebels' side or not, the Chamberlain refused to tell him. "Stop trembling," Tanaka said. "The revolt's over." He introduced himself. "I deeply regret," he said, "that so much inconvenience has been caused."

The rebellion was now confined to Major Hatanaka and a few officers and men, all in and around the NHK building. Brandishing his revolver, Hatanaka was still insisting on broadcasting – especially now that the all clear had sounded. Morio Tateno, on one pretext or another, was still refusing to let him do so, and soon the Imperial Guards outside the NHK building were withdrawn.

As the sound engineer, Shizuto Haruna, who had returned to the NHK building after his release from the guardroom, remembers, a Chamberlain, "wearing shabby clothes, looking almost like a beggar", arrived later that morning with the precious record. He had deliberately assumed his disguise so that rebellious troops would not think he was from the Palace, and search him. Out of sight from Major Hatanaka, preparations for the Emperor's broadcast now began.

Morio Tateno remembers that one final telephone call came through – for Major Hatanaka. It must have been from Eastern Army Command, perhaps from General Tanaka himself, for Hatanaka straightened up, said, "yes, sir," several times, and, on hanging up, muttered to himself: "It's all over." He then left the building, with his faithful supporter, Lieutenant-Colonel Shiizaki. Outside, in a fit of rage, Shiizaki drew his sword, and slashed wildly at a pine-tree. General Anami was finally dead, and the Yokohama Guards, still on the rampage, had set fire to Baron Hiranuma's house before returning to Yokohama.

Hatanaka, pushing his motorcycle, and Lieutenant-Colonel Shiizaki, holding his horse, were finally apprehended distributing leaflets outside the Imperial Palace. These read:

"Our intention is to protect the Emperor and to preserve the national polity despite the designs of the enemy ... We pray that the Japanese people and the members of the Armed Forces will appreciate the significance of our action and join with us to fight for the preservation of our country and the elimination of the traitors around the Emperor, thus confounding the enemy's schemes." The few passers-by glanced at the leaflets, but showed no interest in reading them.

After their arrest, in a final act of defiance, Hatanaka shot himself, while Shiizaki committed "seppuku" with his sword. On Hatanaka's body, the kempei found a poem he had written: "I have nothing to regret now that the dark clouds have disappeared from the reign of the Emperor." A wake for the two men would be held that night, attended by most of the staff officers from the War Ministry.

Now, at regular intervals, all over Japan, radio announcements warned that the Emperor would be speaking at noon. Everyone must listen. In factories, offices, hospitals, village squares, radio sets were got ready, and street committees spread the word that the entire population was to be marshalled for this unprecedented event. In the NHK studio, a brief row flared as Haruna tested the quality of the record by playing a few seconds of the speech in advance. "I had to do this," he said, "to get the overlapping right." The Imperial Household Minister objected. "He looked dispproving and uptight," Haruna recalls. Another Palace Chamberlain said: "It's wrong to test the Emperor's voice." At the time, of course, the Emperor was still a living God, and "one shouldn't test a God. I said: 'just let me do it my way,' and the NHK Director, who was standing by, told the Imperial Household Minister: 'do let this young man get on with his job.'"

"A broadcast of the highest importance is about to be made," said an NHK announcer a few seconds before noon. "All listeners please rise."

There was a brief pause, and the national anthem, "Kimigayo", was played. "His Majesty the Emperor," said the announcer, "will now read his Imperial Rescript to the people of Japan. We respectfully transmit his voice."

Hirohito listened, in the safety of his bunker. In the whole of Japan, he was probably the only able-bodied Japanese to do so sitting down.

CHAPTER TWENTY-TWO

Those who listened to the Emperor's broadcast at noon on August 15, 1945 – and they must have been fifty million at least, out of a total population of seventy-five million – never recovered from the shock of actually hearing "the Voice of the Crane", nor did they ever forget the impact of the speech, or the circumstances under which they heard it.*

Akiro Kurosawa, the world-famous director, then a young, up-and-coming film-maker compelled to make propaganda films and beset by censorship problems, had been ordered to report to his studio, to hear Hirohito speak.

"I'll never forget the scenes as I walked the streets that day," [1] he wrote later. "On the way from Soshigaya to the studio in Kinuta, the shopping street looked fully prepared for the 'honourable death of a hundred million'.

"The atmosphere was tense, panicky. There were even shopkeepers who had taken their Japanese swords from their scabbards and were staring at them."

Robert Guillain, by this time interned with other "hostile aliens" in the comparative safety of a mountain village, "saw people in my corner of the village gather around radio sets, not in each house, but in groups in their 'tonarigumi' [civil defence] leaders' houses. [2] No one in these troupes of pantalooned housewives and runty elders clustered around the blue-and-white pennants of their civil-defence sections knew what the sovereign was going to say ... People clustered in the doorways because the houses were too small to hold them all ... Silence. And then that voice never heard before. A little hoarse, slow, too

* See Appendix for the text of the Emperor's speech.

controlled, the voice of someone reading a speech. Surprise: for all practical purposes, no one understood a word of it! The sovereign was speaking the learned and solemn language reserved to the Son of Heaven alone; an antique, almost Chinese, language that had little in common with the language the people spoke and was made even more unintelligible by the fact that while the people may sometimes have read Imperial proclamations, they had never before heard one spoken by the Emperor himself. As soon as he finished speaking, an official commentator had to come on with a vernacular translation of what the Emperor had said. Only then was his speech really understood."

After it was over, the *Domei* reporter, Matsuo Kato, recalls,[3] "people huddled together in the ruins [of Tokyo]. There was no leadership to overcome the mass inertia." Kato remembers the "dull, vacant stares of the people" but also their "distinct sense of relief. In a way, it was like a miraculous and unexplained cure after a long illness. Newspaper editors and staff behaved like canaries released from a cage . . ."

Kurosawa witnessed similar signs of relief: "When I walked the same street back to my home afterwards, the scene was entirely different. The people in the shopping street were bustling about with cheerful faces as if preparing for a festival the next day." Reflecting on the alternative, the "honourable death of a hundred million" that many Japanese expected the Emperor to announce, Kurosawa wrote: "If the Emperor had called for our 'honourable deaths', these people in the street would probably have done as they were told and died. And I would probably have done likewise. The Japanese see self-assertion as immoral and self-sacrifice as the sensible course to take in life. We were accustomed to this teaching and had never thought to question it. In wartime we were all deaf-mutes . . ."

Guillain remembers the shock – and relief – caused by Hirohito's high-pitched, incantatory broadcast: "When the announcer came on to explain the Emperor's speech, the people remained stiff and silent for a few moments more in the intensity of concentration. Then it was over. They had understood, and the sobbing broke out . . . Something huge had just cracked: the proud dream of Greater Japan. They scattered and hid to weep in the seclusion of their wooden houses. Absolute silence prevailed in the village. As you walked down the street, all you saw through the doors left open in the August heat was an occasional tear-stained face that turned quickly away as you passed." All over Japan, civilians remained in their homes for several days, weeping ceaselessly.

General Anami was not the only one to prefer death to surrender: among the notable suicides were General Sugiyama and his wife, Admiral Onishi, the "father" of the "kamikaze" concept (he could have taken no other action without losing face to an intolerable degree), General Honjo, Hirohito's former Chief ADC, General Tanaka, the Eastern Army Commander who had nipped the Imperial Guards conspiracy in the bud, and several other high-ranking officers. A number of lesser-known Army and Navy officers also killed themselves, some within yards of the Imperial palace walls and gates, deliberately facing in the Emperor's direction. But on the whole there were far fewer such deaths than expected. There were, however, continuing signs of rage: the Navy's "special attack corps" flew over Tokyo several times that day, dropping leaflets which said: "Don't surrender, don't believe the Imperial Rescript, it was a false document;" and there were short-lived mutinies at the midget submarine base at Yokosuka, near Tokyo, and at a Military Cadets School at Sanatan. Very quickly, kempei and Navy police removed the propellers from those planes which were still serviceable, in order to prevent "kamikaze" attempts on the US Occupation Force advance guard, expected at any moment.

It was only later that the ambiguity of the Emperor's speech became apparent. As Guillain noted: "How odd the proclamation was, and how Japanese in spirit! How prudently it dealt with the future, how careful it was not to tarnish the book of Japanese history with the forbidden word 'surrender' . . . Not once was the word 'defeat' mentioned. Should the military, in the future, have occasion to rewrite history to their liking, they will be able to cite the proclamation as witness that Japan had ended the war only because of the inhumanity of her enemies and that, even though his armies were intact, her Emperor had agreed to end the carnage because he wished to be not only the saviour of Japan but the defender of human civilization." This view is shared by Russell Braddon, the biographer of Shoichi Yokoi, the Japanese soldier who hid in the Guam jungles for twenty-two years rather than surrender: "The Emperor didn't mention unconditional surrender, only that he had decided to put an end to the war and that fighting must stop. So little like surrender did the Rescript sound to our captors that, then and there, they told us, all men go home. Instead of beating us, they bowed. Instead of killing us off, they began to feed us up."

The final tragedy, Guillain noted, "reserved one more surprise for us. Seventy-five million people were supposed to have died to the last man. Even the poorest of them swore, and doubtless believed, that they would commit harakiri rather than surrender. And when, after averting its face to weep, Japan looked up again – it entered tranquilly into its defeat. There seemed a disconcerting facility in that acceptance; the page was turned with seeming effortlessness. And on Japan's new face was a glimmer of something that had not been seen in a very long time: the special Japanese smile." The police, "who had so long made us feel the weight of their hate and petty persecution", visited each foreigner, bowing endlessly and offering their amiable services; the civil defence leaders smiled, and handed out sake and new clothes to the foreigners; so did Foreign Ministry officials, obsequiously calling on neutral Embassy diplomats and urging them to visit prisoner-of-war camps the inspection of which they had constantly refused in the past. There were even smiles from the man in the street." Travelling back to Tokyo, Guillain noted that, "as though the courtesy and hospitality of a long-vanished Japan had been reborn, amiable volunteers kindly offered their assistance. 'Can I help you carry your luggage? Can you find your way? Everything has changed so, hasn't it?'

And my unpaid guide gestured towards the ruined station, towards the ravaged plain that was once Tokyo, and he laughed that Japanese laugh ... Even the press smiled. With a single twist, all the newspapers turned their coats at once. In only a week, the famous *Nippon Times* [formerly the *Tokyo Times and Advertiser*], fascistic and militaristic before, became a champion of democracy, parliamentary government and the people's rights; having shouted itself hoarse about 'American bestiality', here it was informing its readers of the impatiently awaited invaders' generosity of soul and protesting that only rude and stupid Japanese provincials could imagine that an American soldier was a gangster in uniform."

There now took place one of the strangest conspiracies not just of the Showa era, but of Japan's 2,600-year-old dynasty – a tragi-comic episode of the kind Japanese directors like Kurosawa have drawn on to make their epic films: though seldom referred to, it was certainly discussed within the privacy of the Palace, for Prince Takamatsu himself had a small part in it. Whether Hirohito, too, looked on it with approval, or detached amusement, or even hostility, will in all probability never be known, for the basis of this plot was never publicly raised in his presence, though it was later officially acknowledged. Most likely, he approved of what took place, as a means of preserving the "Emperor-system" should the Americans have been sufficiently foolish, or bold, to dissolve the Imperial dynasty and proclaim a Japanese Republic – as many Japanese, at the war's end, felt they might.

It all began at a Naval Air base in Kyushu, Japan's southernmost island, shortly after the Emperor's surrender speech. Navy Captain Minoru Genda, once Admiral Yamamoto's chief aide, a close friend of Prince Takamatsu (and, according to many military experts, the real brains behind the Pearl Harbour planning), convened one last parade of all the officers and men of his beloved 343 Squadron. He told them that he, like many officers, had believed at first that the Emperor had been tricked into proclaiming the end of the war by "evil advisers".

But, after flying to Tokyo to consult with senior Navy Ministry officials, Genda told them, he was now convinced that the Emperor had indeed decided to end the war. "If we were to continue fighting," he said, "this would be against the Emperor's will." He ended his harangue emotionally ("I will never see you again, farewell") – hinting rather broadly that, rather than witness the occupation of Japan, he was going to commit "seppuku". He then asked the officers and NCOs (about 200 in all) to stay behind. He wanted to take them into his confidence, he said. At eight that evening, he, Genda, would commit suicide. Did anyone wish to join him in this act? About twenty people raised their hands.

"Don't make an emotional, spur-of-the-moment decision," Genda urged them. "Think about it. There's nothing dishonourable about changing your minds."

Eventually some twenty-three officers and NCOs congregated at eight o'clock. Genda told them they should first write farewell letters to their families. They did so. Ritual cups of saké were drunk, and brother officers exchanged toasts. The mood was grim. Genda then explained his real motive in bringing them together. "I apologize for putting you through this kind of test," he said, "but there was no alternative. What I have to propose is a mission far more important than death. It begins right now."

On his lightning visit to Tokyo just after the Emperor's speech, Genda told them, he had been entrusted with an extraordinary secret: the Imperial Navy intended to kidnap a small child of royal blood, hide him in a remote place where the occupation forces would never find him, bring him up as the rightful heir and wait until the time was ripe to restore him to the throne. It was a plan culled straight from medieval legend, but it also had some actual historical precedents, and had been devised by some of the Navy Ministry's brightest officials and staff officers, with what was left of their secret fund "treasure chest".

Genda, together with a small, dedicated group under his command, would become the chosen instrument to preserve

Japan's Imperial dynasty. From the start (the scheme was first discussed a few weeks before the actual surrender) Prince Taka-matsu had been aware of it, had approved it and suggested that Genda was the right man for the job. The officer entrusted with the overall planning was Rear-Admiral Tomiyoka, who had briefed Genda on the broad lines of the scheme, earmarked the necessary funds, and told him to gather a team together.

In the context of August 1945, the plan, for all its romantic overtones, made practical sense: almost all senior military men were convinced that, at best, Hirohito would be compelled to abdicate; at worst, the entire Imperial Family might be punished, dispersed and exiled. But this, Tomiyoka argued, was but a temporary crisis, for America and the Soviet Union were bound to fall out sooner rather than later, and eventually fight a war, and then Japan would once more have a chance of being restored to greatness. The important point was to maintain, in hiding, a member of the exalted Meiji family who would continue to be steeped in the age-old Japanese Imperial tradi-tions, and so be ready to assume the role of Emperor once more favourable conditions prevailed. Given the state of the world, Genda told his men, this might not be long delayed – but they should assume it might be a lifelong mission. From now on this small group was to be an élite secret society, and the lives of all its members had to be subordinate to the task of hiding, raising, educating and maintaining in suitable comfort the small boy who would later become the new Emperor. They might marry, take jobs, achieve prominent positions in the new Japan, but their ultimate loyalty, in all circumstances, must be to the secret heir to the throne, and they had to be prepared to sacrifice their fortunes, their well-being, and if necessary their lives to this ideal.

As a first step, Genda elaborated, a suitable hiding-place must be found, and a suitable family let in on the secret. The selection of this was all-important, for such a family had to be able to impart to the young Prince not only Japan's traditional "bush-ido" values but the Shintoist precepts and rites they wished to keep alive. The chosen élite of 343 Squadron should approach the task as if it were a fully-fledged military operation. There and then, the Navy plotters dispersed, with secret funds, trucks, petrol, blankets and food. They established a secure communications link, with Genda masterminding the entire operation.

Eleven days after Hirohito's surrender speech, they had found a possible hiding-place – a remote, hilltop village on Kyushu island called Gokonosho. But Genda was not happy with the local population. He doubted whether they could be trusted, and he could find no reliable locals to assume the role of "parents". Reluctantly, the idea of Gokanosho was dropped, and eventually Genda settled on another location, a remote spot on the sparsely-populated coast. Here, he decided, a house would be built. There was ample land for the creation of a vegetable garden, and plenty of fish in the sea, so the future Emperor would not starve.

What Genda did not know was that another military group (from the Army) had not only had the same idea, but made far more advanced preparations. They had selected their future Emperor, and obtained permission, at the highest level, to go ahead with their scheme.

The mastermind behind this parallel conspiracy was a senior War Ministry official, Hirose. His candidate was the seven-year-old Prince Kitashirakawa, the grandson of the other Prince Kitashirakawa, a daredevil pilot who had died in France in a car-crash in 1923 in mysterious circumstances. The boy's father, Nagahisa Kitashirakawa, had also met a violent death: at a pre-war air display, a pilot had lost control of his plane which had crashed into the spectators' stand, killing him instantly. At the time of the surrender, Emperor Meiji's great-grandson was living with his grandmother, mother and a small retinue of servants and ladies-in-waiting in a large house near Mount Fuji belonging to a prominent entrepreneur called Tanaka who had business connections with the Imperial Family. The latter had taken refuge there to escape from the bombing, which had destroyed all of the Kitashirakawa family's valuable Tokyo property.

The Army plotters had not only found the boy, but also enlisted the help of the young Prince's grandmother, Princess Fusako, the second of Emperor Meiji's four daughters. Her younger sister Nobuko had married Prince Asaka (one of the perpetrators of the "rape of Nanking"), and her youngest sister was married to Prince Higashikuni, who was about to become Japan's first post-war Prime Minister. Princess Fusako had even provided the conspirators with a letter confirming her knowledge and approbation of the scheme.

The rank-and-file of the small secret group entrusted with young Prince Kitashirakawa's hiding-place were hand-picked members of the Nakano Spy School. One of its graduates, Colonel Ichiro Kubota, became the executive officer responsible for the whole scheme, and he devised a plan reflecting his own background in the world of espionage.

It so happened that Kubota knew a wealthy ham manufacturer called Takuzo Imanari who was himself a staunch patriot. He decided to bring Imanari into the plot, and hide the young Prince in Imanari's village, Rokkamachi, some 400 kilometres north-west of Tokyo. At least, Kubata argued, the young Prince would never be short of food in Rokkamachi.

But, when Kubota reached Rokkamachi, he found a somewhat shifty Imanari, who appeared to be having second thoughts about the whole affair. No mean interrogator, Kubota questioned Imanari on his apparent reticence, and what he discovered angered him: Imanari admitted that, at the request of the Japanese Foreign Ministry, he had been hiding one VIP in his village ever since the surrender: the Burmese nationalist leader, U Ba Maw, wanted by the British as a leading Japanese collaborator.

The plotters mulled over this discovery, and finally came to the conclusion they had no choice but to put their hope in Imanari. But another product of the Nakano Spy School, Inomata, decided the risks of hiding two such important people in the same place were far too great. Inomata had, in the immediate pre-war period, been a fully-fledged Japanese Intelligence agent in Germany and the USSR, under the alias of Joji Imura. Now, after raising funds from his former fellow pupils at Nakano (who thought he was laying plans to hide the son of one of the most influential Japanese war criminals), Inomata set out for Hiroshima, determined to talk local municipal officials there into providing him with genuine identity papers for a seven-year-old boy. He picked the place deliberately because its archives had been entirely destroyed.

It proved to be more difficult than he had anticipated, for he encountered one of those indomitable Japanese bureaucrats who fussed over every detail and was determined to go by the book, despite the calamity that had recently struck. Under his Imura alias, Inomata said he was a distant relative of a family, the Kimuras, that had been wiped out in the bombing – all but their small son, Michio, who was lying seriously wounded in hospital. He needed new identity papers.

The bureaucrat was either extremely obtuse or very suspicious – perhaps both. It was most unusual for identity papers to disappear without a trace. Was he quite certain the parents were dead? How could he be sure?

Inomata said their house had been at the very epicentre of the explosion.

Then how was the boy alive, the bureaucrat asked.

He eventually allowed Inomata to fill in a form but, when the latter handed it in, he was asked for *his* identity papers.

"I don't have any," Inomata said. "They were destroyed in one of the Tokyo raids."

"Without papers," the bureaucrat said, "I can't do a thing."

How could he be so heartless, Inomata asked. The boy was badly burnt and would probably die. Did the clerk want him cremated anonymously, like an animal? Hadn't his family suffered enough?

Eventually the clerk relented, and made out papers for Michio Kimura, born March 31, 1938, of a military arsenal worker who had got married and fathered a son in Okinawa (another place, Inomata knew, where no one was likely to check the records).

The real Prince, a lively seven-year-old with a beautiful younger sister call Hatsuko, was still living with the Tanaka family in the country, under reasonably enviable circumstances: because of Princess Fusako's close connections with Hirohito, the Tanaka house was guarded by the police and by a company of Japanese infantry. Additional rations were provided by the Japanese Foreign Ministry, from its allocation for foreign diplomats. In all, Princess Fusako's retinue consisted of about thirty people – but the US Occupation soon put a stop to their various privileges: the soldiers were demobilized, the police transferred to other duties. The ladies-in-waiting drifted away, and a few weeks after the end of the war Princess Fusako returned to Tokyo. But her house was tiny, and the small Prince remained in the country. Inomato and Kubota (who had finally rallied to Inomata's plan) decided there was no harm in his remaining there for the time being. They set about finding a suitable house, and suitable companions and environment, for him – and ran into the same difficulties as Genda's group had experienced. Just before the War Ministry's operations came under close US Occupation scrutiny, before the final demobilization and disbandment of the Japanese Imperial Army, Hirose obtained 500,000 yen from its secret funds for his purpose.

While the plot to keep an Emperor "replacement" developed, Japanese representatives signed the surrender terms aboard the *Missouri* in Tokyo Bay on September 2, and on September 8 General MacArthur, the "Supremo", arrived in Tokyo, establishing his headquarters in the Dai Ichi building recently vacated by the Eastern Corps Commander. MacArthur, who moved into the US Embassy residence, furnishing it, his aide Faubion Bowers recalled, with "rather hideous wicker furniture from the Philippines", came to Japan with the advance guard of a force which, at its peak, numbered over a million men (by mid-1946 it had been reduced to 400,000, half in Korea, half in Japan). MacArthur's headquarters alone numbered 5,000, and in the early Occupation days several hundred US officers took over local government and administrative duties.

As time passed, and as the US Occupation became an accepted state of affairs, plans for the boy-Prince's survival as an "alternate" Emperor evaporated: the Occupation turned out to be very different from the brutally repressive régime the plotters had anticipated – and some of them were caught up in new, civilian interests: to acquire sufficient funds to maintain the young Prince in the requisite luxury, Kubota used the money to start a small toy factory, and Inomata invested in a plumbing business. They, too, had taken an oath to dedicate their lives to perpetuating the Meiji dynasty, and saw this as a first step in providing the Prince with a regular income. They were better plotters than businessmen, however, and, far from generating new income for the young Prince's upkeep, both their ventures went bankrupt. Worse still, British Intelligence, with the help of the newly arrived US Counter-Intelligence Corps (CIC), began actively looking for U Ba Maw.

At the start of the US Occupation of Japan, the CIC was almost obsessively concerned with the continued underground existence of extremist Japanese military groups, plotting the assassination of high-ranking US officers and guerrilla warfare against the Occupation forces. Though CIC officers did uncover large numbers of arms caches, such covert anti-American activity was largely a figment of their imagination. Colonel Kubota, because of his Nakano Spy School antecedents, did attract their attention, however: informers told CIC agents that his toy-manufacturing activities seemed to be a front for something else. The CIC put Kubota under surveillance, and shortly afterwards arrested him.

Faced with the prospect of the Prince's future hiding-place being discovered, Kubota did not hesitate: he betrayed U Ba Maw. On the pretext of finding him a safe, clandestine passage to North Korea, Kubota lured the former Burmese head of state to Tokyo. Kubota arranged a banquet for him. At its conclusion, a squad led by the British Military Attaché arrested him. So anxious was Kubota to conceal all traces of the plot that he ordered his wife to burn Princess Fusako's precious letter.

But in any case, even a short while after the start of the US Occupation, things were not turning out quite as the plotters had expected: it was becoming increasingly difficult to imagine that Japan would ever require a new Emperor. Some of the Army and Navy conspirators dropped out. Young Prince Kitashirakawa grew up, first under the Allied Occupation, then in the "new" Japan, without ever realizing he had almost been spirited away, and only learnt of the Genda and Kubota plans years later. Now a commoner, and a senior Toshiba executive, he retains close links with the Imperial Family.

Even the U Ba Maw story has an ironic twist, for in the long run – with both India and Burma about to become fully-fledged, sovereign states – the British were compelled to release him, and he became, briefly, the "father" of Burmese independence: he never forgave the Japanese, though, for delivering him into the hands of his enemies.

Kubota, Inomata and many of the other plotters simply faded away, but Minoru Genda, the brilliant ex-Navy pilot, artisan of Pearl Harbour and would-be kamikaze, ended his career as Chief of Staff of Japan's post-war Self-Defence Air Force; after retirement, he became a prominent backbencher in the ruling LDP. He too had studied the Imperial family tree assiduously, and by an odd coincidence had also selected young Prince Kitashirakawa as the best possible candidate. But Genda, too, was overcome by events – and never even approached the boy's family.

In 1981, at the Togo temple in Harajuku, retired Air Marshal Genda staged a "dissolution celebration" for all those plotters who had once helped him on his romantic quest to prepare a young Meiji descendant to assume the Japanese throne: the survivors of the twenty-three officers and NCOs who had sworn a suicide oath with Genda, that fateful night in August 1945, were a cross-section of the new, prosperous post-war Japan: they included an airline pilot, a businessman, the owner of a bookshop, and several former Self-Defence Air Force officers. In a short speech, Genda told them: "Our greatest success was in holding back and not kidnapping the Prince. Our mission has been accomplished."

Asked about Genda's romantic plot, many years after the war, Prince Takamatsu merely said that "something like it might well have proved necessary". That must have been Hirohito's view too. In the event, it was the US Occupation policy towards the Emperor and its belief in the "Emperor-system" as an essential factor of stability in Japanese society that eventually made the Genda and the Nakano Spy School conspiracies redundant.

Immediately after his surrender speech, Hirohito had no means of knowing this, nor had the victorious Allies quite made up their minds about him. There were so many other problems: Japan's towns were flattened, her people starving, her economy in ruins. How to nurse Japan back to normalcy without, at the same time, reviving her aggressive, military tendencies, how to get Japan to accept defeat without provoking a desperate "were-wolf" backlash * were far more important preoccupations. Soviet entry into Japanese-controlled Manchuria, in the last six days of the war, further complicated matters: after Potsdam, the Allies knew they were on a collision course with the Soviet Union.

It so happened that, in this new equation, Hirohito's role would become paramount: he quickly realized this, and rode out the storm with consummate skill. His talent for self-preservation astonished those who had assumed that catastrophic defeat necessarily brought in its wake the abdication of the Emperor. In the astonishing Occupation years, marked from the start by unexpectedly cordial US–Japanese collaboration, the biggest collaborator was Hirohito himself.

---

* "Werewolf" commandos were the young Nazi extremists who – briefly – threatened to continue the war after Germany's surrender.
[1] Akira Kurosawa, *Something Like an Autobiography*. Knopf, 1982.
[2] Robert Guillain, *I saw Tokyo burning*, ib.
[3] Matsuo Kato, *The Lost War*, ib.

CHAPTER TWENTY-THREE

As hundreds of thousands of American, Australian, British and New Zealand soldiers poured into Japan, and as MacArthur's huge headquarters staff began administering the country, some of the earlier, secret plans for maintaining the "Emperor-system" in a defeated Japan discussed and elaborated by Kido and Konoye from 1944 onwards now became reality. Two days after the surrender, Higashikuni himself, Hirohito's uncle (by marriage to Toshiko, Emperor Meiji's youngest daughter), whose name had been so frequently mentioned, became Japan's first post-war Prime Minister, as Kido and he had secretly determined he would: an early Supreme Command, Allied Powers (SCAP) confidential report on him noted that he had been removed from his China command after the Nanking atrocities, had pioneered the growth of Japanese air power, was "militaristic and nationalistic, a daredevil who drives his car alone in the Tokyo streets", and was known as a "tough disciplinarian, self-willed, stubborn, somewhat erratic, admired in the Army for his strength of character and independence and directness of speech".

As deputy Premier, Minister without Portfolio, and real power behind the scenes, Higashikuni chose Prince Konoye. The presence of a "royal" and a "near royal" to head the government was dictated by the need to impress on the Japanese people that the "Emperor-system" still functioned, even in such difficult, even humiliating times. Significantly, other members of the Imperial Family were sent to Army Commands throughout Japan to explain the meaning of the Emperor's speech and directives.

In the short space of time between Hirohito's surrender speech, the arrival of the occupation forces advance-guard and the signing of the Japanese capitulation aboard the *Missouri* on September 2, Hirohito was in limbo: like all Tokyo residents, he must have felt immense relief that the bombing had stopped, but for him this did not mean that the worst was over. B-29s continued to fly over Tokyo, an ominous reminder of the occupation to come. On August 30, Empress Nagako mentioned the situation in a letter to Crown Prince Akihito, still in his mountain hide-out. "Here every day B-29 bombers and fighters fly over noisily from morning till evening" she wrote. "To my regret, the B-29 is a great aircraft. I'm writing this in the library, and as I look up, lots of them are flying over us as I write. How are you doing? I'm very pleased you're fit and fine in this heat. We've not seen each other for a long time but you must have heard the voice of His Majesty. Your father was worried so much every day but Japan was saved for ever. A lot of people come to the Palace every day with thanks and apologies. You also should think over what the Emperor said in a great Rescript. Study hard and endure the unendurable, without making any mistakes. Train your body: we have to establish a great nation, to turn bad luck into good."

In the almost unreal first few days of peace, Hirohito was chiefly concerned with his own immediate future: should he abdicate now or later? Would the Allies insist on his departure, and, perhaps, his indictment as a war criminal? Furthermore, in a country where "custom compels senior leaders to take responsibility for serious mishaps involving their organizations" (to quote the *Washington Post*'s story about the resignation of Japan's Defence Minister following a collision between a Japanese submarine and a fishing vessel in 1988), it was unthinkable to many Japanese, including some of those closest to him, that he should remain on the throne after what had happened to Japan; and indeed Professor Hata, a leading historian of this period, describes Hirohito's survival as nothing short of miraculous. But his status as Emperor also compelled him to think hard about the probable fate of his closest subordinates. Having accepted the terms of the Potsdam Declaration, he knew the Allies intended to punish Japanese war criminals severely. Trials of captured Japanese military commanders had already begun in the Philippines before the actual war had even ended. At first, he could hardly bear to talk about these. On August 29, he told Kido: "It is so painful and unbearable to leave all the war criminals in the hands of the Allies. Is there any way I can take the whole responsibility by retiring from the throne?"

Kido replied that although "this sacred consideration" was "very moving", "the Allies won't be content with this. Foreigners," Kido added, "could have a different approach to things." Besides, to abdicate risked "abasing the Emperor-system and as a result it could provoke the idea of republicanism and democracy. So we have to be very careful and see what the Allies will do." Even before August 15, Kido had correctly concluded that the Emperor was safer from prosecution if he remained on the throne, and that to abdicate would be regarded as an admission of guilt. It is clear, from his subsequent behaviour, that Hirohito very quickly realized this too.

At first, however, the war criminals issue began to assume even more importance, in Hirohito's mind, than his own uncertain fate. To Higashikuni, his new Prime Minister, in early September, Hirohito again returned to the subject of war criminals. Some advisers were urging that Hirohito should insist that they be tried and sentenced by Japanese courts, but Hirohito would not even consider this option. "The so-called war criminals," he told Higashikuni, "especially those in positions of responsibility, are only being loyal to the nation, so it is unbearable to execute them in the name of the Emperor. Is there no way of reconsidering this?" On September 13, Higashikuni replied there was indeed no alternative. In any case, he told Hirohito, "MacArthur wants a Nuremberg-style court".

Konoye had no such misgivings. Shortly before the end of the war (in June 1945) he had told his former aide, Tomita: "I would like revenge; I would like to make a sweeping round-up of all the intriguers who have brought Japan to this defeat and the selfish profit-seekers who have accused us as traitors. I am better qualified than you to perform such a cruel job. Maybe I should be Home Minister."

At this stage, with Australia, New Zealand, the Soviet Union, the Netherlands and China firmly in favour of Hirohito's trial as a war criminal, France undecided, and the British Foreign Office largely following the views of Americans like Grew and Stimson, the Emperor's future was in Truman's hands – and the die was by no means cast: Hirohito's responsible behaviour, in the closing stages of the war, gave additional strength to the already dominant "Tokyo lobby" determined to keep him on the throne, but both Congressmen and Senators, responding to public opinion and the wishes of their constituents, lobbied for his arrest – and passed a joint resolution demanding that he be tried as a war criminal.

In Britain's House of Commons, a newly elected Labour MP, James Callaghan, later to become Prime Minister, devoted his maiden speech to a reasoned appeal to "get rid of him". Chiang Kai-chek felt the same way. Australia, closer to the war than the rest of the Allies (it was the only non-Asian country which had actually been bombed by Japan except for a daring, quixotic, submarine-launched airplane mission that dropped bombs on coastal Oregon in early 1942 in a vain attempt to start a forest fire) was extremely irritated by Britain's pro-Hirohito stand. In the list of sixty-four major war criminals established by the Australian Foreign Ministry, Hirohito was number seven – but only because the names were listed in alphabetical order. Even before the end of the war, the Australian government had insisted that Hirohito be made to sign the surrender document aboard the *Missouri*. "There is undoubtedly a small but influential school of thought in some Allied countries which is prepared to save the face of the Emperor," a government memorandum read. "To this we are resolutely opposed." Another External Affairs Ministry report, forwarded to SCAP, which turned it over to the IMTFE prosecution, read: "Attempts have been made to absolve Hirohito from responsibility for the actions of Japan in entering the recent conflict on the ground that he was forced into declaring war by the militarist faction. The fact is that he was not at any time forced under duress to give written approval. He could have refused and supported his protests by abdication or hara-kiri. It is being suggested now that he will abdicate. How much more to the point it would have been if he had taken a forceful stand against those of his ministers who were intent on making war. He could have notified them that in the event of Japan entering the war he would publicly show his disapproval in either of the above-mentioned ways. It may be true that Hirohito never believed in war, but is his crime not greater because he approved of something in which he did not believe?" The hara-kiri suggestion was naive, displaying abysmal ignorance of Japanese ways: an Emperor did not commit hara-kiri, for the spilling of royal blood would have been a sacrilegious act.

Some Washington analysts were opposed to Hirohito's prosecution not because they felt he was innocent, but because they argued that to proceed in that way would lead, paradoxically, to many major war criminals going scot-free. If the Emperor *did* assume full responsibility for everyone and everything, and was punished, how could the brutal prisoner-of-war camp commandants and the instigators of the Bataan death march be made accountable for their actions?

The US State Department cast its net wide in the search for an answer: among the experts, a Columbia University professor, Homer H. Dubs, an authority on Japan, in a report to Grew, urged that Hirohito be dethroned. "It makes no difference whether he was inclined towards peace or war," he wrote. "It is the office, not the individual, that is important in Japanese eyes: the essential matter is to remove from the minds of the Japanese people their belief in the sanctity of the Emperor. That cannot be done unless the Allies prove to them that they are able to uproot even their divine rulers."

Presciently (his report is dated August 13, 1945), Dubs noted that "the present US practice of refraining from criticizing or blaming or touching the Emperor in any way plays into the hands of the nationalistic Japanese. They can declare to their people that even Americans respect and are awed by the inviolable mikado." Dubs' radical view was that, since the dynasty was more important than any of the lives of the individuals who made it up, "it is important that Hirohito be prevented from being given imperial honours by a descendant who is himself an Emperor". One unusual – and, by Japanese standards, at least, highly blasphemous – suggestion was that the three sacred objects handed down throughout the ages by the Sun-Goddess Amaterasu, the mirror, sword and necklace, be "de-sacralised" by exhibition, under American sponsorship, in major museums all over the world, and shown to be "mere artefacts".

Hirohito's fate was also a matter of immediate concern to his younger brothers: Prince Chichibu heard the Emperor's broadcast in his country home – and immediately returned to Tokyo, despite his worsening tuberculosis. On August 30, Prince Takamatsu, the third brother, called on Kido and "asked about the future of the Imperial Family". Professor Hata feels that both Chichibu and Takamatsu may have been responding to a call that never came, and were preparing themselves for a possible role as Regents. There were – as Empress Nagako wrote to her son – touching demonstrations of loyalty in the vicinity of the Palace in those immediate post-surrender days. But there were also anti-Hirohito demonstrations, unthinkable in the pre-August 15 era, now watched by unarmed Tokyo police (who had replaced the Imperial Guards) and their US Military Police colleagues. For the first time, there was a spate of anti-Hirohito editorials in the new, post-war Japanese press, some (but not all) translated from American papers.

Higashikuni himself had earlier believed that it would be impossible for Hirohito to remain on the throne. He accepted the Premiership, he was to tell a reporter in 1965, because Kido had told him "only you can do it" and because the Emperor, "who looked so tired, and had lost so much weight", had asked him "gloomily: will you be the next Prime Minister? I finally couldn't resist." But Higashikuni imposed one condition, immediately accepted by the Emperor: he would not go aboard the *Missouri* and sign the armistice. "I said: 'I won't go,'" Higashikuni told Ando. "If I'm compelled to go I'll resign. I don't mean to bow there and sign documents." No Imperial family member was to be directly involved in this disgraceful episode of Japanese history.

In his 1965 interview, Higashikuni also revealed one important detail: whereas it is the accepted view that Hirohito himself decided to visit MacArthur, Higashikuni clearly stated the initiative was his. "I wanted the idea to appear to come from the Emperor," Higashikuni said, "as his idea, not mine. The Emperor behaved very modestly in front of MacArthur and MacArthur was pleased and flattered." While the substance of that first dialogue between the two men is by now established, no complete version exists. Then, as later, there was an understanding on both sides to keep the talks secret.

MacArthur kept his part of the bargain with a vengeance, not even bothering to brief his President, or the State Department. In subsequent meetings the Japanese Foreign Ministry carefully debriefed the Emperor's interpreter, and records of their conversations exist – but have never been accessible for perusal.

It is highly likely, Professor Hata believes, that during this first meeting MacArthur persuaded the Emperor not to abdicate. If Hirohito *did* toy with the notion of retirement in those first three weeks of peace, there was precious little talk of it *after* his September 27 meeting with MacArthur. And it is from that date onward, as the *New York Times*' Hanson Baldwin, then a young reporter in Tokyo, put it, that there evolved "a tacit agreement on the Emperor's part to be MacArthur's junior partner in the surrender and occupation". The victim of this new Imperial policy was to be Prince Konoye, the very man who saw himself as the stern judge set over Japanese war criminals.

Before July 12, 1945, because of his "suspect" anti-war views, Konoye had been kept at arms' length from the Palace, and, except for one meeting, in February 1945, had not seen Hirohito directly for three years. As deputy Prime Minister, Konoye was now charged with drafting a new, democratic constitution, and he set about his task with considerable energy and purpose. But, as a loyal kinsman whose links with the Imperial Family went back several centuries, he was also determined to protect the Emperor – however much he may have disapproved of his immediate pre-war conduct. The way he embarked on this defence virtually guaranteed his own downfall.

Unlike Hirohito, Prince Konoye did not behave modestly in MacArthur's presence, or "bow deeply like a servant". He tended to think, at this stage, that he and MacArthur were on the same side, and assumed that MacArthur knew all about his attempts to prevent Japan from going to war on December 7, 1941.

MacArthur *did* know about Konoye, but his knowledge, culled from aides' reports, was highly selective: to SCAP, Konoye was the man who had thrown Japanese troops into China in 1937, had "invented" the "Greater Asian Co-prosperity Sphere", and established fascistic, one-party rule in Japan. SCAP staff were unaware of Konoye's role in trying to convince Hirohito, and Tojo, not to go to war with the US – and they remained highly suspicious of his "summit" initiative with Roosevelt, proposed just before Pearl Harbor.

Konoye's first meeting with MacArthur was brief, and formal. When he requested a second audience (granted on October 4, 1945), he was kept deliberately waiting for twenty minutes, and at first an aide announced MacArthur was "too busy" to see him. Only when Konoye threatened to walk out rather than talk to a subordinate did MacArthur's schedule, miraculously, become less encumbered. But what Konoye had to say only confirmed SCAP in its prejudices against him.

For Konoye's defence of Hirohito took an unacceptable form: all responsibility for the war, Konoye told MacArthur bluntly, lay with the militarists and the ultra-nationalists. Had he stopped there, it would have been an unexceptionable, though hardly original, argument. But Konoye went on to defend the "zaibatsu", the large industrial conglomerates MacArthur was determined to break up. These, Konoye said, along with the feudal nature of the Imperial institution, "had always acted as a brake on the militarists". It was the "leftist element in the Imperial Japanese army, exploiting the military clique, that drove Japan to war". They were the sole culprits.

He then embarked on the same speech he had made to Hirohito in February 1945 – warning MacArthur of the spectre of Japanese Communism. If the Court institutions and the "zaibatsu" were liquidated along with the military clique and the ultra-nationalists, Japan would be Communism's easy prey. This was particularly unwelcome: some of SCAP's staff were "New Deal" liberals, and to them Konoye sounded like an unreconstructed, hard-line reactionary. Not knowing enough about his past, or about his dramatic change of heart in 1941, they saw his warning, coming as it did in advance of the "cold war", as a deliberate attempt to pull the wool over their eyes.

MacArthur listened politely, but spoke gruffly, in a clipped, soldierly tone, when Konoye started asking pointed questions about the composition of the future Diet and the organization of government, making it clear that these were issues to be decided by SCAP alone. Here again, Konoye misunderstood the nature of his role, assuming that he, Konoye, was to have a major part in reshaping post-war Japan, with MacArthur as a partner. MacArthur was prepared to defer to an Emperor, but not to Konoye, an ideal scapegoat, who could so easily be blamed for Japan's entry into the war with China – the crucial decision which had led, in the long run, to Pearl Harbor.

Konoye told MacArthur that he was "ready to serve the nation to the best of his ability", unaware that the meeting had only reinforced the Supremo in his belief that Konoye was not to be trusted, and should be got rid of as quickly as possible. Reflecting SCAP's anti-Konoye views, a spate of articles almost immediately appeared in the US press. The *New York Times*, in an editorial reprinted in Tokyo's papers, wrote that, if Konoye was given a role to play in post-war Japan, this was tantamount to "making Quisling President of Norway, Laval President of France and Goering chief of the Allied Powers in Europe".

Far from being Japan's post-war justiciar, Konoye now became the target of US investigators determined to bring war criminals to book. With little inside knowledge of the inner crises around the throne in 1941, SCAP specialists focused on those whose names had surfaced, again and again, in the events leading up to Pearl Harbor. Konoye's name was high on the list, since he had been Prime Minister three times, had ushered in the "Greater Asia Co-prosperity Sphere" and had been in charge of the government at the time of the "Marco Polo" incident which had led to full-scale war with China. (Another prominent pre-war figure in SCAP's sights was Kiko Hirota, also a former Prime Minister – and also, ironically, a spirited opponent of war with America from 1941 onwards.)

A day later, Konoye's fate was sealed. Higashikuni had scored several points in his brief dealings with SCAP. He had successfully argued against the introduction of US military "scrip", and against direct military control. "Japan shouldn't be like Hawaii or the Philippines," Higashikuni told Ando later. "Japan was defeated but Japan was still Japan." Faced with a determined, self-confident, princely Prime Minister, the SCAP authorities had wavered – but they stood firm on the principle of removing from public office all those regarded as "militarists". When they asked Higashikuni to dismiss his own Interior Minister on such grounds, Higashikuni refused – and, on October 5, 1945, resigned. Konoye, now an embarrassment to Hirohito, was not included in the next government, headed by Mamoru Shigemitsu, formerly Higashikuni's Foreign Minister. Konoye was still blithely unaware of the gathering clouds around him. On October 8, he obtained a meeting with George Atcheson, MacArthur's top civilian adviser, to discuss the new Japanese constitution. On October 11, Hirohito brought Konoye into the Privy Seal Secretariat as an adviser on constitutional reform, almost certainly to give him something to do and keep him out of harm's way. On October 17, he held a press conference on constitutional reform, largely attended by US and British correspondents, in which he hinted that the Emperor would gladly become a constitutional monarch along British lines.

But, very shortly afterwards, the word went out from SCAP that Konoye was in serious trouble. Highly responsive to MacArthur by this time, Hirohito became increasingly inaccessible to Konoye, and SCAP declared him persona non grata – no member of SCAP staff was to have any dealings with him.

A month later, Konoye was interrogated for three hours by the US Strategic Bombing Survey team. Though a British Embassy official, D. MacDermot, forwarding the transcript of Konoye's interrogation to the Foreign Office, later wrote that "one of the American generals who has interviewed Konoye several times described him to me as a rat who was quite prepared to sell anyone to save himself, and even went so far as to call his master, the Emperor, 'the major war criminal'", the actual transcript contains no such allegations.

On the contrary: with his misguided sense of loyalty to Hirohito, Konoye failed to itemize the differences between them in 1941, failed to give his version of his resignation in October 1941, failed above all to rise above generalities – all in his obsessive concern to protect the Emperor. The nearest he came to implicit criticism of Hirohito was in answer to a question, asking him to spell out what "efforts" were made to terminate the war. "Just as finally the end of the war was brought about by the Emperor," Konoye replied, "so at that time efforts were made to persuade the Emperor, particularly through Kido, who was close to him, to put an end to the war" – implying that the final decision had been Kido's rather than Hirohito's, and that the Emperor might, had he wished, have ended the war earlier.

Partly because Konoye was determined to keep his answers vague, in order not to implicate the Emperor, partly because he was ill at ease and unused to being cross-examined, he made a deplorable impression. Throughout, he hedged and prevaricated, blaming the military and his faulty memory, never once covering the dramatic details of his break with Hirohito in September 1941, his confrontation with Tojo in October, or his comments to his staff at the time – who would have corroborated his version of events. Partly out of princely arrogance, partly because he was unprepared for the committee's onslaught, he failed to provide a cogent defence of his own actions from September 1941 onwards – or any indication of the sweeping nature of the change that came over him in the last three months before Pearl Harbor. The circumstances of the interrogation were also unusual: unlike other witnesses, Konoye was not questioned in Tokyo, but aboard a US Navy gunboat in Tokyo harbour. His interrogators pointedly called him "Mr. Konoye". "It was horrible," he told Tomita afterwards, "like a prosecuting attorney taking a deposition from a criminal." He could not understand it. "Perhaps," he told Tomita, "the attitude of the US Occupation staff is affected by the fact that there are so many Jews in MacArthur's Headquarters . . . They are not just antipathetic towards the Imperial Family but seek some pretext to destroy it. They also seem to be plotting the communization of Japan." Ironically, he pointed out to Tomita that, while the militarists had treated him as a traitor from 1941 onwards for trying to prevent a war, he was now being treated like a war criminal by SCAP.

On November 22 Konoye finally saw Hirohito, and submitted his outline for constitutional reform. He also formally asked Hirohito to relinquish his princely title. The Emperor by this time had become distant, less interested in any of Konoye's plans or problems, aware that Konoye was now on SCAP's "black list".

By November 1945, despite his successful initial meeting with MacArthur, Hirohito was not fully reassured as to his own fate: SCAP investigators were closing in on suspected war criminals in high places. They actually arrested a member of the

Imperial Family, the elderly, inoffensive Prince Nashimoto, the former Field Marshal and chief priest at the sacred Isé shrine, and the last person to have had a say in the running of the war. Perhaps some SCAP officials wanted to show Hirohito he was not himself immune from prosecution.

Konoye reacted badly: "Does not the Government do anything when an Imperial Prince is imprisoned?" Konoye asked Tomita. "The way things are, I doubt whether the [Japanese] press would do anything if the Emperor himself were arrested. I must ask Nashimoto why he didn't kill himself for the sake of the Emperor and Japan." (After a few weeks in detention, Prince Nashimoto was released; he had faced his ordeal with unexpected cheerfulness, carrying out his prisoner's chores with a broad smile, treating the whole experience as a huge joke.)

Then, on December 6, came the final blow: Konoye was ordered, by SCAP, to report to Sugamo prison as a suspected war criminal on December 16.

Kido, similarly notified, was more serene. "Everything is as expected," he noted in his Diary, "and I am not disturbed." The only thing that mattered, he told Konoye, was to keep the Emperor from being charged — and who better could ensure this than he and Konoye?

Konoye disagreed. If he tried to explain why he had acted as he had as Prime Minister, he told Kido, this would not prevent the Emperor from being charged. "The responsibility of the Supreme Command would still lie with the Emperor as Commander-in-Chief," he said. "If the United States has already made up its mind to punish the Emperor, I feel helpless to defend him." Perhaps he also felt that he could not explain the rationale of his own behaviour from 1937 onwards without heavily implicating Hirohito — and that the prospect of betraying the Emperor in this way was intolerable. In any case, he told friends, he could not bear the humiliation of standing in court as a suspected war criminal. He again returned to his immediate pre-war record. To a *Mainichi* reporter, he said: "Before the war I was ridiculed for being indecisive, during the war I was rebuked as an escapist peacemaker, and after the war accused of being a war criminal. I am a child of fate."

In contrast, Kido displayed no such introspection: though he suspected, even before December 6, that he was likely to be accused as a war criminal, he did not let this prospect interfere with his overriding responsibility: lifelong service to the Emperor. He continued to provide Hirohito with good advice. On September 29 (two days after his visit to MacArthur), Hirohito complained about virulent attacks on him in the American press. "I can pretend not to notice," he told Kido. "I can also reveal my true feelings through a newspaper reporter or to MacArthur directly." Kido advised him to do no such thing. "Americans in general," he told the Emperor, "have considerable misunderstanding of Japan's attitude. So if we try to defend ourselves, it could make matters worse." It was important to ignore the attacks and let everything die down. Hirohito followed his advice.

On November 12, Hirohito expressed the wish to commune with his ancestors at the Isé shrine, to inform them of his calamitous defeat and beg their forgiveness. Again, it was Kido who made the arrangements with SCAP, obtaining MacArthur's special clearance, and who carefully supervised the travel arrangements. It was Hirohito's first trip outside Tokyo since the end of the war and Kido worried about possible hostile demonstrations. He was relieved when, at Numazu station, where the Imperial train stopped for six minutes, there were none, for "if a mob threw stones, there was nothing we could do". But "the six minutes passed quickly. It wasn't the stereotyped pre-war welcome. Some people stood and bowed, but they were natural. I was glad to see the people and the Imperial Family coming close together." At another station, "a widow displayed a picture of her late army officer husband. I watched her face and thought she was a true Japanese and my eyes were moist."

After formally quitting his job as Lord Privy Seal, but staying on as a "special temporary employee of the Imperial Household", Kido had received various presents from the Emperor:

20,000 yen in cash, a barrel of Imperial sake and tinned goods. "The great sacred mercy makes me shed tears," Kido noted. He received more presents when, along with other former peers, he submitted his formal request to become a commoner on November 24.

Unlike Konoye, who was kept at a distance and ignored, Kido received further marks of esteem from Hirohito after December 6: five days before going to jail, Kido was summoned to dine with the Emperor. Kido declined at first, on the grounds that, as he was under suspicion as a war criminal, he could "contaminate" the Emperor.

Hirohito replied to the Chamberlain who conveyed this apology that "in the eyes of the Americans he may be a criminal but he is a devoted servant of his country. If he is reluctant to come, have the food sent to him." A Palace car came to fetch Kido from his home for his last dinner with Hirohito.

Kido received more gifts, including "a big table" from the Empress, and doughnuts she had baked herself. Kido noted that, in the course of their conversation "the Emperor told me various stories in all directions" – he rambled on, disjointedly, clearly upset by Kido's impending fate.

There was one last meeting, the day before Kido reported to Sugamo prison. Hirohito's final words to him were: "This time I am very sorry. Take care of your health. I think you understand my feelings completely as we have talked to each other always. So please explain it fully to them [the other prisoners]."

In this characteristically oblique way, the Emperor was conveying a crucial message to Kido: he was to be his eyes and ears inside the prison, using his intuitive knowledge to interpret the Emperor's viewpoint, and make sure it was understood. Unsaid but implicit was Hirohito's mute plea to protect him, come what may, from involvement in the trial.

In his country home, ignored and rejected by Hirohito, Konoye was making very different preparations: he made peace with his brother, a musician who had spent the war years in

Germany, and from whom he had been estranged; he settled his family and private affairs, and dictated a brief political testament. "I have made many political blunders, beginning with the China war," it began,

and I feel my responsibility for them deeply. The air is ringing with false charges and misunderstanding. Whatever you say, people accuse you of evasion and lying. I refuse to engage in mudslinging with people who will say anything to boost themselves. It makes no difference to me if people do not understand me. I am convinced that some time in the future I will be judged with justice and exonerated.

The fervour and hatred that accompany war, the excessive arrogance of the victors and the extreme servility of the losers, the rumours because of intentionally false accusations and misunderstandings – all these together are called "public opinion". Eventually, I hope that in the court of the Gods, a just judgment will be passed on me. I find it intolerable, however, to stand in an American court as a so-called war criminal.

The very fact that I did feel responsibility for the China war made the task of effecting a settlement [with the US] all the more crucial to me.

Concluding that the only remaining chance to achieve a settlement of the war in China was to reach an understanding with the US, I did everything in my power to make the negotiations a success. It is regrettable that I am now suspected by the same US of being a war criminal.

I believe those who know me well know what my aspirations were. I believe that even in the US I have friends who understand me.

At a dinner with his two closest friends on December 14, Konoye allowed some of his bitterness towards Hirohito to seep through. He calmly informed them of his intention to die. "Tell the Emperor," he said, "to do the same when they come and get him."

At dawn on December 15, he killed himself: a Prince of the Royal blood was not supposed to spill it, and Konoye swallowed a cyanide capsule. His funeral was sparsely attended. As his biographer, Yoshitake Oka, noted, "a number of people who should have been there excused themselves. In the normal course of events, ten thousand people would have shown up. There were a few hundred." The Emperor never attended funerals, barring those of his immediate family, but on this occasion he did not even send a representative, or write an immediate note of condolence to his family. As Mark Gayn, a correspondent in Tokyo for the *Chicago Sun*, wrote at the time, "the Emperor, unsure he would not himself be brought to trial as a war criminal, will not blacken himself by sympathy for a man upon whom for so long he had depended for guidance". According to one reliable contemporary report, Hirohito's only apparent reaction to Konoye's death was annoyance: he promptly spread the word that all those summoned to Sugamo prison should unfailingly obey.

Apart from his political testament, Konoye left behind an annotated copy of Oscar Wilde's *De Profundis*, a work – and by a writer – he much admired. The passage he had underlined on New Year's Day, 1945, read: "The people used to say of me that I was too individualistic . . . Indeed, my main crime came not from too great individualism of life, but from too little" – another oblique reference to the real cause of his death: his determination to protect Hirohito at all costs, in character with his conception of his Princely role.

Perhaps Konoye, with his keen sense of irony, would have appreciated the absurdity of his own death: forty-three years later, Robert Fearey, a former SCAP official, gave this account of the events leading up to it. Shortly before Konoye's notification that he would stand trial as a war criminal, he said, "Atcheson* called me into his office, and told me, 'I've had a call from General MacArthur and he has noticed that all these major war criminals have been arrested and tried, or are about to be tried, in Germany, and here we have arrested no major war criminals in Japan, they're still walking the streets. This

* MacArthur's civilian deputy with ambassadorial status.

isn't right. So would you please draw me a list of 10 to 12 – or whatever the number was – of people who should be arrested, and then arrest them.' Together with Herb Norman, a Canadian working for the Intelligence branch of SCAP, we drew up a list of ten people we thought should be arrested as major war criminals, and gave it to Atcheson who gave it to MacArthur, and the next day they were arrested, headlines all over the place.

"Maybe a week later, MacArthur said, 'there must be more than ten.' So I produced another list, and on it was Prince Konoye, not because we felt he was a war criminal who should be tried and convicted, but because he had been Prime Minister at critical phases over many years when Japan had gone into North China, and his involvement was important from the military point of view. The understanding between us was that we would get word to Prince Konoye that we did not regard him as a war criminal like the others, that we only wanted him as material witness and felt we had to do this because of the positions he had held."

In other words, he was only included in the second war criminal suspects' list because of his knowledge of the past. "I am afraid," Fearey added, "that word of this did not get to Prince Konoye in time. Someone forgot to tell him."

CHAPTER TWENTY-FOUR

The very day Kido and Konoye received their notification to report to Sugamo prison, the American contingent of the International Military Tribunal for the Far East (IMTFE) left the US by air for Tokyo. Their leader, Joseph B. Keenan, a gang-busting attorney who had helped topple Al Capone, and was to become the IMTFE's chief prosecutor, knew nothing about Japan. A close friend of Franklin Roosevelt and of J. Edgar Hoover, he was no favourite of Truman's, who appointed him so that he should no longer haunt the White House corridors.

It turned out to be a disastrous choice. A lecher and secret drinker who was frequently unintelligible in court in the afternoons, Keenan alienated some of the best American legal brains already at work at SCAP in Tokyo. His courtroom manner irritated the President of the Court, Sir William Flood Webb, the able but crotchety Chief Justice of the State of Queensland, who had already presided over one war crimes trial in the Philippines. It also completely baffled the Japanese defence lawyers. Keenan showed contempt for Japanese customs in little ways, such as refusing to remove his outdoor shoes when he entered Japanese homes or restaurants.

A striking physical resemblance to the great comedian, W. C. Fields, provoked hilarity, but otherwise there was nothing funny about Keenan. He was a meddler as well as a consistent publicity-grabbing bully, slavishly subservient to MacArthur at all times. Under him, the so-called independence of the judiciary was a mockery. This highly idiosyncratic, unattractive figure dominated IMTFE proceedings from 1946 to 1948, making life a misery for all those who crossed him.

Before leaving for Tokyo, Keenan had told reporters in Washington that, in his view, Hirohito clearly deserved to stand trial. According to an Associated Press story "Keenan disclosed Emperor Hirohito may join in the prisoners dock as a war criminal" (*sic*), i.e., be made to stand trial. As Robert Dohini, a member of his prosecution team, recalls, "Emperor Hirohito was the subject of special interest before we left the US and, as far as the other sixteen of us were concerned, he was 'number one' on the list in consideration for trial. Right up to the time our plane left, we were led to think we were going to try the Emperor.

"It was virtually as we boarded the plane that we learnt, from a letter delivered to Keenan by President Truman practically at the airport, that we should lay off Hirohito, and that meant laying off the whole Imperial Household as well. I was told, personally: do not attempt to interrogate any of them."

Truman's letter to Keenan was part of a policy battle fought out between bureaucrats in Washington and Tokyo. Only a few days before (November 29) a top secret directive from the Joint Chiefs of Staff to MacArthur indicated that they at least had an open mind about the Emperor's responsibilities. Referring to Hirohito "as a person and not to the Emperor institution as such", their note read:

Whether Hirohito is to be tried as a war criminal is of great interest to the United States. The US Government's position is that Hirohito is not immune from arrest, trial, and punishment as a war criminal.

It may be assumed that when it appears that the Occupation can proceed satisfactorily without him, the question of his trial will be raised.

It may also be assumed that if such a proposal will serve a purpose, it may be raised by one or more of our allies. It's clear we mustn't delay in collecting the evidence, necessary whether he is eventually tried or not, since any decision not to try him should be made in the light of all available facts . . .

Assembly of evidence must be conducted with strict security safeguards to avoid disclosure either of the evidence itself or of the fact that such evidence is being assembled.

This was certainly not MacArthur's view, and may have led to the hasty note delivered to Keenan as he boarded the plane to Tokyo. Atcheson spelled out with considerable frankness the advantages and disadvantages of prosecuting Hirohito. In a report to the State Department dated January 8, 1946, he wrote:

It's clear Hirohito is not immune from trial as a war criminal but treatment of him as a war criminal cannot be divorced from our overall objective in Japan.

If we are prepared not only for indefinite occupation but huge expenditures on economic aid, and also on increasing the size of forces in Japan for any contingency that may arise, then we can adopt a strongly aggressive political policy, try the Emperor as a war criminal and encourage the complete abolition of the emperor system. Even some Japanese argue that if he had sufficient power to stop the war, he had the authority to prevent it.

But, Atcheson pointed out, the Emperor was "useful, obeyed by officials and people . . .

. . . I am reliably informed that Hirohito is considering abdication at some time in the not too distant future. An important element in such planning is the fear he may be named as a war criminal. This would result in the elimination of a leader to whom Japan is accustomed, and to whom, strangely enough, most of the common people are grateful for bringing them peace.

Thus if we decide to continue to use the Emperor indefinitely he should be given some indication that we regard his continuing on the throne desirable.

MacArthur followed this up with his own views to the Joint Chiefs of Staff, dated January 25, making Atcheson's points with almost caricatural emphasis. His extraordinary letter is worth quoting almost in full:

If he is tried, great changes must be made in occupational plans and due preparation therefore should be accomplished in preparedness before the actual action is initiated. His indictment will unquestionably cause a tremendous convulsion among the Japanese people, the repercussions of which cannot be overestimated. He is the symbol which unites all the Japanese. Destroy him and the nation will disintegrate.

The whole of Japan can be expected, in my opinion, to resist the action either by passive or semi-active means. They are disarmed and therefore represent no special menace to trained and equipped troops. But it is not inconceivable that all government agencies will largely cease, and a condition of underground chaos and disorder amounting to guerrilla warfare in the mountains or outlying areas result. I believe all hope of introducing modern democratic methods would disappear and that when military control finally ceased some form of intense regimentation probably along communistic lines would arise from the mutilated masses. This would present an entirely different problem of occupation from that now prevalent. It would be absolutely essential to greatly increase the occupational forces. It is quite possible that a minimum of one million troops would be required which would have to be maintained for an indefinite number of years.

By brandishing the threat of administrative chaos, guerrilla warfare, the growth of Japanese Communism and the need to maintain a million-strong garrison in Japan on a war footing for years to come, MacArthur effectively eliminated the idea of putting Hirohito on trial.

Whether he actually believed in his dire predictions or simply blackmailed Truman and the Chiefs of Staff into submitting to his own will is another matter. Even Grew, that arch-defender of the Imperial system, had been less sanguine: in July 1944, after the OSS had reported rumours that Hirohito was about to leave Tokyo for the comparative safety of Manchuria, Grew noted that "one could argue that if he flees the country he will be considered to have abdicated. The question whether the [occupation] military government should therefore set up another member of the Imperial family as the Emperor's successor or should treat the Emperor-instituiton as having been terminated should be decided after our occupation of Tokyo." Around this time, Washington even toyed with the idea of encouraging an exile Japanese group along "Free French" lines, called the "International Japanese Peoples' Liberation Alliance", to be underwritten by the OSS and the Office of War Information (OWI) and later used as the nucleus of a free "democratic" post-war government. The reason the project was dropped was not because it was feared that the end of the "Emperor-system" would lead to armed chaos, but because the OSS felt such a group would be dominated by Communist exiles.

Both the Atcheson and the MacArthur letters were deliberately ambiguous: MacArthur enumerated the consequences, as he said he saw them, of the end of the "Emperor-system". But at no time was this radical solution given serious thought. What many people − including the Emperor's own intimates − had in mind was Hirohito's abdication in favour of Akihito, and the setting up of a Regency under either Chichibu, Takamatsu or Mikasa, Hirohito's younger brothers. Had such a series of events taken place, there is no certainty that any of the consequences outlined by Atcheson and MacArthur would have occurred. In the recent past, Chichibu, Takamatsu and Konoye had all calmly contemplated Hirohito's abdication as an option. Leading Japanese historians, and many Japanese who experienced the trauma of surrender at first hand, agree in retrospect that a state of complete apathy prevailed immediately after Hirohito's August 15 speech, and that Hirohito's removal from the throne would not have led to any violent or lasting upheaval, especially if a Regency had been established. Even the romantic "boy Emperor" conspiracy devised by the Nakano Spy School and Imperial Navy stalwarts − among the toughest, most uncompromising advocates of continuing clandestine action after the war − showed that their plans were long-term and non-violent. In short, everything points to MacArthur blatantly using his position as Supreme Commander to compel not only Truman, but also America's allies, to accept Hirohito's continued presence on the throne because this was what he wanted, especially after their meeting of September 27, 1945. And it was MacArthur, more than any other single person, who made official the theory of the "Emperor as puppet". In another report, MacArthur wrote that it would be

. . a disaster to indict Hirohito as a war criminal since he had been from the beginning to the end a puppet, a complete "Charlie McCarthy"* who had neither begun the war nor stopped it. At every point he had acted automatically on advice and he could not have done otherwise. The Cabinet meeting which ended the war was as much staged as those which began it.

This, over the years, became the officially accepted view: it ignored some of the evidence to the contrary readily available in the Kido diaries, and some key portions of the Sugiyama memorandum. But comparing Hirohito to a top-hatted doll also meant denying the Emperor his one claim to greatness: the manner in which he had ended the war. It was a price Hirohito's apologists were prepared to pay.

As Donihi pointed out, the Emperor's immunity to prosecution had to extend to members of his family, for it would not have been possible to spare the Emperor while pursuing his close relatives. So several Princely figures who might otherwise have found themselves in the dock as "class A" criminals were spared, among them Prince Asaka, who had commanded troops during the rape of Nanking.

A further deal made behind the scenes turned the IMTFE proceedings into a ghoulish farce. Before leaving Ping Fan, as the Soviets advanced into Manchuria in the final four days of the war, the infamous General Ishii, of "Unit 731", ordered forty live "marutas" held there in readiness for experiments to be injected with prussic acid and cremated; their ashes and thousands of containers containing specimens were dumped in the Sungari river.

* The celebrated ventriloquist Edgar Bergen's dummy.

From Harbin, Ishii fled to Pusan in Korea. He returned to Tokyo just after the end of the war and took a room in the Wakamatsu Hotel opposite the Tokyo Military Hospital in the Shinjuku district: there, while Empress Nagako was watching B-29s ferry in US Occupation troops, Ishii was busy disposing of the grisly "maruta" specimens kept until then in the Tokyo Military Hospital.

If ever anyone deserved to be labelled a "grade A" war crimes suspect, it was Ishii. US Army Colonel Murray Sanders, sent to Tokyo immediately after the war to investigate "Unit 731's" activities, many years later said that his contact in Tokyo, Colonel Ryohi Nahito, after considerable pressure, "laid out the table of organization: it started with the Emperor and branched off into various departments – the War Ministry, Chief of Staff, Army Medical Affairs Department, etc."

Through Nahito, Ishii, by now in hiding, petitioned Sanders for full immunity in return for the entire "Unit 731" scientific data on chemical and biological warfare. According to Sanders (who died in 1986): "MacArthur agreed to immunity for all in return for all the [Unit 731] information. I had MacArthur's word we would not prosecute." In January 1946 Ishii emerged from hiding. A year later, two US scientists, Edwin Hill and Joseph Victor, came to Japan and debriefed Ishii and others. Their report contains the following euphemism: "Such information could not be obtained in our own laboratories because of scruples attached to human experimentation."

MacArthur kept his word, and Keenan raised no objections: neither Ishii, nor any of his subordinates, were ever arraigned before IMTFE. The "Unit 731" issue did surface, very briefly, during the IMTFE court proceedings. A US prosecutor, referring to documents supplied by China, noted, early in the trial, that "the enemy's 'TAMA' [Japanese codename for 'Unit 731'] Detachment carried off their civilian captives to a medical laboratory, where their reactions to poisonous serums were tested. This detachment was one of the most secret units. The number of persons slaughtered by this detachment cannot be ascertained."

Webb asked for further evidence: "This is something entirely new, are you going to leave it at that?"

"We do not at this time anticipate introducing evidence on that subject," the prosecutor replied. Webb concluded there was none, and dismissed this particular indictment, calling it, doubtless in good faith, "mere assertion unsupported by any evidence". "Unit 731" was never mentioned again at the trial.

Ishii died of cancer at a ripe old age; several "Unit 731" specialists have written that, after a "decent interval", he was invited to lecture US Army specialists at Camp Detrick, Virginia, the US Army's chemical warfare headquarters, and this has never been officially denied.

Since Hirohito was not on trial, and since the defendants did their best to shield him at all times, his name was rarely mentioned during the interminable IMTFE proceedings. Before the actual start of the trial (on May 3, 1946), Keenan had made his attitude very clear: when Sir William Webb asked him why the Emperor had not been indicted, Keenan replied that everyone knew that, throughout the pre-war period, "the Emperor had been in the power of gangsters". At a preparatory meeting of prosecutors, he also stressed his "hands off" policy where the Emperor was concerned. A British member of his team asked: "Is that a decision or a proposal?" Keenan replied: "The policy has been decided. I am asking for your agreement." When the British lawyer said: "I can't go along with this sort of thing," Keenan replied: "It's in the interest of all the Allied nations to carry out occupation policy smoothly; that is also the will of SCAP. If you gentlemen are unable to agree with SCAP policy, feel free to pack your bags and go home." In the course of time, some eventually did.

A few months into the trial, however, the question arose: should the Emperor be called upon to testify? Hardly unexpectedly, both MacArthur and Keenan were adamant in their opposition. In November 1947 Webb absented himself from Tokyo on leave: the decision not to involve the Emperor in any way was taken in his absence. Webb was privately of the opinion that Hirohito should have been in court along with the other accused.

A final attempt to involve Hirohito in IMTFE proceedings was made in the course of the trial by Edward P. Monaghan, of the prosecution team's investigative division. In a note to Keenan, Monaghan pointed out that there were reliable reports that Hirohito had kept a diary ever since he was a child. Since this diary would throw considerable light on the events leading up to Pearl Harbor, Monaghan suggested the Palace should be subpoenaed to turn over the Emperor's diary to the court. Keenan's reaction was predictable: in a handwritten note appended to Monaghan's request, he wrote: "There are important matters of policy involved in suggestion; it concerns matters other than the need for dependable evidence. If any action should be taken on this it would be only after specific orders from the highest authority in SCAP. I believe that there are strong reasons why any such request should be denied." Keenan's official reply was as follows:

CONFIDENTIAL; MEMO FOR EDWARD P. MONAGHAN, CHIEF INVESTIGATIVE DIVISION I.P.S.
FROM: JOSEPH B. KEENAN, CHIEF OF COUNSEL, I.P.S.

The obvious matters of policy involved in procuring a thing as personal as a diary from the Emperor of Japan are so outstanding that at any stage of the proceedings it would have been difficult to have obtained consent to any demand for production of same.

Particularly at this stage of our proceedings, with our case in chief already in, we could not expect to have serious considerations given thereto.

It is, therefore, my conclusion that the matter should be dropped.

For all his determination to protect Hirohito, even Keenan occasionally became carried away in the heat of cross-examination. Whenever this happened, almost comically, realizing that the reply to his question might implicate Hirohito, he would cease his line of questioning. A classic example of this technique occurred during his cross-examination of Kido. By rights, Kido's prosecuting counsel should have been asking the questions, but Keenan, despite his imperfect knowledge of the Kido dossier, was not prepared to let a subordinate occupy centre stage when a well-known figure was being cross-examined.

Keenan was trying to prove that Kido knew about Pearl Harbor. An IMTFE report (based on a *New York Times* story) had stated that the Emperor, in admiral's uniform, had spent the night of December 7–8, 1941, monitoring radio transmission from Admiral Yamamoto's flagship.

Keenan must have remembered this.

KEENAN: I am suggesting there was a little gathering over there at the palace, to find out how this attack on Pearl Harbor was going?

KIDO: I know nothing about that.

KEENAN: That is all.

He was, however, expert in putting words into the accuseds' mouths that would exonerate the Emperor, and reinforce Mac-Arthur's "puppet" thesis. An example came while he was questioning Kido about the September 6, 1941 "Gozen Kaigi".

In reply to Keenan's question ("did the Emperor have anything to do with the decision of the September 6 Imperial Conference?") Kido indulged in a lengthy, convoluted, hedging explanation. Keenan cut him short.

KEENAN: All right, then, the answer is that it wasn't really a decision of the Emperor at all. It was a decision formally made in his name but made by other people. Is not that perfectly plain?

KIDO: In plain language, yes.

The only time when IMTFE court proceedings looked as if they might call Hirohito's entire role into question came towards the end, on December 31, 1947. By this time public interest in the trial had waned, both in Japan and abroad. Tojo was in the middle of a long statement, winding up his own defence proceedings, and had just stated that Hirohito had consented, "though reluctantly, to the war", when a Japanese defence lawyer acting for Kido interrupted him. "Did you ever make any suggestion or take action against the Emperor's will for peace?" he asked.

Tojo was taken aback. "No," he said, "I didn't. None of us [Japanese] would dare act against the Emperor's will."

The reply may not have been significant to the handful of Western reporters present, but to the experts it was a crucial, and damning, admission: it made nonsense of the "Emperor as puppet" theory so dear to MacArthur, and to Keenan, implying as it did that, had Hirohito really wanted to prevent war, he could have acted accordingly, and been obeyed by all, including arch-militarists like Tojo. Webb immediately pounced on Tojo's reply: with some glee, he said (and his remark, though addressed to the court as a whole, was unmistakably directed at Keenan): "Well, you know the implications from that reply." The following day the chief Soviet Prosecutor, outside the courtroom, requested that Hirohito be indicted as soon as possible.

All this could not have occurred at a less propitious time: six days before, on Christmas Day, 1947, with Keenan's blessing, one of his Japanese aides, Ryukushi Tanaka, had called on Prince Takamatsu, told him that the Emperor had nothing to worry about and that the court proceedings would come to an end without involving him. Keenan ingratiatingly intended this information to be unofficially conveyed to Hirohito himself.

Ryukushi Tanaka was the same huge, bullet-headed army officer who had monitored the departure of the Chinese warlord Chang Tsu-lin's train from Peking in 1928 and had been, in the thirties, the "control" of "Eastern Jewel", the famous Japanese spy; he had fallen on hard times in recent years. Because of a long-standing feud with Tojo, and genuine doubts about the wisdom of going to war against the US, he had been placed on the reserve, and his anguish at the course of events had led to insomnia, depression and a spell in a mental home. "As a result," he wrote later, "I was branded as a lunatic by my enemies."

In 1946, he had been routinely questioned by IMTFE staff, and a young American lieutenant, Robert Honidi, realized his immense potential as a prosecution witness. He introduced him to Keenan, who attached him to his personal staff. Tanaka became Keenan's court jester, pimp, and adviser on Japanese matters. In his new role as arch-collaborator, he was viewed as an abject traitor and turncoat by the Japanese "establishment" and the now demobilized military hierarchy. But his usefulness to the Emperor as well as to Keenan was never denied, for Tanaka professed intense feelings of personal loyalty to Hirohito and claimed that his only reason for becoming a prosecution witness in the first place had been to protect the Emperor's name. He provided damning evidence against Tojo and other generals, invariably adopting the MacArthur-Keenan line that the Emperor had been nothing but a puppet, manipulated at all times by the military.

Now, with the "puppet" theory suddenly in jeopardy, Keenan stepped in with terrier-like zeal. He told his Japanese secretary to telephone Tanaka, who lived in the country, and summon him back to Tokyo in the middle of the night.

Tanaka, many years later, told what happened next (in an article in a Japanese magazine dated August 1965). Professor Hata, who has himself made a special study of both Tanaka and the events he described, and fleshed out Tanaka's account with his own additional investigation, confirms that, for all Tanaka's controversial personality, his account is completely accurate.

An agitated Keenan, on January 1, 1948, told Tanaka the only way out was to reach Tojo in Sugamo prison and force him to retract his statement. "A few days later," Tanaka wrote, "I went to court and met Tojo and asked him to do this. But Tojo was stubbornly against my suggestion. He said: 'What I said is what I believe about the Imperial family and I cannot go back on it.'" Tanaka then sought a meeting with Tojo's Japanese defence counsel. "To my embarrassment," wrote

Tanaka, "another of his lawyers tried to prevent this from taking place."

There was only one course left open, and that was to get the Palace itself to put pressure on Tojo. "On the evening of January 3," Tanaka wrote, "with a Keenan aide, I went to see Yasumaya Matsudaira, the Imperial Household Minister." (Professor Hata supplies additional details here. Tanaka, he says, went round to Matsudaira's house late at night, hammered on the door in vain, and finally climbed over the wall to gain entry.)

Matsudaira agreed to co-operate: he told Tanaka he himself would visit the court. With his innate understanding of the way Tojo's mind worked, and fully aware of Kido's special role as the Emperor's representative inside Sugamo, Matsudaira knew that the person to put pressure on Tojo was Kido. The following day, January 4, he saw Kido, explaining everything. Kido agreed to help. "Kido talked to Tojo and told him of Keenan's intention [to protect Hirohito at all costs]," Tanaka wrote. "He was still reluctant but Kido tried very hard to persuade him and eventually Tojo understood and reluctantly agreed."

On January 6 a carefully rehearsed charade was played out in the IMTFE court. Keenan was asking Tojo questions about Pu Yi, the Manchukuo puppet emperor, and suddenly digressed, as Tojo had been warned he would.

KEENAN: While we are discussing the subject matter of emperors, it might be an appropriate moment to ask you a few questions on the relative positions of yourself and the Emperor of Japan on the matter of waging war in December of 1941. You have told us that the Emperor on repeated occasions made known to you that he was a man of peace and did not want war, is that correct?

TOJO: I was then speaking to you of my feeling toward the Emperor as subject, and that is a quite different matter from the problem of responsibility, that is, the responsibility of the Emperor.

KEENAN: Well, you did make war against the United States, Great Britain and the Netherlands, did you not?

TOJO: War was decided on in my cabinet.

KEENAN: Was that the will of Emperor Hirohito, that war should be instituted?

TOJO: It may not have been according to his will, but it is a fact that because of my advice and because of the advice given by the High Command, the Emperor consented – though reluctantly – to the war.

INTERPRETER: The first part should be corrected: it might have been against the Emperor's will.

TOJO: The Emperor's love and desire for peace remained the same right up to the very moment when hostilities commenced, and even during the war his feelings remained the same. The Emperor's feeling in this regard can be clearly ascertained from the Imperial Rescript on December 8, 1941, declaring war ... That is to say, the Imperial Rescript contains words to this effect: this war is indeed unavoidable and is against my own desires.

As Seiichi Yamazaki, Keenan's personal secretary, noted later, "what people saw there was just a fake play ... conducted by the mutual agreement of Keenan and Tojo." Arnold Brackman, author of *The Other Nuremberg*, was present in court as a young UP correspondent. He wrote later: "Thus, the most volatile crisis during the trial was contained as a result of a secret agreement between the Allied chief of counsel and the most-wanted war criminal in the dock." Though it has never been proved, many experts believe that a generous private settlement to Tojo's family was part of the deal.*

* After first publication of the book, a number of critics alleged that my account of the pressure put on Tojo was fallacious, and that my interpretation of his exchange in court was based on my faulty interpretation of Japanese, a language famous for its ambiguities. One of the witnesses I had sought out, while researching the book, was Aristides George Lazarus, one of the IMTFE defense counsel for Field Marshal Shunreku Hata, the highest-ranking military defendant. (Hata was acquitted.) Alas, I failed to locate him in time. Fortunately, this distinguished lawyer himself commented on the book, in a letter to the *Far Eastern Economic Review*. His testimony, of immense importance, throws additional light on what happened.

Two days later, on January 8, Keenan was the guest of honour at a banquet given for him at Atami, the hot spring resort, by four leading Japanese members of the "peace faction", including the former Prime Minister, Reijiro Wakatsuki, and General Ugaki. Tanaka was present. Here, Keenan announced: 'The Emperor's innocence has been determined.' There was much emotional rejoicing, and innumerable sake toasts were drunk. Afterwards, Keenan called for the services of a geisha. Ruefully, Tanaka noted that he ended up paying for the girl, because, Keenan said, "I'm your guest here".

Tanaka was also shown new consideration: on January 15 he was invited to meet young Crown Prince Akihito. The Imperial Household Minister, Yasumasa Matsudaira,† was present. He told Tanaka that the Emperor had read articles about Tanaka in the Japanese press, and "shown displeasure" in the past at Tanaka's role. But now, Matsudaira said, he had explained Tanaka's real role to the Emperor. "Everything is now all right."

On November 12, 1948, Webb finally handed down the court's verdict: none of the accused was acquitted; seven were sentenced to death by hanging. These included Tojo, for whom the sentence could hardly have come as a surprise, but also Matsui, the general who had been nominally in charge at the "rape of

---

"Halfway through the trial, President Truman sent a high-level official to ask me to undertake 'a mission of the utmost importance to the future security of America'. The mission: to save Hirohito because his trial and execution would cause Japan to descend into chaos. I accepted the mission, though I was warned the US would disown me if the details were publicly disclosed. With Hata, I arranged that the military defendants, and their witnesses, would go out of their way during their testimony to include the fact that Hirohito was only a benign presence when military actions or programmes were discussed at meetings that, by protocol, he had to attend. With a little subterfuge, I visited Gen. Tojo in Sugamo Prison and I flattered him by stating that I left it entirely up to him how best to lend support to Truman's decision to save the emperor. He obviously appreciated my approach and when I closed my meeting with him, I bluntly told him that his cooperation could not be counted on to save him from execution or even delay it. He nodded his head vigorously in agreement. He carried out the mission perfectly and submitted to the hangman's noose with his lips sealed – an officer, a gentleman and a patriot to the end. When the trial ended, the record was so favourable to Hirohito that not one of the Allied powers even suggested that the previously scheduled trial and execution of the emperor be carried out."
† No relative of Tsuneo Matsudaira, the former Imperial Household Minister.

Nanking" in 1937, and Kito Hirota, the former Prime Minister, who many SCAP officials felt should not have been indicted in the first place. A petition on his behalf quickly brought 300,000 signatures. Kido was sentenced to life imprisonment.

All those sentenced behaved with extraordinary dignity and stoicism. Tojo's lawyer reported: "His mind is eased very much by the verdict, knowing that he has given no additional trouble to the Emperor." The Japanese press was less respectful. "What are the feelings of the Emperor?" asked the *Kokusai Times*. "He cannot continue to conceal his responsibility for war crimes." A few provincial papers called for his abdication as an apology to the Japanese people. The most scathing editorials, expectedly, were in *Akahata* (Red Flag), the Communist daily. But some of the bitterest implicit criticism arising out of Hirohito's immunity came from one of IMTFE's defence counsels, Owen Cunningham – and from members of the Tribunal, including Webb himself. "If the prosecution wanted the truth as to individual responsibilities, why did they not call the Emperor of Japan to the witness stand?" Cunningham asked. "Did they not have the courage to do so? ... No one can accept the prosecution's theory that the Emperor was the puppet of Tojo." In a dissenting opinion, the French member of IMTFE, Henri Bernard, wrote: "It cannot be denied, the declaration [of war] had a principal author who escaped all prosecution and of whom, in any case, the present defenders could only be considered as accomplices."

It was Webb's own opinion, not read out in court, but distributed to the press, that caused the most stir: "The immunity of the Emperor, as contrasted with the part he played in launching the war in the Pacific, is I think a matter which the Tribunal should take into consideration in imposing sentences," he wrote. He compared the Emperor to "the leader in the crime" granted immunity from prosecution. "His immunity was, no doubt, decided upon in the best interests of all the Allied Powers." Refuting the argument (not advanced in court, but used by Hirohito himself in his initial meeting with MacArthur) Webb said: "No ruler can commit the crime of launching aggressive war and then validly claim to be excused for so doing because his life would otherwise have been in danger."

It was known that there had been acrimonious arguments among the judges on the number of death sentences to be handed down, and that Webb, who had been against any death penalties whatever (on the grounds that all the accused, whatever their own responsibilities, had been "accomplices"), had been overruled. MacArthur could have commuted the sentences, but chose not to interfere.

Hirohito was known to be stunned by the verdicts, especially the life sentence on Kido. But he was determined, by this time, to remain on the throne. In a deliberate move to show that he would not be swayed by adverse Japanese press comment, or calls to abdicate, he sent Hidenori Terasaki, one of his personal interpreters – the same Terasaki who, as a Washington-based diplomat and intelligence chief, had engineered the last-minute Roosevelt letter to him – to see William J. Sebald, MacArthur's political adviser. He conveyed a personal verbal message from the Emperor to MacArthur. Notwithstanding the sentences passed at IMTFE, he had "definitely" decided not to abdicate.

On the night of December 22 the hangings started. All but Hirota shouted "Banzai" – their final homage to the Emperor. It was all over by 0230 hours, December 23. That day, Hirohito closeted himself alone in the Palace library, seeing no one. It happened to be Crown Prince Akihoto's fifteenth birthday, and all celebrations were cancelled.

Before leaving Japan, shortly afterwards, Keenan was received in audience by Hirohito and the Empress, given a signed photograph and a handbag for his wife. A well-known Tokyo Art Gallery owner in Ginza gave him a topaz "for his effort in contributing to the Emperor's innocence".

CHAPTER TWENTY-FIVE

"The peaceful beginning of the occupation of Japan," wrote Kazuo Kawai, the American-educated political scientist,[1] "will always remain something of a mystery. The United States expected resistance and treachery. To their amazement, both sides discovered that the other was not what they had been led to believe."

The post-war behaviour of the Emperor of Japan, and his adaptability, came as the greatest surprise of all. Almost overnight, his uniforms and white chargers were seen no more, and his bewildered Japanese subjects discovered the existence of a resolutely civilian Emperor, full of middle-class virtues and gauche affability, whom they could stare at and even talk to with impunity.

Overnight, too, the still powerful Imperial Household Ministry (later to become an "Agency") started projecting the image of an Imperial Family of almost caricatural ordinariness: pictures were released showing Hirohito, with his wife and son, seated round a plain dining-room table, enjoying a simple meal, or reading *The Stars and Stripes*, the US military newspaper, or watering flowers in the garden. There were even pictures of his humble, somewhat frayed indoor slippers. The change was less publicized, but equally dramatic, among lesser members of the Imperial Family: shortly after the war nothing differentiated Prince Mikasa, for instance, from other students at Tokyo University. He wore shabby clothes, and rode around on a motorcycle. Prince Takamatsu tended his own vegetable garden.

Cynical Tokyo-based correspondents who witnessed all this knew that it was deliberately contrived. For behind the Emperor's new look was a July 1946 directive from the SNWCC (State/Navy/War/Coordinating Committee) in Washington to Mac-Arthur, defining the "preservation of the Imperial system" as official US policy. "A direct attack on the Imperial system," this report read, "would weaken the democratic elements and, on the contrary, strengthen the extremists, both communist and militarist. The Supreme Commander is therefore ordered to assist secretly in popularizing and humanizing the Emperor. This will not be known to the Japanese people."

Hirohito dutifully acceded to the change, at what must have been considerable personal cost. When, in the heady first few days of the Occupation, a US army sergeant found the Emperor's white charger in the Palace stable, and rode him cowboy-style through the Palace grounds, Hirohito resented this not just as an intrusion of privacy but as an intolerable example of lèse-majesté, a humiliating, personal affront which, he felt, should have been severely punished. But the need to co-operate – and collaborate – overcame all other considerations. The new Constitution, American-imposed and reading like a translation from a foreign language (Konoye's draft, experts said later, would have been an improvement), guaranteed human rights, political liberties, and put an end to Japan's "right of belligerency", disbanding all her armed forces, and turning Japan into a parliamentary democracy. The Emperor became a constitutional monarch with only ceremonial powers, on the British model, "a symbol of the state and of the unity of the people". On New Year's Day, 1946, in a broadcast speech, he formally renounced his "divinity". Shintoism ceased being a state religion. "Feudalism" in all its forms was eradicated. Many Japanese, including those acceptable to SCAP, felt that, in many ways, the liberal practices foisted on Japan went too far. As Shigeru Yoshida, shortly to be Japan's durable post-war Prime Minister, later wrote in his memoirs: SCAP "initially allowed the trade union movement workers a degree of freedom in political activity that was not warranted by any economic needs".

Hirohito did what he had to do, both to make the Occupation

as palatable as possible for his people and to ensure the survival of the "Emperor-system" under the Occupation framework. In return, SCAP not only began economic aid to Japan on a huge scale, sending massive quantities of food in the first years, but also did its utmost to restore the Emperor's image. Not only was he immune from prosecution for war crimes: SCAP collaborated in forging the historical image of Hirohito that has persisted to this day. *Stars and Stripes* was careful not to run stories on the Emperor's wartime role; the brutal, and at times racist, anti-Hirohito propaganda, that had been a feature of the Second World War, was replaced by propaganda of another sort, extolling the Emperor as a democratically-minded, peace-loving, decent man, caught up against his will in a regrettable militaristic adventure he had always deplored. Reporters like Russell Brines, AP's correspondent in Tokyo before and after the war, had sufficient pre-war experience to know this was a distortion of the facts, but the Hirohito issue, he wrote, was "too hot to handle: his trial would hardly have accomplished much, except to salve international wounded feelings or, perhaps, to keep the record straight".[2]

As they came to see the Emperor at close quarters in the immediate post-war months, the foreign press corps in Tokyo, many of them former war correspondents exposed to copious wartime propaganda, found it difficult to adjust to the new situation. Most reacted with scorn, disbelief and patronizing condescension. To Mark Gayn, of the *Chicago Sun*, Hirohito came across as "a pathetic little man, compelled to do a distasteful job, desperately trying to control his disobedient voice and face and body". He described him on one of his earliest appearances as "about five feet two, in a badly cut, grey striped suit, with trousers a couple of inches too short . . . He has a pronounced facial tic, and his right shoulder twitches constantly. When he walks, he throws his right leg a little sideways, as if he has no control over it. He was obviously excited and ill at ease, and uncertain what to do with his arms and hands."[3] To Russell Brines, the Emperor was "short, slight, round-shouldered", with such poor coordination "that he seemed constantly on the verge of toppling over".

The contrast between Hirohito's martial wartime image and his pathetically clumsy public appearances encouraged some of the less experienced members of the foreign press in the wholly mistaken belief that the Emperor *was* a figure of fun, that he might well have been a puppet and a creation of the military machine. At one of his first public appearances, Brines noticed, under pouring rain, "the Emperor of Japan and his soggy subjects stared at each other in mutual embarrassment. Then he reached suddenly for his battered fedora, thought better of it, dropped his hand and tried to smile. He then grinned, seized his hat and waved it lustily. The crowd cheered and everybody relaxed . . . The huge contrast between his current appearance and the military presence [the Japanese] had gotten used to puzzled the public. He was a little man who had to be told by his entourage what to do."

Because of the discretion of Japanese newsreel and, later, TV networks, the Emperor's off-the-cuff remarks on these public appearances were generally not recorded or, at least, broadcast. One newsreel, however, shows him desperately attempting to make small talk with a factory worker.

"I gather you were in the bombing," Hirohito says.

"No," the worker replies, without using any of the formal ultra-respectful form of speech usually de rigueur, "I wasn't."

"Ahso desuka," says Hirohito, visibly at a loss as to how to extricate himself. "Well . . ." (rapidly losing interest in the proceedings), "we must all pull together."

In retrospect, Hirohito managed the transition from "divine" ruler to constitutional monarch with only ceremonial powers, from uttering sybilline speeches to deferential courtiers in an archaic language to facing steelworkers in factories, with infinite patience and a good deal of hard work. No wonder he sought refuge in polite clichés and empty formulas: he had to learn to speak a new language. The first time he went up to a small boy and asked him where his father and mother were, Court officials were amazed – he had actually managed to speak to him in colloquial Japanese! Later, Hirohito was to tell officials that his problem was that he lacked the vocabulary for use in everyday life. He never did master the art of small talk, and, later, with the advent of television, TV crews filming him were ordered to turn off the sound to avoid his possible embarrassment and ridicule. For all his new visibility, he still managed to keep aloof: he was used to American Generals shaking him by the hand, or GIs asking him for autographs. He could not prevent this kind of familiarity, though he never became used to it, and hated it, but he was determined to keep his own people at the proper distance. A Court Chamberlain described how, on a factory inspection tour, Hirohito came face to face with a trades union delegation. Their leader thrust out a hand, and said: "I would like to shake your hand on behalf of all Japanese workers." Hirohito kept his arms at his sides. He retreated a step, and, bowing slightly, said: "Let's do it the Japanese way." The Japanese worker bowed back: the formalities had been preserved.

Hirohito's physical co-ordination may sometimes have been lacking, but he was not always the figure of fun Americans so scornfully described. An equally revealing moment, on film, came years later, in 1975, during the Hirohito visit to Disneyland. An adult Mickey Mouse moved close to him, and seemed about to lay a friendly, reassuring arm on the startled Emperor. With split-second timing, and unexpected agility, Hirohito stepped smartly aside. Mickey Mouse did not lay an arm on an Emperor, even in the interests of better US–Japanese relations.

His faculty for stating the obvious, on his early "walkabouts", became legendary. On his first official visit outside Tokyo, in Hiroshima, he looked around him through his thick glasses and said sententiously: "There seems to have been considerable damage here." As Russell Brines noted, "he always said things like that. His conversation consisted of inanities in a high voice. His face was covered in moles, he often needed a shave, his shoes were scuffed." Among the press, his walk-abouts became known as "ahso desuka" visits because that was his invariable response to any situation.*

Brines, with his experience of pre-war Japan, knew that Hirohito "was far from the impotent or ignorant puppet that he was portrayed". But most of the other correspondents failed to realize that the scuffed shoes, the ill-fitting suits, the almost clownish demeanour were all part of an elaborate defence mechanism: they were ways of indicating that the Emperor, in this unprecedented and painful situation, was facing up to the Occupation in characteristic Japanese fashion. "The Japanese had learnt to protect themselves while bowing to authority," wrote Kawai. "They rolled with the punch." Hirohito showed them how to do it.

In private he was far less humble, and more articulate. In a letter to his son, Akihito, dated September 9, 1945, he revealed both his inner strength and his true feelings about the lost war:

Thank you for your letter. I'm pleased to know your spirit is strong. Japan is facing a lot of trouble but I am all right, don't worry.

I should have mentioned earlier about the decision I made this time but I hesitated to do so because I couldn't contradict your teacher too much. Let me explain about the reason for Japan's defeat: the Japanese people rely on imperial Japan too much and looked down on the United States and Britain and our military put too much emphasis on the spirit and forgot about science.

At the time of the Meiji emperor, there were brilliant generals in the army and navy but this time Japan was just like Germany in World War One.

The military were arrogant and didn't look at the situation from a wider point of view. They only knew how to go forward, not how to retreat.

I thought that if we continue the war, we would be unable to

* "Indeed", "is that so", "how interesting".

protect the three divine items and have to kill people.

So, swallowing our tears, I chose the way to save the Japanese race from extinction. It's getting cold so please take care of yourself,

from father.

So soon after the surrender speech, here, in a letter to a twelve-year-old that would escape the scrutiny of SCAP, he was conveying that he had been betrayed by incompetent military commanders who had under-estimated the fighting capacity of the enemy. No mention of his personal responsibility in acquiescing to, and starting, the war; no apparent guilt; a disparaging reference to his generals. The image-building was not confined to SCAP . . .

In the immediate aftermath of surrender, Hirohito also returned to his pet subject: his high regard for the British Royal Family, and his wretchedness at having to declare war on Britain. He found it necessary to jog Kido's memory, on September 26, 1945: "Don't you recall, when I issued the declaration of war, I mentioned to Tojo that this was a very painful decision for me . . . I felt as though my intestines had been severed by a knife." Later, he returned to the subject. On a visit to Japan in January 1946, Sir George Sansom, a British diplomat with previous experience of Japan, was invited to meet Hirohito at a private audience, but thought it advisable to decline; before he left, however, the Imperial Household Minister sent him Hirohito's personal message to King George VI, hoping for early, normal relations between Japan and Britain to be restored, stressing that he had "done his utmost to avoid war", and apologizing for British suffering because of loss of lives and property. There was a very good reason for this highly unusual piece of diplomacy: Hirohito was aware that Lord Mountbatten, a frequent visitor to Buckingham Palace, held strong views about Japan in general and Hirohito in particular, despite the fact that he had been part of the Prince of Wales's retinue on the visit to Japan in 1922, and a recipient of the then Crown Prince's lavish hospitality. Mountbatten had been among those who had wanted Hirohito to sign the surrender document himself and, as US Army General Henry H. Arnold noted at the time, he thought the entire Imperial Family were "morons, inbred and degenerate", and believed "the royal family should all be liquidated".[4]

Hirohito's sudden exposure to crowds of all kinds, after years of seclusion, must have been an almost unbearably traumatic experience. Shizuto Haruna, the same sound engineer who had recorded Hirohito's surrender speech, recalls one of the Emperor's early post-war appearances in the Mitsukoshi department store. Because of the crowd of (mostly American) press, Hirohito was unable to reach the microphone stand, and Haruna found himself thrusting a microphone into the Emperor's face in one of the aisles, indeed getting so close to Hirohito that a Palace Chamberlain grabbed his jacket in order to pull him away. This, the diminutive Haruna suddenly recalled as he pushed and shoved, was the same "living God" whose voice had never been heard prior to August 15, 1945, on whom ordinary citizens had not even dared to gaze, the "divine monarch" he was not permitted to look at during the August 14 recording session.

There were many such instances of lèse-majesté becoming part of the accepted Royal routine. Communist demonstrators gathered at Hibiya Park to boo the Emperor. Yoshio Shiga, the Japanese Communist Party leader and editor of *Red Flag*, attacked Empress Nagako for "leading Japanese womanhood on the path of reaction and feudalism". There were even "rice riots" around the Imperial palace, organized by the JCP, recently legalized, to compel the Imperial Household to release its stocks to the people. As one American reporter recalled, they fell silent when a car, with Empress Nagako inside, made its way through the crowd to enter the Palace gates – and some of the demonstrators even bowed.

At the end of 1946, Hirohito wrote a poem, urging his people not to forget their past:

The pine is brave
that changes not its colour,
bearing the snow.
People too
like it should be.

He was, as Brines pointed out, "telling them to bear the 'snow' of Occupation without being transformed by it".

Gayn, who enjoyed extremely good relations with Japanese Communist leaders in this immediate post-war period, paints a depressing picture of a "highly reactionary" group around MacArthur determined to protect the pre-war status quo while paying lip service to change, quoting MacArthur's influential aide, General Bonner Fellers, as saying: "Hirohito is no more of a war criminal than Roosevelt. As a matter of fact, if you examine the record closely . . ." Gayn felt that the walk-abouts, the deliberate projection, under American sponsorship, of Hirohito as a democratic constitutional monarch, keenly interested in his subjects' welfare, was "a shameful conspiracy against the Japanese people".

There was one American with privileged access to the Imperial family from 1947 onwards, the only foreigner within the Palace walls to witness the Emperor's transformation at first hand: Elizabeth Grey Vining, a Quaker and author of children's books, was selected by the Imperial Household to become Crown Prince Akihito's English teacher. It was Hirohito's idea, she wrote later. "An American tutor was not imposed by the Occupation, and [the Emperor] didn't even consult the Prince's official educational specialists." Hirohito had specified he wanted "a woman, a Christian, but not a fanatic" – the most important requisite of all being that whoever was selected must have had no experience of pre-war Japan.[5]

Originally engaged on a two-year contract, Elizabeth Vining proved so satisfactory to the Imperial Family that it was renewed twice, and would have been a third time, but she declined the offer. In addition to her hours with Akihito, she also gave

English lessons to the Empress and to other members of the Imperial Family. Arriving in Tokyo in October 1946, she found conditions inside the Palace reflected the poverty and destruction outside: there were quonset huts inside the Palace grounds, the Peers' School (Gaikushin) was cold, damp and dirty, the Emperor and Empress still lived in the Library above their air raid shelter, and, that winter, young Prince Akihito suffered from chilblains.

The Empress may, however, have been less impressed with Elizabeth Vining than was Hirohito. She approached SCAP and suggested that, instead of continuing to receive instruction from Miss Vining, Crown Prince Akihito be educated in the United States "in an American school" and then go to Britain as a student. Senior SCAP officials debated this possibility at length. Finally William H. Sebald, MacArthur's political adviser, told the State Department in Washington:

I am against Prince Akihito's schooling in the US. I am inclined to believe it would be an almost impossible adjustment for one who has been brought up in the atmosphere of Japanese Court life. To be suddenly placed, at an early age, and with only rudimentary English, in an alien country and among boarding school boys would be a traumatic experience.

Sebald cited possible "reactions [among the boys] owing to the war . . . Because of the possibility of embarrassing incidents in the US arising out of racial discrimination, quite aside from the hangover from wartime animosities, the Prince's sojourn here could be a source of constant concern". He also worried that Akihito could develop an anti-American bias as the result of unpleasant experiences in the US, just like the former Japanese Foreign Minister, Yosuke Matsuoka, "who became violently anti-American as a result of indignities in his youth as a student of a coastal North-Western University". For these reasons, he also advised that Akihito go to Britain as a university student rather than to the US, because it would lessen charges of "US colonialism".

In the event, Vining stayed with her "Jimmy", as she called him in the class-room. At first, she found Akihito shy, introspective and somewhat narrow-minded and humourless. Communication was difficult: "his interests in those [early] days were almost entirely confined to fish and I felt they needed broadening," she wrote. But under her expert tuition he was transformed into an outgoing, fun-loving extrovert, mingling with commoners of his own age on easy terms. Apart from his passion for fish, tennis and riding, he was "fond of travel, history, adventure, cowboys. He dislikes school stories, stars, plants, aeroplanes, machines of any kind."

Vining turned out to be the ideal courtier – deferential, always on call when needed. This is probably why her book is so singularly uninformative. Though tantalizingly full of references to intimate dinners with Hirohito and the rest of the Imperial family, games of snap with the Emperor and so on, these events are invariably described with the discretion of an Imperial Household employee: they were "happy informal evenings with the Empress so gracious and charming, the Emperor smiling benevolently on his children and making occasional comments". We are never told what these comments were.

Vining drew all her knowledge of pre-Occupation Japan from Japanese sources within the Palace, never questioning what she was told. For this reason she is sometimes revealing despite herself. In her book, for instance, she refers to Marquis Kido, then languishing in Sugamo prison as ". . . the Lord Privy Seal who had been closest of all to the Emperor and who was *generally said to have deceived the Emperor by withholding important information from him*".*

Since Vining had only occasional contacts with SCAP, and was careful not to act as its "eyes and ears" within the Palace, or take any guidance from SCAP officials, this monstrous slur on the man to whom Hirohito owed so much could only have been the result of what was passed on to her by top Palace sources, possibly by members of the Imperial Family themselves.

* Author's italics.

It was all part of the image-building process and the rewriting of history: since Hirohito had to be perceived as completely blameless, all crimes committed in earlier times had nothing to do with him, his subordinates alone were to blame. Whether Kido himself ever discovered how his lifelong, devoted service to the Emperor was denigrated in this way in the interests of Hirohito's new image is unlikely, but even Kido, as time went on, must have been surprised by what he read in the newspapers. He still kept a diary. From it we learn that, in October 1951, he conveyed a note to the Imperial Household Minister, Matsudaira, for Hirohito's special attention. Kido had come to believe that the Emperor was responsible for the war, and should therefore abdicate. Kido added that, if this occurred, "the families of the dead and the war criminals would feel rewarded". Otherwise, the Imperial Family "would turn out to be the only ones to have evaded all responsibility for the war". Shortly afterwards, with Japan a sovereign country after her 1951 Peace Treaty with the United States, Kido, along with all the other remaining IMTFE prisoners, was freed. For the rest of his life, he kept a dignified silence about the past, his contacts with the Imperial family now few and far between.

In later years, the horror of war and his friendship for Britain became Hirohito's familiar leitmotivs in his annual sessions with the small group of "court correspondents" licensed by the Imperial Household Agency to cover the Emperor's activities. On August 29, 1963, he told them: "I have no comment to make: I rather regret my past sixty years. I couldn't do anything great. From now on, I want to make a great effort to help the people, contribute to international understanding and world peace." Nine years later, in 1971, he told them: "I had a similar feeling on my Golden Anniversary. When I think back, I feel really ashamed." Again and again, he referred to his friendly Buckingham Palace connection. "My most memorable time was during my visit to the British Royal Family," he said in 1969. "The Prince of Wales was roughly my age. It was like a second home. King George V kindly explained British constitutional politics to me. Since then I have always thought how I should behave as a leader of a constitutional monarchy ... When I went to Europe, I thought we should not go to war. When the war started, I was always thinking how I could end it." Inexorably returning, in these brief, formal meetings, to his European trip, he said that the Verdun battlefield "was even grimmer than I expected. I thought: this must never happen again". Asked in 1975 about his best – and his worst – experience, he replied: "I was on the throne a long time, and had many experiences of all kinds. My most meaningful experience was my European trip with the Empress, and then the United States trip I'm about to go on." He mentioned the 1960 Tokyo Olympics and Osaka Fair as some of the highlights of his life. "The worst of course, without doubt, was everything connected with the Second World War." In September that same year, he told his "court correspondents" that "I always wish I could live like the general public, though it's rather difficult under the present situation. I think I am not so different from ordinary people". On January 22, 1984, the occasion of his diamond wedding, he praised the "invisible assistance of the Empress". "When I think back, a lot happened in the past sixty years, but the Empress was always cheerful, made my family happy and supported my mind. I'm really thankful." Two months later, he said that he enjoyed most "meeting my grandchildren, walking, observing animals and plants. What I really hated during sixty years are matters relating to the Second World War. What I feel most pleased about is to see that Japan has recovered from the defeat and established a prosperous society by its own efforts."

For the first time ever during the Occupation years, the Emperor's personal fortune came under public scrutiny. MacArthur duly broke up the pre-war "Zaibatsu", and the Imperial fortune was regarded as the "Imperial Household-Zaibatsu". SCAP released its findings to the press. Hirohito's assets consisted of 1,500 million yen, made up of holdings in land, timber and property, as well as 330 million yen in cash. Jewellery was not included, and SCAP added that "Imperial property was markedly undervalued".

Yomiuri Hochi published its own evaluation of the Emperor's fortune, listing 2 million yen worth of jewellery, 3 million of silver and 309 million yen in gold bullion. "The Imperial Household," it wrote, "is a financial clique whose interests are connected with those of imperialism by the holding of national bonds and shares of various chartered banks, monopolistic companies and aggressive commercial concerns. The Imperial Family is also the biggest landowner." It suggested that the extensive Palace grounds be opened to the public "to help with the housing shortage".

Yomiuri Hochi also listed overseas stocks held by the Imperial Household in Korean and Taiwanese banks, the assets of the South Manchurian Railway (owned largely by the Emperor), and the Oriental Colonial Company. Among the assets owned by the Imperial Household, it listed the Imperial Hotel opposite the Palace, the Hokkaido Coalmining and Steamship Company, the NYK and OSK companies, Konto Electric Supply, a large number of Mitsubishi shares, six railway companies, the Japan Lumber Company and the Hakone hot springs, as well as overseas debentures totalling 25 million yen. There were also reports that the Imperial Household held up to 60 per cent of the stock of the Bank of Japan and 22 per cent of the Yokohama Specie Bank, which had specialized in overseas investments in Japanese-occupied areas during the war.

The Imperial Household was stripped of most of these assets, but there were some that may have escaped SCAP's scrutiny: as the war turned against Japan, in 1943 and 1944, it was widely rumoured that the Emperor, responding to expert advice and acting through overseas intermediaries, had transferred some of his fortune abroad, into Switzerland and Latin American banks in countries like Argentina which were sympathetic to the Axis. A SCAP report, dated July 19, 1948, said that "Japanese public and private assets located in neutral and Latin American countries have not been adequately controlled and are a proper interest of SCAP". Some SCAP specialists believed that Imperial Household assets spirited out of Japan in the war years totalled £41 million (1945 value) – £8·5 million in Switzerland and £14 million in Latin America, mostly from Yokohama Specie bank holdings abroad. Nothing was ever done to recover these missing millions and by 1951 the Occupation had come to an end. Throughout, MacArthur showed a marked disinclination to investigate the Emperor's overseas assets.

Becoming a constitutional monarch meant, in effect, becoming a salaried official. The sum granted Hirohito as a salary and to cover all expenses in 1945 came to 32 million yen. Of this 8 million yen was the Emperor's salary, the rest went towards the upkeep of the palaces and the officials' salaries. The Emperor's land, farms, forestry and other tangible assets were handed over to the state. The Imperial Palace, and the priceless Akasaka Palace site, where close members of the Imperial Family continue to live to this day, were not included in the list. More affected than the Emperor himself were his relatives. While members of his immediate family continued to draw stipends, the Imperial Family's payroll was restricted to a handful of people: Princely cousins, almost overnight, found themselves, owing to SCAP's land reform, and crippling capital levies on their other assets, deprived of their farms, other property, and inevitably of the police and army protection that had been routinely provided. They were given a final lump sum payment, out of the Emperor's own fortune, but all those young enough to do so had now to work for a living. Some Princely living standards dropped dramatically.

Ordinary Japanese reacted to all this with considerable interest. In the US Military Archives at Suitland, Virginia, where the SCAP records are kept, there are three large cardboard boxes somewhat mistakenly labelled "military intelligence". They contain thousands of letters written to MacArthur during the Occupation years; all have been translated. They must have provided intelligence of a crude kind, for some of them consist of anonymous denunciations of former "militarists" or "thought police" holding posts in the new Administration, or embarking on new and lucrative careers as black marketeers and racketeers. Many refer to Hirohito and the "Emperor-system", and most ask MacArthur not to treat him as a war criminal. Though a small minority branded Hirohito as "the worst war criminal of all", the majority of letter-writers asked MacArthur to "forgive" him. Typical was a letter from a former kamikaze pilot volunteer, "friendly to the United States". "The Imperial family is beyond criticism," it read. "This is the national Japanese feeling, for the last 3,000 years. So if you tamper with the Imperial system or the Emperor himself . . . this will be the world's biggest tragedy." Other writers complained that, despite the changes, some schools were still indulging in "extreme Shintoist military education". The process of turning Japan into a democracy, one Tokyo citizen wrote, was like "trying to grow cherry blossom on a plum tree".

Gradually, as the Japanese came to terms with their new political environment, the Emperor's public schedule eased somewhat. By 1948 he was no longer front-page news, except when something important occurred, like the opening of the Diet. Taboos were broken, for commoners were allowed to look down on Hirohito from the visitors' gallery, and Komakichi Matsuoka, a leading member of the House of Representatives, refused to meet him. Some Diet members did not bow to the Emperor, and the President of the Senate failed to attend an audience with him before the inauguration ceremonies. By and large, however, Japanese newspaper editors were careful to eliminate even factual stories that reflected adversely on the Emperor and the Imperial Court.

Imperceptibly, as Japan recovered from destruction and defeat, the lot of the Japanese people improved – and the Imperial Household itself became less austere. As early as 1947 Elizabeth Vining describes her farewell lunch at the Palace before returning to the US on leave. There was "French gourmet food", and with dessert "an eagle carved out of ice to feed an eaglet", symbolizing "the American tutor bringing refreshment to the Crown Prince". Later, in 1949, she attended another Imperial Family party, and this time a string band played at lunch. As Mrs. Matsudaira, widow of the former Japanese Ambassador in London and Washington, and Prince Chichibu's mother-in-law, whispered during dinner, "It's all come back."

[1] Kazuo Kawai, *Japan's American Interlude*, University of Chicago Pres, 1960.
[2] Russell Brines, *MacArthur's Japan*, Lippincott, NY, 1948.
[3] Mark Gayn, *Japan Diary*, William Sloane Association, NY, 1948.
[4] Philip Ziegler, *Mountbatten*, Collins, London, 1985.
[5] Elizabeth Vining, *Windows for the Crown Prince*, Michael Joseph, 1962.

CHAPTER TWENTY-SIX

By 1950, the predictions of the Navy and "Spy School" plotters, who had briefly decided to hide and raise a "boy Emperor" at the end of the war, had come true in one respect: the "cold war" between the Soviet Union and the United States had begun in earnest, and, since June 25, a "hot war" was raging in Korea. John Foster Dulles, America's hyper-active assistant to the Secretary of State, Dean Acheson, and Truman's peripatetic envoy, felt that Japan was too valuable an ally in the cold war to be indefinitely treated as a second-class, occupied nation, and that the time had come for her to assume major international responsibilities. Though he was careful never to overstep his constitutionally defined role, Hirohito played an important, if little-known, part in bringing about this state of affairs.

As Professor Hata points out, a certain amount of friction had over the years developed between the Emperor and MacArthur. The Supremo's favourite Japanese was no longer the Emperor, but Shigeru Yoshida, the Prime Minister whom MacArthur met no less than seventy-six times during his six years in Tokyo. MacArthur never travelled outside the capital, except for one weekend in Yoshida's country home, and lived and worked in an overwhelmingly American environment; he only met sixteen Japanese during his entire tenure of office as Supreme Commander.

Yoshida and MacArthur agreed on almost everything – including the need to adhere strictly to Japan's post-war constitution banning the re-estabishment of her armed forces, and to respect her economic priorities. But Hirohito shared Dulles's view that Japan should be allowed to rearm, and even be host nation, not only to the United States, but to other Western forces; both men wanted Japan to become a fully-fledged member of the Western Alliance, long before such a notion became acceptable to the rest of the world.

By this time, of course, Hirohito's ceremonial status and diminished role meant that he had no means of bringing pressure to bear, even indirectly, on the Japanese government, but his personal views did carry considerable weight, especially with prominent Americans. Hirohito and Dulles met several times, and it was as a result of these meetings, Professor Hata believes, that Dulles was reinforced in his conviction that Japanese rearmament and membership of the Western Alliance, necessary to Western security as a whole, would also be acceptable to the Japanese people. In 1950–51, the CIA was predicting the Soviet Union's imminent entry into the Korean War: if this happened, Japan needed to rearm fast.

Dulles, of course, got his way. As Yoshida later wrote: "Rearmament was for Japan out of the question at that time." But the United States insisted, and written into the US–Japan Security Treaty, signed immediately after the conclusion of the San Francisco Peace Treaty (which brought Japan's Occupation status to an end), was the preamble that the US, "in the interests of peace and security, is precisely willing to maintain certain of its armed forces in and around Japan, in the expectation, however, that Japan will itself increasingly assume responsibility for its own defence against direct and indirect aggression". There is no doubt that this form of words was only reluctantly accepted by Yoshida, conscious of the additional economic burden the "Self-Defence Forces" would entail, while Hirohito himself was far more enthusiastic about the principle of Japanese rearmament. Hata is also convinced that Hirohito was much less concerned than Yoshida about the future of Okinawa, the offshore island administered after the war by the US, and used as an important American military base. Hirohito, he says, was prepared to concede such rights indefinitely.

The circumstances of MacArthur's departure from Tokyo, on

April 16, 1951, also show how far Hirohito had moved since that historic, humiliating September 27, 1945 meeting. SCAP wanted Hirohito to see MacArthur off at the airport. This, Palace officials felt, was out of the question. On the contrary, they wanted MacArthur to call on Hirohito at the Palace to take his leave. MacArthur refused point-blank. Eventually, a compromise solution was accepted: Hirohito agreed to call on MacArthur at the US Embassy residence where they had met for the first time. The niceties were preserved: Hirohito presented MacArthur, on departure, with two valuable silver vases.

Later (on April 22, 1952) Hirohito was to tell Dulles that MacArthur's resignation came as a "big shock" but that he had been reassured by Dulles's proven determination to protect Japan from Communist encroachment. "Is there a danger," Hirohito asked, "that the United States will change its policy towards Communism in Asia which is bolstered by the Soviet Union?" Dulles reassured him that there would be no change. The San Francisco Treaty heralded Japan's return to the international community of nations: in 1956 she became the 80th member of the United Nations; in 1958 the last US ground troops left Japan; in 1969 Okinawa became once more part of Japan.

Though the discreet Dulles–Hirohito meetings marked the Emperor's return to international respectability, it was a long time before he re-entered the world scene publicly. In the intervening years, he grew old gracefully, performing the duties of a ceremonial head of state, attending poetry reading competitions, athletics meetings, sumo wrestling championships, and visiting every Japanese province except for Okinawa. It was 1971 before he travelled to Bonn, Brussels, Paris and London. The only major anti-Hirohito demonstration staged by Asian students was in Bonn. In 1975, he made a much-publicized, and highly successful, state visit to the USA.

By the 1970s, the Japanese "economic miracle" had transformed the nation: by the early part of the decade, Tokyo was one of the most modern – and largest – capitals in the world.

Though the skeletons of victims of the 1945 air raids continued to surface in excavations during the Tokyo building boom, the war years seemed very remote indeed, even to those who had lived through them. It was impossible, now, not to look down on the Emperor: along the vestigial palace moat, separated by only a few hundred yards of carefully tended lawns, huge modern skyscrapers towered over the Imperial Palace grounds. Out of respect for the Imperial Family, however, there were no neon lights or hoardings, those hallmarks of modern Japan.

In advance of the Emperor's 1975 visit to the USA, and especially for American consumption, a "pictorial history" was put out by Kodansha, the large Japanese publishing house. Photographs showed Hirohito in still slightly baggy dark suits and rather gaudy silk ties, but also in white shorts and straw hat, very much the middle-class Japanese seaside holiday-maker. The Empress, "an accomplished artist", also featured in the book, her paintings and kimono designs fulsomely praised.

The "pictorial history" included a rare informal glimpse of Hirohito, interesting not only for the details it revealed about his daily life, but for the image it intentionally projected of him as an almost over-emphasized ordinary person. "He is an avid TV fan," the text read, "one of the many indications that far from being shackled by tradition and cut off from ordinary life, he is in good touch. His day begins at 7 a.m. Apparently he rises earlier but refrains from leaving his room to avoid disturbing those who wait on him. At 7 a.m. on the dot he presses the buzzer by his bed to let the attendants know he is up.

"His bedroom, which no attendant is allowed to enter in his presence, is in the Western style, with an ordinary bed and red carpeting. Fukiaga Palace, his private residence, has only one room done in the Japanese style – the Empress's sitting-room.

"He wears old, comfortable suits. He is careless of dress, tends to leave things where he took them off, likes grey, dislikes brown, wears suspenders, is not dismayed that some suits are shiny with wear. The Empress selects his ties.

"She joins her husband in the living-room for Western-style

breakfast – bread, oatmeal, eggs, vegetable salad and milk from the Imperial dairy farm. He watches the NHK TV drama serial at 8.15 a.m., and is also a keen viewer of sumo wrestling, tennis, baseball, glued to the set but only for the last hour of the day's sport. He videotapes important events, and watches TV news. At 10 a.m. he leaves for the Outer Palace, weather permitting he walks to work. The Empress invariably sees him off, at the bottom of the steps, bows politely as he lifts his hat in response, then she watches until he starts to disappear round the corner 50 yards away, when she bows again. At this point, the Emperor always turns and waves his hat at her."

Lunch, said the "pictorial history", consists of "sushi, sandwiches or noodles, often in his office, and dinner is early – at 6 p.m. His doctors insist on a low-fat diet, with plenty of green vegetables. All vegetables and fruit come from the Imperial farm, and are organically grown without any chemical additives. His French-trained chef prepares a mixture of Western and Japanese dishes, and menus are established two weeks in advance." The "pictorial history" omits the fact – confirmed by Court reporters with access to Palace officials – that the practice of food-tasting, an age-old Imperial custom originally introduced to prevent would-be murderers from poisoning the Emperor, was still adhered to: a Court physician sampled a tiny portion of whatever was served. The imperial stools were analysed daily.

After dinner, the Emperor and Empress "watch TV, read till 9.30 p.m. and so to bed. For the curious", the anonymous author added archly, "it might be of interest that the Emperor has absolute sovereignty over the channel section but knows which programs the Empress enjoys". Occasionally, "Hirohito listens as his wife sings Schubert 'lieder', accompanying herself on the piano."

On Sundays, "they go for a two hour stroll, the grandchildren visit at least once a week. His biology research is on Thursdays and Saturdays." Whenever he goes to the country, "he carries a magnifying glass around his neck".

By the standards of the British Royal Family, even before age and illness restricted his activities, Hirohito led a singularly leisurely life. Until poor health prevented it, he continued reading State documents – some of which required his ceremonial seal, three and a half inches high and made of solid gold. Though three different stamps were affixed to all the papers that came under his scrutiny ("read", "endorsed", "approved") endorsement and approval were, of course, mere formalities.

Perhaps inevitably, after the relative informality of the Occupation years, with brash American servicemen photographing Hirohito and even demanding autographs from him, the age-old Palace formalities were gradually reintroduced. The Imperial Household Agency officials, always sticklers for protocol, their real power curtailed and now restricted exclusively to Palace functions, saw to that. Their intense conservatism and insistence on archaic protocol were a constant source of irritation to the younger members of the Imperial Family, including Akihito himself. "They still behaved," says one member of the Imperial Family, "as though they were living in the thirties."

Some rituals were immutable: the French Ambassador, Bernard Dorin, has described how, in 1987, he was carefully rehearsed in the art of the slight, medium and deep bows before being admitted into the Imperial presence to present his credentials. The Imperial Household Agency Chamberlain taking him through his paces told him to keep his eyes downcast in Hirohito's presence, for "one does not look at the Sun". The Emperor's welcoming speech was in archaic Japanese and he enquired after the health of "my esteemed brother, President Mitterrand".

Until he became seriously ill, Hirohito received briefings on foreign affairs twice a week; in the last years of his life, he spent summers in his new country house in Hasu, winters in Shunoda, also in a brand-new mansion. He continued to attend athletics meetings and poetry competitions, planted trees and occasionally received foreign guests, but by and large his official workload was slight.

There was none of the subliminal promotion of industry that forms such an important part of the activities of British Royalty, especially on visits abroad. Japanese Imperial Family members are far too polite to say so openly, but it is clear that they regard the unabashed promotion of British goods as hopelessly vulgar. They are also baffled by the British Royal Family's press coverage.

While there is a great deal of interest in who Hirohito's grandson will marry, for instance, the Japanese press handles things differently: a small group of correspondents, specially vetted by the Imperial Household Agency, are kept on a very tight rein. They have a small club-house within the Palace grounds, and their job is largely confined to reproducing official press communiqués (prepared in a large "newsroom" in the Imperial Household Agency building) in their respective papers: the phenomenon of "paparazzi" around the Imperial Family simply does not exist, the discreet but vigilant Japanese police screen sees to that; besides, members of the Imperial Family scarcely ever indulge in the kind of behaviour that delights the tabloids; they lead extremely secluded lives, and access to the Akasaka Palace grounds, that huge, walled-in compound where the Emperor's closest relatives live, is severely restricted. Ultra-sophisticated electronic surveillance protects all Imperial residences, and special clearance has to be obtained from the Imperial Household Agency to film even *outside* the Palaces: any breach of the regulations leads to the speedy appearance of police cars.

If anything, says the Court reporter, Toshiya Matsuzaki, the atmosphere inside the Palace became increasingly formal as the Emperor became older. Every year, right up to 1989, the year he died, Hirohito invited the surviving members of his Peers' School class to tea, but the occasion had none of the bantering informality a similar event would have elsewhere and was in fact, one contemporary of the Emperor's admitted, rather an ordeal, for Hirohito's conversation was as limited as ever and inevitably focused on classmates who had died in the intervening twelve months.

Hirohito treated his staff, including his personal interpreters, courteously, but impersonally. Court correspondents, even those who covered the Palace over decades, were never "recognized" by name, though some of them, when they came to retire, found themselves recipients of the Order of the Rising Sun, second class.

In public, Hirohito seemed good-natured, but in the privacy of the Palace, one Court reporter says, tantrums were frequent, and his bad temper was feared. A stickler for strictly-observed routine, he was angry when it was disturbed: on his rare official engagements, he required a detailed schedule long in advance and was irritated when changes were made. He was, like almost all "royals", fanatical about punctuality: once, when a valet brought him his frock coat (required for the formal opening of Parliament) at the very last minute, he became very angry indeed.

In many respects, says another Court reporter who observed him since just after the war, Hirohito really was the absent-minded scientist, indifferent to the way he looked, only relaxing in the company of other scientists, comfortable only in old clothes, or in his laboratory coat, and never happier than when talking to fellow-experts about prehistoric cuttlefish or the habits of sea spiders. "He really was meant to be a university professor," says a former ambassador who observed him at close quarters. Most of Hirohito's light-hearted comments were concerned, in some way or other, with biology and science. A delegation from the Royal Society called on him just before his trip to Britain in 1971, after he had been formally re-instated as a member (his name had been struck off after Pearl Harbor), and he conducted his fellow-scientists on an extensive tour of his Palace laboratory. "He took a malicious delight in placing a live chameleon on my neck to show how it would change colour," remembers one member of that delegation. He was also capable of quite earthy enjoyment of biological details. During his subsequent visit to the London Zoo, in 1971, he showed great interest in the pandas there, and was particularly curious about their unsuccessful mating habits. The head keeper's theory – "they mistook the orifice" – delighted him. Though he did not actually burst into raucous laughter, he clearly indicated, by his facial expression, that he found this a comically apt description. In general, those who met him say, he was perfectly at ease only with marine biologists of his own stature with whom he was able to share a common interest. In a scientific conversation with a visiting Soviet marine biologist, a Court interpreter recalls, there was nearly a breakdown in communications because – in the absence of a Russian translator – no exchange seemed possible. Hirohito surprised his entourage – and the visitor – by breaking into halting Latin. Soon he and the Russian were exchanging names of prehistoric underwater animals in the kind of Latin used exclusively by scientists, and they got on famously. But small talk was always an effort. At one reception, an Imperial Household Agency official went up to a Japanese-speaking ambassador, and said: "Please go and talk to him, he's such a nice old gentleman."

During his trip to Europe as Crown Prince, in 1921, Hirohito ordered a pair of shoes from Lobb's, and then, with typical thrift, had them copied by the famous Otsuka shoe shop in Tokyo. It was the same with his suits: before the war patterns were sent to a Savile Row tailor but, since the Emperor could not be touched, the results were sometimes grotesque. A Tokyo tailor made the Emperor's suits from 1941 onwards. Before the end of the war, "by Appointment" signs were as coveted by leading Japanese shopkeepers as they are in Britain, but this practice was discontinued in 1950: the Imperial Household Agency decided that, "in the interests of democracy", and to avoid the risk of excessive commercialization, the Emperor should not make his preferences known. But special brands of "Imperial saké" and "Imperial cigarettes" continued to be manufactured, to be distributed as gifts.

Television played an enormous part in his post-war existence. There were aspects of Japanese everyday life he could only have learnt about from watching TV. In his occasional chats with

Court correspondents Hirohito admitted as much, even discussing soap operas with them. His favourite was *Oshin*, a well-made series about the life of an ordinary Japanese family at the turn of the twentieth century. "I didn't realize how hard those times were," Hirohito told Court reporters, "especially for women." One man asked him if he did not find what he saw on television strange. "Not at all," Hirohito answered. "I've found it very useful." Had he not been an assiduous TV-watcher, he would probably have answered differently when, on his seventy-eighth birthday, a Court reporter asked him if he found life was tiring. "It's more exhausting to be a 'salaryman' in the Marinuchi district riding a packed train for hours every day," Hirohito replied.

On his trips abroad, especially to the US, Hirohito's simple sense of fun delighted his guests. Visiting the Rockefeller estate in Williamsburg, he was told that legend had it that anyone sitting under a certain tree was sure of becoming rich. Grinning, he immediately made a beeline for it. He showed genuine interest in anything to do with agriculture, driving a combine harvester, or picking up and closely examining a piglet on a farm, with every sign of enjoyment. He overcame his dislike of small talk in his meeting with Gerald Ford (they discussed American football and the Japanese passion for baseball, and Hirohito explained the finer points of sumo wrestling). "I watch the championships every year," he said, "but I never back one team against another, not in public at least."

Quintessentially Japanese in his love of exotic fish dishes, Hirohito was particularly fond of eels, and sea-slugs. His one regret was that Imperial Household regulations forbade him to sample the famous "fugu", the Japanese delicacy that has to be handled by expert cooks because it contains lethal poison. One of the rare glimpses of truly informal, unposed family life was provided by a member of the Imperial Household, who overheard the Emperor, the Empress and the Imperial physician, Dr. Sugimura, discuss the pros and cons of eating "fugu".

"May I eat 'fugu'?" Hirohito asked his doctor.

"Certainly not," Sugimura replied.

"Why not?" Hirohito asked. "This particular 'fugu' was given to me by my son. Surely there's no danger involved when they're handled by expert 'fugu' chefs."

A long discussion followed. Dr. Sugimara was adamant, the Emperor insistent. Finally Empress Nagako put a stop to it. "That's enough about 'fugu'," she told both men. "Please stop arguing about it."

Apart from Elizabeth Vining's portrait of him as a charming but obedient schoolboy brought up in almost the same isolation as his father had been (she tried in vain to persuade Court officials that he would be better off living with his parents, or at least sharing a house with his younger brother) few people beyond his immediate family circle feel they really know Akihito, beyond the fact that he is an expert on fish, an excellent tennis-player and skier, and the first Crown Prince ever to marry a commoner. Though Michiko Shoda, the daughter of a rich flour-mill owner, was known to be one of the leading contenders for Akihito's hand, the fact that she was a commoner was at first regarded as an insuperable bar – and it is well-known that the hidebound Imperial Household Agency chiefs (and Empress Nagako) were not pleased.

Mainichi Shimbun's book commemorating the fiftieth year of Hirohito's rule[1] showed how respectful the Japanese media remain, as far as their Imperial Family is concerned: *Mainichi* – in common with other leading newspapers – agreed on an embargo on the whole subject of Akihito's chosen fiancée until the official announcement was made. A reporter then rushed to the newsroom, shouting: "'It was Michiko-san after all.' He was sobbing. The editor, too, was in tears."

The former *New York Times* Tokyo correspondent, Clyde Haberman, attended a press conference given by Prince Akihito and Princess Michiko in 1986, shortly before their departure for a brief US visit. "As they chatted," he wrote, "they were surrounded by government bureaucrats of various pinstripes.

Shepherded to and fro by chamberlains, they looked like glass-encased butterflies." But both are reported to have minds of their own: Michiko has had several disagreements with Imperial Household officials, and insisted on bringing up her son Hiro, now twenty-nine, at home; Akihito is also said to be determined, as Emperor, to force into retirement large numbers of crusty Imperial Household officials and make the Imperial Palace a less formal place, more in touch with everyday life at the close of the twentieth century. But traditions die exceedingly hard: Prince Hiro, third in line to the succession, has been of marriage-able age for years, but is certainly not entirely free to select the bride of his choice: a committee composed of leading Imperial Household officials, the Prime Minister, Emperor Akihito and other family representatives, is expected to approve a list of suitable candidates, and the requirements are draconian: Hiro's bride has to have perfect sight, an impeccable background and past with no hint of scandal (or previous boyfriends), and she must be no taller than her husband-to-be.

The discretion shown towards Akihito by the Japanese press also extends to Hirohito's second son, Prince Hitachi (a courtesy title, this — his name at birth was Masahito), and to Hirohito's three surviving daughters — Kazuko, Atsuko and Takako. Kazuko, fifty-nine in 1988, has been, since her widowhood, the high priestess of the Sacred Isé shrine; Atsuko is the wife of a prominent businessman of aristocratic lineage; Takako married a banker, and lived with her husband in Washington DC for several years. The Emperor's daughters were all compelled by tradition to relinquish their Imperial titles on marriage, and they seldom attract the attention of Japan's gossip columnists. Though Hirohito gave his formal approval to their marriages, protocol forbade him to attend their actual marriage ceremonies, which took place outside the Imperial Palace.

For most of his life, Hirohito had been remarkably fit, but on April 29, 1987, during a banquet held in his honour on his birthday, he felt sick, and left the table. His condition declined, and later that year he underwent major surgery. The operation took place in the Imperial Palace clinic, a small but ultra-modern hospital; and, while the medical reports were uninformative, it was clear that he had undergone an operation for stomach cancer, part of his colon being removed. Though he recovered sufficiently to wave to crowds on the occasion of his birthday in 1988, and managed to fulfil some official functions, like the ceremonial planting of rice, that year, he was clearly a very ill man. Newspapers reported that Hirohito was suffering from a slowly-evolving but inoperable tumour of the pancreas. The Imperial Household Agency refused to comment, and his 1987 operation highlighted its still extraordinarily secretive character.

Hirohito himself was kept in ignorance of his condition. When he started reading newspapers during his convalescence he learnt more from them than he had from Imperial Household Agency officials, and he became extremely angry. One Court reporter said that Imperial Household officials were stunned by his rage. Dr. Yashiko Moriaka, the surgeon who had operated on the Emperor, complained to journalists that he was not able to examine Hirohito alone: court officials and Court-appointed physicians got in his way. Court reporters were told that Hirohito's first words to his staff after resuming consciousness were to tell them to switch on the television set so that he could watch the sumo wrestling. On their first visit to him, his granddaughters presented him with a giant teddy bear.

I watched him at one of his last public appearances, his eighty-eighth birthday, April 29, 1988. On that day tens of thousands of Japanese, mostly in groups, were ushered into the Palace in eager, but tightly-disciplined groups, herded into the rectangular space outside its low-lying post-war wing, an understated piece of architecture that looks like the outside of a school, or maybe a particularly expensive gymnasium. A policewoman announced on a loudspeaker the imminent arrival of the Emperor. His immediate family lined up behind a bulletproof glass bay, and then, shuffling slightly, Hirohito appeared. "How good of you to come," he said over the loudspeaker. "I thank you and wish you happiness in your lives." This was repeated three times at forty-five minute intervals – the time it took to clear the grounds of the Palace and bring in fresh visitors. The Emperor looked tired; his face and hands, covered in liver spots, were so thin one could see the bones beneath the skin; and his delivery was slightly slurred – ill-fitting false teeth appeared to be the trouble.

Contingency plans in the event of Hirohito's death had been in existence for years. Inevitably, they were brought up to date after his 1987 operation. In government circles and behind the scenes in the media this was code-named "X-day" (the Empress's death being referred to as "Y-day") and with typical Japanese thoroughness almost everything was meticulously planned, in a series of conferences attended by Government and Imperial Household Agency representatives, and, later, by editors and TV network executives.

The elaborate instructions that went out to all networks covered the eventuality of the Emperor's dying during the night. In this case, a special programme was to be broadcast immediately, until the end of broadcasting time that day; if it occurred after 6 a.m., the special programme was to continue for the next twenty-four hours (for "Y-day" the programmes were slightly shorter).

During this time, there were to be no commercials, no commercially sponsored condolences, and no songs, comedies, drama or sport; in the subsequent mourning period, lasting at least three days, programmes were to be suitably tailored to take the Emperor's death into account. The major broadcasting networks already had, in readiness, hours and hours of special programmes about the Emperor and his life and times. The initial announcement of his death was to be restricted to the time and cause, and the Emperor's age, with no detailed discussion of the ailments leading up to it. TV announcers were to wear black, reporters dark blue or dark grey suits; cameramen were allowed navy blue blazers. Black ties were to be worn by all. A list of special interviewees had been drawn up a long time in advance, though many of those initially approached appear subsequently to have declined the honour: they were concerned that, if they said anything that might be considered disrespectful about the Emperor, the extremist right-wing groups that profess fanatical devotion to him – and desire a return to a more authoritarian "Emperor-system" – might take reprisals.

Publishing companies made equally detailed preparations: newspapers and types of magazines, all had their special issues ready. Banks, stock markets, cinemas, theatres and nightclubs were to remain closed during the official mourning period.

The Emperor's death was of vital concern to the printing, publishing, paper and incense trades, for one uniquely Japanese reason. With Hirohito's death, the Showa era came to an end, and Hirohito after January 7, 1989 was renamed Emperor Showa. All official Japanese stationery, letterheads, calendars, documents, bills, etc., up to that day, carried the "Showa" date: 1988, for instance, was "the 63rd year of Showa". This meant that, overnight, all diaries, documents and official letter heads had to be reprinted.

At the time of Emperor Taisho's death in 1926, a huge upheaval had been caused in the publishing and printing trades (and many small purveyors of New Year cards ruined, for, as Taisho's death was announced on Christmas Day, out of respect for the late Emperor almost all Japanese refrained from sending each other New Year greetings cards which failed to take his death into account: this could have been interpreted as a disrespectful attitude).

In Hirohito's case, speculation about his health led to certain stock market upheavals as early as 1987: with incense being consumed in enormous quantities, shares in a small chemical firm (which had lain dormant for years) suddenly rocketed – and stayed high; shares in paper, publishing and printing firms also rose in anticipation. By and large, Japanese diary-manufacturers, in anticipation of Hirohito's death before December 31, 1988, refrained from marketing "Showa" calendars for 1989.

Far more important than stock market fluctuations, however, were the political decisions that were taken in the wake of

Hirohito's death. The Emperor's burial ceremonies, traditionally occur several weeks after the actual death, and the problems facing the Takeshita Government were many. A source of considerable controversy not only in political circles, but throughout Japan, was the ritual envisaged for both the many burial ceremonies and the enthronement of the new Emperor. Was Hirohito to be buried as an ordinary citizen – as the Opposition parties wanted – or in a series of elaborate Shinto ceremonies, as the direct descendant of Amaterasu, the Sun Goddess? The nature of the enthronement ceremonies was also under review: when Taisho died, Hirohito presided over no less than sixty Shinto ceremonies, and it was nearly two years before the enthronement took place. But, in 1926 and 1928, the Emperor was still a "living God". The Imperial Household Agency, and the politicians, had to agree on a ceremonial that would be sufficiently awesome to take account of the mystical bond between the Emperor and the Japanese people, yet also take account of his post-war status as an ordinary human being.

Because of the militancy of the small but dynamic right-wing ultra-nationalist movements which want a return to age-old religious and "Imperial" traditions, this controversy threatened to lead to a full-scale political crisis, and to clashes with left-wingers: the right-wingers' black vans, a feature of down-town Tokyo, which routinely patrol the city with loud-speakers blaring reactionary slogans, are a sombre reminder that not all Japanese adhere to the post-war democratic ideals. The nature of the funeral and enthronement ceremonies provided a crucial test: had Japan made a clean sweep of its pre-surrender past, or was there still a strong element, par-ticularly among the conservative LDP rank-and-file, influential enough to insist on archaic ceremonies that underlined Japan's uniqueness, as a country of "divine" origins? Akihito almost certainly favoured a simple, citizen's funeral ceremony for his father, and an equally low-key enthronement ceremony for himself, but the LDP conservatives and the traditionalist Im-perial Household Agency represent a formidable coalition – and wanted ceremonies to compare with those of 1926 and 1928.

There were several reasons for this. For all Japan's post-war recovery and emergence as a leading world power, the Showa era was also a low point in her history: hugely colourful, traditional ceremonies marking the beginning of another Imperial "era" would, in the traditionalists' view, help exorcize the past; the LDP has, increasingly, felt that the Imperial system, even in its modified, post-war form, is a binding element in Japanese society, and that the emphasis should be on more, not less, respect for the monarchical system. It believes that this is a feeling shared by Japan's "silent majority", and that to skimp on pageantry, and ceremonial, simply fuels the anger of the people while at the same time alienating ordinary middle-of-the-road voters.

The funeral ceremonies on February 24, 1989, attended by 163 Heads of State and Government (including Prince Philip, Belgium's King Baudouin, King Juan Carlos of Spain and King Carl Gustav XVI of Sweden, Presidents Aquino, Bush and Mitterrand as well as King Hussein of Jordan) turned out to be a judicious mixture of civil and Shintoist rites – the latter held behind an opaque black curtain and watched only by the late Emperor's family, Palace Officials and Shinto priests. The Empress – confined to a wheelchair for several months – was too sick to attend.

The Shintoist rites took place inside Shinjuku Gyoen, a park once reserved for Imperial use. Sea bream, birds, mountain potatoes and melons were offered to the spirit of the late Emperor; his favourite personal effects, including his microscope and his Mickey Mouse watch, were buried with him.

Stringent security precautions had been in force throughout Tokyo for at least a week. Tiny groups of leftwingers protested, but there was no major mishap, except for the rain and freezing cold. Some 200,000 people, far less than the expected crowd of 800,000, lined the five-mile procession route. The traditional ox-drawn hearse was replaced, for security reasons, by a huge vehicle. As the *Financial Times* noted, "great pains were taken to satisfy the demands of nationalists who wanted a traditional

Shinto ceremony and others who insisted on a clear separation of church and state . . . Bored mourners retreated frequently from the funeral hall to adjacent marquees for tea, where the conversations were often so lively that officials circulated with signs pleading for silence."

In the Japanese calendar, Emperor Showa's funeral took place on the 48th day of Heisei, as Emperor Akihito decided to name his new era. Heisei means achieving peace. Whatever changes occur in Japan during the Heisei era, it is unlikely to be as memorable as Showa – the very name a reminder of Japan's extraordinary rise, fall and resurrection, and of one man's miraculous survival.

---

[1] *Mainichi Shimbun, Fifty Years of Light and Dark*, 1985.

EPILOGUE

While there have been relatively few books about Emperor Hirohito, there have been scores about Japan's economic miracle and her post-war emergence as a world power. It is a cliché that Japan, from the 1960s onwards, acquired an immensely greater reputation as an exporter and industrial innovator than she obtained through the brutal conquest and occupation of most of Asia from 1931 to 1945. Not even the most rabid Japanese nationalist would today suggest that the Emperor of Japan has a divine right to rule the world through *Hakko Ichiu*, but it is universally recognized that Japanese names like Honda, Mitsubishi, Sanyo, Sony and Toyota do, indeed, straddle "the eight corners of the world", as do Japanese banks (nine out of ten of the world's largest), property conglomerates, hotel and even restaurant and hairdressing salon chains, and the yen itself.

It would be absurd to argue that the "Emperor-system" has been directly responsible for this extraordinary leap forward: since January 1946, Hirohito's status as the "symbol of unity of the Japanese people" was so understated that few of the seminal books chronicling Japan's astonishing recovery even mention him. Unlike other monarchies, which unabashedly promote their nation's goods and services, the Imperial Family keeps such a low profile that it never stoops to such practices. Just as Hirohito once noted, in one of his brief, somewhat stilted conversations with Japanese Court correspondents, that he never allowed himself to express his preference in public for individual sumo wrestlers, so he never "put out more flags" for any of Japan's major conglomerates. On his 1975 visit to the United States, he visited Disneyland and model farms, not factories with Japanese connections.

For all this discretion and reluctance to beat the Japanese drum, the "Emperor-system", even in its post-war incarnation, has been a constant, if muted, factor in Japanese politics and society: it is almost as if the old Imperial values have been taken over by the major Japanese conglomerates, and adapted to present-day economic realities. As the tide of war turned inexorably against Japan in January 1944, Kido had noted in his diaries: "Looking over the future trend of the world, I believe that we must preserve and cultivate our real power in the State for about a hundred years before embarking on conquest again." It has taken Japan considerably less than a hundred years to achieve her goals, and again and again one is confronted with strange, sometimes risible, parallels between traditional, pre-war rites and present-day practices. The Yakusuni Shrine, dedicated to the spirits of all dead warriors, has a parallel in mercantile, "salaryman" Japan, where the ashes of many deserving lifelong employees of some major corporations are often laid to rest in "corporation shrines". At annual pilgrimages conducted at these sites, the "heroic conduct" of these hardy former fighters is celebrated; their exploits in promoting the greatness and profitability of the firms for which they devoted their lives, their health often impaired by excessive work, travel and drinking in the pursuit of markets, profits and contracts, are recalled with all the hyperbole of heroic, wartime Japan.

Sometimes, in the course of Japan's economic miracle, the past has intruded with almost comical intensity. Take, for instance, the moment former Corporal Shoichi Yokoi returned to Japan after twenty-eight years in hiding in the jungles of Guam, obeying to the letter his commanding officer's 1944 injunction to evade capture by the enemy. On February 2, 1972, on Japanese soil, and fighting back his tears, Yokoi insisted on carrying out his military duties to the last. "Yokoi Shoichi, reporting back from Guam," he told the astounded TV teams awaiting him at Tokyo airport, "shamefully alive, to report how the war was lost. I have brought back the rifle [still in working order, and intact except for the absence of its wooden butt, eaten by termites] given me by His Gracious Majesty. I am now returning it to His Imperial Majesty. I am deeply ashamed at my failure to serve His Majesty." (Hirohito's predictable reaction was: "It must have been very hard for him. I hope he gets a good rest now.")

Those Japanese who had not experienced the Second World War could not understand Yokoi's behaviour. Yokoi, in turn, was shocked to discover that the "chrysanthemum taboo" no longer prevented the Japanese press from publishing photographs of the Emperor. Traditionalists, and, inevitably, the ultra-nationalist, right-wing groups, felt inordinately proud of Yokoi, the obscure NCO from the supply company of the 38th regiment, who had used his skills as a tailor to fashion shoes and clothes out of twine and bark, and had survived far longer than Robinson Crusoe in a far more hostile environment, intent all these years on fighting a one-man war and, above all, on avoiding the ultimate shame of capture.

But had there ever been, in the Japanese consciousness, the notion of surrender? In a perceptive introduction to a book on Shoichi Yokoi,[1] Russell Braddon argues not. As he points out, nowhere in Hirohito's surrender speech was surrender, or even defeat, specifically mentioned, only that "the fighting had to stop". And, as Clyde Haberman of the *New York Times* reflected, in a valedictory piece on leaving his three-year Tokyo assignment, "anyone living in Japan could be forgiven the impression that World War Two began on August 6, 1945, when the United States dropped an atom-bomb on Hiroshima. Precious little is said about the misery that Japan had inflicted throughout Asia for years . . . Hiroshima and Nagasaki enabled the Japanese to convince themselves that they, possibly along with the Jews, were the war's prime victims."

This in turn explains why the Japanese educational system is intent on perpetuating a version of events that not only absolves Japan from any blame for the horrors of the Second World War but also promotes the concept of Japan as victim. The former Education Minister, Masayuki Fujio, also felt that Japan's textbooks were "not sufficiently patriotic". That Japan had nothing to be ashamed of during the war is the message rammed home by any number of politicians from the ruling party: on April 22, 1988, the Land Agency Minister, Seisuko Okuno, told assembled veterans' representatives at a ceremony at the Yakusuni Shrine that Japan's war with China was not "a war of aggression. Japan fought in order to secure its safety." In any case, he went on, "the white races had turned Asia into a colony". "Japan was by no means the aggressor nation." Because the Japanese Government was intent on better relations with China, the ensuing outcry forced Okuno to resign. What few people realized was that a senior representative of Emperor Hirohito was present on this occasion, and that the presentation of sacred Imperial gifts to the Yasukuni Shrine (bales of precious raw silk out of which banners would be made) was indeed the pretext for the ceremony.

The Japanese nationalists' desire to return to a balmy pre-Hiroshima era, affirming the sacred nature of the Emperor as an inescapable part of Japan's national heritage, without which there can be no true greatness, has been seen, variously, as hopelessly romantic nostalgia (exemplified by Yukio Mishima and his theatrical end) and as a clash between those who accept Japan's new internationalism and those who reject it. For all his artistic greatness, however, Mishima is, in a sense, irrelevant: what we see, in present-day Japan, is a totally illogical, irrational attitude towards the "Emperor-system", not just among arrant nationalists, but across the Japanese spectrum.

On the one hand there is the "official" doctrine, affirming the myth of Hirohito's innocence. It extends beyond Japan, to most Western academic circles, and is backed by the generations of diplomats following the example of Joseph C. Grew, for almost all Western ambassadors in Tokyo – charmed by the younger members of the Imperial Family they have been privileged to meet, absorbed in this fascinating, in many respects forward-looking, élitist society – dismiss any other view as revisionist nonsense.

Japanese attitudes towards the Emperor are, indeed, based on popular conceptions and myths which are not only questionable but, above all, inconsistent: for, while every effort is made to isolate him from the 1931–45 events, it is now increasingly fashionable to maintain that the events themselves were pre-ordained and were nothing to be ashamed of: in a book on the fiftieth anniversary of the Showa era, *Mainichi Shimbun* referred to the events leading up to Pearl Harbor as follows:

We would be indiscreet to maintain Japan was forced into war by subtle US diplomatic manoeuvres. But with President Ford defending the US right to intervene militarily in the Middle East if the US is threatened with the strangulation of oil supply in 1975, then what was so unusual about Japan defending the same right in 1941?[4]

Such an assertion pleases Japanese readers, little versed in the background to events (for Japanese history-books carry next to nothing about what really happened). It ignores, of course, the fact that Japan needed oil mainly to sustain her huge military build-up. And the analogy would only be valid if – prior to 1973, the year of the oil crisis – the United States had overrun large parts of Central and Latin America and behaved with extreme cruelty there for years. The point could also be made that, though President Ford may have barked, the US did not bite: the hallmark of American policy in the Middle East has been, in fact, a growing disengagement which many critics regard as unworthy of a nation with international responsibilities.

In the same way, the Emperor's role as father-figure to the great Japanese "family" has seldom been questioned. Just before his US trip, in 1975, *Newsweek*'s Bernard Krisher was granted a rare interview. He asked: "What are the particular ingredients Your Majesty feels have contributed to the 2,000-year survival of the Imperial tradition?"[5]

Hirohito answered: "Because, throughout history, the Imperial Family has always given first thought to the welfare of the people."

In the light of the incredible sacrifices imposed on the Japanese from 1937 onwards, it was an extraordinary reply. Even more extraordinary, perhaps, was that it was accepted at its face value, both in Japan and the United States, and that no indignant editorial underlined the hypocritical nature of such an assertion.

To want to have it both ways is human: in contemporary Japan, this desire reaches absurd proportions. No country has ever exploited more strenuously than Japan the rules governing free trade. At the same time, to justify stringent limits to foreign imports, Japanese officials, with a straight face, invoke Japan's "uniqueness": imports of European skis are limited because they are "unsuitable" for Japan, given the "uniqueness" of Japanese snow; imports of American and Charolais beef are equally unsuitable, because of the "uniqueness" of the Japanese digestive system; Japanese rice is ten times more costly than the world price, but imports are banned "because rice is the core of our spiritual civilization". Japanese neurologists have even postulated the "uniqueness" of the Japanese brain, and scientists have erected whole theories on such "uniqueness" stemming from distant evolution itself – the so-called "European races" evolving from chimpanzees, the Japanese from "oriental" primates such as orang-utangs. One of the taboos every foreign businessman, however ignorant of Japanese customs, is drilled to observe is that it is bad form ever to refer to Japanese ethnic origins. It is accepted by leading anthropologists that, behind the legends of Amaterasu and her divine progeny, is the reality of the colonization of what is now Japan by Chinese and Korean invaders. Japanese susceptibilities are such that this must never be mentioned, even in sophisticated company. Japanese attitudes towards the Koreans in their midst should by rights attract the indignant attention of anti-racists and do-gooders of all kinds. Twenty thousand Koreans died at Hiroshima, but only long after the end of the war was a monument finally erected to them – and it stands outside Hiroshima's "peace Park".

The individual behaviour of some Japanese reflects this double scale of values. On his visits to foreign capitals, the former

Premier, Nakasone, was an "internationalist", almost a liberal. At home, he was a staunch nationalist, who encouraged the setting-up of the "Japanology Institute" whose director, Takeshi Umehara, believes that Western civilization is like a disease threatening the modern world. Until his death, no foreign artist was more adulated in France than the Japanese painter, Fujita. No Franco-Japanese event in Paris was complete without him, and this highly publicity-conscious, fashionable painter never let an opportunity slip to air his views on the need for close bonds between the two countries. He was, to judge from newspaper cuttings, "Monsieur Japon" in Paris. It would come as something of a surprise to many of the well-meaning French socialites, who lionized him and bought his paintings to learn how rabidly Fujita had used his artistic talents as a propagandist for Japanese militarism and an Axis victory. Yet, the war over, he assumed his place in French high society as though nothing had happened.

This, perhaps, is a function of Japanese "uniqueness": that it justifies a double scale of values, and that no moral stigma can be attached to any behaviour relating to "foreigners". Since this "uniqueness" is the foundation on which Japanese society is built, and since it determines Japanese relations with the outside world, the "Emperor-system" assumes far more importance than, say, the British, Dutch or Swedish monarchy in relation to its peoples. As Yuji Kishida, a Freudian psychologist (quoted by Ian Buruma in the *New York Times*) wrote: "The Japanese are able to cope with modernization not because their identity is based on firm principles but because of the illusion that all Japanese are connected by blood . . . Japanese identity is threatened when foreigners are assimilated in our midst . . . the core of this belief is the fact that all Japanese believe they are related by blood to the emperor . . . as long as we believe that, the Japanese identity won't be threatened." [6]

Once this is realized, the Emperor's real past becomes something of a family secret, not to be divulged to outsiders. Part of the Japanese "uniqueness" has been the ability not only to accept, over the years, a version of history, and of the Emperor's role, which is palpably, demonstrably false, but to impose it on the rest of the world.

[1] *The Last Japanese Soldier*, translated by Ruri Corley Smith with an introduction by Russell Braddon, Tom Stacey, London, 1972.
[2] *Hogaku Jiho* (Law Review), August 1970.
[3] Inouye, *The Emperor's Responsibilities*, ib.
[4] *Mainichi Shimbun* Editorial staff, *Fifty years of light and dark*, Tokyo, 1975.
[5] *Newsweek*, September 29, 1975.
[6] *New York Times*, April 12, 1987.

APPENDIX A

The Emperor's surrender speech (recorded August 14, 1945;
broadcast August 15, 1945).

To Our good and loyal subjects:

After pondering deeply the general trends of the world and
the actual conditions obtaining in Our Empire today, We have
decided to effect a settlement of the present situation by resorting
to an extraordinary measure.

We have ordered Our Government to communicate to the
Governments of the United States, Great Britain, China and the
Soviet Union that Our Empire accepts the provisions of their
Joint Declaration.

To strive for the common prosperity and happiness of all
nations as well as the security and well-being of Our subjects is
the solemn obligation which has been handed down by Our
Imperial Ancestors, and which We lay close to our heart.
Indeed, We declared war on America and Britain out of Our
sincere desire to ensure Japan's self-preservation and the stabilization of East Asia, it being far from Our thought either to
infringe upon the sovereignty of other nations or to embark on
territorial aggrandizement. But now the war has lasted for
nearly four years. Despite the best that has been done by
everyone – the gallant fighting of military and naval forces, the
diligence and assiduity of Our servants and the devoted service
of Our one hundred million people, the war situation has
developed not necessarily to Japan's advantage, while the general
trends of the world have all turned against her interest. Moreover, the enemy has begun to employ a new and most cruel

bomb, the power of which to do damage is indeed incalculable, taking the toll of many innocent lives. Should We continue to fight, it would not only result in an ultimate collapse and obliteration of the Japanese nation, but also it would lead to the total extinction of human civilization. Such being the case, how are We to save the millions of Our subjects; or to atone Ourselves before the hallowed spirits of Our Imperial Ancestors? This is the reason why We have ordered the acceptance of the provisions of the Joint Declaration of the Powers.

We cannot but express the deepest sense of regret to our Allied nations of East Asia, who have consistently cooperated with the Empire towards the emancipation of East Asia. The thought of those officers and men as well as others who have fallen in the fields of battle, those who died at their posts of duty, or those who met with untimely death and all their bereaved families, pains Our heart night and day. The welfare of the wounded and the war-sufferers, and of those who have lost their homes and livelihood, are the object of Our profound solicitude. The hardships and sufferings to which Our nation is to be subjected hereafter will be certainly great. We are keenly aware of the inmost feelings of all ye, Our subjects. However, it is according to the dictate of time and fate that We have resolved to pave the way for a grand peace for all the generations to come by enduring the unendurable and suffering what is insufferable.

Having been able to safeguard and maintain the structure of the Imperial State, We are always with ye, Our good and loyal subjects, relying upon your sincerity and integrity. Beware most strictly of any outbursts of emotion which may engender needless complications, or any fraternal contentions and strife which may create confusion, lead ye astray and cause ye to lose the confidence of the world. Let the entire nation continue as one family from generation to generation, ever firm in its faith of the imperishableness of its divine land, and mindful of its heavy burden of responsibilities, and the long road before it. Unite your total strength to be devoted to the construction of the future. Cultivate the ways of rectitude; foster nobility of spirit; and work with resolution so as ye may enhance the innate glory of the Imperial State and keep pace with the progress of the world.

Imperial Seal affixed.

The 14th day of the 8th month of the 20th year of Showa.

BIBLIOGRAPHY

Agawa, Hiroyuki: *The Reluctant Admiral*, Kodansha, 1982.

Beasley, W. G.: *The Modern History of Japan*, Tuttle, 1963.

Bergamini, David: *Japan's Imperialist Conspiracy*, William Morrow, 1971.

Brackman, Arnold C.: *The Other Nuremberg*, William Morrow, 1987.

Brocade Banner, the story of Japanese nationalism, Civil Intelligence Section, GHQ Far Eastern Command, Sept. 1946.

Brines, Russell: *MacArthur's Japan*, Lippincott, NY, 1948.

Butow, Robert: *Tojo and the Coming of the War*, Princeton University Press, 1961.

Coffey, Thomas M.: *Imperial Tragedy*, World Publishing Co., 1970.

Connors, Lesley: *The Emperor's Adviser, Kinmochi Saionji*, Croom Helm and Nissan Institute for Japanese Studies, 1987.

Craigie, Sir Robert: *Behind the Japanese Mask*, Hutchinson, 1945.

Day, David: *The Great Betrayal*, Angus and Robertson, London, 1988.

Feis, Herbert: *The Road to Pearl Harbor*, Princeton University Press, 1950.

Futara, Yoshimori and Saweda, Setsuko: *The Crown Prince's European Tour*, Osaka Mainichi, 1925.

Gayn, Mark: *Japan Diary*, William Sloan Associates, NY, 1948.

Grew, Joseph C.: *Ten Years in Japan*, Hammond Hammond and Co., London, 1945.

Guillain, Robert: *I Saw Tokyo Burning*, John Murray, 1981.

—*Orient Extreme*, Arlea-le-Seuil, Paris, 1988.

Harada, Kumao: *Prince Saionji and the Political Situation*, Iwanami Shoten, 1956.

Hata, Ikuhito: *The Emperor's Five Decisions*, Kodansha, 1984.

IMTFE "Documents Presented in Evidence", prosecution exhibits and trial excerpts, National Archives, Washington DC.

Inouye, Kyoshi: *The Emperor's Responsibilities*, Gendai Hyoronsha, Tokyo, 1975.

James D. Clayton: *The Years of MacArthur*, Houghton Mifflin, 1985.

Japan Times archives, *Japan Times and Advertiser* & *Nippon Times* microfilms, 1940–45.

Johnson, Chalmers: *An Instance of Treason*, Tuttle, 1977.

Kanroji, Osanaga: *The Emperor and Poems and Horses*, Shuken Asahi, 1967.

—*Hirohito, An Intimate Portrait*, Gateway Publishers, Los Angeles, 1975.

Kato, Matsuo: *The Lost War*, Knopf, 1946.

Kawai, Kazuo: *Japan's American Interlude*, University of Chicago Press, 1960.

Kido: *Nikki* (Kido Diaries), Daigaku Shuppankai, 1966.

Kido: Kenkyukai, stenographic record by Mr. Teiichi Suzuki, Daigaku Shuppankai, 1971.

Kodana, Yoshiro: *I was Defeated*, Booth and Fukuda, 1957.

Kurosawa, Akiro: *Something like an Autobiography*, Knopf, 1982.

Lewin, Ronald: *The American Magic: Codes, Cyphers and the Defeat of Japan*, Farrar Straus & Giroux, 1982.

"Magic" Intercepts, (5 vols) Dept. of Defense, Washington DC.

Manning, Paul: *Hirohito, the War Years*, Dodd Mead and Co, NY, 1986.

Mainichi Shimbun (writing staff): *Fifty Years of Light and Dark*, 1985.

May, Henry John: *Little Yellow Gentlemen*, Cassells, 1937.

Minear, Richard: *Victor's Justice*, Princeton University Press, 1971.

Montgomery, Michael: *Imperialist Japan*, Christopher Helm, London, 1988.

Mosley, Leonard: *Hirohito, Emperor of Japan*, Prentice Hall, 1967.

Morgan Young, A.: *Imperial Japan*, William Morrow, 1938.

Morley, James William (editor): *The Fatal Choice: Japan's Advance into South-east Asia*, Columbia University Press, 1980.

Oka, Yoshitake: *Konoe Fumimaro, a Political Biography*, University of Tokyo Press, 1983.

Pacific War Research Society: *Japan's Longest Day*, Kodansha Intl., 1968.

Packard, Jerrold M.: *Sons of Heaven*, Scribners, 1987.

Prange, Gordon W.: *Pearl Harbor, the Verdict of History*, McGraw Hill, 1986.

Price, Willard: *Japan and the Son of Heaven*, Duell Sloan and Pearce, 1945.

Shiroyama, Saburo: *War Criminal: the Life and Death of Koki Hirota*, Kodansha Intl., 1977.

Spector, Ronald H.: *Eagle Against the Sun*, Free Press (Macmillan), 1980.

Steinberg, David Joel: *Philippine Collaboration in World War Two*, Solidaridad Publishing House, Manila, 1970.

Storry, Richard: *A History of Modern Japan*, Pelican, 1961.

Sugiyama Memorandum, Hara Shobo, Tokyo, 1967.

Terasaki, Gwen: *A Bridge to the Sun*, Michael Joseph, 1958.

Toland, John: *The Rising Sun*, Random House, 1970.

Tolischus, Otto: *Tokyo Record*, Reynal and Hitchcock, NY, 1943.

TVS: *Did the Emperor know?* (Documentary).

Vining, Elizabeth: *Windows for the Crown Prince*, Michael Joseph, 1952.

Wilcox, Robert: *The Secret War*, William Morrow, 1987.

Yoshida, Shigeru: *Memoirs*, Houghton Mifflin, Boston, 1962.

INDEX

Abe, Gen. Noburuku, 278
Adachi, Kenzo, 107, 112, 113, 173
Agawa, Hiroyuki, 214
Aizawa, Lt-Col., 158–9, 161
Akahata (Red Flag), Communist daily, 423
Akasaka Palace, 33, 37, 61, 69, 72, 73, 96, 168, 448
Akihito, Crown Prince, 145, 157, 335, 339, 340, 347–8, 422, 430, 431, 453, 458; birth, 142; and H's abdication in favour of, 412; and Elizabeth Grey Vining, 433, 435; education, 434–5; and Imperial Household Agency, 447; marriage, 452
Amaterasu (sun goddess), 78, 395, 457, 465
Anami, Korechika, 85; as War Minister, 355; communiqué of, 359; and Army coup, 360; and Jap. surrender, 356–7, 361–7; seppuku of, 370–1, 373
Anti-Komintern Pact, 189, 216
Army coup (1945), 360, 362, 364, 368–75; *see also* March Plot, May Incident, October Plot
Army mutiny, 158–78
Asahi Shimbun (newspaper), 163
Asaka, Prince, 186, 200–2, 332, 413
Atcheson, George, 406–7, 410, 412, 442
Atholl, Duke of, 54, 57, 61
Attlee, Clement, 359

atom bomb, 343; *see also* Truman, Harry S.
Atsuko, Princess, 453
Australia: and H.'s "guilt", 12; submarine threat, 284; *see also* Strike South Option

B-29s (US bombers), *see* Tokyo, air raids
Bataan death march, 394
Benedict XV, Pope, 57
Bergamini, David, 14
Bernard, Henri, 423
Black Dragon Society (extreme right-wing organisation), 49, 58, 63, 107, 109, 112; and March Plot, 116; Toyama as leader, 136
"Blood Brotherhood Martyrs", 161; *see also* Ketsumeidan Society
Bose, Subhas Chandra, 323
Bowers, Maj. Faubion, 5–6, 10
Boxer Rebellion, The, 22–3
Brackman, Arnold, 421
Braddon, Russell, 379, 462
Brines, Russell, 427–30, 433
Britain: and "triple intervention", 24; and Hong Kong/Shanghai, 41; HMS *Ladybird* incident, 210; and aid to Chiang Kai-chek, 222–3; "in decline", 225; H.'s ambivalence towards, 231; military preparations against, 250; and Japanese option to attack, 254–7; Battle of, 315

474